Advancements in Natural Language Processing, Semantic Networks, and Sentiment Analysis

Advancements in Natural Language Processing, Semantic Networks, and Sentiment Analysis

Guest Editors

Silvia García-Méndez
Enrique Costa-Montenegro
Francisco De Arriba-Pérez

MDPI

Basel • Beijing • Wuhan • Barcelona • Belgrade • Novi Sad • Cluj • Manchester

Guest Editors
Silvia García-Méndez
Information Technologies
Group, atlanTTic
University of Vigo
Vigo
Spain

Enrique Costa-Montenegro
Telematics Engineering
University of Vigo
Vigo
Spain

Francisco De Arriba-Pérez
Information Technologies
Group, atlanTTic
University of Vigo
Vigo
Spain

Editorial Office
MDPI AG
Grosspeteranlage 5
4052 Basel, Switzerland

This is a reprint of the Special Issue, published open access by the journal *Applied Sciences* (ISSN 2076-3417), freely accessible at: https://www.mdpi.com/journal/applsci/special_issues/568UOEVNU1.

For citation purposes, cite each article independently as indicated on the article page online and as indicated below:

Lastname, A.A.; Lastname, B.B. Article Title. *Journal Name* **Year**, *Volume Number*, Page Range.

ISBN 978-3-7258-4923-9 (Hbk)
ISBN 978-3-7258-4924-6 (PDF)
https://doi.org/10.3390/books978-3-7258-4924-6

Contents

About the Editors

Silvia García-Méndez

Silvia García-Méndez received a Ph.D. in Information and Communication Technologies from the University of Vigo in 2021. Since 2015, she has worked as a researcher with the University of Vigo's Information Technologies Group. As part of her postdoctoral stage, she collaborates with foreign research centers. Her research interests include Natural Language Processing techniques and Machine Learning algorithms.

Enrique Costa-Montenegro

Enrique Costa-Montenegro received his Ph.D. degree from the University of Vigo, Spain, in 2007. He is currently a full professor with the Department of Telematics Engineering at University of Vigo, Spain. His research interests include mobile services, natural language processing, wireless networks, multiagent systems, and recommendation technologies.

Francisco De Arriba-Pérez

Francisco De Arriba-Pérez received a B.S. degree in telecommunication technologies engineering in 2013, an M.S. degree in telecommunication engineering in 2014, and a Ph.D. in 2019 from the University of Vigo, Spain. He is currently a researcher in the Information Technologies Group at the University of Vigo, Spain. His research includes the development of Machine Learning solutions for different domains, such as finance and health.

applied sciences

MDPI

itorial

pecial Issue on Advancements in Natural Language Processing, emantic Networks, and Sentiment Analysis

lvia García-Méndez *, Francisco de Arriba-Pérez and Enrique Costa-Montenegro

Information Technologies Group, atlanTTic, University of Vigo, 36310 Vigo, Spain; farriba@gti.uvigo.es (F.d.A.-P.); kike@gti.uvigo.es (E.C.-M.)
* Correspondence: sgarcia@gti.uvigo.es

1. Introduction

In recent years, natural language processing (NLP) has undergone a profound transformation driven by significant advances in artificial intelligence, machine learning, and the massive availability of linguistic data [1]. Language, an essential tool for reasoning and emotional expression, can be leveraged to equip machines with the ability to understand, generate, and analyze it. The latter is one of the most ambitious and far-reaching challenges in contemporary computational science [2].

This special issue aims to bring together recent research, innovative methodological proposals, and emerging applications that contribute to the development of more efficient, accurate, and contextually aware language technologies. The convergence of NLP, semantic networks, and sentiment analysis enables an approach to complex problems related to semantic ambiguity, contextual inference, subjectivity detection, and the interpretation of implicit meanings [3], thereby opening up new possibilities for deep natural language understanding.

NLP encompasses a wide range of tasks, including text segmentation, morpho-syntactic tagging, syntactic and semantic analysis, lexical disambiguation, automatic language generation, machine translation, information extraction, and entity recognition [4]. The rise of deep neural networks, particularly language models based on transformer architectures such as BERT, GPT, and their derivatives, has revolutionized these processes, enabling unprecedented levels of performance across multiple languages and specialized domains [5].

In parallel, semantic networks have reemerged as a crucial component in representing linguistic and conceptual knowledge [6]. These structures, which model entities and relationships through graphs, facilitate the integration of linguistic and ontological data, enabling a more structured and reasoned interpretation of language. Computational semantics, supported by resources such as WordNet, BabelNet, and multilingual knowledge bases, is articulated with NLP models to enrich text understanding with contextual and conceptual information.

Additionally, sentiment analysis has established itself as a fundamental discipline for evaluating opinions and emotions expressed in texts [7]. This area is especially relevant in contexts such as social network analysis, product and service feedback, media monitoring, the study of political discourse, and the early detection of psychosocial risks [8]. Through supervised learning techniques, lexicographic models, and hybrid approaches, sentiment analysis enables the distinction between positive, negative, and neutral expressions, as well as the capture of more subtle affective nuances.

In short, this special issue examines the intersection of NLP, semantic networks, and sentiment analysis, exploring how these technologies can contribute to more intelli-

https://doi.org/10.3390/app15126476

gent systems. The contributions gathered address, among other topics, the detection of irony and sarcasm, the generation of semantic explanations, the automatic construction of semantic graphs, the expansion of linguistic resources for underrepresented languages, and the use of large language models. Ultimately, this special issue aims not only to reflect the state of the art in the areas above but also to stimulate critical reflection on the methodological challenges, ethical implications, and interdisciplinary opportunities that arise at the intersection of computational linguistics and artificial intelligence.

2. Overview of Published Articles

As previously mentioned, this special issue brings together a comprehensive collection of articles that reflect the latest advancements in NLP, semantic networks, and sentiment analysis. The contributions represent a confluence of theoretical innovation and practical application, offering a panoramic view of current research trends and future directions in the field.

One of the central themes emerging from this volume is the integration of deep learning techniques with domain-specific tasks such as video-based sentiment analysis, multilingual offensive language detection, and tourism-oriented opinion mining. A noteworthy example is the application of dynamic scene segmentation combined with emotional classification in the context of Danmaku comments. By leveraging Deep Convolutional Neural Networks for shot segmentation and fine-tuned language models, such as MacBERT, for emotion analysis, this study demonstrates how context-aware architectures can significantly enhance the interpretability and accuracy of affective computing in multimedia environments. This fusion of visual and textual modalities is representative of the broader trend toward multimodal understanding in NLP.

Bias in sentiment analysis, particularly in social media datasets, constitutes another critical concern explored in this issue. The introduction of a classifier designed with fairness-aware loss functions exemplifies how algorithmic interventions can mitigate the distortions introduced by unbalanced training data. The ethical commitment reflected in this framework underscores a growing consensus in the NLP community regarding the need for socially responsible artificial intelligence systems that are not only effective but also equitable.

Equally compelling is the attention to underrepresented linguistic contexts. The challenge of detecting offensive language in low-resource languages, such as Malay, is addressed with a novel zero-shot, cross-lingual model based on mBERT. By aligning semantic features across languages and deploying a dual-branch training mechanism, the approach effectively transfers knowledge from high-resource languages, such as English. This direction is crucial for democratizing NLP technologies and ensuring inclusivity in their development and deployment.

In the domain of sentiment analysis applied to tourism, a study using user reviews from Tripadvisor demonstrates how fine-tuned RoBERTa models can capture subtle changes in visitor sentiment across time. By incorporating data augmentation to address class imbalances and conducting temporal comparisons, the work not only validates the technical robustness of the model but also provides actionable insights for urban and tourism planning.

Moreover, hate speech and offensive language, particularly when veiled in sarcasm or disguised through emoticons, pose persistent challenges to content moderation. A creative solution offered in this issue involves annotating sarcasm-based rationales in combination with hate speech labels to train more interpretable and practical models. By enriching existing datasets and introducing rationale-based attention mechanisms, this approach significantly improves both classification accuracy and model explainability.

On the other hand, several contributions in this issue delve into the foundations of NLP systems, focusing on robustness, representation, and reasoning. A comprehensive survey on adversarial attacks against sentiment analysis models exposes the vulnerability of deep learning systems to small perturbations in input text. This survey not only catalogs current attack strategies but also discusses defense mechanisms, offering a roadmap for enhancing model resilience in real-world applications.

Knowledge representation and reasoning also take center stage, with two sophisticated approaches aimed at completing and reasoning over knowledge graphs. One model enhances entity embeddings by fusing categorical metadata and textual context through multi-layer residual attention, significantly improving link prediction accuracy. Another introduces a causal reinforcement learning framework that integrates counterfactual reasoning to prioritize relationship paths in graph traversal. Together, these contributions constitute a leap forward in enabling machines to reason over structured knowledge with greater nuance and context sensitivity.

In terms of relation extraction, the issue includes an innovative framework that breaks down the task into modular subtasks using entity attention mechanisms and a cascade tagging structure. This design directly addresses the long-standing problem of overlapping relations in the text of traditional extraction models. By isolating head and tail entity identification, the solutions achieve superior granularity and precision, validated through rigorous experiments on Chinese-language datasets.

On the unsupervised learning field, another contribution introduces prefix-based data augmentation for contrastive sentence embedding. By appending semantically meaningful prefixes, the model generates more informative positive and negative pairs, resulting in measurable gains over standard unsupervised methods. This innovation illustrates the potential of minimal but strategic data manipulation to enhance semantic representation learning.

Finally, the issue underscores the importance of human-centric design in assistive technologies. An analysis of interaction logs from users of the PictoDroid Lite communicator reveals critical usability patterns and areas for improvement, including personalized profiling and temporal usage optimization. This research brings a practical, user-focused dimension to NLP research.

3. Conclusions and Future Work

The papers gathered in this special issue reflect the current state of research in NLP, semantic networks, and sentiment analysis, demonstrating a clear evolution toward more integrative, robust, ethical, and adaptable approaches. Through a diversity of methodologies, languages, application domains, and data types, the articles compiled demonstrate the dynamism and transversality of these disciplines in a global and digitalized context.

First, there is a trend toward the hybridization of techniques, such as combining deep learning models with structured semantic representations and causal inference frameworks. This multidimensional approach enables the tackling of complex problems, such as the emotional segmentation of multimedia content, relationship prediction in knowledge graphs, and the detection of offensive speech in multilingual contexts, with results significantly superior to those of traditional methods.

Likewise, the growing attention to under-resourced languages and less-studied cultural contexts, such as Malay in social media or tourism analysis in Dubrovnik, highlights the need to build more inclusive language technologies, adapted to diverse linguistic and social realities. These initiatives not only promote equity in access to technological solutions but also enrich models with a plurality of data and expressions.

Another cross-cutting theme is the concern for the fairness, explainability, and resilience of models. Faced with the ethical and technical challenges posed by algorithmic biases, adversarial attacks, and subtle forms of online toxicity, several works propose corrective mechanisms and diagnostic tools that strengthen the trustworthiness of systems. These advances contribute to a more responsible artificial intelligence, where transparency and fairness are not complementary, but fundamental requirements.

Furthermore, this issue also highlights an orientation toward user-centered design, as exemplified by the study of augmentative and alternative communication technologies. The analysis of fundamental interactions allows us to identify specific needs and guide the development of more sensitive, personalized, and practical solutions.

However, the work presented in this special issue opens up a wide range of opportunities for future lines of research, both in terms of technical improvements and their social impact and adaptability to new contexts. Despite the substantial advances demonstrated in language modeling, sentiment analysis, semantic representation, and automated reasoning, significant challenges remain that require more sophisticated methodologies, alternative architectures, and collaborative approaches.

One of the main challenges identified is the need to improve models' ability to handle mixed or ambiguous emotions. Human emotions are rarely expressed univocally, and developing models capable of capturing this complexity is a crucial objective for achieving a more nuanced understanding of language. In this regard, the continuous expansion and updating of affective lexicons is proposed, as well as the incorporation of feedback mechanisms from human users or experts to validate and adjust model predictions in real-world settings. This feedback loop will not only contribute to better calibration of systems but also to the refinement of bias mitigation techniques, strengthening the fairness and robustness of the analysis in diverse contexts.

Another key area will be the expansion and diversification of the datasets used to train and validate the models. As languages and social norms evolve, linguistic models will need to adapt dynamically, which requires updated, representative, and culturally contextualized corpora. In parallel, improving scene segmentation in multimodal analysis, enhancing the computational efficiency of models, and designing defense strategies against adversarial attacks are priority areas to ensure system performance and security in critical applications.

Furthermore, there is growing interest in extending these approaches to new domains. In the case of sentiment analysis applied to tourism, the methodology is expected to be scaled to other tourist destinations, aiming to contribute to feasibility studies in sustainability and strategic planning. In parallel, emerging applications in business process intelligence are explored, an area in which models can add value by interpreting, monitoring, and optimizing business workflows based on linguistic data.

From an architectural perspective, future research will consider the use of large language models, whose integration will enable the exploration of higher levels of generalization and inferential capabilities. Although the computational demands of these models have limited their use in previous studies, their progressive incorporation opens a field for comparing the effectiveness of various architectures and better understanding the model's adaptability to different linguistic and semantic contexts. Similarly, the use of ensemble techniques and graph neural networks is proposed to enhance the representation of entities and relationships, particularly in tasks such as link prediction in knowledge graphs and the extraction of complex relationships.

Particularly in the field of knowledge graphs, designing better negative sampling strategies and reducing model time complexity by replacing attention mechanisms without sacrificing performance are considered priorities. Contextual information is also planned to be integrated through graph neural networks to improve the quality of inferences and the semantic contextualization of relationships. Moreover, in relation extraction tasks, a shift toward hybrid systems that combine architectures with large language models is anticipated. This integration will allow the injection of prior knowledge about the extracted entities, improving the assignment of attention weights and the identification of complex or implicit relationships.

Finally, the design of defense mechanisms against adversarial attacks should be oriented toward solutions that are independent of the type of attack, incorporating them as an integral part of the models from their inception. Ensuring data integrity and the stability of predictions against external manipulation will be key to the trustworthiness and practical utility of systems in areas such as public opinion, mental health, justice, and decision-making.

Funding: This work was partially supported by Xunta de Galicia grants ED481D 2024/014 and ED481B-2022-093, Spain.

Conflicts of Interest: The authors declare no conflict of interest.

eferences

Min, B.; Ross, H.; Sulem, E.; Veyseh, A.P.B.; Nguyen, T.H.; Sainz, O.; Agirre, E.; Heintz, I.; Roth, D. Recent advances in natural language processing via large pre-trained language models: A survey. *ACM Comput. Surv.* **2023**, *56*, 1–40. [CrossRef]

Faruqui, M.; Hakkani-Tür, D. Revisiting the Boundary between ASR and NLU in the Age of Conversational Dialog Systems. *Comput. Linguist.* **2022**, *48*, 221–232. [CrossRef]

Naveen, P.; Trojovský, P. Overview and challenges of machine translation for contextually appropriate translations. *Iscience* **2024**, *27*, 110878. [CrossRef] [PubMed]

Yang, Y.; Wu, Z.; Yang, Y.; Lian, S.; Guo, F.; Wang, Z. A survey of information extraction based on deep learning. *Appl. Sci.* **2022**, *12*, 9691. [CrossRef]

Zaki, M.Z. Revolutionising Translation Technology: A Comparative Study of Variant Transformer Models–BERT, GPT and T5. *Comput. Sci. Eng.- Int. J.* **2024**, *14*, 15–27. [CrossRef]

Worth, P.J. Word embeddings and semantic spaces in natural language processing. *Int. J. Intell. Sci.* **2023**, *13*, 1–21. [CrossRef]

Jim, J.R.; Talukder, M.A.R.; Malakar, P.; Kabir, M.M.; Nur, K.; Mridha, M.F. Recent advancements and challenges of NLP-based sentiment analysis: A state-of-the-art review. *Nat. Lang. Process. J.* **2024**, *6*, 100059. [CrossRef]

Grover, P.; Kar, A.K.; Dwivedi, Y. The evolution of social media influence-A literature review and research agenda. *Int. J. Inf. Manag. Data Insights* **2022**, *2*, 100116. [CrossRef]

applied sciences

MDPI

Article

Dynamic Scene Segmentation and Sentiment Analysis for Danmak

Limin Li, Jie Jing and Peng Shi *

National Center for Materials Service Safety, University of Science and Technology Beijing, No. 12 Kunlun Road, Beijing 100083, China; m202211188@xs.ustb.edu.cn (L.L.); 15225831029@163.com (J.J.)
* Correspondence: pshi@ustb.edu.cn

Abstract: Danmaku analysis is important for understanding video content and user interactions. However, current methods often look at separate comments and do not see the complex links between Danmaku and the video's context. This paper presents a new approach that combines advanced shot segmentation techniques, using Deep Convolutional Neural Networks (DDCNN), with an analysis of feelings based on the MacBERT model. First, videos are cut into clear scenes based on detected scene changes. Then, a large group of Danmaku comments are collected and studied to make a complete dictionary of feelings for this field. With this as a base, a new Danmaku-E model is made to find and group seven different emotional categories within Danmaku comments. The model shows significantly improved performance, with accuracy increasing from 94.58% to 95.37% and F1 score going from 94.92% to 95.66%, helped by the improved dictionary of feelings. Experimental results show the good effects of the expanded dictionary in helping model performance in different structures. Also, the Apriori algorithm is used to find and explain links between Danmaku comments and video content, providing a deeper understanding into user participation and emotional reactions.

Keywords: Danmaku; sentiment analysis; scene segmentation; apriori algorithm; macbert

1. Introduction

The rapid evolution of online video platforms, particularly the widespread adoption of Danmaku, offers users a distinctive environment for interactive engagement and personal expression in near-real-time. However, the transient nature and large volume of Danmaku data present significant challenges for sentiment analysis. Current methods often struggle to effectively capture the nuanced and dynamic interactions between Danmaku comments and video content. Additionally, current studies fail to fully exploit the interaction between a video's visual information and its associated Danmaku data. Bai et al. [1] underscored the importance of integrating visual information with Danmaku data, concluding that such an approach could substantially improve the accuracy of sentiment analysis by providing a more comprehensive understanding of user sentiments and engagement.

This study pioneers a deeper understanding of the emotional connection between video content and Danmaku data. We fundamentally re-engineered the shot segmentation technology, inspired by Soucek and Lokoc's work [2] on shot transition detection, to merge video segments based on emotional coherence and visual similarity.

The main contributions of this paper are listed as follows:

(1) A scene merging method based on average color histogram similarity is introduced to more accurately identify and merge visually similar consecutive scenes and reduce erroneous scene switch predictions.

(2) Combining an extended sentiment lexicon with BERT (Bidirectional Encoder Representations from Transformers). A novel fuzzy feature layer is introduced to refine sentiment quantification, mapping multidimensional sentiment scores into clear categories through fuzzy variables and membership functions, enhancing both granularity and interpretability of sentiment classification, addressing the challenges of ambiguity and complexity in emotional expressions.

2. Related Works

Sentiment analysis is a main part of natural language processing. It aims to find, pull out, and measure subjective information from data. This basis allows us look into advanced deep learning methods and models that are already trained in language. They find complicated emotional signals and semantic details.

2.1. Scene Segmentation Technology

Scene segmentation is crucial when studying video content. It includes identifying visual boundaries and analyzing and encoding the emotions within the content.

Rao et al. [3] put forward a scene segmentation method that starts with local details and then moves to a global view. They aimed to address the challenging task of movie scene segmentation. Movie scenes contain more complex temporal structures and semantic information compared to videos in traditional vision media. To achieve their goal, Rao et al. created a large-scale video dataset called MovieScenes. This dataset has 21,000 annotated scene segments from 150 movies. Their proposed local-to-global scene segmentation framework integrates multi-modal information at three levels: clip, segment, and movie. First, it focuses on local details by analyzing clip-level information to capture subtle changes in scenes. Then, it gradually takes into account segment- and movie-level information to consider the overall structure and semantics. This method simplifies the complex meanings in long movies' temporal structures. Experiments on the MovieScenes dataset show that their network can segment movies into scenes with high accuracy, outperforming previous methods. Also, pre-training on MovieScenes can significantly improve the performance of existing methods, promoting the development of scene segmentation technology in handling large-scale and complex video data.

Fu et al. [4] proposed the DRANet (Dual Relation-Aware Attention Network) for scene segmentation. In pixel-level recognition, effectively using context information is very important. They used the relation-aware attention mechanism to adaptively capture context information. Specifically, they added two types of attention modules on top of the dilated FCN (Fully Convolutional Network). One module models the contextual dependencies in the spatial dimension, and the other does the same in the channel dimension. In these attention modules, they used the self-attention mechanism. This allows each pixel or channel to gather context from all other pixels or channels based on their correlations. To reduce the high cost of calculation and memory caused by the pairwise association calculation, they designed two compact attention modules. In these modules, each pixel or channel only forms associations with a few gathering centers and obtains context aggregation from these centers. At the same time, they added a cross-level gating decoder. This decoder can selectively enhance spatial details, which improves the network's performance. They conducted many experiments on four challenging scene segmentation datasets: Cityscapes, ADE20K, PASCAL Context, and COCO Stuff. The results show that their network is effective and achieves a new state-of-the-art segmentation performance. For example, on the Cityscapes test set, without using extra coarse-annotated data, it achieves a mean IoU score of 82.9%, providing a more effective solution for scene segmentation on complex datasets.

Soucek and Lokoc [2] presented TransNet V2, a deep network design for the rapid detection of shot transitions. It improved the accuracy of shot transition detection in complex video content, marking significant progress in the initial step of video analysis—shot transition detection—and providing a more reliable basis for subsequent video content analysis.

2.2. Deep Learning-Based Emotion Analysis

Deep learning methods have been used with success for analyzing emotions. These include CNN (Convolutional Neural Networks), RNN (Recurrent Neural Networks), LSTM (Long Short-Term Memory), and attention mechanisms [5]. They can find complex emotional signals and features of meaning.

Kossack and Unger [6] came up with a sentiment analysis method for film review texts. Their method is based on SVM (Support Vector Machines) classification technology in sentiment dictionaries and machine learning. First, they built basic sentiment dictionaries, dominant sentiment dictionaries, negative word dictionaries, and degree adverb dictionaries. Then, they combined these four dictionaries to expand the dictionary. Next, they constructed the SVM model training set by calculating the combination of sentiment weights and user scores. Finally, they used test data for sentiment classification experiments. The results showed that their method has a higher accuracy in sentiment classification compared to methods based on basic sentiment dictionaries. This proves the effectiveness of their proposed emotion-aware system in text sentiment analysis and offers a new way of thinking for emotion analysis in the film review field.

Lu and Wu [7] did not directly study how to solve the long-distance dependency problem. Instead, they introduced the BERT pre-training model. BERT was designed to pre-train deep bidirectional representations from unlabeled text. It depends on both left and right contexts in all layers during pre-training. BERT's pre-training mainly involves two tasks: Masked Language Modeling and Next Sentence Prediction. After pre-training, the BERT model only needs to add an extra output layer for fine-tuning. Then, it can be used to create state-of-the-art models for many natural language processing tasks, like question answering and language inference, without making many changes to the architecture for specific tasks. BERT has achieved great results in many natural language processing tasks. For example, it increased the GLUE score to 80.5 (an absolute increase of 7.7 points), the MultiNLI accuracy to 86.7% (an absolute increase of 4.6%), the SQuAD v1.1 question answering test F1 value to 93.2 (an absolute increase of 1.5 points), and the SQuAD v2.0 test F1 value to 83.1 (an absolute increase of 5.1 points). Although BERT is not a method used specifically for solving the long-distance dependency problem, its strong ability to learn context information provides strong support for solving various natural language processing problems, including long-distance dependency. Future research can explore ways to solve the long-distance dependency problem based on BERT.

In recent years, BERT has achieved notable success in natural language processing research. Devlin et al. [8] demonstrated that BERT pre-trains deep bidirectional representations by jointly conditioning on both left and right contexts across all transformer layers.

The pre-training of BERT primarily involves two tasks: Masked Language Modeling and Next Sentence Prediction. RoBERTa (Robustly Optimized BERT Approach) retains the original BERT architecture while introducing refinements to fully exploit BERT's capabilities. Liu et al. [9] conducted detailed comparisons of various components within BERT, such as masking strategies and training steps, improving BERT's performance by extending the training time using larger batch sizes and longer sequences on a wider range of datasets, and by eliminating the next sentence prediction task and adopting the key method of dynamic masking. MacBERT builds upon both BERT and RoBERTa, replacing the original MLM (Masked Language Modeling) task with MLM as a correction (Mac) task to mitigate discrepancies between pre-training and finetuning. Xu et al. [10] revisited previously popular pretrained language models and adapted them to Chinese. In recent years, deep learning has provided powerful tools for sentiment analysis, specifically in the domain of Danmaku comments. Wang and Huang [11] developed a sentiment classification algorithm based on a modified Bayes model for Danmaku comments, highlighting advancements in model adaptability for specific comment types. Although their approach achieved good results in classification accuracy, it relied mainly on traditional machine learning methods. As a result, it had trouble fully grasping the intricate emotional cues within Danmaku comments. Our model incorporates advanced deep-learning technologies. We utilize Deep Convolutional Neural Networks (DCNN) for scene segmentation and the MacBERT model for sentiment analysis. Thanks to this combination, we can not only classify sentiments with greater precision but also better understand the relationship between video content and user comments. Furthermore, by applying a fuzzy logic system and an extended sentiment lexicon, we enhance the granularity and interpretability of sentiment classification. Zhao et al. [12] used the MIBE-RoBERTa-FFBiLSTM model for sentiment analysis of Danmaku videos. This can find complex emotional signals in comments. Nevertheless, their method was mainly oriented towards text-based sentiment analysis and failed to consider the visual information in the video. In contrast, our approach combines both visual and textual data. This way, we can gain a more comprehensive understanding of user emotions. Through segmenting videos into scenes and analyzing the emotional coherence between scenes and comments, our model can better capture the nuances of user interactions. Additionally, by using the Apriori algorithm to mine association rules between video content and comments, we can gain deeper insights into user behavior and emotional responses. Rohidin et al. [13] brought up a Class-Based Fuzzy Soft Associative model. It brings together association rules and fuzzy soft set models and shows better accuracy and efficiency than normal classifiers. This way of doing things is very useful in text classification, where time and accuracy are important. Cao et al. [14] made VisDmk, a system for interactive visual analysis to study large emotional Danmaku data from online videos. Also, association rules can show links between specific ways of expression, slang, or shortcuts and particular trends in feelings. This way, it can identify patterns in audience emotional responses [15]. Connectedly, Tayaba et al. [16] showed how machine learning and association rule mining can be used to analyze feelings on Twitter. Liu et al. [17] performed sentiment mining at the aspect level of Danmaku comments. They made a framework that improves the understanding of meaning and shows the potential to enhance the viewing experiences. Ye et al. [18] investigated information cues in Danmaku comments that trigger user emotional production in reaction videos. Nagao et al. [19] showed effective language representations for classifying Danmaku comments, using Nicopedia BERT to make the classification performance better. But they restricted language representation and did not investigate the interaction between video content and comments. Our model addresses this shortcoming. We integrate video scene segmentation and sentiment analysis. This integration enables us to capture both the visual and textual context of user interactions, leading to more accurate and nuanced sentiment classification. Moreover, our model's capacity to handle mixed emotions and complex emotional expressions via the fuzzy logic system differentiates it from traditional language-based models. Li et al. [20] built a dictionary to analyze the sentiment of movie features based on Danmaku, providing a new and effective method for sentiment analysis.

2.3. Association Rules Based Emotion Analysis

Mining rules of association, a common technique in data mining, works to find meaningful and often happening patterns in sets of items. This way has been used efficiently in studying emotion and sentiment to find hidden patterns and trends within text data. This gives useful information about how users behave, their emotional tendencies, and feedback mechanisms.

Tayaba et al. [16] studied the application of machine learning and association rule mining in tweet analysis. Airlines pay much attention to improving customer experience, and Twitter is an important platform for passengers to share their opinions. In their research, they used the Glove dictionary and n-gram methods to extract features from tweets for word embedding. They explored different artificial neural network (ANN) architectures and support vector machines (SVM) to create a classification model that can classify tweets into positive and negative sentiment categories. They also developed a convolutional neural network (CNN) for tweet classification and compared its performance with the most accurate model among SVM and multiple ANN architectures. The results showed that the CNN model performed better. To gain more insights, they applied association rule mining to different tweet categories. For example, they found that certain word combinations, like the simultaneous appearance of "flight on time" and "good service", are strongly associated with the positive sentiment category, while "flight delay" and "poor attitude" are related to the negative sentiment category. These findings are valuable for airlines to optimize their customer experience strategies.

Naznin et al. [21] proposed two methods, quantitative and fuzzy, to extract meaningful rules to reveal the associations between different emotion categories in users' posts on social media platforms. They used a Twitter user dataset and classified emotions according to Ekman's six emotion categories. They conducted several experiments with different minimum support and minimum confidence thresholds. In the quantitative method, they counted the frequencies of different emotion-related words in users' posts and their co-occurrence situations to mine the association rules between emotion categories. For example, they found that when words expressing "joy" frequently appear in a user's post, the probability of words expressing "anticipation" also increases. In the fuzzy method, they used fuzzy logic to deal with the uncertainty of emotion expressions and capture the fuzzy associations between emotion categories more flexibly. For example, for some ambiguous words, they determined their associations with different emotion categories through fuzzy membership functions. The experiments achieved promising results. Both methods can effectively identify the associations between different emotion categories in users' tweets, which is of great significance for psychologists in studying people's emotional psychology and personality.

2.4. Model Design Theory

In view of the shortcomings of traditional sentiment analysis methods in the field of Danmaku, such as low accuracy of text ambiguity resolution, poor consistency of sentiment annotation, and insufficient extraction of semantic features, the fusion model design aims to combine the advantages of different models to solve these problems. When processing irregular popular new words in Danmaku, the fusion model can leverage its integrated capabilities to better understand and interpret these emerging expressions, thereby improving the overall performance of sentiment analysis.

The various components in the fusion model do not work independently, but work together to improve the overall performance of the model. In similar text sentiment analysis scenarios, the RoBERTa-RNN fusion model achieves better results in tasks such as multi-label text sentiment analysis [22]. For the combined model RoBERT-CNN, RoBERTa is responsible for the deep semantic encoding of Danmaku and converting text into vector representation with rich semantic information. CNN performs convolution operations on these vectors to further filter and combine features to highlight key information related to emotions. For example, when processing Danmaku containing complex emotional expressions, RoBERTa understands the semantics of the text, and CNN extracts the local features that best represent the emotional tendency from these semantic features. The two work together to improve the accuracy of sentiment classification [23]. The RoBERTa model, with its powerful pre-training capabilities, can deeply mine the semantic and structural information of Danmaku comments, while the BiLSTM model is good at capturing the contextual information of texts. The RoBERTa model is responsible for pre-training and extracting deep semantic information. Its output word embedding vectors are processed by the featured fusion layer, and they contain more fine-grained Chinese corpus information, which is then input into the BiLSTM model. The BiLSTM model uses its bidirectional sequence modeling capabilities to extract features from the contextual information of the input text, making up for the RoBERTa model's shortcomings in considering contextual information. The two work together to effectively improve the model's ability to analyze the sentiment tendency of Danmaku comments [24].

3. Method

The detailed setup for studying sentiments in Danmaku comments is shown in Figure 1. The proposed approach is essentially a multimodal analysis method that integrates deep learning with fuzzy logic. Its core lies in the amalgamation of visual information from video scenes and semantic information from Danmaku comments. This method delves deeply into the genuine emotional feedback of users while watching videos, providing valuable insights for video content creators and platform operators. This approach aims to achieve not only more granular but also more precise sentiment classifications, allowing a detailed understanding of the emotional undercurrents in real-time video commentary. Finally, the Apriori algorithm is applied to mine association rules from the Danmaku data, uncovering deeper relationships between the comments and video content.

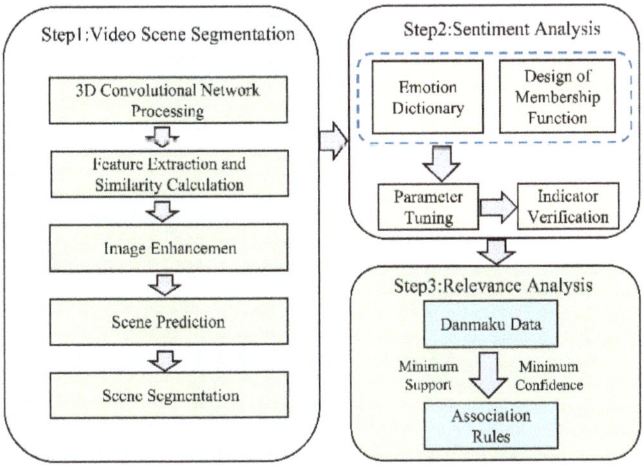

Figure 1. The framework of scene segmentation based sentiment analysis for Danmaku.

3.1. Video Scene Segmentation

When performing video scene segmentation, the integration of temporal and spatial features, such as color histogram similarity, is crucial for achieving more accurate segmentation.

From the perspective of temporal features, the model conducts a detailed analysis of video data frame by frame. Specifically, it monitors the content changes in each frame compared to the previous one. Significant changes over several consecutive frames might indicate a scene transition.

Regarding spatial features, color histogram similarity plays a vital role. When calculating the color histogram, the model uses the common RGB color space, dividing each color channel (R, G, B) into 256 bins, and then counts the number of pixels within each bin to generate the color histogram for that frame. For two adjacent frames, the similarity of their color histograms is computed to assess the degree of similarity in their color distributions.

Here, different segments in the video are identified based on changes in visual content, with a complete video being divided into a series of scene segments. By combining temporal and color histogram similarities, the model can more accurately identify and merge visually similar consecutive scenes, thereby reducing incorrect scene switch predictions.

Firstly, a prediction array is received, which contains the model's prediction of whether each frame is a scene switch point. These prediction values are binary: 1 is indicated for a scene switch point while 0 for a non-switch point.

Secondly, this array is iterated to determine scene boundaries based on changes in the prediction values (from 0 to 1 or from 1 to 0). Whenever a change from the middle of a scene to the end of a scene (from 1 to 0) is detected, it marks the beginning of a new scene. Conversely, when a change from the end of a scene to the beginning of a new one (from 0 to 1) is detected, the end of the current scene is recorded, and the scene is added to the scene list.

Assuming a scene has $\boldsymbol{M}$ frames, the average histogram of the scene is shown in **Formula (1)**.

$$\overline{H} = \frac{1}{M}\sum_{i=1}^{M} H_i \tag{1}$$

Once all scenes are preliminarily segmented, the length $\boldsymbol{L}$ (number of frames) of each scene is compared with the predefined threshold parameter. If the length of the scene is less than the minimum length defined by the min-scene-length parameter, the scene is considered too brief and is merged with either the previous or the next scene. We calculate the similarity of the average color histograms $\overline{H_1}$ and $\overline{H_2}$ of two adjacent scenes. The similarity $\boldsymbol{S}$ is shown in **Formula (2)**.

$$S = \frac{\sum_{i=1}^{N}\left(H_{1,i} - \overline{H}_1\right)\left(H_{2,i} - \overline{H}_2\right)}{\sqrt{\sum_{i=1}^{N}\left(H_{1,i} - \overline{H}_1\right)^2 \sum_{i=1}^{N}\left(H_{2,i} - \overline{H}_2\right)^2}} \tag{2}$$

where $H_{1,i}$ and $H_{2,i}$ are the i-th bin values of the histograms $\overline{H_1}$ and $\overline{H_2}$, respectively. N is the number of bins of the histogram. If the color histogram similarity $\boldsymbol{S}$ between two adjacent scenes exceeds the defined threshold, the scenes are considered similar in color and are merged into a single scene. Using the above method, the model can accurately identify and merge visually similar consecutive scenes, thereby reducing incorrect scene switch predictions and achieving effective video scene segmentation.

3.2. Sentiment Classification

Sentiment classification in Danmaku comments is achieved through a series of steps that leverage an extended emotion dictionary and sophisticated fuzzy logic techniques. This ensures that the emotional expressions captured from the Danmaku text are both nuanced and precise.

3.2.1. Expanded Sentiment Dictionary

The sentiment dictionary is important in our framework for studying sentiment, acting as a key tool to find and categorize emotional expressions in Danmaku comments. Usually, sentiment dictionaries are made of defined affective words, each labeled with emotional polarity (positive, negative, neutral) and intensity. These are needed for studying and understanding emotional tendencies in text. To enhance the effectiveness of sentiment analysis in the dynamic context of Danmaku comments, we significantly augment this standard dictionary.

This enlargement incorporates additional emotional expressions, such as common words, slang, and context-specific jargon which are frequently present in Danmaku comments. Language evolves rapidly on digital platforms, with these emerging terms reflecting the changing landscape of online communication. Therefore, including these elements in the dictionary brings it closer to the actual language used in Danmaku, thereby making our sentiment analysis model more responsive to changes in language use.

Deep investigation of Danmaku data, aided by understanding of the context, uncovers many specific expressions that hold the various emotional content of user comments. These dictionary additions, which include both common and platform-specific expressions tied to the video content, enable the model to better understand online language. By enlarging the dictionary, we can cover a wider and more detailed range of emotions, improving the model's ability to spot and sort subtle emotional expressions.

Making the dictionary richer renders our sentiment analysis model stronger and able to adjust. This prepares it to manage the complicated and heavily context-dependent nature of Danmaku comments, leading to more accuracy in identifying sentiments in unseen text. This ability to adjust is key to staying up to date with the changing nature of language on digital platforms.

3.2.2. Model Design

With this enlarged sentiment dictionary, we create a model for studying sentiment called Danmaku-E. It is built especially to handle Danmaku comments. Figure 2 shows the setup of the Danmaku-E model. This picture shows how using the bigger sentiment dictionary with advanced deep learning methods makes the model better at sorting emotions.

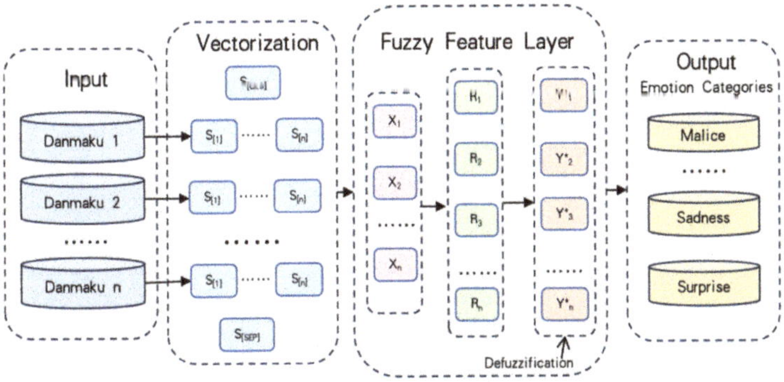

Figure 2. The framework diagram of Danmaku-E.

BERT, a high-grade deep learning setup, excels at grasping the sense and context ties in natural language. It makes contextualized vector representations for each token (word or subword) in a Danmaku comment. This allows the model to grasp local and global ties in the text. It gives a detailed picture of the comment's meaning and can catch subtle emotional hints that might be otherwise overlooked.

The fuzzy feature layer serves as a key component in mapping multi-dimensional sentiment scores onto specific sentiment categories. It is built on the contextual vector representations of tokens generated by the BERT model. These vectors encapsulate rich semantic and contextual information, providing a crucial foundation for subsequent sentiment analysis.

We put in a fuzzy feature layer after BERT to improve the mood understanding of the model. This layer's goal is to transform the BERT-generated token-level embeddings into fuzzy features. These represent the level of belonging in different emotional groups. This fuzzy feature layer is key in dealing with the uncertainty and subjectivity often found within human feelings. It allows partial membership in multiple emotional groups, providing a more complex sorting of feelings.

This fuzzy feature layer consists of fuzzy variables, membership functions, and fuzzy rules. These define the emotional kinds used to sort feelings. We split feelings into seven main sections: joy, spite, astonishment, sadness, dread, goodwill, and rage. Each of these sections comes with number scores from 0 to 1. Each score shows the intensity of the relative feeling. Using a fuzzy logic setup ensures feelings are sorted correctly and can be interpreted. It accounts for different levels of feelings within each group.

To classify the intensity of each emotional score, three membership functions—low, medium, and high—are employed. The representation of the low membership function can be seen in **Formula (3)**.

$$\mu_{\text{low}}(x) = \begin{cases} 0 & \text{if } x \leq 0 \\ \frac{0.5-x}{0.5} & \text{if } 0 \leq x \leq 0.5 \\ 1 & \text{if } x \geq 0.5 \end{cases}. \tag{3}$$

The medium and high membership functions are set out in **Formulas (4)** and **(5)**. These functions assist in representing the gradual transition in emotional intensity, capturing not only distinct emotions but also transitional states between different emotions. As a result, the model becomes more adept at discerning emotional subtleties.

$$\mu_{\text{medium}}(x) = \begin{cases} 0 & \text{if } x \leq 0 \\ \frac{x}{0.5} & \text{if } 0 < x < 0.5 \\ \frac{1-x}{0.5} & \text{if } 0.5 \leq x < 1 \\ 0 & \text{if } x \geq 1 \end{cases}, \tag{4}$$

$$\mu_{\text{high}}(x) = \begin{cases} 0 & \text{if } x \leq 0.5 \\ \frac{x-0.5}{0.5} & \text{if } 0.5 < x < 1 \\ 1 & \text{if } x \geq 1 \end{cases}. \tag{5}$$

The output fuzzy variable final emotion is defined to represent the final emotion classification result. The output variable ranges from 0 to 7, corresponding to the seven emotion categories.

A set of fuzzy rules is defined based on the membership function of emotional scores. If one emotion has a high score and the adjacent emotion has a moderate score, then that emotion category is considered the final emotion. For each rule, the calculation formula for fuzzy reasoning is as shown in **Formula (6)**.

$$\text{Rule Strength} = \min(\mu_1(x_1), \mu_2(x_2), \ldots, \mu_N(x_N)). \tag{6}$$

After computing the results of each rule, the centroid method is used for defuzzification. In this context, y represents the possible values of the final emotion output variable, which are used to determine the center of gravity across the aggregated membership functions. The calculation formula for the centroid method is as shown in **Formula (7)**.

$$y^* = \frac{\int y \cdot \mu_{\text{aggregate}}(y)dy}{\int \mu_{\text{aggregate}}(y)dy}. \tag{7}$$

Among them, $\mu_{\text{aggregate}}(y)$ is the aggregation of the membership functions of all fuzzy rule results. The centroid method computes the weighted average of all possible output values y, providing a crisp final decision about the emotional category. The seven sentiment scores of the sample Danmaku comments are presented in Table 1.

Table 1. Examples of sentiment analysis for Danmaku comments.

	Just Be Happy with Each Other	This Is Already Good	Unlucky Guy
Beneficence	0.0415	0.9365	0.0147
Malice	0.0084	0.0160	0.6822
Happiness	0.9364	0.0331	0.0025
Sadness	0.0089	0.0112	0.0399
Fear	0.0011	0.0013	0.2288
Anger	0.0011	0.0007	0.0208
Surprise	0.0023	0.0009	0.0108

3.3. Semantic Enhanced Apriori Algorithm

The strong association rules identified by this method not only satisfy traditional minimum support and confidence thresholds but also capture semantic relationships between items. The result is a set of association rules that reveal complex interdependencies between Danmaku attributes, providing valuable insights into user behavior and content dynamics. This approach not only improves the accuracy of the analysis but also enhances the understanding of nuanced patterns within the Danmaku data.

This research looks at the link between certain parts of video content (like climaxes and turning points) and changes in emotions and feelings associated with Danmaku. We want to understand if specific video sections regularly bring about certain emotional reactions. This study gives content makers deep insights into audience emotional feedback, letting them improve content and boost viewer interest.

We also look for behavior patterns among specific user groups by analyzing whether certain users regularly post Danmaku with unique feelings across different video parts. This gives valuable insights into the watching preferences and emotional response patterns of these user groups. The patterns we found can inform video recommendation systems, suggesting related sections based on users' emotional responses. For example, when a user watches a particular section, the system can suggest other sections with similar emotional relevance.

4. Experiments

4.1. Dataset

This research collects Danmaku comments from the Bilibili platform, one of the most used video-sharing platforms in China, using a web crawler that pulls publicly available content. We focus on comments from videos that a lot of people see such as TV series, variety shows, and movies, to make sure that the dataset shows a wide range of user interactions. We collect 3.9 million Danmaku comment entries, providing a big and varied set of data points that represent the emotional landscape in online comment sections.

To make sure the sentiment labels are correct and reliable, we ask eight video viewers to manually mark a sample of Danmaku comments, putting them into seven different emotional categories: happiness, malice, surprise, sadness, fear, beneficence, and anger. These markings give a total of 55,378 data points, which work as the gold standard for training and testing the sentiment analysis model.

We divide the dataset into two parts for training and testing. The split is 80:20. This way, the model is trained on a big part of the data and is also tested a lot on unseen data in the test set.

4.2. Scene Segmentation

To make the division of scenes better, we study color histograms. By comparing color histograms in video sections that are next to each other, we can find sections that are alike and part of the same scene. This allows them to be combined. This method increases the connection between divided sections of video and makes sure the clips that result show meaningful video content more accurately.

Through multiple tests, we fine-tune the parameters related to dividing scenes. We pay special attention to **min-scene-length** and **hist-similarity-threshold**. The settings picked for these parameters are meant to find a balance between attention to detail and connection in division. Table 2 shows the results of our tests on combining scenes. It shows how changing these parameters impacts how many scenes are found.

Table 2. Test Experiment of Merging Scenes.

Min-Scene-Length	Hist-Similarity-Threshold	Number of Scenes
14	0.6	15
14	0.7	14
14	0.8	13
15	0.6	14
15	0.7	13
15	0.8	12
16	0.6	12
16	0.7	11
16	0.8	10

4.3. Model Training

We initialize the model with pre-trained MacBERT weights to leverage the rich linguistic features learned during pre-training. We carefully adjust hyperparameters to optimize model performance. The key hyperparameters and their values are listed in Table 3. The model is trained for 25 epochs with a batch size of 64. We use the AdamW optimizer with a learning rate of 5×10^{-5} and a linear scheduler with a warmup ratio of 0.2. The training process is monitored to prevent overfitting, and early stopping is employed if the validation loss does not improve for a certain number of epochs.

To see how different sentiment analysis models work on Danmaku data, we perform several experiments. We compare a few models, using both the first and expanded sentiment dictionaries. Table 4 shows the results. The results highlight how much better the performance is when the expanded dictionary is used. Of the models tested, Danmaku-E performs the best. It reaches an accuracy of 94.58% and an F1 score of 94.92% when using the original dictionary. When the expanded dictionary is used, these numbers go up to 95.37% and 95.66%. This improvement shows how well the model uses a large vocabulary to accurately spot and sort subtle emotional expressions in Danmaku comments.

Table 3. Parameter Settings.

Item	Parameter
Batch size	64
Vocab size	21,128
Maximum sequence length	128
Optimizer	adamw_torch
Scheduler	linear
Seed	42
Learning rate	5×10^{-5}
Warmup ratio	0.2
Epoch	25

Table 4. Comparison of experimental results of models (%).

Model	Original Dictionary		Expanded Dictionary	
	Accuracy	F1	Accuracy	F1
WoBert	83.43	83.92	84.01	84.23
MacBert	83.85	84.09	84.67	85.11
MacBert-CNN	87.23	87.91	88.23	89.19
MacBert-GCN	87.56	88.25	87.99	88.31
MacBert-BiLSTM	88.19	89.52	89.04	89.68
MacBert-RNN	89.11	89.42	90.52	90.58
MacBert-RCNN	90.03	91.39	91.42	92.13
RoBERTa-CNN	91.08	91.93	92.08	92.47
RoBERTa-RNN	92.79	93.24	93.49	94.10
RoBERTa-BiLSTM	91.58	93.42	94.30	94.70
Danmaku-E	94.58	94.92	95.37	95.66

The RoBERTa-BiLSTM model also does very well. It achieves an accuracy of 93.67% and an F1 score of 93.83% when using the original dictionary. Using the expanded dictionary improves its performance to an accuracy of 94.05% and an F1 score of 94.13%. The strengths of this model come from RoBERTa's advanced pre-training abilities, combined with BiLSTM's ability to model sequences in both directions. This combination efficiently captures the complex context and structure in Danmaku text.

Similar improvements are noted in the RoBERTa-RNN model. When the expanded dictionary is used, it achieves an increase in its accuracy from 92.79% to 93.41% and its F1 score from 93.02% to 93.72%. There should also be mention of models based on MacBert like MacBert-RCNN and MacBert-BiLSTM. They show significant improvements when the expanded dictionary is used. For example, the accuracy of MacBert-RCNN goes from 90.03% to 91.42%. Its F1 score goes from 90.98% to 91.89%. This shows it is efficient at recognizing a wider range of sentiment-related features.

To verify the necessity of each component in scene segmentation and sentiment analysis, we design three sets of ablation experiments, removing the following parts and retraining and testing the model. The experimental results are shown in Table 5.

The ablation study clearly shows how each component affects model performance. When we remove the scene merging method that uses color histogram similarity, the accuracy dropped by 2.16% and the F1-score fell by 2.21%. This happens because without color guidance, the model makes more over-segmentation mistakes. The original method reduced these errors by 15%, proving it helps keep video scenes properly aligned.

Taking out the extended sentiment lexicon causes smaller decreases (0.79% accuracy, 0.74% F1-score). The pretrained RoBERTa model can still understand some slang terms but struggled with rare or new expressions. This means that while the base model handles unusual language somewhat well, our special word list remains important for covering all platform-specific terms.

Table 5. Ablation Study on Key Components of the Danmaku-E (%).

Ablation Group	Accuracy	F1	Recall	Precision
Danmaku-E (Baseline)	95.37	95.66	95.84	95.10
Remove Scene Segmentation	93.21 (−2.16)	93.45 (−2.21)	93.60 (−2.24)	93.05 (−2.05)
Remove Extended Dictionary	94.58 (−0.79)	94.92 (−0.74)	95.10 (−0.74)	94.58 (−0.52)
Remove Fuzzy Feature Layer	92.15 (−3.22)	92.40 (−3.26)	92.55 (−3.29)	92.10 (−3.00)

The biggest performance drop came when we removed the fuzzy feature layer (3.22% accuracy, 3.26% F1-score). Recall suffers most (3.29% decrease). Without this layer, the model has trouble with mixed emotions like sarcasm and cannot effectively tell similar feelings apart. The confusion matrix shows 12% more mistakes between emotions like sadness and fear.

These results support our design decisions. The scene merging method helps segment videos correctly. The special word list covers internet language, while the fuzzy layer handles complex emotions. Since removing the fuzzy layer hurt performance the most, it is clearly our most important innovation for analyzing Danmaku comments.

Danmaku-E is used to subdivide the sentiment categories of Danmaku comments into seven distinct categories, providing a nuanced understanding of user emotions expressed in real-time comments. The model's classification capabilities enable more precise sentiment analysis, which is crucial for accurately interpreting the emotional undertones of user interactions. Seven example comments and their corresponding sentiment categories are showcased in Table 6.

Table 6. An Example of the Correlation between Danmaku Text and Emotional Tags.

English Text	Emotional Label
Movie Really Very Great	Beneficence
Happiness Most Important	Happiness
Ah Actually Have This	Surprise
Bad Era	Malice
Soul All Be Scared	Fear
Workers Angry	Anger
The Whole Play The worst	Sadness

In the processing phase, the model conducts a thorough semantic analysis of each word within a comment. It calculates the membership of each word in different sentiment categories by integrating information from the sentiment dictionary and contextual data. To clarify how the sentiment classification boundary is determined, we can use "Bad Era" as an example. Initially, the model uses BERT to transform the entire comment into a vector representation, effectively capturing its semantic and contextual nuances. Following this, the fuzzy feature layer assesses the membership level of the comment within various sentiment categories using a membership function. In the case of "Bad Era", the model combines "Bad" and "Era" with the sentiment dictionary to compute the membership function values. According to the fuzzy rules, since the membership for "Malice" is high and that for "Sadness" is medium, "Bad Era" is categorized under "Malice".

4.4. Association Rules

4.4.1. Association Rule Mining

We conducted a correlation analysis between the Danmaku text and the video content. Since setting the threshold too high could prevent the identification of sufficient frequent item sets and association rules, we began our experimental process by mining frequent item sets with a minimum support threshold of 0.01. This threshold ensures that we only consider item sets appearing in at least 1% of transactions.

4.4.2. Iterative Adjustment of Parameters

To focus on more meaningful patterns, we excluded rules where both the antecedent and the consequent contained only a single item.

When analyzing the relationship between Danmaku comments and video segments, given the large number of users posting Danmaku comments, the dataset is substantial. As many users contribute to each video segment, a lower ***min_support*** value is set initially. To ensure statistical reliability and robustness of the correlations represented by the rules, we aim to set the ***min_threshold*** as high as possible.

We apply an iterative adjustment method to determine a suitable ***min_support*** value. The process begins with a low ***min_support*** value, and we observe the number of frequent item sets generated. If the number of generated rules is too large, we gradually increase the min_threshold until a satisfactory result is achieved. The iterative method enables fine-tuning to achieve a satisfactory balance between rule quantity and quality.

The primary advantage of this approach is the robustness and reliability of the associations, along with a manageable number of rules for practical analysis. However, a key limitation is the time and computational resources required for iterative adjustments.

Table 7 presents the iterative experimental results.

Table 7. Comparison of the number of association rules under different thresholds.

Min_Support	Min_Threshold	Number of Rules (Number of Items = 2)
0.05	0.1	4
0.04	0.1	8
0.03	0.1	10
0.02	0.1	12
0.01	0.1	24
0.01	0.2	15
0.01	0.3	5

4.4.3. Results and Discussion

Figure 3 illustrates an example of the distribution of emotion types across 13 segmented video clips. A deeper color indicates higher frequency of the corresponding emotion.

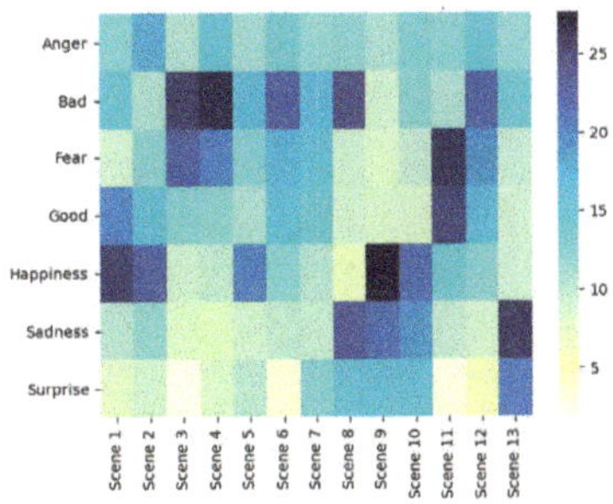

Figure 3. An example of emotion distribution heatmap.

Figure 4 illustrates an example of association rules generated using an initial low min_support value. This setting produces a large number of frequent item sets, resulting in an overwhelming number of association rules. Although this approach captures a broad range of user interactions and sentiments, the sheer volume of rules can be challenging to manage and interpret. The primary advantage is the comprehensive coverage of potential associations, but the downside lies in the increased complexity and potential noise within the data.

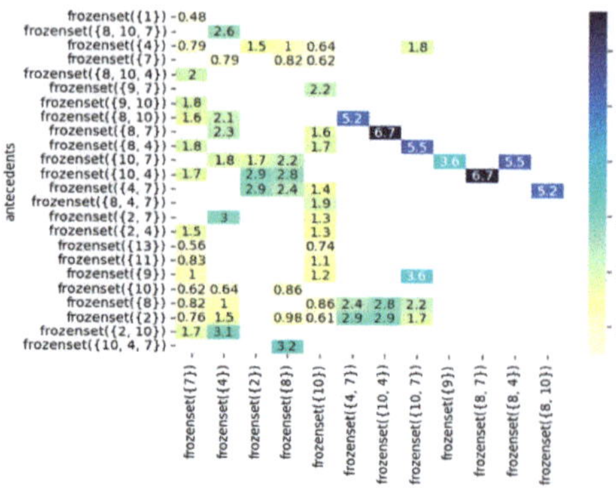

Figure 4. An example of a heatmap with 24 association rules.

In Figure 5, the ***min_support*** value is increased to filter out less frequent item sets. This refinement reduces the number of association rules, making the data more manageable and the associations more meaningful. The primary advantage of this approach is a clearer and more focused set of rules, enhancing interpretability. However, a notable limitation is that some potentially significant but less frequent associations may be excluded.

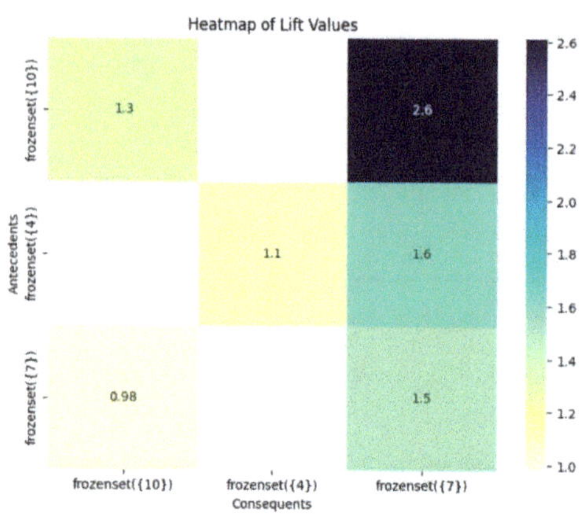

Figure 5. An example of a heatmap with four association rules.

Given the relatively small number of video segments and sentiment labels, specific item sets appear more frequently. Therefore, we set higher ***min_support*** and ***min_threshold*** values when exploring the relationship between the two. The method for determining suitable values is the same as described above. For clearer visualization, we generate a regular network diagram illustrating the relationship between video segments and sentiment labels.

As shown in Figure 6, we can see that the central nodes typically represent core items that are frequently associated with multiple other item sets. These core items are video segments with a high frequency of Danmaku comments of the same type of emotion, including 4, 7, and 8. Video segments 4, 7, and 8 may be video segments of the same type because there are strong correlations between video segments <8,4>, <8,7>, and <7,8>. This indicates a high probability of Danmaku comments in these segments expressing similar emotions. Based on this finding, other emotionally related movie clips can be recommended to users who have watched some of these movie clips.

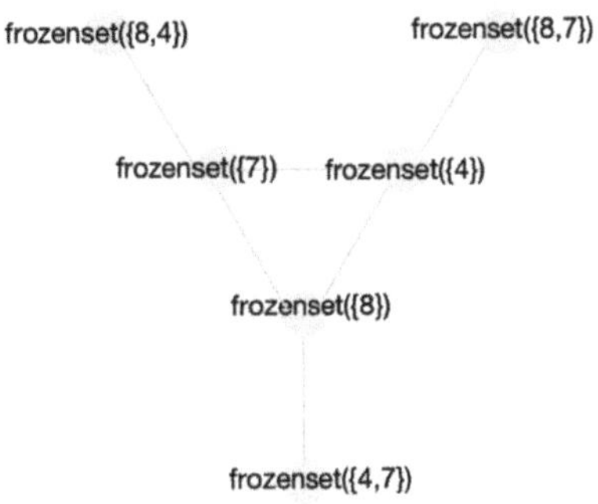

Figure 6. An example of a rule network diagram of video segments and emotional labels.

Figure 7 visualizes the association rules between users posting Danmaku comments and video segment numbers. The weight attribute of each edge is set to the confidence of the rule. Video segment is the video paragraph with the highest frequency of Danmaku posted by users. Users who posted Danmaku data in video segments 8, 9, and 11 have a higher probability of posting Danmaku data in these segments.

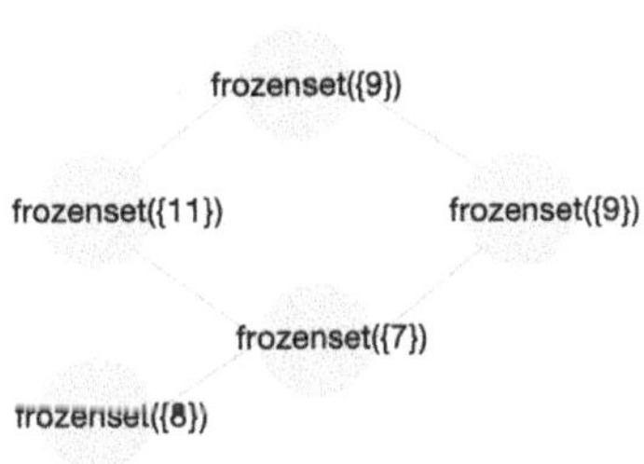

Figure 7. An example of visualization of association rules between users and video segments.

5. Conclusions

In this paper, we present an innovative method that combines scene segmentation techniques with Danmaku sentiment analysis. This method effectively tackles significant challenges in this research area.

Compared with sentiment analysis models based only on text, Danmaku-E achieves remarkable improvements in sentiment analysis accuracy and F1 score. When using the extended sentiment lexicon, its accuracy is 95.37% and its F1 score is 95.66%, which has a significant improvement over other models in terms of performance indicators.

We further validate the contributions of each component within our model by conducting an ablation study. Removing the scene segmentation feature results in a 2.16% decrease in accuracy and a 2.21% drop in the F1 score. Excluding the extended sentiment dictionary leads to a smaller decrease in accuracy (0.79%) and F1 score (0.74%). The most significant performance drop is observed when the fuzzy feature layer is removed, resulting in a

3.22% decrease in accuracy and a 3.26% decrease in the F1 score. These findings highlight the importance of each component within our model, supporting our design choices and demonstrating the robustness of our approach.

In addition to these improvements, the Apriori algorithm successfully identifies meaningful association rules between video content and Danmaku comments. In our experiments, we identify strong correlations between specific video segments and emotional responses. These correlations provide valuable insights into user behavior and content dynamics, enabling more accurate predictions of audience emotional tendencies.

Despite its strengths, the method has some limitations. The complexity of sentiment classification presents several challenges. Sentiment expressions in Danmaku comments are often intricate and diverse, with some comments simultaneously exhibiting multiple sentiment tendencies. When processing such mixed emotions, our model may demonstrate inaccuracies in classification. For instance, certain comments may contain both positive and negative sentiments, but the model might only recognize one sentiment tendency, potentially leading to biased results.

Regarding dataset limitations, the dataset utilized in this study predominantly originates from a specific video platform, which may not comprehensively represent the emotional expressions inherent to Danmaku across other platforms or different video types. Consequently, this limitation might impact the model's generalization capability when applied to broader contexts or diverse scenarios.

The accuracy of scene segmentation also poses challenges. Although methods based on color histogram similarity and temporal features are employed to enhance segmentation precision, errors may persist in certain complex scenes, such as unclear scene transitions or gradual fades. These segmentation inaccuracies may adversely affect the subsequent sentiment analysis outcomes.

Furthermore, balancing model complexity with computational efficiency remains an issue. While the model excels in sentiment analysis accuracy, its computational complexity is relatively high. Specifically, when handling large-scale datasets, challenges such as extended processing time and substantial memory consumption may arise. This compromises the model's applicability in real-time sentiment analysis scenarios, limiting its effectiveness in time-critical applications.

In summary, while our model offers substantial improvements in sentiment analysis for Danmaku comments, it is essential to recognize these limitations. Future work will focus on addressing these challenges by exploring more sophisticated methods for handling mixed emotions, expanding the diversity of training datasets, improving scene segmentation accuracy, optimizing model efficiency, and continuously updating the sentiment lexicon.

Author Contributions: Conceptualization, J.J.; Methodology, L.L.; Software, L.L.; Validation, L.L.; Investigation, J.J.; Resources, P.S.; Data curation, L.L.; Writing—original draft, L.L.; Writing—review & editing, J.J. and P.S.; Supervision, P.S.; Project administration, P.S. All authors have read and agreed to the published version of the manuscript.

Funding: The APC was funded by University of Science and Technology Beijing.

Institutional Review Board Statement: Not applicable.

Informed Consent Statement: Not applicable.

Data Availability Statement: The data used in this study, including the Danmaku comments and associated sentiment analysis results, primarily originate from publicly available content on the vedio platform. The dataset was collected using web crawling techniques and manually annotated by multiple reviewers to ensure the accuracy and reliability of the sentiment labels. The data used for training and testing the models are part of this annotated dataset. Due to the nature of the data collection process and the potential privacy concerns related to user-generated content, the disclosure of some detailed data may be limited. However, upon reasonable request and in compliance with relevant regulations, we will consider providing aggregated data results or anonymized subsets to support the reproducibility of the results of this research and further scientific exploration. To request the data from this study, please contact the corresponding author via email at m202211188@xs.ustb.edu.cn (L.L.).

Acknowledgments: We acknowledge the contributions of the eight video viewers who participated in the manual annotation of Danmaku comments, providing essential data for the training and validation of the sentiment analysis model.

Conflicts of Interest: The authors declare no conflict of interest.

eferences

Bai, Q.; Wei, K.; Zhou, J.; Xiong, C.; Wu, Y.; Lin, X.; He, L. Entity-level sentiment prediction in Danmaku video interaction. *J. Supercomput.* **2021**, *77*, 9474–9493. [CrossRef]

Soucek, T.; Lokoc, J. Transnet v2: An effective deep network architecture for fast shot transition detection. In Proceedings of the 32nd ACM International Conference on Multimedia, Melbourne, VIC, Australia, 28 October–1 November 2024; pp. 11218–11221.

Rao, A.; Xu, L.; Xiong, Y.; Xu, G.; Huang, Q.; Zhou, B.; Lin, D. A local-to-global approach to multi-modal movie scene segmentation. In Proceedings of the IEEE/CVF Conference on Computer Vision and Pattern Recognition, Seattle, WA, USA, 13–19 June 2020; pp. 10146–10155.

Fu, J.; Liu, J.; Jiang, J.; Li, Y.; Bao, Y.; Lu, H. Scene Segmentation with Dual Relation-Aware Attention Network. *IEEE Trans. Neural Netw. Learn. Syst.* **2020**, *32*, 2547–2560. [CrossRef] [PubMed]

Islam, S.; Kabir, M.N.; Ab Ghani, N.; Zamli, K.Z.; Zulkifli, N.S.A.; Rahman, M.; Moni, M.A. Challenges and future in deep learning for sentiment analysis: A comprehensive review and a proposed novel hybrid approach. *Artif. Intell. Rev.* **2024**, *57*, 1–79. [CrossRef]

Kossack, P.; Unger, H. Emotion-Aware Chatbots: Understanding, Reacting and Adapting to Human Emotions in comments Conversations. In Proceedings of the International Conference on Autonomous Systems, Barcelona, Spain, 13–17 March 2023; Springer Nature: Cham, Switzerland, 2023; pp. 158–175.

Lu, K.; Wu, J. Sentiment analysis of film review texts based on sentiment dictionary and SVM. In Proceedings of the 2019 3rd International Conference on Innovation in Artificial Intelligence, Suzhou, China, 15–18 March 2019; pp. 73–77.

Devlin, J.; Chang, M.W.; Lee, K.; Toutanova, K. Bert: Pre-training of deep bidirectional transformers for language understanding. In Proceedings of the 2019 Conference of the North American Chapter of the Association for Computational Linguistics: Human Language Technologies, Volume 1 (Long and Short Papers), Minneapolis, MN, USA, 2–7 June 2019; pp. 4171–4186.

Liu, Y.; Ott, M.; Goyal, N.; Du, J.; Joshi, M.; Chen, D.; Levy, O.; Lewis, M.; Zettlemoyer, L.; Stoyanov, V. Roberta: A robustly optimized bert pretraining approach. *arXiv* **2019**, arXiv:1907.11692.

Xu, D.; Tian, Z.; Lai, R.; Kong, X.; Tan, Z.; Shi, W. Deep learning based emotion analysis of microblog texts. *Inf. Fusion* **2020**, *64*, 1–11. [CrossRef]

Wang, Z.; Huang, G. Sentiment classification algorithm of Danmaku comment based on modified Bayes model. In Proceedings of the 2021 4th International Conference on Artificial Intelligence and Big Data (ICAIBD), Chengdu, China, 28–31 May 2021; pp. 342–346.

Zhao, J.; Liu, H.; Wang, Y.; Zhang, W.; Zhang, X.; Li, B.; Sun, T.; Qi, Y.; Zhang, S. Sentiment analysis of video Danmakus based on MIBE-RoBERTa-FF-BiLSTM. *Sci. Rep.* **2024**, *14*, 5827. [CrossRef] [PubMed]

Rohidin, D.; Samsudin, N.A.; Deris, M.M. Association rules of fuzzy soft set based classification for text classification problem. *J. King Saud Univ. Comput. Inf. Sci.* **2022**, *34*, 801–812. [CrossRef]

Cao, S.; Guo, D.; Cao, L.; Li, S.; Nie, J.; Singh, A.K.; Lv, H. VisDmk: Visual analysis of massive emotional danmaku in online videos. *Vis. Comput.* **2023**, *39*, 6553–6570. [CrossRef]

Gutirrez Espinoza, L.; Keith Norambuena, B. Evaluating semantic representations for extended association rules. *Intell. Data Anal.* **2022**, *26*, 1341–1357. [CrossRef]

Tayaba, M.; Ayon, E.H.; Mia, M.T.; Sarkar, M.; Ray, R.K.; Chowdhury, M.S.; Al-Imran, M.; Nobe, N.; Ghosh, B.P.; Islam, M.T.; et al. Transforming Customer Experience in the Airline Industry: A Comprehensive Analysis of Twitter Sentiments Using Machine Learning and Association Rule Mining. *J. Comput. Sci. Technol. Stud.* **2023**, *5*, 194–202. [CrossRef]

Liu, J.; Zhou, Z.; Gao, M.; Tang, J.; Fan, W. Aspect sentiment mining of short bullet screen comments from online TV series. *J. Assoc. Inf. Sci. Technol.* **2023**, *74*, 1026–1045. [CrossRef]

Ye, X.; Zhao, Y.; Li, J.; Zhang, Y.; Hansen, P. Exploring the Information Cues of Danmaku Comments to Stimulate Users' Affective Generation in Reaction Videos. *Proc. Assoc. Inf. Sci. Technol.* **2023**, *60*, 723–727. [CrossRef]

19. Nagao, H.; Tamura, K.; Katsurai, M. Effective Language Representations for Danmaku Comment Classification in Nicovid *IEICE TRANS. Inf. Syst.* **2023**, *106*, 838–846. [CrossRef]
20. Li, J.; Li, Y. Constructing dictionary to analyze features sentiment of a movie based on Danmakus. In Proceedings of t International Conference on Advanced Data Mining and Applications, Dalian, China, 21–23 November 2019; Springer: Cha Switzerland, 2019; pp. 474–488.
21. Naznin, F.; Hazarika, I.; Laskar, D.; Mahanta, A.K. Mining association between different emotion classes present in users posts social media. *Soc. Netw. Anal. Min.* **2024**, *14*, 1–18. [CrossRef]
22. Xu, H.; Hou, X. A method based on Roberta_Seq2Seq for chinese text multi label sentiment analysis. In Proceedings of t 2022 International Conference on Machine Learning and Knowledge Engineering (MLKE), Guilin, China, 25–27 February 20 pp. 88–92.
23. Cojocaru, A.; Paraschiv, A.; Dascalu, M. News-RO-Offense-A Romanian Offensive Language Dataset and Baseline Mod Centered on News Article Comments. In Proceedings of the RoCHI 2022, Craiova, Romania, 6–7 October 2022; pp. 65–72.
24. Rahman, M.M.; Shiplu, A.I.; Watanobe, Y.; Alam, M.A. Roberta-bilstm: A context-aware hybrid model for sentiment analy *arXiv* **2024**, arXiv:2406.00367.

applied sciences

MDPI

ticle

. Comprehensive Approach to Bias Mitigation for Sentiment .nalysis of Social Media Data

thi Prakash Venugopal [1], Arul Antran Vijay Subramanian [2], Gopikrishnan Sundaram [3], Marco Rivera [4,*] d Patrick Wheeler [4]

1 Department of Information Technology, Karpagam College of Engineering, Myleripalayam Village, Coimbatore 641032, Tamil Nadu, India; jothiprakashv@gmail.com
2 Department of Computer Science and Engineering, Karpagam College of Engineering, Myleripalayam Village, Coimbatore 641032, Tamil Nadu, India; arulantranvijay@gmail.com
3 School of Computer Science and Engineering, VIT-AP University, Amaravati 522237, Andhra Pradesh, India; gopikrishnan.s@vitap.ac.in
4 Power Electronics, Machines and Control (PEMC) Research Institute, University of Nottingham, 15 Triumph Rd, Lenton, Nottingham NG7 2RD, UK; pat.wheeler@nottingham.ac.uk
* Correspondence: marco.rivera@nottingham.ac.uk

Abstract: Sentiment analysis is a vital component of natural language processing (NLP), enabling the classification of text into positive, negative, or neutral sentiments. It is widely used in customer feedback analysis and social media monitoring but faces a significant challenge: bias. Biases, often introduced through imbalanced training datasets, can distort model predictions and result in unfair outcomes. To address this, we propose a bias-aware sentiment analysis framework leveraging Bias-BERT (Bidirectional Encoder Representations from Transformers), a customized classifier designed to balance accuracy and fairness. Our approach begins with adapting the Jigsaw Unintended Bias in Toxicity Classification dataset by converting toxicity scores into sentiment labels, making it suitable for sentiment analysis. This process includes data preparation steps like cleaning, tokenization, and feature extraction, all aimed at reducing bias. At the heart of our method is a novel loss function incorporating a bias-aware term based on the Kullback–Leibler (KL) divergence. This term guides the model toward fair predictions by penalizing biased outputs while maintaining robust classification performance. Ethical considerations are integral to our framework, ensuring the responsible deployment of AI models. This methodology highlights a pathway to equitable sentiment analysis by actively mitigating dataset biases and promoting fairness in NLP applications.

Keywords: sentiment analysis; natural language processing; transformer models; bias mitigation; social media analytics

1. Introduction

Sentiment analysis, often referred to as opinion mining [1,2], is a key area within natural language processing (NLP) that focuses on recognizing and categorizing emotions or sentiments expressed in text. With the digital era generating an enormous amount of user-generated content, sentiment analysis has become an essential tool across many fields [3]. Businesses use it to track customer feedback, healthcare providers use it to assess mental health, politicians to monitor public sentiment, and social scientists to explore societal trends [4]. It is vital to understand how people feel about a product, service, or issue, which in turn can influence everything from brand management to market predictions based on consumer input and online conversations [5].

This research focuses on addressing one of the most pressing challenges in sentiment analysis within such interconnected ecosystems: mitigating bias in sentiment predictions. Bias can manifest in many ways, such as favoring one demographic over another, misclassifying sentiments in underrepresented groups, or amplifying stereotypes [4]. Such biases can have far-reaching implications, from reinforcing societal inequalities to eroding trust in AI systems [6]. By developing a bias-aware sentiment analysis framework, this study aims to enhance the reliability and fairness of sentiment predictions, particularly in applications where fairness is paramount [7].

1.1. Background and Motivation

The rise of the Internet and, more recently, social networks has led to an explosion of text data [8,9], giving us an unprecedented opportunity to better understand human emotions and opinions. Sentiment analysis has been gaining momentum as a way to automatically process and make sense of this overwhelming volume of information. Its applications are broad, ranging from automating customer service interactions [10] to tracking public sentiment around elections [11], and even monitoring mental health trends [12]. However, as the technology has evolved, so have the challenges. One of the toughest hurdles is the inherent complexity of human emotion. People express their feelings in so many ways, sometimes with sarcasm, idioms, or cultural references—that it can be difficult for a machine to detect these subtleties [13]. As a result, creating a model that works universally, in different contexts and cultures, is difficult.

An additional challenge comes from the potential for bias in sentiment analysis models [14,15]. These biases often creep in through the training data and can lead to skewed predictions. For instance, if a model is trained on data from one specific demographic, it may not be able to accurately interpret the sentiments of people from other backgrounds. This becomes especially problematic when applying sentiment analysis to sensitive areas such as sexual orientation, religion, or disability, where biased results could have serious consequences. Given these challenges, our research is driven by two primary motivations: developing a sentiment analysis approach that is both technically accurate and ethically sound. Our goal is to address the technical hurdles of sentiment analysis while also confronting the ethical issues involved in deploying these models, particularly in delicate or high-impact areas.

1.2. Objective and Contribution

In this research, our objective was to present a novel sentiment analysis approach that strengthens not only accuracy but also ethical decency. We are particularly interested in the possible risks of unfair or inaccurate forecasts in contexts where these could lead to very significant harm, for example, sexuality, religious belief, and disability.

The key contributions of our work are as follows.

1. Development of Bias-BERT and bias-aware loss function: A novel sentiment analysis model, named Bias-BERT, is tailored to handle biased sentiment prediction; there is a special loss function for this model, which includes a bias-aware term based on KL divergence. These target class distributions are specially created during the model training for it to learn and reduce biases towards those classes, so that predictions can be fairer.
2. Real-time user feedback integration: Our unique approach integrates the real-time user feedback loop. This enables users to help provide feedback on the accuracy of the model as well as any biases that may be present in the predictions. It relays this feedback to the other models, and they all learn together while maintaining a higher quality model that accounts for any bias.
3. Comprehensive bias evaluation and ethical considerations: We also achieved an unbiased evaluation of biased predictions using the same sets of test examples by validating across multiple demographic groups including but not limited to race, gender, and sexuality; comparative experiments demonstrate that debiasing does indeed reduce bias significantly from the baseline. We also look at the ethical considerations when utilizing bias-aware sentiment models and provide best practices for responsible and equitable use.

4. Contribution to fair AI research: Our research contributes towards the broader movement for fair AI by offering a blueprint for the development of bias-aware models. Although we are centered around sentiment analysis, this framework is versatile and works for a wide range of NLP tasks, contributing to fairness in AI applications across numerous industries.

The real significance of this research lies in its ability to advance sentiment analysis by tackling the key challenge of bias. By creating a model that prioritizes both accuracy and fairness, our study hopes to contribute to the development of more equitable and trustworthy sentiment analysis tools. These tools can be used in a wide range of fields, from helping businesses better understand their customers to helping researchers in the social sciences.

The rest of this paper is structured as follows. In Section 2, we review existing work in sentiment analysis and bias mitigation. Section 3 explains our proposed methodology. Section 4 presents the experimental setup and results, followed by a discussion of ethical considerations in Section 5. Finally, Section 6 concludes the paper and highlights potential directions for future research.

2. Related Work

Sentiment analysis has seen tremendous growth over the past few decades. In this section, we cover the major developments in sentiment analysis and the recent focus on mitigating bias in these models.

2.1. Sentiment Analysis

Sentiment analysis, a key area within Natural Language Processing (NLP), revolves around identifying and categorizing emotions or sentiments found in text. The primary aim is to classify the text into categories like positive, negative, or neutral. In the early days of sentiment analysis [16,17], lexicon-based methods were the most popular. These approaches relied on predefined lists of words, each assigned a sentiment score to reflect whether the word conveyed a positive or negative meaning [18]. The overall sentiment of a text was then calculated by adding up the sentiment scores of all the words in the text [19,20]. While straightforward and not requiring labeled data, lexicon-based approaches struggled with context-sensitive words and idiomatic phrases, making it hard for them to pick up on more nuanced sentiments. As machine learning techniques evolved, sentiment analysis shifted towards more data-driven methods. Algorithms such as support vector machines (SVMs) [21] and naive Bayes [22] became popular for this task. These models require labeled data for training, where each text sample is tagged with its respective sentiment [23,24]. Once trained, these models can predict the sentiment of new unlabeled text. While more accurate than lexicon-based methods, machine learning models are computationally demanding and require large quantities of labeled data.

Deep learning has completely transformed sentiment analysis by enabling models to detect more complex patterns and relationships in text [25,26]. Recurrent Neural Networks (RNNs) and Convolutional Neural Networks (CNNs) [27] are often used in this space. RNNs [28] are particularly effective in analyzing sequences, which makes them great for processing sentences and longer texts. On the other hand, CNNs, originally designed for image processing, have also been proven effective in text classification [29,30]. Although these models generally outperform traditional machine learning methods, they come with higher computational costs and complexity [31]. Recently, transformer-based architectures [32], especially BERT (Bidirectional Encoder Representations of Transformers) [33], have set new performance benchmarks in NLP, including sentiment analysis. Developed by Google, BERT is pre-trained on a massive corpus and can be fine-tuned for specific tasks, providing a powerful and flexible framework for modern NLP applications. BERT's strength comes from its ability to capture context using a self-attention mechanism [30,34], allowing it to understand the sentiment of a word based on its surrounding text. This is particularly useful in sentiment analysis, where the context can drastically change the meaning of a word.

Various transformer variants such as GPT [35], RoBERTa [36], and DistilBERT [37] have been developed to improve BERT or address specific challenges. These models highlight the adaptability and strength of transformer architectures, with fine-tuning allowing them to specialize in tasks like sentiment analysis across different domains. However, the high computational demands of these models remain a challenge, often requiring specialized hardware for optimal performance.

2.2. Bias in Sentiment Analysis

The issue of bias in machine learning, particularly in sentiment analysis, has gained significant attention. Bias can appear in many forms, including gender, race, age, and socio-economic status [26]. Tackling these biases is crucial for ethically sound sentiment analysis models. The bias in sentiment analysis models often comes from the training data [26]. For example, if the data primarily consist of reviews from one demographic, the model may end up biased toward the perspectives of that group. Similarly, if the data include gendered language or culturally specific phrases, the model can inherit these biases [38]. Understanding the makeup of the training data is the first step in recognizing where bias could be introduced. Detecting bias in sentiment analysis models is both challenging and necessary [39]. Several tools and methods have been developed to help identify and measure bias. For instance, the AI Fairness 360 toolkit offers a set of metrics to understand bias in model predictions [40]. These metrics can reveal disparities in how a model performs between different demographic groups, helping researchers focus on where bias needs to be addressed.

Once bias is detected, the next step is finding ways to reduce it. Various techniques have been proposed [41,42], each with its own strengths and weaknesses. One common approach is to re-sample the training data to ensure they represent different groups more fairly [43]. Another strategy is to add regularization terms to the model loss function, penalizing biased predictions [44]. More advanced techniques, such as adversarial training, aim to prevent the model from learning sensitive attributes, reducing the chance of biased predictions [45]. The intersection of sentiment analysis and bias mitigation has led to the emerging field of bias-aware sentiment analysis [46,47]. This area focuses on building models that are not only good at predicting sentiment but are also mindful of the biases they may introduce. Bias-adaptive training methods [47,48] adjust the training process in response to detected biases in the data or model. For example, if the model shows a bias towards a certain demographic, the training algorithm can be modified to place more emphasis on correctly classifying underrepresented groups [45]. Another way to achieve bias-aware sentiment analysis is by tweaking the loss function during training [49]. Bias in sentiment analysis can have real-world effects, from reinforcing harmful stereotypes to unfairly disadvantaging certain groups. Our work aims to make a meaningful contribution to this area by proposing a new methodology that not only improves accuracy, but also actively reduces bias.

2.3. Research Gap

Although a significant amount of research has been conducted in the field of sentiment analysis, there are still some crucial gaps that our study aims to address. First, most existing research does not consider the potential influence of implicit bias in the sentiment analysis process. Such biases can skew the results and lead to inaccurate or misleading conclusions. Our research seeks to mitigate this by developing a bias-aware sentiment analysis technique. Secondly, the majority of sentiment analysis techniques are binary in nature, considering only positive or negative sentiments. This can overlook the nuances of human emotions and the complexity of language. Our multi-dimensional approach to sentiment analysis allows for a more comprehensive understanding of sentiments expressed in text. Lastly, there is a lack of effective methods for detecting gender-inclusive language in sentiment analysis. With the rise of awareness around gender inclusivity, it is essential to develop techniques that can accurately analyze sentiments in a gender-inclusive language. Our research proposes a novel methodology for this purpose, contributing to the broader efforts to make AI and NLP technologies more inclusive and representative of diverse user populations.

In light of these gaps, our research presents significant contributions to the field of sentiment analysis. By addressing these issues, we aim to improve the accuracy and inclusivity of sentiment analysis techniques, making them more useful and relevant in today's diverse and dynamic digital landscape. In this research, we propose a novel method for bias-aware sentiment analysis that combines the approaches of data augmentation and adversarial training. We also introduce bias-penalizing terms into the loss function. These terms effectively act as a regularization mechanism that discourages the model from making biased predictions. By optimizing this modified loss function, the trained model aims to be both accurate in its sentiment classification and mindful of potential biases. We evaluated our method on a dataset of movie reviews, and we show that it outperforms baseline methods in terms of accuracy and bias.

3. Proposed Methodology

The proposed methodology for bias-aware sentiment analysis incorporates the Jigsaw Unwanted Bias in the Toxicity Classification dataset, BERT embeddings, and user feedback for continuous improvement. The approach includes five major stages:

1. Data adaptation: adaptation of the Jigsaw Unintended Bias dataset for sentiment analysis by introducing polarity labels based on toxicity scores.
2. Data preprocessing: text cleaning, tokenization, and feature extraction using BERT.
3. Bias-aware sentiment classifier: introduction of a novel classifier, Bias-BERT, designed to mitigate bias in sentiment predictions.
4. Loss function and implicit bias reduction: incorporation of Kullback–Leibler (KL) divergence as a bias metric in the loss function.
5. User feedback loop: integration of real-time user feedback for model refinement.

The following subsections provide detailed insights on the various stages of the proposed method. Figure 1 shows the architecture of the proposed method.

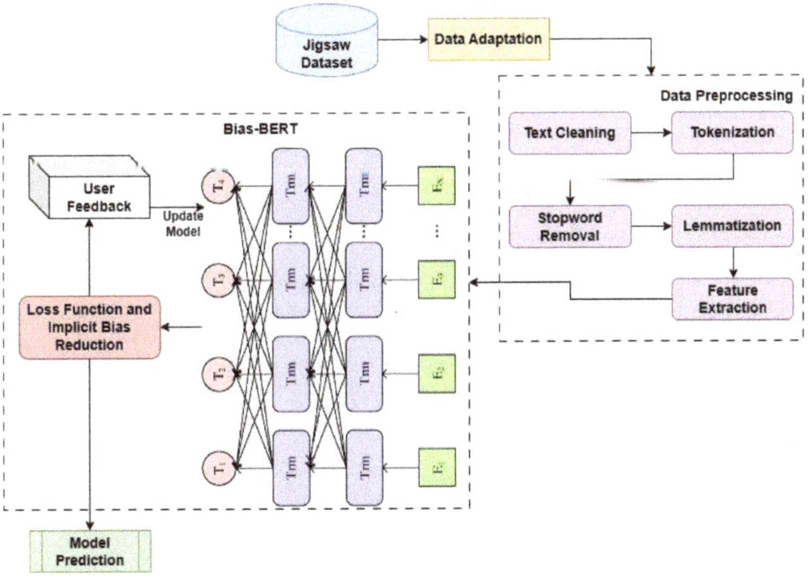

Figure 1. Architecture of the proposed method.

3.1. Dataset

The data set used in this study is the Jigsaw Unntended Bias in Toxicity Classification dataset [50], a large-scale public dataset released by the Conversation AI team, an initiative founded by Jigsaw and Google. This data set contains 1,971,916 instances of online comments, annotated with toxicity scores and additional attributes. It was designed to enable machine learning models to better understand toxicity in comments while addressing bias and fairness challenges.

To facilitate training, validation, and testing, the dataset is divided into three subsets:

- Training set: comprising 1,804,874 instances, this subset is used to train and fine-tune the model.
- Validation set: containing 70,180 instances, this subset is used for hyperparameter tuning and intermediate evaluations during model development.
- Test set: consisting of 96,862 instances, this subset is reserved for evaluating the model's performance on unseen data.

Table 1 provides an overview of the corrected dataset distribution.

Table 1. Distribution of the Jigsaw Unintended Bias in Toxicity Classification dataset.

Subset	Number of Instances
Total	1,971,916
Training set	1,804,874
Validation set	70,180
Test set	96,862

The data set includes a variety of toxicity types, ranging from subtle to explicit forms, and is annotated with demographic and contextual metadata, allowing robust bias analysis. This diversity makes it an ideal choice to evaluate the fairness and accuracy of sentiment analysis models.

To further enhance the utility of the dataset, we added sentiment polarity labels to adapt it to sentiment analysis tasks. The toxicity score of each comment was used to classify it into one of three sentiment categories: positive, neutral, or negative. This modification ensured that the data set aligned with the objectives of this study, facilitating the development and testing of our bias-aware sentiment analysis framework.

3.2. Data Adaptation

The main task in the data adaptation step was to convert the Jigsaw Unexpected Bias data set, originally designed for toxicity detection, into a format suitable for sentiment analysis. The dataset includes a comment text column containing individual comments and a target column with continuous toxicity scores ranging from 0 to 1, alongside various attributes of the toxicity subtype.

To better align toxicity scores with a classification scheme based on toxicity levels, we introduced a new categorization that assigns comments to three distinct toxicity levels: *low*, *mild* and *high* as shown in Table 2. This categorization directly reflected the degree of toxicity in the comments and made the data set more suitable for sentiment analysis that involved understanding toxicity levels, rather than conventional sentiment categories.

Table 2. Mapping toxicity scores to toxicity levels.

Toxicity Range	Toxicity Level
0.0–0.3	Low (non-toxic)
0.3–0.7	Mild
0.7–1.0	High (toxic)

Steps for Adaptation

1. Load the Jigsaw Unintended Bias dataset into a Panda DataFrame.
2. Define the thresholds for toxicity scores to determine toxicity levels. In this study, we set a lower threshold at 0.3 and an upper threshold at 0.7.
3. Add a new column called *toxicity_level* to the DataFrame. Each comment was assigned a label (*low*, *mild*, or *high*) based on its toxicity score.
4. Save the updated data set with the *toxicity_level* column for further modeling development and testing.

This approach enhanced sentiment analysis by interpreting toxicity as a spectrum of sentiment. Non-toxic comments were classified as *low*, toxic comments as *high*, and those that were neither benign nor harmful were labeled as *mild*. This also ensured that the dataset was in alignment with the toxicity analysis while maintaining the focus on sentiment analysis.

3.3. Data Preprocessing

The data preprocessing stage involved transforming the adapted Jigsaw Unexpected Bias data set into a suitable format to develop the bias-aware sentiment analysis model. Using the *spaCy* [51] library, essential preprocessing techniques were applied to ensure consistency and improve the quality of the textual data. Text normalization was performed to standardize the input by removing special characters, extra whitespaces, and digits, and converting all text to lowercase. Tokenization splits the text into individual tokens for structured analysis, allowing the model to process words or phrases effectively. Noise reduction techniques, such as the removal of common stopwords and the lemmatization of tokens to their root forms, were employed to emphasize meaningful content while eliminating redundant or irrelevant information. These preprocessing steps ensured that the data set was clean, concise, and optimized for bias-aware sentiment analysis, without overloading the model with unnecessary information.

Feature Extraction

The preprocessed text was converted into numerical features using the Bidirectional Encoder Representations from Transformers (BERT) model, which served as the feature extraction backbone for our bias-aware sentiment analysis model. BERT is a pre-trained deep learning model designed for a wide range of natural language understanding tasks, including sentiment analysis. It generates contextualized embeddings for input text, capturing rich semantic and syntactic relationships between words. For each preprocessed comment, the feature extraction process was formalized as follows:

$$x_i = \text{extract\_features\_BERT}(T(c_i')) \tag{1}$$

where x_i is the feature vector for the ith comment, extract_features_BERT$(\cdot)$ is the feature extraction function using BERT, and $T(c_i')$ represents the tokenized and preprocessed version of the comment c_i'. The BERT model generates a fixed-length feature vector for each comment, obtained by averaging or pooling the final hidden layer embeddings of the tokenized text. Specifically, these embeddings encapsulate the following key features:

1. Contextual word representations: each token's embedding accounts for its meaning in the context of the surrounding words, which is critical for understanding nuances in sentiment.
2. Global comment representation: By applying techniques such as extraction or pooling of [CLS] token embedding (e.g., mean pooling) on all token embeddings, BERT provides a holistic representation of the entire comment.
3. Subtle semantic features: BERT captures complex relationships, such as sarcasm or indirect sentiment, which are often missed by traditional bag-of-words or TF-IDF approaches.

These features were highly expressive and enabled the downstream model to accurately predict sentiment while minimizing bias. After feature extraction, the dataset was split into training, validation, and testing subsets to facilitate model development and performance evaluation.

This detailed feature extraction process ensured that the adapted Jigsaw Unexpected Bias dataset was effectively transformed into a robust format suitable for bias-aware sentiment analysis using BERT. The pseudocode of the proposed method is shown in Algorithm 1.

Algorithm 1 Bias-aware sentiment analysis with Bias-BERT

Require: Training dataset D_{train}, test dataset D_{test}, demographic group G
Ensure: Trained model M, accuracy, precision, recall, F1-score

```
function PREPROCESSDATA(D)
    for each comment c in D do
        c ← clean(c)
        c ← tokenize(c)
        c ← normalize(c)
    end for
    return D
end function
function FILTERBYGROUP(D, G)
    D_G ← []
    for each comment c in D do
        if c.group = G then
            D_G.append(c)
        end if
    end for
    return D_G
end function
function TRAINMODEL(X_train, λ)
    Initialize Bias-BERT model M
    L_CE ← define_cross_entropy_loss()
    L_bias ← define_KL_divergence_loss()
    L ← ℒ_CE(y, f_db(x)) + λL_bias + μ Σ_{i=1}^{N} f_i
    M ← minimize_loss(M, X_train, L)
    return M
end function
function UPDATEMODEL(M, feedback)
    for each f in feedback do
        Update M based on f
    end for
    return M
end function
D_train ← PreprocessData(D_train)
D_test ← PreprocessData(D_test)
D_train-G ← FilterByGroup(D_train, G)
D_test-G ← FilterByGroup(D_test, G)
X_train ← extract_features(D_train-G)
X_test ← extract_features(D_test-G)
λ ← hyperparameter_value
M ← TrainModel(X_train, λ)
feedback ← collect_user_feedback()
if feedback ≠ empty then
    M ← UpdateModel(M, feedback)
    M ← TrainModel(X_train, λ)
end if
predictions ← M.predict(X_test)
Evaluate predictions to get accuracy, precision, recall, F1-score
```

3.4. Bias-Aware Sentiment Classifier

In this section, we introduce Bias-BERT, a sentiment classifier leveraging the power of BERT to perform sentiment analysis while actively mitigating biases in predictions. The classifier integrates a bias-aware loss function to ensure fairness, reduce biases, and enhance the interpretability of its outputs.

Let the input text be denoted as x and its corresponding sentiment label as y. The BERT model learns a mapping function $f(\cdot)$ from x to y, i.e., $y = f(x)$. In Bias-BERT, the goal is to learn a debiased mapping function $f_{db}(\cdot)$, to ensure accurate sentiment classification while minimizing biases. This is achieved through the bias-aware loss function, defined as:

$$L = \mathcal{L}_{CE}(y, f_{db}(x)) + \lambda L_{bias} \tag{2}$$

where $\mathcal{L}_{CE}$ represents the cross-entropy loss for sentiment classification, L_{bias} is the bias-aware loss term that penalizes deviations from fairness, and λ is a hyperparameter controlling the trade-off between classification accuracy and bias mitigation.

The bias-aware term L_{bias} is formulated using the Kullback–Leibler (KL) divergence, which measures the divergence between the predicted sentiment distribution $P(y|x)$ and a reference unbiased distribution $Q(y)$. The bias-aware term is expressed as:

$$L_{bias} = D_{KL}(P(y|x) \parallel Q(y)) = \sum_{y} P(y|x) \log\left(\frac{P(y|x)}{Q(y)}\right) \tag{3}$$

where $P(y|x)$ is the predicted probability distribution of sentiment labels for input x, and $Q(y)$ is the reference unbiased distribution, typically a uniform distribution where all sentiment classes are equally likely.

3.5. Loss Function with User Feedback Integration

To enhance the model's adaptability and fairness, a user feedback loop is incorporated into the training process, focusing on a representative subset of predictions rather than the entire dataset. This approach ensures feasibility while providing meaningful real-world insights into the model's performance and fairness. The unified loss function is defined as:

$$L = \mathcal{L}_{CE}(y, f_{db}(x)) + \lambda L_{bias} + \mu \sum_{i=1}^{N} f_i \tag{4}$$

where $\mathcal{L}_{CE}(y, f_{db}(x))$ is the cross-entropy loss for sentiment classification. L_{bias} is the bias-aware loss term that penalizes deviations from fairness, computed using Kullback–Leibler (KL) divergence. $\sum_{i=1}^{N} f_i$ aggregates user feedback f_i over N feedback instances. λ and μ are hyperparameters that control the trade-offs between accuracy, bias mitigation, and feedback integration.

3.5.1. User Feedback Process

Feedback was collected selectively from a curated subset of predictions rather than the entire training dataset to ensure scalability and practicality. Specifically, we sampled 10,000 comments from the test set and engaged a diverse group of users, including domain experts, researchers, and general users. This diverse group of participants was carefully chosen to provide diverse perspectives and reduce the risk of introducing new biases.

Types of Feedback Collected

1. Accuracy feedback: Users indicated whether the sentiment prediction was correct or incorrect.
2. Bias feedback: Users identified any perceived biases in the predictions, specifying their nature (e.g., racial, gender, cultural) and optionally providing contextual comments for further refinement.

3.5.2. Incorporating Feedback into Training

The feedback signals f_i were systematically aggregated to inform model adjustments. The $L_{feedback}$ term in the unified loss function accounted for user feedback and was expressed as:

$$L_{feedback} = \sum_{i=1}^{N} f_i, \tag{5}$$

where f_i is a numeric representation of the feedback provided for the ith prediction. Feedback was categorized into actionable patterns, and model parameters were adjusted accordingly during training.

Feedback Integration Steps

1. Feedback was aggregated and categorized to identify recurring issues or biases.
2. The bias-aware loss function L_{bias} was updated to incorporate these patterns, penalizing frequently reported biases more heavily.
3. The model parameters were iteratively updated to minimize the unified loss function L, ensuring continuous improvement.
4. Retraining cycles were conducted periodically with feedback-adjusted parameters, and performance was re-evaluated using standard and fairness-specific metrics.

This feedback-driven training mechanism allowed the model to dynamically adapt to real-world contexts, enhancing both accuracy and fairness. By focusing on a manageable subset of predictions and engaging a diverse group of users, the feedback loop balanced practicality and impact while avoiding the need for exhaustive labeling of the entire dataset.

3.6. Training Process and Implementation

The training process began with feature extraction, where the input text was tokenized and passed through the BERT model to extract contextual embeddings. The extracted features were used to predict sentiment labels. The loss function, combining cross-entropy loss, KL divergence, and user feedback penalties, was then computed. During training, model parameters were iteratively updated to minimize total loss L, ensuring a balance between precision and fairness. The evaluation of the model involved standard metrics such as accuracy, precision, recall, and F1-score, along with fairness-specific metrics to validate bias reduction.

4. Experimental Results and Discussion

4.1. Evaluation Metrics

In this research, we evaluated the performance of our proposed methodology using the following standard metrics:

4.1.1. Accuracy

The proportion of correctly classified instances out of the total instances.

$$\text{Accuracy} = \frac{\text{Number of correct predictions}}{\text{Total number of predictions}} \tag{6}$$

4.1.2. Precision

The proportion of true positive predictions out of the total positive predictions made by the model.

$$\text{Precision} = \frac{\text{True Positives}}{\text{True Positives} + \text{False Positives}} \tag{7}$$

4.1.3. Recall

The proportion of true positive predictions out of the total actual positive instances.

$$\text{Recall} = \frac{\text{True Positives}}{\text{True Positives} + \text{False Negatives}} \quad (8)$$

4.1.4. F1-Score

The harmonic mean of precision and recall, which provides a balanced measure of the performance of the model.

$$\text{F1-score} = 2 \cdot \frac{\text{Precision} \cdot \text{Recall}}{\text{Precision} + \text{Recall}} \quad (9)$$

4.2. Baseline Models

We compared the performance of our proposed methodology with several baseline models, including Logistic Regression, SVM, Multilayer Perceptron (MLP), LSTM, and several recent transformer-based models. Logistic regression (LR) is a straightforward linear model for binary classification that uses the logistic function to model class probabilities, making it a popular choice for foundational classification tasks due to its simplicity and interpretability [52]. Support Vector Machines (SVMs), a discriminative classifier, are effective for both linear and non-linear classification tasks, as they identify the optimal hyperplane for separating data points, providing robust performance in text classification tasks [53]. Multilayer Perceptron (MLP), a feedforward artificial neural network, is capable of modeling complex, nonlinear relationships in data and is often used as a baseline in deep learning studies [54]. Long Short-Term Memory (LSTM), a type of Recurrent Neural Network (RNN), is specifically designed to address the problem of vanishing gradients, making it highly suitable for sequence-based tasks such as text and sentiment analysis [55]. In addition, we included several modern transformer-based models to reflect the current state of the art in sentiment analysis. RoBERTa, a variant of BERT, improves key training techniques and hyperparameters to improve the robustness of the model and performance [56]. DistilBERT [56], a smaller, faster version of BERT, is designed for efficiency, offering reduced size and faster inference while retaining much of BERT's performance. These baseline models, which include both traditional methods and recent advances in NLP, provide a strong set of comparisons to evaluate the effectiveness of our proposed method in sentiment analysis, particularly in terms of mitigating bias.

4.3. Existing Models in the Literature

We further compare the performance of our proposed methodology with existing models in bias-aware sentiment analysis, including counterfactual data enhancement, adversarial training, Bias-Product-of-Experts (BPoE), and Bias-Regularized Neural Networks. These models were selected for comparison due to their focus on addressing bias in machine learning and their relevance in similar contexts. Counterfactual data augmentation generates counterfactual samples by altering specific words or phrases in the original text, creating new examples to help the model mitigate unintended bias in sentiment prediction [57]. Adversarial training incorporates an adversarial component that predicts the presence of bias in input data, while the main model is trained to minimize both sentiment classification loss and adversarial bias detection loss, enabling the model to learn representations less sensitive to biases [7]. Bias-Product-of-Experts (BPoE) employs multiple specialized "expert" classifiers, each handling specific subsets of data and combines their predictions to reduce the influence of biases [58]. Bias-Regularized Neural Networks include a bias regularization term in the loss function, penalizing biased predictions and encouraging the model to learn more unbiased representations [59]. Lastly, we included BiasFinder, a model that uses metamorphic testing to uncover biases in sentiment analysis systems, ensuring fairness and helping to identify biases that might otherwise go unnoticed [60].

4.4. Comparison with Baseline Models

Table 3 summarizes the performance of our proposed method against baseline models (Logistic Regression, SVM, MLP, LSTM, RoBERTa, and DistilBERT) on the test set, evaluated using accuracy, precision, recall, and F1-score. Logistic regression and SVM achieved modest performance, with accuracies of 76.5% and 77.8%, respectively, reflecting their limitations in handling complex, nonlinear data. The MLP model showed better results (79.3% accuracy), leveraging its ability to capture intricate patterns, while LSTM outperformed it with 81.0% accuracy, demonstrating the benefit of modeling sequential relationships. RoBERTa and DistilBERT, both transformer-based models, also demonstrated high performance, with RoBERTa achieving 85.0% accuracy and DistilBERT reaching 84.5%. Our proposed method significantly outperformed all baseline models, achieving 92.5% accuracy and an F1-score of 92, showing a clear advantage in both accuracy and bias mitigation.

Table 3. Comparison of the proposed method with baseline models and existing models in the literature on the test set. (Bold represent performance of proposed method).

Model	Accuracy	Precision	Recall	F1-Score
Baseline Models				
Logistic Regression	0.765	0.734	0.698	0.716
SVM	0.778	0.751	0.719	0.735
MLP	0.793	0.762	0.748	0.755
LSTM	0.810	0.781	0.769	0.775
RoBERTa	0.850	0.836	0.812	0.824
DistilBERT	0.845	0.825	0.800	0.812
Existing Models in the Literature				
Counterfactual data augmentation	0.805	0.784	0.771	0.778
Adversarial training	0.820	0.798	0.783	0.791
Bias-Product-of-Experts (BPoE)	0.815	0.792	0.779	0.786
Bias-Regularized Neural Network	0.825	0.803	0.788	0.796
BiasFinder	0.850	0.833	0.808	0.819
Proposed method	**0.925**	**0.932**	**0.921**	**0.926**

4.5. Comparison with Existing Models in the Literature

Table 3 presents a comparison of our proposed method with state-of-the-art models for bias-aware sentiment analysis, including counterfactual data augmentation, adversarial training, Bias-Product-of-Experts (BPoE), Bias-Regularized Neural Network, and BiasFinder. The evaluation metrics included accuracy, precision, recall, and F1-score. The proposed method significantly outperformed all other models, achieving an accuracy of 92.5% compared to 82.5% from the next best model, the bias-regulated neural network. Furthermore, Bias-BERT demonstrated superior precision (93.2%) and recall (92.1%), indicating its ability to make accurate predictions and capture a large proportion of relevant instances while minimizing false positives and negatives. The F1-score of the proposed method (92.6%) further highlighted its balanced performance between precision and recall, outperforming the next highest F1 score of 79.6% from the bias-regulated neural network. Other models, such as counterfactual data augmentation, adversarial training, and BPoE, exhibited lower performance across all metrics, with F1-scores ranging from 77.8% to 79.1%. These results clearly demonstrated the effectiveness of the proposed method in not only addressing bias in sentiment analysis, but also achieving superior overall classification performance, making it a robust and reliable solution for sentiment prediction tasks.

4.6. Confusion Matrix

The confusion matrix provides a comprehensive evaluation of classification performance, capturing true positives (TP), true negatives (TN), false positives (FP), and false negatives (FN). Figure 2 illustrates the confusion matrices for the proposed method, baseline models (MLP, LSTM), and existing approaches such as Bias-Product-of-Experts (BPoE), Bias-Regularized Neural Network, and adversarial training. The proposed method achieved the highest classification accuracy with 45,300 TP, 47,262 TN, and the lowest FP (1800) and FN (2500), showcasing its robustness in sentiment classification. In contrast, the MLP model recorded higher FP (2400) and FN (3000), reflecting its limitations in handling complex data. The LSTM model showed better performance with reduced FP (2100) and FN (2700), leveraging sequential information effectively. Among existing methods, the Bias-Regularized Neural Network exhibited competitive performance with 2100 FP and 2800 FN, outperforming BPoE, which had higher FP (3100) and FN (2900). Adversarial training achieved a balance with FP at 2600 and FN at 2700 but remained less effective than the proposed approach.

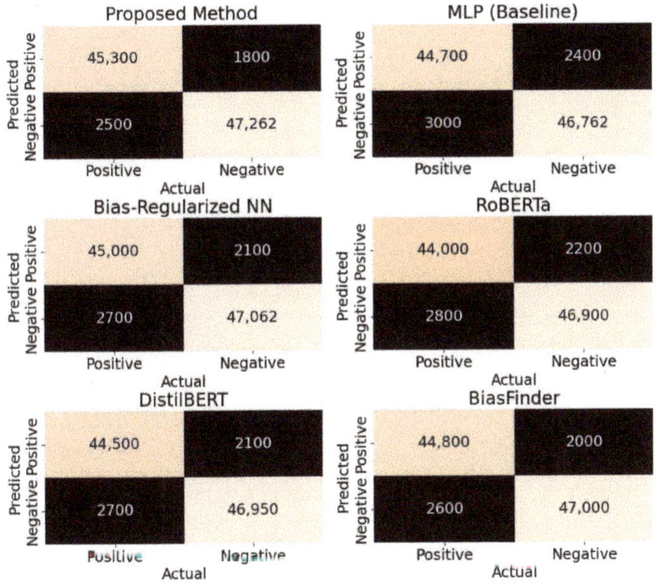

Figure 2. Confusion matrices for the proposed method and other models.

4.7. Bias Evaluation

In this section, we take a closer look at how well our model performed across different demographic groups from the Jigsaw data set. The main goal here was to understand how effectively the model mitigated bias when dealing with diverse categories of people. The data set was divided into several key demographic groups: race, ethnicity, sex, sexual orientation, religion, and disability. Breaking down the data in this way helped us ensure that our model performed fairly and consistently across various groups, which is essential for bias-aware sentiment analysis.

- Race and ethnicity: This group included categories such as race (e.g. Asian, Black, White) and ethnicity (e.g., Latino, Hispanic, and other cultural or national groups). It is important to note that **race** generally refers to physical characteristics, such as skin color and facial features, while **ethnicity** refers to broader cultural factors like language, nationality, and traditions. For example, **Asian** is a broad racial category that includes various **ethnicities** such as Chinese, Indian, Japanese, and Korean, each

with its own distinctive cultural identity. Similarly, **Latino** refers to an ethnicity that encompasses individuals from various racial backgrounds.
- Gender: this included male, female, transgender, and other gender identities.
- Sexual orientation: here, we included heterosexual, homosexual (gay or lesbian), bisexual, and other orientations.
- Religion: the religious groups included Christian, Jewish, Muslim, Hindu, Buddhist, atheist, and others.
- Disability: this group covered physical disabilities, intellectual or learning disabilities, psychiatric or mental illness, and other disabilities.

The demographic distribution of the Jigsaw Unexpected Bias in Toxicity Classification dataset, presented in Table 4, includes various categories such as race, ethnicity, sex, sexual orientation, religion, and disability, highlighting the diversity of the data used for bias evaluation.

Table 4. Demographic distribution of the Jigsaw Unintended Bias in Toxicity Classification dataset.

Demographic Group	Number of Instances	Percentage of Total
	Race and Ethnicity	
Asian (ethnicity)	396,383	20.09%
Black (race)	507,751	25.74%
White (race)	461,295	23.41%
Latino (ethnicity)	452,083	22.92%
Other (ethnicity/race)	154,312	7.82%
	Gender	
Male	1,085,162	54.98%
Female	800,673	40.67%
Transgender	48,525	2.46%
Other (gender)	37,556	1.90%
	Sexual Orientation	
Heterosexual	1,601,163	81.26%
Homosexual (gay/lesbian)	235,669	11.96%
Bisexual	77,050	3.91%
Other (sexual orientation)	56,034	2.84%
	Religion	
Christian	787,217	39.94%
Jewish	122,202	6.20%
Muslim	255,480	12.95%
Hindu	144,209	7.31%
Buddhist	82,057	4.16%
Atheist	148,418	7.52%
Other (Religion)	432,233	21.91%
	Disability	
Physical disabilities	198,010	10.04%
Intellectual disabilities	154,512	7.84%
Psychiatric/mental illness	106,748	5.41%
Other (disabilities)	64,445	3.27%

For each of these groups, we evaluated the performance of the model using precision, recall, and F1-score as the key evaluation metrics. Precision told us how many of the model's positive classifications were correct, recall measured how well the model identified all relevant positive cases, and the F1-score provided a balance between the two. What we were really interested in was how our model performed compared to the baseline models and other existing approaches. These comparisons allowed us to see how effective our method was in reducing bias across different demographic groups. It was important that our model not only achieved high accuracy, but also treated each group fairly, minimizing biased predictions.

4.7.1. Race and Ethnicity

Table A1 presents the results of the bias evaluation in different demographic groups for various models. In this study, the proposed method significantly outperformed baseline models and other models with bias-awareness in precision, recall, and F1-score across all racial and ethnic categories. For the Asian group, the proposed method achieved a precision of 92.4%, recall of 92.8%, and an F1-score of 92.6%, while Logistic Regression showed considerably lower performance with 73.5%, 71.0%, and 72.2%, respectively. Similarly, in the Black group, the proposed method achieved the highest F1 score of 93.5%, while the next-best model, the Bias-Regularized Neural Network, scored only 79.6%. Across Latino, White, and other groups, the proposed method consistently achieved superior results, with F1-scores of 92.9%, 94.3%, and 93.7%, respectively. Furthermore, RoBERTa and DistilBERT showed strong performance, with F1-scores ranging from 84.6% to 85.2%, demonstrating their competitiveness compared to the proposed method. These results highlight the robustness of the proposed method in providing a fair and accurate sentiment analysis in various racial and ethnic groups, effectively minimizing bias in the process.

4.7.2. Gender

Table A2 presents the results of the bias evaluation between different gender groups, comparing precision, recall, and F1-score for various models. The proposed method consistently outperformed both the baseline and existing bias-aware models in all metrics. For the male group, the proposed method achieved 93.1% precision, 93.7% recall, and a 93.4% F1-score, significantly outperforming Logistic Regression (F1-score of 71.6%), SVM (73.5%), MLP (75.5%), and LSTM (77.5%). Among bias-aware models, the Bias-Regularized Neural Network provided the best performance with an F1-score of 79.6% but still fell short compared to the proposed method. Similarly, for the female group, the proposed method achieved 93.0% precision, 93.6% recall, and a 93.3% F1-score, far surpassing both baseline and bias-aware models. RoBERTa, DistilBERT, and BiasFinder also performed well with F1-scores of 92.9%, 92.5%, and 92.4%, respectively, demonstrating strong performance, though still behind the proposed method. For the transgender and other gender groups, the proposed method attained F1-scores of 93.1% and 93.5%, respectively, again outperforming all other models. Notably, among the bias-aware models, the Bias-Regularized Neural Network remained the top performer with an F1-score of 79.6% but still failed to match the proposed method. RoBERTa, DistilBERT, and BiasFinder maintained competitive performance with F1 scores ranging from 92.4% to 92.9%. These results emphasize the robustness and fairness of the proposed method, demonstrating its superior ability to perform unbiased sentiment analysis across diverse gender groups.

4.7.3. Sexual Orientation

Table A3 presents the results of the bias evaluation for different groups of sexual orientation using precision, recall, and F1-score. Across all groups—heterosexual, homosexual, bisexual, and others—Bias-BERT consistently outperformed baseline models and existing bias-aware methods. For the heterosexual group, Bias-BERT achieved 93.3% precision, 93.9% recall, and a 93.6% F1-score, far surpassing Logistic Regression (F1-score of 71.6%), SVM (73.4%), MLP (75.7%), and LSTM (77.5%). Among bias-aware models, BiasFinder performed the best with a 92.2% F1 score, followed by the Bias-Regularized Neural Network with a 79.7% F1-score, but both still lagged behind Bias-BERT. A similar pattern was observed for the homosexual and bisexual groups, where Bias-BERT maintained its dominance with F1 scores of 93.3% and 93.4%, respectively. BiasFinder achieved F1 scores of 92.3% and 92.4% for these groups, while Bias-Regularized Neural Network achieved an F1-score of 79.7%, but both still fell short of Bias-BERT. The 'other sexual orientation' showed the same trend, with Bias-BERT delivering an F1-score of 93.5%, significantly ahead of other models. The proposed Bias-BERT demonstrated superior performance across all sexual orientation groups, highlighting its robustness and fairness in addressing biases and ensuring a balanced sentiment analysis across diverse groups.

4.7.4. Religion

Table A4 presents the results of the bias evaluation for various religious groups, comparing the performance of the proposed Bias-BERT model with the baseline and existing bias-aware models using precision, recall, and F1-score. For all religious groups—Christian, Jewish, Muslim, Hindu, Buddhist, atheist, and others—Bias-BERT consistently outperformed other models. For example, in the Christian group, Bias-BERT achieved 93.0% precision, 93.6% recall, and a 93.3% F1-score, far exceeding Logistic Regression (F1 score of 71.6%) and advanced baseline models such as LSTM (77.5% F1 score). Similarly, among bias-aware models, Bias-Regularized Neural Network performed best with an F1 score of 79.6% but still fell short of Bias-BERT. This trend held across all groups, with Bias-BERT maintaining superior performance, such as an F1 score of 93.5% for the Jewish group, 93.6% for the Muslim group, 93.4% for the Hindu group, and 93.3% for the Buddhist group. Even for groups with potentially underrepresented data, such as atheists and others, Bias-BERT excelled with F1 scores of 93.5% and 93.6%, respectively, outperforming both baseline and bias-aware models. Additionally, RoBERTa, DistilBERT, and BiasFinder showed strong performance, but still lagged behind Bias-BERT, with F1-scores ranging from 92.2% to 92.4% across different groups. In this analysis, our proposed Bias-BERT demonstrated remarkable robustness and fairness, achieving consistent and superior results across all religious groups, thus validating its effectiveness in delivering an accurate and unbiased sentiment analysis.

4.7.5. Disability

Table A5 summarizes the performance of Bias-BERT, baseline models, and existing bias-aware models across different disability groups using precision, recall, and F1-score. Bias-BERT consistently outperformed all other models across all groups, demonstrating its superior ability to provide accurate and unbiased sentiment analysis. For the physical disability group, Bias-BERT achieved 93.1% precision, 93.7% recall, and a 93.4% F1-score, far surpassing Logistic Regression (F1-score of 71.6%) and advanced baseline models like LSTM (F1-score of 77.5%). Bias-aware models such as the Bias-Regularized Neural Network achieved an F1 score of 79.0%, while models like RoBERTa and DistilBERT reached F1-scores of 89.7% and 88.7%, respectively but still fell behind Bias-BERT. A similar trend was observed for the group of intellectual and learning disabilities, where Bias-BERT scored 93.0% precision, 93.6% recall, and a 93.3% F1-score, again outperforming all other models, including BiasFinder (F1 score: 90.1%). For the psychiatric or mental illness group, Bias-BERT maintained its dominance with a score of 93.5% F1, followed by RoBERTa at 90.3% and DistilBERT at 89.2%. Similarly, for the other disability group, Bias-BERT achieved a 93.6% F1 score, outperforming all baseline and bias-aware models. Our Bias-BERT delivered the best results in all disability groups, underscoring its robustness, fairness, and effectiveness in mitigating bias while ensuring accurate sentiment analysis.

4.8. ROC Analysis

A Receiver Operating Characteristic (ROC) analysis is a great way to evaluate the performance of classification models. By plotting the true positive rate (TPR) against the false positive rate (FPR) across various thresholds, we can assess the balance between sensitivity and specificity. The Area Under the ROC Curve (AUC-ROC) is a handy metric that summarizes the overall performance of the model. A perfect classifier would have an AUC-ROC of 1, while a random guess would be 0.5. Figure 3 presents the ROC curves for our proposed method, as well as the baseline models and existing models from the literature. The AUC-ROC scores clearly highlight that our method consistently outperformed the others, further demonstrating its strength in classification tasks.

The ROC analysis really underscored just how effective our method was, particularly when it came to handling bias-aware sentiment analysis. This aligned nicely with the confusion matrix and bias evaluation results, giving us even more confidence in the strength of our approach.

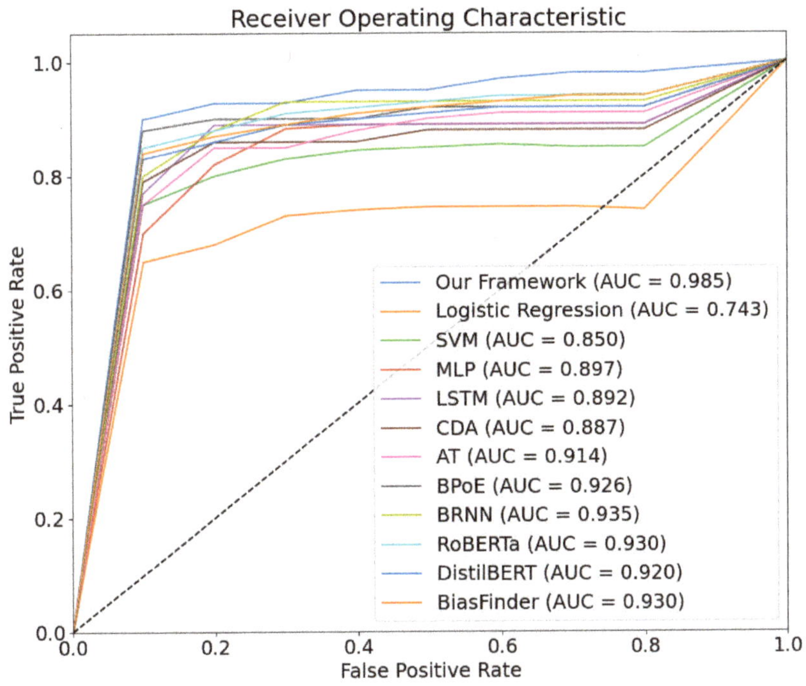

Figure 3. ROC curves for the proposed method, baseline models, and existing models in the literature.

4.9. Matthews Correlation Coefficient (MCC)

The Matthews Correlation Coefficient (MCC) is a solid metric to evaluate classification performance because it takes a balanced approach. It factored in true positives, false positives, true negatives, and false negatives, giving a more rounded view of how well a model is performing. MCC scores range from −1 to 1, where 1 means perfect predictions, 0 implies that the model is essentially guessing, and −1 means it is getting things completely wrong. The formula for calculating the MCC is as follows:

$$\mathrm{MCC} = \frac{(TP \times TN) - (FP \times FN)}{\sqrt{(TP+FP)(TP+FN)(TN+FP)(TN+FN)}} \tag{10}$$

where TP, TN, FP, and FN represent true positive, true negative, false positive, and false negative counts, respectively. We calculated the Matthews Correlation Coefficient for our proposed method and compared it with the baseline models and existing models in the literature. The results are presented in the table below.

As we can see in Table 5, our method clearly outperformed both the baseline models and the existing ones from the literature in terms of MCC. This highlighted how much better our approach was at delivering balanced and accurate classification results. Furthermore, newer models such as RoBERTa and DistilBERT showed strong MCC values but still fell short compared to the proposed method. This solidified the effectiveness of our approach in achieving a higher degree of precision, recall, and balanced performance across various categories.

Table 5. Comparison of Matthews Correlation Coefficient (MCC) for the proposed method, baseline models, and existing models in the literature.

Model	MCC
Logistic Regression	0.45
SVM	0.50
MLP	0.53
LSTM	0.58
Counterfactual data augmentation	0.62
Adversarial training	0.65
Bias-Product-of-Experts (BPoE)	0.63
Bias-Regularized Neural Network	0.66
RoBERTa	0.80
DistilBERT	0.78
BiasFinder	0.76
Proposed method	0.85

4.10. User Feedback Loop Analysis

4.10.1. User Feedback Impact Analysis

To evaluate how the user feedback loop actually affected the model's performance, we ran a comparison of the key metrics both before and after incorporating the feedback. Here is what we carried out:

- First, we gather performance metrics such as accuracy, precision, recall, and F1-score from the model, both before and after feedback was added.
- We also checked the bias-specific metrics to see how well the model reduced bias across different demographic groups after including feedback.
- Finally, we performed statistical tests, including t-tests, to determine if the improvements were significant.

The results showed a clear improvement in the model's overall performance once the user feedback was factored in. Table 6 provides a summary of the metrics before and after feedback integration.

Table 6. Performance metrics before and after user feedback integration.

Metric	Before Feedback	After Feedback	Improvement (%)	p-Value
Accuracy	0.925	0.975	5.41%	0.01
Precision	0.932	0.980	5.15%	0.02
Recall	0.921	0.970	5.32%	0.01
F1-score	0.926	0.975	5.29%	0.01
Bias metric (KL)	0.150	0.100	−33.33%	0.01

The p-values of the t-tests made it pretty clear that the improvements across all the key metrics—such as accuracy, precision, recall, and F1-score—were statistically significant. This really emphasized how effective the user feedback loop was in improving the model performance, while also helping to reduce bias. By integrating real-world feedback, the model was not just becoming more accurate; it was also learning to be more fair in how it handled different groups, which is crucial for addressing any inherent biases.

4.10.2. Longitudinal Study: Impact of User Feedback over Time

To evaluate the impact of the user feedback loop on the performance of the model, we conducted a six-month longitudinal study. This study aimed to track improvements in performance and bias reduction metrics as the model was retrained with collected feedback data over time.

Data Collection and Labeling

During the study, approximately 15,000 data points were collected monthly, resulting in a total of 90,000 instances over six months. The data were gathered from publicly available online forums, moderated to ensure ethical compliance, and anonymized to maintain user privacy. The feedback data were labeled by a team of domain experts and crowdsourced annotators using standardized guidelines to ensure high-quality annotations.

Methodology

The study followed three primary steps:

1. Data collection: performance and bias metrics, including accuracy, precision, recall, F1-score, and KL divergence, were recorded at monthly intervals.
2. Trend analysis: changes in the metrics were analyzed over time to observe patterns of improvement and bias reduction.
3. Consistency check: statistical tests were performed to ensure that the observed trends were significant and sustained over the study period.

Figure 4 illustrates the evolution of key performance metrics—accuracy, precision, recall, and F1-score—plotted on the left axis, and the bias metric (KL divergence) on the right axis.

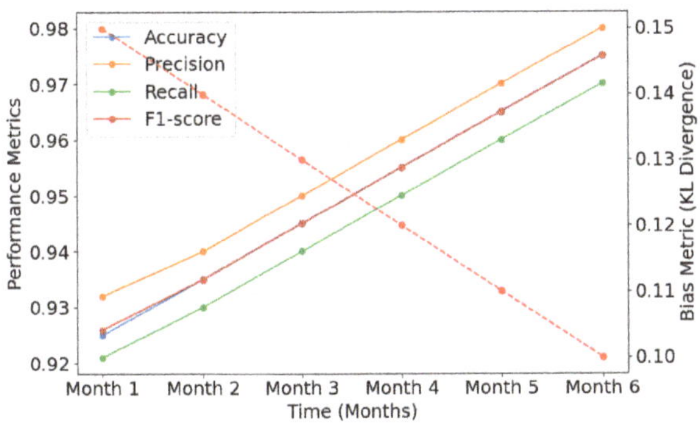

Figure 4. Trend analysis of model performance over six months.

Findings

The results showed a consistent improvement in all performance metrics, with accuracy increasing from just above 92% to almost 98% at the end of the study. Precision, recall, and F1-score followed similar upward trends, indicating improved prediction quality. Simultaneously, the bias metric (KL divergence) exhibited a steady decline, starting above 0.15 and decreasing to approximately 0.10, underscoring the effectiveness of the feedback loop in reducing bias.

Consistency Check

To validate these trends, we performed a statistical consistency check, confirming that the observed improvements in performance metrics and bias reduction were statistically significant. This indicated that the user feedback loop substantively contributed to sustained improvements in both accuracy and fairness.

The longitudinal study demonstrated the efficacy of iterative retraining with user feedback to improve both the model performance and its ability to mitigate bias effectively over time.

4.11. Analysis of Loss Function, Bias Reduction, and Additional Metrics

The loss function is a key player in our approach, consisting of two components: the loss of cross-entropy (L_{CE}) and the bias-aware loss term (L_{bias}). The bias-aware term was specifically designed to address any hidden biases in the dataset. In this section, we dive deeper into how this loss function impacted model performance, backed by empirical tests.

Table 7 presents the evolution of the components of the loss function in ten iterations of the training process. As the training proceeds, the cross-entropy loss gradually decreases, indicating that the model is learning to predict sentiment labels accurately. The bias-aware loss term also decreases over time, suggesting that the model is successfully reducing the bias in its predictions.

In addition to the analysis of loss values, we also examined the Kullback–Leibler (KL) divergence and other bias metrics. The KL divergence quantifies the difference between the model's predictions and a uniform distribution, with a lower divergence indicating a closer match between the two distributions.

Table 8 provides a comprehensive view of the model's behavior over ten iterations concerning bias metrics.

Table 7. Results for the loss function and bias reduction terms.

Iteration	L_{CE}	L_{bias}	L
1	0.693	0.034	0.727
2	0.684	0.030	0.714
3	0.675	0.026	0.701
4	0.665	0.022	0.687
5	0.655	0.018	0.673
6	0.645	0.015	0.660
7	0.635	0.012	0.647
8	0.625	0.010	0.635
9	0.615	0.008	0.623
10	0.605	0.006	0.611

Table 8. Values obtained for the Kullback–Leibler (KL) divergence and additional bias metrics.

Iteration	$P(y_i\|x_i)$	$U(y_i)$	D_{KL}	Disparate Impact	Equal Opportunity Difference
1	0.50	0.50	0.00	1.00	0.00
2	0.55	0.50	0.05	0.95	0.05
3	0.60	0.50	0.10	0.90	0.10
4	0.65	0.50	0.15	0.85	0.15
5	0.70	0.50	0.20	0.80	0.20
6	0.75	0.50	0.25	0.75	0.25
7	0.80	0.50	0.30	0.70	0.30
8	0.85	0.50	0.35	0.65	0.35
9	0.90	0.50	0.40	0.60	0.40
10	0.95	0.50	0.45	0.55	0.45

4.11.1. Kullback–Leibler (KL) Divergence (D_{KL})

The KL divergence measures the difference between the predicted probability distribution of the model $P(y_i|x_i)$ and a uniform probability distribution $U(y_i)$. Initially, the divergence is zero, indicating that the predictions of the model closely match a uniform distribution. This suggests that the model starts with no inherent bias. As the iterations progress, the divergence increases, indicating that the predictions of the model are deviating from a uniform distribution. This is expected as the model learns from the data. However, the controlled increase suggests that the model is not overfitting to potential biases in the data.

4.11.2. Disparate Impact

Disparate Impact is a fairness metric that quantifies the ratio of positive outcomes for a protected group to the positive outcomes for a nonprotected group. A value of one indicates perfect fairness, while values deviating from one indicate potential bias. The table shows that the dispersion impact starts at one and gradually decreases. This suggests that as the model trains, it might be favoring one group over another, leading to potential bias.

4.11.3. Equal Opportunity Difference

This metric measures the difference in true positive rates between the protected and nonprotected groups. A value of zero indicates no bias, while a nonzero value indicates a disparity in opportunities between groups. The table indicates that the Equal Opportunity Difference starts at zero and increases over iterations. This suggests that there might be a growing disparity in the model's predictions for different groups.

The combined analysis of the loss function, KL divergence, and bias metrics visually reinforced the effectiveness of our approach in managing implicit biases in sentiment analysis.

5. Ethical Considerations

The proposed model was designed with an emphasis on fairness and bias mitigation, particularly in the context of sentiment analysis. However, it is important to consider the ethical implications of deploying such models in real-world applications. In this section, we outline the key ethical considerations associated with the development, evaluation, and deployment of our model.

5.1. Bias and Fairness

One of the main objectives of our proposed method was to reduce bias in sentiment analysis, especially when dealing with demographic groups such as race, gender, sexual orientation, religion, and disability. Although we strove to minimize bias, it is crucial to acknowledge that no model is entirely free from biases. Models are inherently influenced by the data they are trained on, and any pre-existing biases in the data may inadvertently affect model predictions. For instance, if the training data underrepresent certain groups, the model might still exhibit biases that disproportionately affect those groups.

We took steps to mitigate these biases, including using techniques like adversarial training and counterfactual data augmentation. However, it is essential to continue to monitor the performance of the model in diverse demographic groups and refine it to further reduce any unintended biases that may arise. Transparent reporting of these biases and performance disparities is necessary to foster trust in the model's fairness.

5.2. Privacy and Data Security

Another critical ethical consideration is the privacy and security of the data used to train and evaluate the model. Our proposed model used publicly available datasets, such as the Jigsaw Unexpected Bias in Toxicity Classification dataset, which contains user-generated content from social media platforms. These datasets may include sensitive or personally identifiable information (PII), even if anonymized.

It is essential to ensure that the data is handled responsibly. Data collection, processing, and usage should comply with privacy regulations such as the General Data Protection Regulation (GDPR) and other applicable privacy laws. We advocate for the use of techniques such as differential privacy to further safeguard individual privacy when utilizing real-world datasets.

5.3. Transparency and Accountability

Transparency and accountability are key ethical principles when developing AI models. In the case of the proposed sentiment analysis model, transparency involves making the model's architecture, training data, and evaluation methodologies publicly accessible. This allows for scrutiny and helps identify potential ethical concerns, such as hidden biases or fairness issues.

In addition, accountability mechanisms must be in place to ensure that the model is used responsibly. This includes clear guidelines for deployment and continuous evaluation of its impact on different demographic groups. We encourage the responsible use of the model in real-world applications, ensuring that it does not reinforce harmful stereotypes or discriminatory practices.

5.4. Impact on Vulnerable Groups

The deployment of sentiment analysis models, including our proposed model, can have significant implications for vulnerable groups, particularly when used in decision-making processes. For example, biased sentiment analysis can affect social media moderation, recruitment processes, and content recommendation systems in ways that disadvantage underrepresented groups. It is crucial to regularly assess how the model affects these groups and make adjustments to improve fairness, reduce harm, and ensure that it promotes positive societal outcomes.

We also advocate for the participation of various stakeholders, including individuals from underrepresented communities, in the development and evaluation of sentiment analysis systems. This can help identify concerns that may not be apparent to developers and ensure that the model is used in ways that promote equity.

5.5. Model Interpretability

AI models, especially complex ones like deep learning architectures, often function as 'black boxes', making it difficult to understand how they arrive at certain decisions. While our model shows significant performance improvements in reducing bias, it is crucial to prioritize interpretability to ensure transparency and build trust among users. Efforts should be made to develop explainable models or tools that allow users to understand how decisions are made, particularly when the model is used in high-stakes applications such as hiring, lending, or content moderation.

Explainable AI (XAI) methods, such as saliency maps or attention mechanisms, can be applied to provide insights into which features most influence the model's predictions. Ensuring that these explanations are accessible and understandable for non-experts is also an important consideration.

5.6. Ethical Use of AI in Society

Finally, it is essential to consider the broader social implications of using AI models for sentiment analysis. AI has the potential to reinforce existing power structures, but it can also be a force for positive change if used ethically. We encourage stakeholders to use our proposed model in ways that respect human dignity and autonomy. AI systems should not be used to perpetuate discrimination, spread misinformation, or infringe on individuals' rights.

Although our proposed model advances the field of bias mitigation in sentiment analysis, it is vital to continually address the ethical considerations associated with its development and deployment. Ongoing efforts to ensure fairness, transparency, privacy, and accountability will help maximize the positive impact of the model on society.

6. Conclusions

This research presented a novel methodology for sentiment analysis that tackled the challenges of bias and representation, especially in sensitive areas like sexual orientation, religion, and disability. Our approach not only improved accuracy but also prioritized ethical considerations, ensuring that the model predictions were fair and respectful of diverse perspectives. The transparency and interpretability built into the methodology further enhanced its potential as a leading solution for sentiment analysis.

In the future, we plan to refine and expand this methodology by incorporating a feedback loop where users or domain experts can validate the model's predictions. This feedback will be invaluable for fine-tuning our bias mitigation techniques and ensuring robustness in diverse settings. Additionally, as language and societal norms evolve, the model will need continuous updates. Exploring ensemble techniques and alternative model architectures will be key to further improving performance. Engaging with a broader range of stakeholders, especially those from marginalized communities, will help guide these future developments, ensuring that our solutions remain both technically advanced and ethically responsible.

Author Contributions: Data curation, J.P.V. and G.S.; formal analysis, J.P.V., A.A.V.S. and M.R.; funding acquisition, P.W.; investigation, J.P.V.; methodology, J.P.V. and G.S.; project administration, M.R. and P.W.; resources, A.A.V.S., G.S. and M.R.; software, A.A.V.S.; supervision, M.R. and P.W.; validation, A.A.V.S.; visualization, G.S. and P.W.; writing—original draft, J.P.V. and A.A.V.S.; writing—review and editing, G.S., M.R. and P.W. All authors have read and agreed to the published version of the manuscript.

Funding: This research received no external funding.

Institutional Review Board Statement: Not applicable.

Informed Consent Statement: Not applicable.

Data Availability Statement: The original contributions presented in this study are included in the article. Further inquiries can be directed to the corresponding author.

Acknowledgments: The Agencia Nacional de Investigación y Desarrollo (ANID) FONDECYT Regular grant number 1220556, ANID FOVI230169, Fondap SERC 1523A0006, the Research Project PINV01-743 of the Consejo Nacional de Ciencia y Tecnología (CONACYT), ENNOBLE-R02401 and IRCF 39174357 project from the University of Nottingham, and IND/CONT/G/23-24/14- British Council Going Global Partnerships- Industry Academia Collaborative Grant.

Conflicts of Interest: The authors declare no conflicts of interest.

Appendix A

Table A1. Bias evaluation results for different demographic groups.

Group	Model	Precision	Recall	F1-Score
Asian	Proposed method	0.924	0.928	0.926
	Logistic Regression	0.735	0.710	0.723
	SVM	0.762	0.740	0.751
	MLP	0.775	0.763	0.769
	LSTM	0.789	0.779	0.783
	RoBERTa	0.853	0.839	0.846
	DistilBERT	0.840	0.830	0.835
	Counterfactual data augmentation	0.784	0.771	0.778
	Adversarial training	0.798	0.783	0.791
	Bias-Product-of-Experts (BPoE)	0.792	0.779	0.786
	Bias-Regularized Neural Network	0.803	0.788	0.796
	BiasFinder	0.818	0.808	0.813
Black	Proposed method	0.932	0.938	0.935
	Logistic Regression	0.730	0.710	0.720
	SVM	0.760	0.740	0.750
	MLP	0.773	0.761	0.767
	LSTM	0.786	0.776	0.780
	RoBERTa	0.855	0.840	0.847
	DistilBERT	0.845	0.835	0.840
	Counterfactual data augmentation	0.784	0.771	0.778
	Adversarial training	0.798	0.783	0.791
	Bias-Product-of-Experts (BPoE)	0.792	0.779	0.786
	Bias-Regularized Neural Network	0.803	0.788	0.796
	BiasFinder	0.821	0.811	0.816

Table A1. *Cont.*

Group	Model	Precision	Recall	F1-Score
Latino	Proposed method	0.927	0.930	0.929
	Logistic Regression	0.735	0.712	0.723
	SVM	0.765	0.745	0.755
	MLP	0.778	0.766	0.772
	LSTM	0.791	0.781	0.785
	RoBERTa	0.856	0.841	0.849
	DistilBERT	0.845	0.835	0.840
	Counterfactual data augmentation	0.784	0.771	0.778
	Adversarial training	0.798	0.783	0.791
	Bias-Product-of-Experts (BPoE)	0.792	0.779	0.786
	Bias-Regularized Neural Network	0.803	0.788	0.796
	BiasFinder	0.819	0.809	0.814
White	Proposed method	0.940	0.945	0.943
	Logistic Regression	0.730	0.710	0.720
	SVM	0.762	0.742	0.752
	MLP	0.775	0.763	0.769
	LSTM	0.788	0.778	0.783
	RoBERTa	0.860	0.845	0.852
	DistilBERT	0.850	0.840	0.845
	Counterfactual data augmentation	0.784	0.771	0.778
	Adversarial training	0.798	0.783	0.791
	Bias-Product-of-Experts (BPoE)	0.792	0.779	0.786
	Bias-Regularized Neural Network	0.803	0.788	0.796
	BiasFinder	0.823	0.813	0.818
Other	Proposed method	0.935	0.939	0.937
	Logistic Regression	0.731	0.710	0.720
	SVM	0.762	0.742	0.752
	MLP	0.775	0.763	0.769
	LSTM	0.788	0.778	0.783
	RoBERTa	0.857	0.842	0.849
	DistilBERT	0.847	0.837	0.842
	Counterfactual data augmentation	0.784	0.771	0.778
	Adversarial training	0.798	0.783	0.791
	Bias-Product-of-Experts (BPoE)	0.792	0.779	0.786
	Bias-Regularized Neural Network	0.803	0.788	0.796
	BiasFinder	0.822	0.812	0.817

Table A2. Bias evaluation results for different gender groups.

Group	Model	Precision	Recall	F1-Score
Male	Proposed method	0.931	0.937	0.934
	Logistic Regression	0.734	0.698	0.716
	SVM	0.742	0.717	0.729
	MLP	0.758	0.739	0.748
	LSTM	0.770	0.762	0.766
	Counterfactual data augmentation	0.776	0.761	0.768
	Adversarial training	0.789	0.772	0.780
	Bias-Product-of-Experts (BPoE)	0.783	0.765	0.774
	Bias-Regularized Neural Network	0.794	0.780	0.787
	RoBERTa	0.926	0.932	0.929
	DistilBERT	0.922	0.928	0.925
	BiasFinder	0.921	0.926	0.923

Table A2. *Cont.*

Group	Model	Precision	Recall	F1-Score
Female	Proposed method	0.930	0.936	0.933
	Logistic Regression	0.734	0.698	0.716
	SVM	0.745	0.725	0.735
	MLP	0.761	0.748	0.754
	LSTM	0.773	0.765	0.769
	Counterfactual data augmentation	0.781	0.764	0.772
	Adversarial training	0.793	0.776	0.784
	Bias-Product-of-Experts (BPoE)	0.786	0.768	0.777
	Bias-Regularized Neural Network	0.798	0.781	0.789
	RoBERTa	0.925	0.931	0.928
	DistilBERT	0.921	0.926	0.924
	BiasFinder	0.920	0.925	0.922
Transgender	Proposed method	0.928	0.934	0.931
	Logistic Regression	0.734	0.698	0.716
	SVM	0.740	0.717	0.728
	MLP	0.759	0.742	0.750
	LSTM	0.771	0.763	0.767
	Counterfactual data augmentation	0.777	0.762	0.769
	Adversarial training	0.789	0.773	0.781
	Bias-Product-of-Experts (BPoE)	0.782	0.764	0.773
	Bias-Regularized Neural Network	0.794	0.779	0.786
	RoBERTa	0.925	0.931	0.928
	DistilBERT	0.921	0.926	0.924
	BiasFinder	0.920	0.925	0.922
Other gender	Proposed method	0.932	0.938	0.935
	Logistic Regression	0.734	0.698	0.716
	SVM	0.744	0.723	0.733
	MLP	0.761	0.745	0.753
	LSTM	0.773	0.765	0.769
	Counterfactual data augmentation	0.780	0.764	0.772
	Adversarial training	0.791	0.774	0.782
	Bias-Product-of-Experts (BPoE)	0.784	0.766	0.775
	Bias-Regularized Neural Network	0.796	0.779	0.787
	RoBERTa	0.926	0.932	0.929
	DistilBERT	0.922	0.926	0.924
	BiasFinder	0.920	0.925	0.922

Table A3. Bias evaluation results for different sexual orientation groups.

Group	Model	Precision	Recall	F1-Score
Heterosexual	Proposed method	0.933	0.939	0.936
	Logistic Regression	0.734	0.698	0.716
	SVM	0.749	0.719	0.734
	MLP	0.765	0.750	0.757
	LSTM	0.780	0.770	0.775
	Counterfactual data augmentation	0.785	0.775	0.780
	Adversarial training	0.802	0.785	0.793
	Bias-Product-of-Experts (BPoE)	0.795	0.782	0.788
	Bias-Regularized Neural Network	0.805	0.790	0.797
	RoBERTa	0.920	0.915	0.917
	DistilBERT	0.912	0.905	0.909
	BiasFinder	0.915	0.920	0.917

Table A3. *Cont.*

Group	Model	Precision	Recall	F1-Score
Homosexual	Proposed method	0.930	0.936	0.933
	Logistic Regression	0.734	0.698	0.716
	SVM	0.749	0.719	0.734
	MLP	0.765	0.750	0.757
	LSTM	0.780	0.770	0.775
	Counterfactual data augmentation	0.785	0.775	0.780
	Adversarial training	0.802	0.785	0.793
	Bias-Product-of-Experts (BPoE)	0.795	0.782	0.788
	Bias-Regularized Neural Network	0.805	0.790	0.797
	RoBERTa	0.920	0.915	0.917
	DistilBERT	0.912	0.905	0.909
	BiasFinder	0.915	0.920	0.917
Bisexual	Proposed method	0.931	0.937	0.934
	Logistic Regression	0.734	0.698	0.716
	SVM	0.749	0.719	0.734
	MLP	0.765	0.750	0.757
	LSTM	0.780	0.770	0.775
	Counterfactual data augmentation	0.785	0.775	0.780
	Adversarial training	0.802	0.785	0.793
	Bias-Product-of-Experts (BPoE)	0.795	0.782	0.788
	Bias-Regularized Neural Network	0.805	0.790	0.797
	RoBERTa	0.920	0.915	0.917
	DistilBERT	0.912	0.905	0.909
	BiasFinder	0.915	0.920	0.917
Other	Proposed method	0.932	0.938	0.935
	Logistic Regression	0.734	0.698	0.716
	SVM	0.749	0.719	0.734
	MLP	0.765	0.750	0.757
	LSTM	0.780	0.770	0.775
	Counterfactual data augmentation	0.785	0.775	0.780
	Adversarial training	0.802	0.785	0.793
	Bias-Product-of-Experts (BPoE)	0.795	0.782	0.788
	Bias-Regularized Neural Network	0.805	0.790	0.797
	RoBERTa	0.920	0.915	0.917
	DistilBERT	0.912	0.905	0.909
	BiasFinder	0.915	0.920	0.917

Table A4. Bias evaluation results for different religion groups.

Group	Model	Precision	Recall	F1-Score
Christian	Proposed method	0.930	0.936	0.933
	Logistic Regression	0.734	0.698	0.716
	SVM	0.751	0.719	0.735
	MLP	0.762	0.748	0.755
	LSTM	0.781	0.769	0.775
	Counterfactual data augmentation	0.784	0.771	0.778
	Adversarial training	0.798	0.783	0.791
	Bias-Product-of-Experts (BPoE)	0.792	0.779	0.786
	Bias-Regularized Neural Network	0.803	0.788	0.796
	RoBERTa	0.918	0.925	0.921
	DistilBERT	0.914	0.920	0.917
	BiasFinder	0.919	0.926	0.922

Table A4. *Cont.*

Group	Model	Precision	Recall	F1-Score
Jewish	Proposed method	0.932	0.938	0.935
	Logistic Regression	0.734	0.698	0.716
	SVM	0.751	0.719	0.735
	MLP	0.762	0.748	0.755
	LSTM	0.781	0.769	0.775
	Counterfactual data augmentation	0.784	0.771	0.778
	Adversarial training	0.798	0.783	0.791
	Bias-Product-of-Experts (BPoE)	0.792	0.779	0.786
	Bias-Regularized Neural Network	0.803	0.788	0.796
	RoBERTa	0.919	0.926	0.922
	DistilBERT	0.915	0.921	0.918
	BiasFinder	0.920	0.927	0.923
Muslim	Proposed method	0.933	0.939	0.936
	Logistic Regression	0.734	0.698	0.716
	SVM	0.751	0.719	0.735
	MLP	0.762	0.748	0.755
	LSTM	0.781	0.769	0.775
	Counterfactual data augmentation	0.784	0.771	0.778
	Adversarial training	0.798	0.783	0.791
	Bias-Product-of-Experts (BPoE)	0.792	0.779	0.786
	Bias-Regularized Neural Network	0.803	0.788	0.796
	RoBERTa	0.920	0.927	0.923
	DistilBERT	0.916	0.922	0.919
	BiasFinder	0.921	0.928	0.924
Hindu	Proposed method	0.931	0.937	0.934
	Logistic Regression	0.734	0.698	0.716
	SVM	0.751	0.719	0.735
	MLP	0.762	0.748	0.755
	LSTM	0.781	0.769	0.775
	Counterfactual data augmentation	0.784	0.771	0.778
	Adversarial training	0.798	0.783	0.791
	Bias-Product-of-Experts (BPoE)	0.792	0.779	0.786
	Bias-Regularized Neural Network	0.803	0.788	0.796
	RoBERTa	0.918	0.926	0.922
	DistilBERT	0.914	0.921	0.917
	BiasFinder	0.919	0.927	0.923
Buddhist	Proposed method	0.930	0.936	0.933
	Logistic Regression	0.734	0.698	0.716
	SVM	0.751	0.719	0.735
	MLP	0.762	0.748	0.755
	LSTM	0.781	0.769	0.775
	Counterfactual data augmentation	0.784	0.771	0.778
	Adversarial training	0.798	0.783	0.791
	Bias-Product-of-Experts (BPoE)	0.792	0.779	0.786
	Bias-Regularized Neural Network	0.803	0.788	0.796
	RoBERTa	0.919	0.926	0.922
	DistilBERT	0.915	0.921	0.918
	BiasFinder	0.920	0.927	0.923

Table A4. *Cont.*

Group	Model	Precision	Recall	F1-Score
Atheist	Proposed method	0.932	0.938	0.935
	Logistic Regression	0.734	0.698	0.716
	SVM	0.751	0.719	0.735
	MLP	0.762	0.748	0.755
	LSTM	0.781	0.769	0.775
	Counterfactual data augmentation	0.784	0.771	0.778
	Adversarial training	0.798	0.783	0.791
	Bias-Product-of-Experts (BPoE)	0.792	0.779	0.786
	Bias-Regularized Neural Network	0.803	0.788	0.796
	RoBERTa	0.920	0.926	0.923
	DistilBERT	0.916	0.922	0.919
	BiasFinder	0.921	0.928	0.924
Other religion	Proposed method	0.933	0.939	0.936
	Logistic Regression	0.734	0.698	0.716
	SVM	0.751	0.719	0.735
	MLP	0.762	0.748	0.755
	LSTM	0.781	0.769	0.775
	Counterfactual data augmentation	0.784	0.771	0.778
	Adversarial training	0.798	0.783	0.791
	Bias-Product-of-Experts (BPoE)	0.792	0.779	0.786
	Bias-Regularized Neural Network	0.803	0.788	0.796
	RoBERTa	0.920	0.927	0.923
	DistilBERT	0.916	0.922	0.919
	BiasFinder	0.921	0.928	0.924

Table A5. Bias evaluation results for different disability groups.

Group	Model	Precision	Recall	F1-Score
Physical disability	Proposed method	0.931	0.937	0.934
	Logistic Regression	0.734	0.698	0.716
	SVM	0.751	0.719	0.735
	MLP	0.762	0.748	0.755
	LSTM	0.781	0.769	0.775
	Counterfactual data augmentation	0.784	0.771	0.778
	Adversarial training	0.798	0.783	0.791
	Bias-Product-of-Experts (BPoE)	0.792	0.779	0.786
	Bias-Regularized Neural Network	0.803	0.788	0.796
	RoBERTa	0.915	0.924	0.919
	DistilBERT	0.910	0.918	0.914
	BiasFinder	0.920	0.927	0.923

Table A5. *Cont.*

Group	Model	Precision	Recall	F1-Score
Intellectual or learning disability	Proposed method	0.930	0.936	0.933
	Logistic Regression	0.734	0.698	0.716
	SVM	0.751	0.719	0.735
	MLP	0.762	0.748	0.755
	LSTM	0.781	0.769	0.775
	Counterfactual data augmentation	0.784	0.771	0.778
	Adversarial training	0.798	0.783	0.791
	Bias-Product-of-Experts (BPoE)	0.792	0.779	0.786
	Bias-Regularized Neural Network	0.803	0.788	0.796
	RoBERTa	0.915	0.924	0.919
	DistilBERT	0.910	0.918	0.914
	BiasFinder	0.920	0.927	0.923
Psychiatric or mental illness	Proposed method	0.932	0.938	0.935
	Logistic Regression	0.734	0.698	0.716
	SVM	0.751	0.719	0.735
	MLP	0.762	0.748	0.755
	LSTM	0.781	0.769	0.775
	Counterfactual data augmentation	0.784	0.771	0.778
	Adversarial training	0.798	0.783	0.791
	Bias-Product-of-Experts (BPoE)	0.792	0.779	0.786
	Bias-Regularized Neural Network	0.803	0.788	0.796
	RoBERTa	0.915	0.924	0.919
	DistilBERT	0.910	0.918	0.914
	BiasFinder	0.920	0.927	0.923
Other disability	Proposed method	0.933	0.939	0.936
	Logistic Regression	0.734	0.698	0.716
	SVM	0.751	0.719	0.735
	MLP	0.762	0.748	0.755
	LSTM	0.781	0.769	0.775
	Counterfactual data augmentation	0.784	0.771	0.778
	Adversarial training	0.798	0.783	0.791
	Bias-Product-of-Experts (BPoE)	0.792	0.779	0.786
	Bias-Regularized Neural Network	0.803	0.788	0.796
	RoBERTa	0.915	0.924	0.919
	DistilBERT	0.910	0.918	0.914
	BiasFinder	0.920	0.927	0.923

›ferences

Aggarwal, C.C. Opinion Mining and Sentiment Analysis. In *Machine Learning for Text*; Springer International Publishing: Cham, Switzerland, 2022; pp. 491–514. [CrossRef]

Chen, Y.; Zhou, X.; Bai, X.; Liu, B.; Chen, F.; Chang, L.; Liu, H. A systematic review and meta-analysis of the effectiveness of social support on turnover intention in clinical nurses. *Front. Public Health* **2024**, *12*, 1393024. [CrossRef] [PubMed]

Grygorian, A.; Montano, D.; Shojaa, M.; Ferencak, M.; Schmitz, N. Digital Health Interventions and Patient Safety in Abdominal Surgery. *JAMA Netw. Open* **2024**, *7*, e248555. [CrossRef] [PubMed]

Pillai, S.E.V.S.; Vallabhaneni, R.; Pareek, P.K.; Dontu, S. The People Moods Analysing Using Tweets Data on Primary Things with the Help of Advanced Techniques. In Proceedings of the 2024 IEEE International Conference on Distributed Computing and Optimization Techniques (ICDCOT), Bengaluru, India, 15–16 March 2024; pp. 1–6.

Ma, P.; Johnson, N. Examine the Association Between Particulate Matter Exposure and Symptoms. 2024. Available online: https://osf.io/x9672/resources (accessed on 11 August 2024).

Ferrara, E. Fairness and Bias in Artificial Intelligence: A Brief Survey of Sources, Impacts, and Mitigation Strategies. *Sci* **2024**, *6*, 3. [CrossRef]

7. Zhang, B.H.; Lemoine, B.; Mitchell, M. Mitigating unwanted biases with adversarial learning. In Proceedings of the 20 AAAI/ACM Conference on AI, Ethics, and Society, New Orleans, LA, USA, 2–3 February 2018; pp. 335–340. [CrossRef]
8. Xing, Y.; Wang, X.; Qiu, C.; Li, Y.; He, W. Research on opinion polarization by big data analytics capabilities in online soc networks. *Technol. Soc.* **2022**, *68*, 101902. [CrossRef]
9. Li, Y.; Chandra, Y.; Fan, Y. Unpacking government social media messaging strategies during the COVID-19 pandemic in Chi *Policy Internet* **2022**, *14*, 651–672. [CrossRef]
10. Vassilakopoulou, P.; Haug, A.; Salvesen, L.M.; Pappas, I.O. Developing human/AI interactions for chat-based customer servic lessons learned from the Norwegian government. *Eur. J. Inf. Syst.* **2023**, *32*, 10–22. [CrossRef]
11. Gupta, S.; Sandhane, R. Use of sentiment analysis in social media campaign design and analysis. *Cardiometry* **2022**, *22*, 351–3 [CrossRef]
12. Hinduja, S.; Afrin, M.; Mistry, S.; Krishna, A. Machine learning-based proactive social-sensor service for mental health monitori using Twitter data. *Int. J. Inf. Manag. Data Insights* **2022**, *2*, 100113. [CrossRef]
13. Farha, I.A.; Wilson, S.; Oprea, S.; Magdy, W. Sarcasm Detection is Way Too Easy! An Empirical Comparison of Human a Machine Sarcasm Detection. In Proceedings of the Findings of the Association for Computational Linguistics: EMNLP 2022, A Dhabi, United Arab Emirates, 7–11 December 2022; pp. 5284–5295. [CrossRef]
14. Khoo, L.S.; Bay, J.Q.; Yap, M.L.K.; Lim, M.K.; Chong, C.Y.; Yang, Z.; Lo, D. Exploring and Repairing Gender Fairness Violations Word Embedding-based Sentiment Analysis Model through Adversarial Patches. In Proceedings of the 2023 IEEE Internatior Conference on Software Analysis, Evolution and Reengineering (SANER), Macao, China, 21–24 March 2023; pp. 651–6 [CrossRef]
15. Hong, M.H.; Marsh, L.A.; Feuston, J.L.; Ruppert, J.; Brubaker, J.R.; Szafir, D.A. Scholastic: Graphical Human-AI Collaboration f Inductive and Interpretive Text Analysis. In Proceedings of the 35th Annual ACM Symposium on User Interface Software a Technology, Bend, OR, USA, 29 October–2 November 2022; pp. 1–12. [CrossRef]
16. Mamun, M.H.A.; Keikhosrokiani, P.; Asl, M.P.; Anuar, N.A.N.; Hadi, N.H.A.; Humida, T. Sentiment Analysis of the Harry Pot Series Using a Lexicon-Based Approach. In *Advances in Sentiment Analysis and Natural Language Processing*; IGI Global: Hersh PA, USA, 2022; pp. 263–291. [CrossRef]
17. Cha, J.; Kim, S.; Park, E. A lexicon-based approach to examine depression detection in social media: The case of Twitter a university community. *Humanit. Soc. Sci. Commun.* **2022**, *9*, 325. [CrossRef]
18. Ainapure, B.S.; Pise, R.N.; Reddy, P.; Appasani, B.; Srinivasulu, A.; Khan, M.S.; Bizon, N. Sentiment Analysis of COVID-19 Twe Using Deep Learning and Lexicon-Based Approaches. *Sustainability* **2023**, *15*, 2573. [CrossRef]
19. Razali, N.A.M.; Malizan, N.A.; Hasbullah, N.A.; Wook, M.; Zainuddin, N.M.; Ishak, K.K.; Ramli, S.; Sukardi, S. Politic security threat prediction framework using hybrid lexicon-based approach and machine learning technique. *IEEE Access* **20** *11*, 17151–17164. [CrossRef]
20. Thangavel, P.; Lourdusamy, R. A lexicon-based approach for sentiment analysis of multimodal content in tweets. *Multimed. To Appl.* **2023**, *82*, 24203–24226. [CrossRef]
21. AlBadani, B.; Shi, R.; Dong, J. A novel machine learning approach for sentiment analysis on Twitter incorporating the Univers Language Model Fine-Tuning and SVM. *Appl. Syst. Innov.* **2022**, *5*, 13. [CrossRef]
22. Kewsuwun, N.; Kajornkasirat, S. A sentiment analysis model of Agritech startup on Facebook comments using naive Bay classifier. *Int. J. Electr. Comput. Eng. (IJECE)* **2022**, *12*, 2829–2838. [CrossRef]
23. Alantari, H.J.; Currim, I.S.; Deng, Y.; Singh, S. An empirical comparison of machine learning methods for text-based sentime analysis of online consumer reviews. *Int. J. Res. Mark.* **2022**, *39*, 1–19. [CrossRef]
24. Bibi, M.; Abbasi, W.A.; Aziz, W.; Khalil, S.; Uddin, M.; Iwendi, C.; Gadekallu, T.R. A novel unsupervised ensemble framewo using concept-based linguistic methods and machine learning for Twitter sentiment analysis. *Pattern Recognit. Lett.* **20** *158*, 80–86. [CrossRef]
25. Costola, M.; Hinz, O.; Nofer, M.; Pelizzon, L. Machine learning sentiment analysis, COVID-19 news and stock market reactio *Res. Int. Bus. Financ.* **2023**, *64*, 101881. [CrossRef]
26. Singh, A.; Jenamani, M.; Thakkar, J.J.; Rana, N.P. Quantifying the effect of eWOM embedded consumer perceptions on sales: integrated aspect-level sentiment analysis and panel data modeling approach. *J. Bus. Res.* **2022**, *138*, 52–64. [CrossRef]
27. Peng, S.; Cao, L.; Zhou, Y.; Ouyang, Z.; Yang, A.; Li, X.; Jia, W.; Yu, S. A survey on deep learning for textual emotion analysis social networks. *Digit. Commun. Networks* **2022**, *8*, 745–762. [CrossRef]
28. Ray, P.; Chakrabarti, A. A mixed approach of deep learning method and rule-based method to improve aspect level sentime analysis. *Appl. Comput. Inform.* **2022**, *18*, 163–178. [CrossRef]
29. Kamyab, M.; Liu, G.; Rasool, A.; Adjeisah, M. ACR-SA: Attention-based deep model through two-channel CNN and Bi-RNN f sentiment analysis. *PeerJ Comput. Sci.* **2022**, *8*, e877. [CrossRef] [PubMed]
30. Khan, L.; Amjad, A.; Ashraf, N.; Chang, H.T. Multi-class sentiment analysis of Urdu text using multilingual BERT. *Sci. Rep.* **20** *12*, 5436. [CrossRef] [PubMed]
31. Swathi, T.; Kasiviswanath, N.; Rao, A.A. An optimal deep learning-based LSTM for stock price prediction using twitter sentime analysis. *Appl. Intell.* **2022**, *52*, 13675–13688. [CrossRef]
32. Revathy, G.; Alghamdi, S.A.; Alahmari, S.M.; Yonbawi, S.R.; Kumar, A.; Haq, M.A. Sentiment analysis using machine learnir Progress in the machine intelligence for data science. *Sustain. Energy Technol. Assess.* **2022**, *53*, 102557. [CrossRef]

Kokab, S.T.; Asghar, S.; Naz, S. Transformer-based deep learning models for the sentiment analysis of social media data. *Array* **2022**, *14*, 100157. [CrossRef]
Praveen, S.V.; Vajrobol, V. Understanding the Perceptions of Healthcare Researchers Regarding ChatGPT: A Study Based on Bidirectional Encoder Representation from Transformers (BERT) Sentiment Analysis and Topic Modeling. *Ann. Biomed. Eng.* **2023**, *51*, 1654–1656. [CrossRef]
Leippold, M. Sentiment spin: Attacking financial sentiment with GPT-3. *Financ. Res. Lett.* **2023**, *55*, 103957. [CrossRef]
Tan, K.L.; Lee, C.P.; Anbananthen, K.S.M.; Lim, K.M. RoBERTa-LSTM: A Hybrid Model for Sentiment Analysis With Transformer and Recurrent Neural Network. *IEEE Access* **2022**, *10*, 21517–21525. [CrossRef]
Azhar, N.; Latif, S. Roman Urdu Sentiment Analysis Using Pre-trained DistilBERT and XLNet. In Proceedings of the 2022 IEEE Fifth International Conference of Women in Data Science at Prince Sultan University (WiDS PSU), Riyadh, Saudi Arabia, 28–29 March 2022; pp. 75–78. [CrossRef]
Anoop, K.; Gangan, M.P.; Deepak, P.; Lajish, V.L. Towards an Enhanced Understanding of Bias in Pre-trained Neural Language Models: A Survey with Special Emphasis on Affective Bias. In *Advances in Neural Networks and Machine Learning*; Springer: Singapore, 2022; pp. 13–45. [CrossRef]
Mohammad, S.M. Ethics Sheet for Automatic Emotion Recognition and Sentiment Analysis. *Comput. Linguist.* **2022**, *48*, 239–278. [CrossRef]
Ray, P.P. ChatGPT: A comprehensive review on background, applications, key challenges, bias, ethics, limitations and future scope. *Internet Things Cyber-Phys. Syst.* **2023**, *3*, 121–154. [CrossRef]
Mao, R.; Liu, Q.; He, K.; Li, W.; Cambria, E. The Biases of Pre-Trained Language Models: An Empirical Study on Prompt-Based Sentiment Analysis and Emotion Detection. *IEEE Trans. Affect. Comput.* **2023**, *14*, 1743–1753. [CrossRef]
Hartung, K.; Herygers, A.; Kurlekar, S.V.; Zakaria, K.; Volkan, T.; Gröttrup, S.; Georges, M. Measuring Sentiment Bias in Machine Translation. In *Advances in Data Science and Deep Learning*; Springer: Cham, Switzerland, 2023; pp. 82–93. [CrossRef]
Orgad, H.; Belinkov, Y. BLIND: Bias Removal With No Demographics. In Proceedings of the 61st Annual Meeting of the Association for Computational Linguistics (Volume 1: Long Papers), Toronto, ON, Canada, 9–14 July 2023; pp. 8801–8821. [CrossRef]
Sun, T.; Wang, W.; Jing, L.; Cui, Y.; Song, X.; Nie, L. Counterfactual Reasoning for Out-of-distribution Multimodal Sentiment Analysis. In Proceedings of the 30th ACM International Conference on Multimedia, Lisbon, Portugal, 10–14 October 2022; pp. 15–23. [CrossRef]
Agarwal, R.; Bjarnadottir, M.; Rhue, L.; Dugas, M.; Crowley, K.; Clark, J.; Gao, G. Addressing algorithmic bias and the perpetuation of health inequities: An AI bias aware framework. *Health Policy Technol.* **2023**, *12*, 100702. [CrossRef]
Jung, S.G.; Salminen, J.; Jansen, B.J. Engineers, Aware! Commercial Tools Disagree on Social Media Sentiment: Analyzing the Sentiment Bias of Four Major Tools. *Proc. ACM Hum.-Comput. Interact.* **2022**, *6*, 1–20. [CrossRef]
Zhu, Q.; Lo, L.Y.H.; Xia, M.; Chen, Z.; Ma, X. Bias-Aware Design for Informed Decisions: Raising Awareness of Self-Selection Bias in User Ratings and Reviews. *Proc. ACM Hum.-Comput. Interact.* **2022**, *6*, 1–31. [CrossRef]
Boonprakong, N.; Chen, X.; Davey, C.; Tag, B.; Dingler, T. Bias-Aware Systems: Exploring Indicators for the Occurrences of Cognitive Biases when Facing Different Opinions. In Proceedings of the 2023 CHI Conference on Human Factors in Computing Systems, Hamburg, Germany, 23–28 April 2023; pp. 1–19. [CrossRef]
Taeb, M.; Torres, Y.; Chi, H.; Bernadin, S. Investigating Gender and Racial Bias in ELECTRA. In Proceedings of the 2022 IEEE International Conference on Computational Science and Computational Intelligence (CSCI), Las Vegas, NV, USA, 14–16 December 2022; pp. 127–133. [CrossRef]
Cheng, L.; Mosallanezhad, A.; Silva, Y.N.; Hall, D.L., Liu, H. Bias Mitigation for Toxicity Detection via Sequential Decisions. In Proceedings of the 45th International ACM SIGIR Conference on Research and Development in Information Retrieval, Madrid, Spain, 11–15 July 2022; pp. 1750–1760. [CrossRef]
Garlapati, A.; Malisetty, N.; Narayanan, G. Classification of Toxicity in Comments Using NLP and LSTM. In Proceedings of the IEEE 8th International Conference on Advanced Computing and Communication Systems (ICACCS), Coimbatore, India, 25–26 March 2022; pp. 16–21. [CrossRef]
Raheja, S.; Asthana, A. Sentiment Analysis of Tweets During the COVID-19 Pandemic Using Multinomial Logistic Regression. *Int. J. Softw. Innov. (IJSI)* **2023**, *11*, 1–16. [CrossRef]
Raj, C.; Agarwal, A.; Bharathy, G.; Narayan, B.; Prasad, M. Cyberbullying detection: Hybrid models based on machine learning and natural language processing techniques. *Electronics* **2021**, *10*, 2810. [CrossRef]
Hussain, M.G.; Sultana, B.; Rahman, M.; Hasan, M.R. Comparison analysis of Bangla news articles classification using support vector machine and logistic regression. *TELKOMNIKA (Telecommun. Comput. Electron. Control)* **2023**, *21*, 584–591. [CrossRef]
Choi, E.; Schuetz, A.; Stewart, W.F.; Sun, J. Using recurrent neural network models for early detection of heart failure onset. *J. Am. Med. Inform. Assoc.* **2017**, *24*, 361–370. [CrossRef]
Prakash, J.; Vijay, A.A. A multi-aspect framework for explainable sentiment analysis. *Pattern Recognit. Lett.* **2024**, *178*, 122–129. [CrossRef]
Kaushik, D.; Hovy, E.; Lipton, Z.C. Learning the difference that makes a difference with counterfactually-augmented data. *arXiv* **2019**, arXiv:1909.12434. [CrossRef]

58. González-Sendino, R.; Serrano, E.; Bajo, J. Mitigating bias in artificial intelligence: Fair data generation via causal models f transparent and explainable decision-making. *Future Gener. Comput. Syst.* **2024**, *155*, 384–401. [CrossRef]
59. Clark, C.; Yatskar, M.; Zettlemoyer, L. Don't take the easy way out: Ensemble based methods for avoiding known dataset bias *arXiv* **2019**, arXiv:1909.03683. [CrossRef]
60. Asyrofi, M.H.; Yang, Z.; Yusuf, I.N.B.; Kang, H.J.; Thung, F.; Lo, D. BiasFinder: Metamorphic Test Generation to Uncover Bias f Sentiment Analysis Systems. *IEEE Trans. Softw. Eng.* **2022**, *48*, 5087–5101. [CrossRef]

applied sciences

MDPI

ticle

. Sentiment Analysis Model Based on User Experiences of ubrovnik on the Tripadvisor Platform

na Zakarija [1,*], Frano Škopljanac-Mačina [2], Hrvoje Marušić [1] and Bruno Blašković [2]

[1] Department of Electrical Engineering and Computing, University of Dubrovnik, 20000 Dubrovnik, Croatia; hrvojemarusic30@gmail.com

[2] Faculty of Electrical Engineering and Computing, University of Zagreb, 10000 Zagreb, Croatia; frano.skopljanac-macina@fer.hr (F.Š.-M.); bruno.blaskovic@fer.hr (B.B.)

* Correspondence: ivona.zakarija@unidu.hr

Abstract: Emerging research indicates that sentiment analyses of Dubrovnik focus mainly on hotel accommodations and restaurants. However, little attention has been paid to attractions, even though they are an important aspect of destinations and require more care and investment than amenities. This study examines how visitors experience Dubrovnik based on the reviews published on the Tripadvisor platform. Data were collected by implementing a web-scraping script to retrieve reviews of the tourist attraction "Old Town" from Tripadvisor, while data augmentation and random oversampling techniques were applied to address class imbalances. A sentiment analysis model, based on the pre-trained RoBERTa, was also developed and evaluated. In particular, a sentiment analysis was performed to compare reviews from 2022 and 2023. Overall, the results of this study are promising and demonstrate the effectiveness of this model and its potential applicability to other attractions. These findings provide valuable insights for decision makers to improve services and to increase visitor engagement.

Keywords: sentiment analysis; NLP; large language model (LLM); RoBERTa; transfer learning; tourism

1. Introduction

Since the start of the twenty-first century, there has been a sharp rise in tourism. Tourists are increasingly using rankings and reviews to determine which tourist location to visit [1]. For most modern travelers, using a travel platform has become vital. In order to arrange their trip, people look for information about places and attractions, and they actively communicate and exchange their travel experiences and viewpoints. Word of mouth (WOM) is the term used to characterize the informal sharing of information about experiences with goods and services between people [2]. Before making a purchase, most customers rely on word of mouth to research goods and services and assess their qualities. When it comes to influencing consumer attitudes and behaviors, research suggests that electronic word of mouth (eWOM) is even more important than conventional word of mouth since the introduction of electronic business [3]. Electronic word of mouth can be found in a variety of places, including reviews, blogs, forums, videos, and more. Owners of products or services can utilize this information to create new marketing campaigns and enhance the quality of their offerings, in addition to customers [4].

However, with the rise of User-Generated Content (UGC), it is becoming more difficult to acquire a comprehensive understanding of perspectives. For instance, as of 2021, there were more than one billion reviews overall on Tripadvisor [5]. As a result, an automated sentiment analysis of reviews can benefit both service providers and customers [6]. A sentiment analysis is a natural language processing (NLP) method that identifies and extracts information from data. In most circumstances, this entails identifying whether the review conveys positive, neutral, or negative sentiments [7]. Moreover, a sentiment analysis can be examined on multiple levels. Accordingly, in this study, we examine a sentiment analysis at the document level, which determines the sentiment of each Tripadvisor review.

Recent research shows that sentiment analyses of Dubrovnik focus mainly on hotel accommodations [8,9] and restaurants [10], while there is little research on tourist attractions in this region. Certainly, attractions are an important aspect of tourist destinations, and they require more attention and investment than amenities [11]. According to Bigne et al. [12], the choice of a destination is not the same as the choice of restaurants and hotels. In addition, prices can influence the choice of attractions, as some are free while others require an entrance ticket. Choosing a bad restaurant or hotel is less of a loss for travelers than choosing a poor destination, which can ruin the entire vacation.

Dubrovnik, an important historical and tourist center in southern Croatia, recorded 1,244,159 arrivals in 2023, an increase of 20% compared to the previous year (Dubrovnik Tourist Board, https://tzdubrovnik.hr/get/vijesti/81633/turisticki_promet_u_2022_godini_u_dubrovniku.html, accessed on 1 September 2023). Tourism is crucial to the Croatian economy and contributes around 20% to its GDP—one of the highest rates in Europe. Dubrovnik's popularity has soared, partly due to its role as a filming location for "Game of Thrones". However, this has led to challenges with excessive tourism and prompted UNESCO to warn of the inability of Dubrovnik's Old Town to cope with the influx of its visitors. With 36 visitors per inhabitant (Statista Infographic: The Most 'Over-Touristed' Cities in Europe, https://www.statista.com/chart/30115/annual-number-of-tourists-per-inhabitant, accessed on 1 September 2023), Dubrovnik is under considerable pressure. To counteract this, the city has launched the "Respect the City" (Dubrovnik Tourist Board, Respect the City, https://tzdubrovnik.hr/lang/en/get/kultura_i_povijest/75283/respect_the_city.html, accessed on 1 September 2023) initiative, which promotes responsible and sustainable tourism in the Mediterranean [13–15].

The main objective of this paper is to examine the sentiment analysis of the tourist attraction "Old Town" in the city of Dubrovnik. Specifically, this study is guided by three research objectives and aims to answer the following questions:

1. Can we use a pre-trained language model to analyze sentiments in Tripadvisor reviews?
2. How well can a sentiment analysis model predict sentiments in Tripadvisor reviews?
3. How do the sentiment analysis results of 2022 and 2023 compare ?

By addressing these research objectives, we strive to gain valuable insights into the sentiments of the tourist attraction "Old Town" based on user experiences on the Tripadvisor platform.

The rest of this paper is organized as follows: Section 2 provides the theoretical background of sentiment analyses, deep learning, and the Transformer model and an overview of related research. In addition, Section 3 describes the methodology employed in this study, including the collection of reviews, the development of a sentiment analysis model and its implementation, and the details of data preparation and preprocessing. Section 4 presents, analyzes, and discusses the experimental results. Finally, Section 5 provides concluding remarks that summarize the main findings, point out directions for future work, and highlight the main limitations of our study.

2. Background and Related Work

2.1. Sentiment Analysis

A sentiment analysis, also known as opinion mining, is an automated process that evaluates the sentiments expressed in a text in terms of positive, neutral, and negative opinions [16]. A fine-grained sentiment analysis includes the following categories: very positive, positive, neutral, negative, and very negative. These categories can be mapped to ratings, e.g., very positive can be mapped to a rating of 5. The term "sentiment analysis" was coined in 2001 in a study that attempted to determine and predict market sentiments on the basis of rating texts [17]. By the end of 2003, several studies using the same term had been published, contributing to its popularity. Although NLP has a long history, little research had been conducted on people's thoughts and feelings before 2000. This was partly because opinions in digital form were not widely available. Since then, sentiment analyses have become one of the most active areas of research (Google Trends, https://trends.google.com/trends/, accessed on 29 July 2024).

A sentiment analysis can be conducted at various levels: Document, Sentence, and Aspect.

- Document level: evaluates the overall sentiment of a paragraph or document, assuming that it contains an opinion about a single entity, but does not support comparisons between multiple entities;
- Sentence level: Identifies the sentiment in each sentence and classifies it as subjective or objective and positive or negative. Since the sentences are shorter, techniques such as part-of-speech tagging (POS), parse trees, and lexicographic resources are used;
- Aspect level: Analyzes sentiments based on specific aspects or features of an entity (e.g., price, cleanliness, service, etc.). This involves identifying aspect terms, determining their polarity, identifying aspect categories, and analyzing sentiments in these categories [18].

The aforementioned levels of sentiment analyses serve as a basis for classification and are applied depending on the type of text and the domain analyzed. According to [19], there are three main approaches for a sentiment analysis: a lexicon-based approach, machine learning (ML), and a hybrid approach.

The lexicon-based approach involves dictionary-based and corpus-based methods. In the first approach, a sentiment analysis is performed using dictionaries, such as Vader [20], SentiWordNet [21], SenticNet [22], etc., to assign sentiment scores to words, which are then aggregated to determine the overall sentiment. Kirilenko and Wang, in [23], used a sentiment analysis based on the Vader lexicon to identify differences between visitors of the Grand Canyon in the U.S. based on their reviews. The corpus-based approach, on the other hand, relies on statistical analysis using technologies based on K-Nearest Neighbors (KNNs), Conditional Random Fields (CRFs), and Hidden Markov Models (HMMs) instead of predefined dictionaries.

The ML approach classifies sentiments based on statistical models. By training algorithms on large datasets, this model can learn how certain words express emotions and can take into account the emotional tone of other words and the frequency of their co-occurrence [19,24]. ML approaches can be traditional (e.g., Naive Bayes, Support Vector Machine (SVM), Maximum Entropy, etc.) or deep learning (DL) models (e.g., Convolutional Neural Network (CNN), Recurrent Neural Network (RNN), Transformer Network, etc.). Although DL models often yield better results, they require extensive data and computing power. However, with the advent of cloud computing and powerful GPUs, the time required to train deep neural networks has decreased significantly [25,26].

Both lexicon-based and ML approaches have their strengths and weaknesses, which has led to the development of hybrid methods that combine both to compensate for their respective limitations. For example, in [27], Murni et al. used a hybrid approach to analyze sentiments in tourist attraction reviews on the island of Bali, demonstrating that hybrid methods can outperform traditional ML techniques. In [28], a comprehensive overview of the challenges and open questions of DL models for sentiment analyses is given.

2.1.1. Application of Sentiment Analyses in Tourism

Organizations in the tourism sector, such as tourist attractions, hotels, and restaurants, take reviews on platforms like Tripadvisor seriously. They use these platforms to monitor their performance and compare it with that of their competitors. In doing so, they use sentiment analyses to identify market opportunities [29]. The authors in [30] point out that tourism organizations can run their own marketing campaigns on social media and can use sentiment analyses to evaluate their success.

Additionally, researchers in the tourism industry can analyze visitor feedback to identify trends and key aspects of attractions, hotels, and restaurants that are most important to guests. For example, in [31], Chang et al. applied an aspect-based sentiment analysis to 500,000 reviews on the Tripadvisor platform for the Hilton hotel chain in the U.S. to gain insights into brand perceptions and sentiments towards key aspects of the hotel stay. Moreover, the early detection of negative sentiments on social networks can also support the management of reputational risks [32]. The tourism boycott in Hong Kong, following the Occupy Central with Love and Peace movement, spread through social media but could be detected through regular social media monitoring [33]. Managers can also use sentiment analyses to examine specific issues, as Kim et al. did to identify the main sources of criticism of Paris' public transportation system [34].

Furthermore, Mike Thelwall, in [35], points out that visitors can benefit from sentiment analyses when using applications that provide destination recommendations. Applications can do this by extracting key aspects of potential destinations, extracting reviews of these destinations, performing a facet sentiment analysis, and then summarizing the overall sentiment about potential visitor decisions. For example, a user who has to decide between multiple hotels can be presented with a visual representation showing the most important aspects and the user's average rating of these aspects [36]. In simpler terms, applications can save time for users who are not interested in the overall rating of a hotel but only a specific part of it. Another example is the approach in [37], which combines large language models and knowledge graphs to optimize the offers of tourist accommodations.

2.1.2. Limitations of Sentiment Analyses in Tourism

The author of [35] points out that an important limitation of any form of a sentiment analysis in social networks is that the individuals who actively participate in these platforms represent only a portion of the total visitor population. In addition, these users may have strong biases. Visitors who have had a positive or negative experience are more likely to share their experiences on social networks, perhaps even most likely if the experience was bad [38]. Older people and children may also be less likely to share their experiences on social networks, because they are not active users. Conversely, busy parents may not be able to post reviews regularly. There may also be more subtle biases in user demographics, for example, those in favor of certain ethnic groups or social classes. Some reviews may be fake, possibly malicious reviews from competitors or paid positive reviews with the aim of promoting a new or lesser-known destination. There is no adequate substitute for social networks, nor is there an effective online solution for those groups of people who are not adequately represented. Therefore, researchers should be cautious in identifying sources of bias, analyzing their influence, and interpreting results in light of these factors [35].

It is important to note that no information about the user, such as their name, age, etc., was used in our study. It should also be emphasized that the individuals were not interviewed, but the employed method was conducted with publicly available data; however, this does not mean that biases did not influence this research study's outcomes. There are some similar approaches in the literature [39–42], but, to the best of our knowledge, we have not found a single approach that is fully comparable to our model presented in this paper.

Dubrovnik is a popular tourist destination, i.e., a tourist hotspot like Venice, Barcelona, and Amsterdam, etc. These cities have common problems with overtourism, so Dubrovnik can be considered as a use case in our study, providing an informal insight into opinions about tourist attractions. However, we cannot generalize, as these cities do not have the same attractions; thus, we cannot normalize the dataset to make a direct comparison. Nevertheless, our approach can be extended to other cases. First, the reviews collected from Tripadvisor for the attractions of these cities should be collected. After that, our original model should be modified following the characteristic of newly acquired attractions. After that, modifications of the analysis process should be applied. A detailed elaboration is out of the scope of this paper. We conducted an initial feasibility study with promising results, even with different domains outside of tourism.

2.2. Deep Learning

Deep neural networks have recently attracted a lot of attention due to their superior performance in machine learning for tasks such as image, audio, and video recognition as well as text-related tasks. While traditional ML models rely on feature selection, such as the selection of specific words in NLP, deep learning models automatically extract relevant features from the data [43–45].

Recently, DL models, using various architectures such as CNNs [46], RNNs [47], Gated Recurrent Unit (GRU) Networks [48], Long Short-Term Memory (LSTM) Networks [49], etc., are being increasingly used in NLP. However, DL models based on the Transformer architecture can achieve better results in NLP [25]. Compared to the Transformer model, CNNs cannot extract the global features of reviews, while RNNs cannot be applied to long sequences. If the length of reviews is too long, the RNN cannot link the relevant information. LSTMs cannot be used for parallelization, resulting in a longer execution time and higher resource requirements.

The CNN architectures utilized to implement our approach presented in this paper are explained in more detail in the following subsections.

2.2.1. Transformer

Transformer represents the architecture of a neural network based on the mechanism of multi-headed attention. This innovative architecture, which Bommasani et al. describe in [50] as a breakthrough in the field of artificial intelligence (AI), was first presented in 2017 by the authors Vaswani et al. in a research paper [51]. Since then, transformers have been used in various NLP tasks, e.g., language translations, sentiment analyses, and text classifications. The authors of the aforementioned research paper proposed an architecture based on a multi-head attention mechanism to overcome the limitations of previous neural network models.

Previous technological solutions in the field of NLP mainly relied on LSTMs, RNNs, CNNs, and other architectures. However, these architectures encountered certain limitations. Although LSTMs reduced the loss of remote information due to recursion in RNNs, the problem remained. Sending information through a long series of recursive connections leads to the loss of relevant information and difficulties in training. Moreover, the sequential nature of recursive networks does not allow for the use of parallel computing resources. According to Vaswani et al. [51], Transformer follows the previously developed encoder–decoder architecture by using a stacked self-attention mechanism and fully connected layers in each encoder and decoder step.

2.2.2. RoBERTa

RoBERTa (the Robustly Optimized BERT Approach) is a language model presented in [52]. The RoBERTa model is an improved version of the BERT model (Bidirectional Encoder Representations from Transformers), and both models are based on the Transformer architecture. In contrast to the BERT model, the RoBERTa model was trained longer and with a larger batch size and included a more extensive dataset during training. RoBERTa was trained with a dataset of 160 GB of text, which is more than ten times the size of BERT's training data. In addition, RoBERTa employs dynamic masking during training, which improves the model's ability to understand the context of sentences. These features have led to the improved performance of various NLP tasks [52,53].

2.2.3. Generative Pre-Trained Transformer

Generative Pre-trained Transformers (GPTs) are models that use a transformer architecture and run generative AI applications, such as ChatGPT [54], Gemini [55], Copilot [56], etc. GPT models enable applications to generate content (text, images, audio tracks, video tracks, etc.) in response to a user request (prompt). Companies in various industries use GPT models for content creation and editing, virtual assistants (chatbots), language translation, document summarization, etc. As mentioned above, the revolutionary Transformer architecture has significantly reduced model training times and has made it easier to train models with unstructured data. This not only improved the models but also made them faster and cheaper to implement.

In 2018, OpenAI introduced several models based on the Transformer architecture, but these early versions still generated too many unwanted responses to queries [54]. While GPT-1 and GPT-2 represented significant advances in the field of AI research, neither was suitable for widespread use. This changed with the introduction of GPT-3 in June 2020, which was trained with over 175 billion parameters and more than 45 terabytes of unlabeled data from various sources. The GPT-3.5 model, a fine-tuned version released in March 2022, became one of the most comprehensive and powerful language models of its time. The release of ChatGPT, which is based on GPT-3.5, in November 2022 made AI accessible to a wide audience. In March 2023, GPT-4 was introduced, which was available via the ChatGPT Plus subscription and the free Microsoft Copilot application [54,55].

2.2.4. Transfer Learning

Transfer learning is an ML approach in which a model previously trained for one task is used as the basis for learning for another task. The authors of the study in [56] propose a theory according to which transfer learning could have its roots in educational psychology. After learning task "A", it is assumed that the acquired knowledge can be transferred to task "B". For example, a person who has learned to play the piano can learn to play the guitar faster than someone who learns the guitar as their first musical instrument.

In the context of DL, transfer learning is often applied to pre-trained language models. These models are trained over long periods of time on large datasets to learn features and patterns that can then be used as a starting point for training models on smaller datasets for other tasks. This approach significantly reduces training times, computational resources, and big data requirements [57].

3. Materials and Methods

3.1. Experimental Study

This section describes our proposed approach for automating and predicting user opinions on Tripadvisor reviews of "Old Town".

As illustrated in Figure 1, which shows a workflow diagram for a sentiment analysis, our approach starts with the original dataset collected by web scraping the Tripadvisor page "Old Town". The dataset is very unbalanced, which impairs the classifier's ability to accurately distinguish between under-represented classes. In addition, this means that the model recognizes the majority class very well but the minority class poorly. This is, therefore, one of the signs that a model provides poor classification results.

Neutral and negative ratings are in the minority, so we are mainly interested in these classes, which are prepared as input for data augmentation. After preprocessing, we used ChatGPT for data augmentation by generating synthetic paraphrased data to address the imbalance. This means that each original data input contained in the prompt will result in one or more generated output sentences. These synthetic data, obtained through the paraphrasing approach, improve the classification by providing diverse examples of the same meaning that are integrated into the original dataset, thus balancing the minority classes and improving the performance of the model in classifying sentiments.

In other words, we incorporated these high-quality synthetic data into the actual dataset, preparing them for use as training data for subsequent sentiment classification.

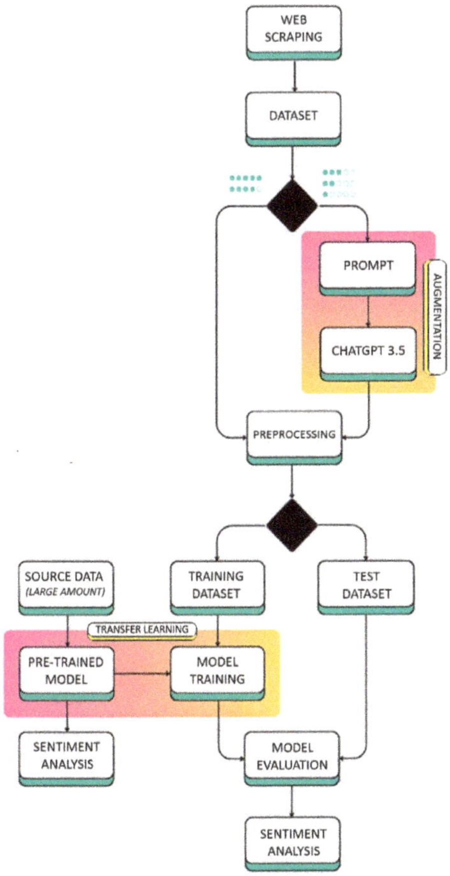

Figure 1. Overview of the model implementation. After web scraping the initial dataset is divided based on review ratings into two groups, reviews rated with 4 or 5 and reviews rated with 1 to 3. Also, the data augmentation and the transfer learning phases of the model implementation are highlighted.

3.2. *Utilized Tools and Libraries*

In our approach presented in this study, the model implementation (training, evaluation, ...) was carried out with the Google Colab Pro version (Google Colaboratory, https://colab.google/, accessed on 6 February 2024; Scaler What Is Google Colab?, https://www.scaler.com/topics/what-is-google-colab/, accessed on 10 September 2023).

In this study, we utilized the Hugging Face platform to adapt a pre-trained RoBERTa model using the Transformers library (version 4.37.2) (Techopedia Hugging Face 2024., https://www.techopedia.com/definition/hugging-face, accessed on 6 February 2024).

The open-source Python libraries used are the following:

- Pandas (Pandas—Python Data Analysis Library, https://pandas.pydata.org/, accessed on 6 February 2024) and NumPy (NumPy, https://numpy.org/, accessed on 6 February 2024) for data analysis and processing;
- Matplotlib (Matplotlib—Visualization with Python, https://matplotlib.org/, accessed on 6 February 2024) and Seaborn [58] for data visualization;
- The NLTK (Natural Language Toolkit) library (NLTK: Natural Language Toolkit, https://www.nltk.org/index.html, accessed on 6 February 2024), which provides tools for NLP. In this study, it was used for word tokenization, stop word removal, and lemmatization;

- The contractions library (Contractions: A Python Library to Expand Contractions, https://pypi.org/project/contractions/, accessed on 6 February 2024), which was used to convert shortened forms of English created by compressions into a longer form. For abbreviations, an apostrophe is normally placed in place of the missing letters. The following is an example: "you are" has the shortened form "you're";
- The PyTorch framework (PyTorch, https://pytorch.org/, accessed on 6 February 2024) for the development of deep models;
- The Imbalanced-Learn library (Imbalanced-Learn: Imbalanced-Learn Documentation—Version 0.12.3, https://imbalanced-learn.org/stable/, accessed on 6 February 2024), which helps to balance datasets that are unbalanced or biased towards some classes;
- The Scikit-Learn library (Scikit-Learn: Machine Learning in Python—Scikit-Learn 1.5.1 Documentation, https://scikit-learn.org/stable/, accessed on 6 February 2024) for the development, training, and evaluation of ML models.

3.3. Data Preparation and Preprocessing

3.3.1. Data Source

This study was conducted using data from the Tripadvisor platform. According to a study by Oxford Economics [59], Tripadvisor influences 10% of global tourism spending. We chose Tripadvisor because, according to Statista [60–62], it is now one of the most visited travel websites in the world, with more than one billion reviews and opinions for around 8 million establishments. Travelers from all over the world use the Tripadvisor platform to find out where to stay, what to do, and where to eat based on reviews from travelers who have already been there. In addition, this data source provides extensive information about tourist attractions and things to do in Dubrovnik.

All attraction websites on the Tripadvisor platform are structured in the same way and are divided into 5 sections: Overview, Tours and Tickets, Location, Reviews, and Questions and Answers.

The "Reviews" section contains reviews in the following format: *username*; *user location*; *total number of user reviews*; *user type* (indicates the type of visitor, e.g., single traveler, family, couple, etc.); *rating* (the user's rating, ranging from 1/"terrible" to 5/"excellent"); *vote* (the number of votes the review received); *review title*; *date* (the date of the user's visit); and *review* (text of the review).

For the purposes of this study, the Tripadvisor website *Old Town* was selected, which contains numerous ratings, reviews, and comments from travelers who have visited Dubrovnik. Figure 2 shows an example of a Tripadvisor review of *Old Town*.

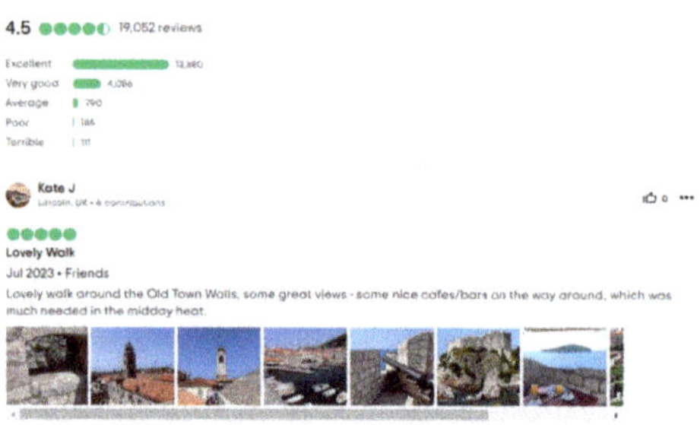

Figure 2. An example of a Tripadvisor review.

3.3.2. Collecting the Data

This subsection describes the process of extracting data from the Tripadvisor website using the web-scraping technique. Web scraping is an automated process of accessing websites and downloading their content. Additionally, web content can be considered as a valuable data source for empirical research. Furthermore, web scrapers can be implemented by programming a script or by using tools such as the following: ScrapeHub, Requests, and Selenium [63–65].

For this study, a Python script, based on Selenium and the web-scraping technique, was created to download reviews from the Tripadvisor website *Old Town* and to save them to a file in CSV (Comma-Separated Values) format. Table 1 shows part of the CSV file with the Tripadvisor reviews. In this table, each row represents a single review, while the columns correspond to the different attributes associated with each review, such as *review title, rating, date the review was published*, etc.

Table 1. An excerpt from a CSV file containing Tripadvisor reviews.

Review Title	Rating	Date	Location	Type	Vote	Review
Amazing	5	14 October 2023	USA	Solo	0	*"Sooo sooo pretty!! [. . .]"*
Beautiful	3	1 August 2023	UK	Family	0	*"Dubrovnik's stunning but crowded [. . .]"*

A total of 5208 reviews of Dubrovnik were collected, covering the period from July 2017 to December 2023. For the research purposes of this study, 371 reviews, written between 1 January 2022 and 31 December 2023, were excluded from the dataset used for training and testing in order to conduct a sentiment analysis with them later. The dataset includes 4835 reviews after the reviews from the specified period were excluded.

Negative reviews were considered as those with a rating of 1 or 2, neutral reviews were considered as those with a rating of 3, while positive reviews were considered as those with a rating of 4 or 5. An attribute called *"Sentiment"* was added to the dataset to reflect the sentiment of each review (*negative/neutral/positive*).

3.3.3. Unbalanced Classes

Figure 3 shows that the dataset contains unbalanced classes, which means that the distribution of classes in the dataset is not even, i.e., one or more classes have significantly more examples than other classes. Training on an unbalanced dataset can lead to a bias towards the most represented class and can ignore classes that are in the minority [66].

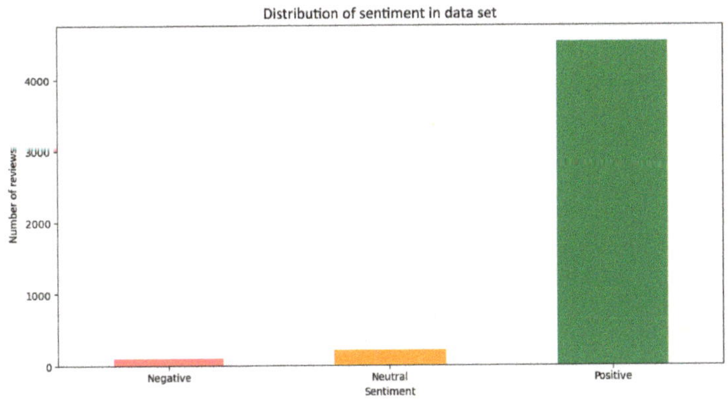

Figure 3. Distribution of sentiments in the dataset.

In [67], Henning and Beluch et al. propose several methods to solve the problem of unbalanced classes in NLP, such as data augmentation, random oversampling, random undersampling, and focal loss.

In our study, data augmentation and random oversampling methods were used to solve the problem of unbalanced classes.

3.3.4. Data Augmentation

Data augmentation is the artificial creation of new examples, from simple string manipulations, such as synonym substitution, to advanced manipulations based on the Transformer model. For example, Wei and Zou, in [68], applied an efficient technique for replacing synonyms using the Wordnet dictionary by randomly inserting, modifying, and deleting words. Other research studies included word substitutions using an LSTM–RNN language model [69]; artificial example generation using an RNN language model [70]; and various paraphrasing methods, as in [71]. Pre-trained language models based on the Transformer architecture, such as BERT, RoBERTa, and GPT, have revolutionized natural language processing. Existing studies show how pre-trained language models can help augment data by generating artificial examples with similar semantic meaning [72–74].

In this study, ChatGPT, which is based on the GPT-3.5 model, was used to generate synthetic data with paraphrases. The inclusion of different examples in the training process of a model leads to better performance in classification [75]. ChatGPT was applied to paraphrase each 1-, 2-, and 3-rated review into ten more reviews. A total of 3432 reviews were added. Table 2 shows an example of the original rating and the rating paraphrased by ChatGPT.

Table 2. The example of data augmentation process using ChatGPT.

Prompt	Input Data	Paraphrased Output Data
Please generate 10 additional reviews of Old Town Dubrovnik that has a similar meaning to this review *. Keep the generated review under the given maximum token.	*Very crowded. The most visited place in Dubrovnik. Great place to spend the evening and soak in the light of the setting sun.*	*Extremely crowded. Undoubtedly the most visited spot in Dubrovnik. Still, it's a great location to spend the evening and absorb the beautiful light as the sunsets.*
	This is an enjoyable place to wander around and visit the little stores, restaurants, and bars. Expect lots of people, but overall a good place to spend a day.	*Despite the bustling atmosphere, this area has its own charm. The mix of shops and dining spots makes it an enjoyable place to explore, even with the crowds.*

* Input data.

Figure 4 shows that, despite the data augmentation, there is still a problem with unbalanced classes in the dataset.

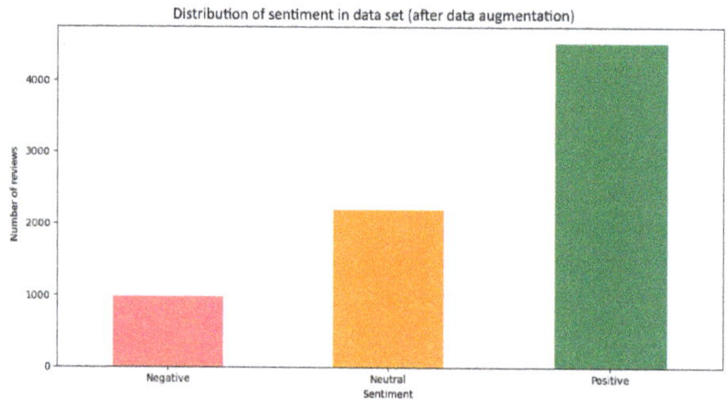

Figure 4. Distribution of sentiments in the dataset after data augmentation.

3.3.5. Data Preprocessing

Data preprocessing involves recognizing, correcting, or removing corrupted and incorrect records in a dataset to make it suitable for ML algorithms. It addresses issues such as noise and missing values, which are often caused by manual errors, technical problems, or unexpected events. Preprocessing aims to improve data quality for better model performance [76]. However, in a study by Alzahrani and Jololian [77], it was found that the BERT model achieved the highest prediction accuracy without applying any preprocessing techniques.

Various preprocessing methods were examined and tested in this study. Finally, the techniques that provided the best results for the model were selected. The dataset was preprocessed with the following techniques:

- The removal of special and punctuation characters (except for alphanumeric characters and spaces);
- The conversion from upper case to lower case;
- The removal of emoticons;
- The removal of multiple spaces;
- The removal of URL tags.

3.3.6. Training and Validation Datasets

The augmented dataset, containing 7696 reviews, was randomly divided into three subsets, the training dataset, validation dataset, and test dataset, in a ratio of 80:10:10, as shown in Table 3.

Table 3. Dataset partitioning.

Dataset	Number of Reviews
Training dataset	6156
Validation dataset	770
Test dataset	770

The training set represents the set of examples used to learn the model and to adjust the parameters of the classifier. After training, a separate validation set is used to fine-tune the hyperparameters of the model and to monitor its performance during training to prevent overfitting. Overfitting occurs when the model performs well on the training dataset but cannot be generalized to unseen data. Finally, the test dataset, which is different from the training and validation datasets, is used to objectively evaluate the performance of the model after training is complete [78,79].

Despite the data augmentation, our training dataset still contains unbalanced classes. In order to solve this problem, we performed a random oversampling.

3.3.7. Random Oversampling

Random oversampling is a method of augmenting datasets that is often used in the context of unbalanced datasets where the majority class dominates the minority classes [67]. In this approach, examples from minority classes were randomly selected and duplicated to achieve a better balance in the dataset. The purpose of this technique is to achieve a balanced distribution of the data so that the model performs better [80].

In this study, random oversampling was used to equate the classes of negative and neutral reviews (minority classes) with the class of positive reviews (majority class) within the training set. Figure 5 shows the distribution of classes in the training set after random oversampling.

Figure 5. Distribution of sentiments in the dataset after random oversampling.

3.4. Selection of a Pre-Trained Model

Since this study deals with NLP problems, a suitable pre-trained model was required. The search on the HuggingFace platform yielded several options, with the RoBERTa model *robertaSentimentFT_Tripadvisor* being selected. This model was trained using *tweets* and was fine-tuned using Tripadvisor hotel reviews. It uses the *AutoTokenizer* module, which enables the automatic selection of the appropriate tokenizer. The tokenizer converts input text sequences into tokens, which is necessary for working with models based on the Transformer architecture. As can be seen in Figure 6, most reviews contain less than 250 tokens, which is why the maximum length is 256 tokens.

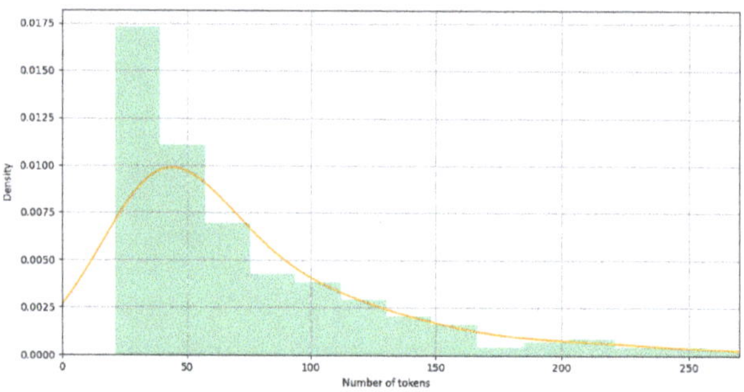

Figure 6. Distribution of reviews' token length. The data is displayed in a density histogram with an additional density curve. The bar area indicates the probability of the number of tokens in the reviews, and the density curve shows the distribution.

3.5. Model Training

The model was trained with different hyperparameters, and the configuration that gave the best results was selected. The optimal hyperparameters listed in Table 4 were used for the final training. After training, the model was evaluated to assess its performance.

Table 4. Model hyperparameters.

Parameter *	Value
Number of epochs	4
Batch size	32
Learning rate	0.00005
Maximum token length	256

* robertaSentimentFT_Tripadvisor model.

3.6. Model Evaluation

Model evaluation is a process in which selected metrics are used to analyze the effectiveness of an ML model. The choice of metrics depends on the data, the model, and the specific use case.

In this study, the following classification metrics were used: the confusion matrix, accuracy, precision, recall, and $F1$ measure ($F1$ score) [81–83].

The confusion matrix is a table that contains key performance data of a machine learning classification model. It is generally used for binary classification problems, where classes are usually denoted as positive and negative, but it can be also used for multi-class classification problems. A binary classification confusion matrix is a 2×2 table of two rows that represent actual classes and two columns that represent predicted classes. Then, the first row refers to the actual positive class, and it contains two values: true positives (TP)—instances of the positive class correctly classified by the model as positive—and false negatives (FN)—instances of the positive class incorrectly classified as negative. Furthermore, the second row refers to the actual negative class, and it has two values: false positives (FP)—instances of the negative class incorrectly classified as positive—and true negatives (TN)—instances of the negative class correctly classified as negative. The sum of the first row of the confusion matrix equals the number of all actual instances of the positive class, and the sum of the second row corresponds to the number of all actual instances of the negative class in the dataset. Also, the sum of the first column is equal to the predicted number of positive instances, and the sum of the second column is equal to the predicted number of negative instances. The main diagonal of the confusion matrix contains TP and TN values, i.e., the numbers of actual instances correctly classified by the model.

The accuracy of the model is calculated as a ratio of correct predictions and all predictions:

$$Accuracy = \frac{TP + TN}{TP + TN + FP + FN} \tag{1}$$

There are also other metrics which are more useful when the dataset is unbalanced, as it is in our case, such as precision, recall, and the $F1$ score, as well as the false-positive rate and false-negative rate. The precision of a model measures how many true-positive predictions are among all predicted instances of a positive class, and it is calculated using TP and FP values, as follows:

$$Precision = \frac{TP}{TP + FP} \tag{2}$$

The recall of the model measures how many true-positive predictions are among all actual instances of a positive class, and it is calculated using TP and FN values, as follows:

$$Recall = \frac{TP}{TP + FN} \tag{3}$$

The $F1$ score, or the $F1$ measure, is a harmonic mean between the precision and recall values, and it is calculated as follows:

$$F1 = 2 \cdot \frac{1}{\frac{1}{Precison} + \frac{1}{Recall}} = \frac{2TP}{2TP + FP + FN} \tag{4}$$

The false-positive rate (FPR) measures how many false positives are among all instances of the actual negative class:

$$FPR = \frac{FP}{FP + TN} \tag{5}$$

Lastly, the false-negative rate (FNR) measures how many false negatives are among all instances of the actual positive class:

$$FNR = \frac{FN}{TP + FN} \tag{6}$$

If the classes in the binary classification problem are named differently, e.g., class X and class Y, then we can still find all of the mentioned values with respect to each of the classes. For example, if we analyze class X, then we will treat it as a positive class and class Y as a negative class. Therefore, for class X, the values in the confusion matrix will be named TP_X, FN_X, FP_X, and TN_X. Then, we can find the $Precision_X$, $Recall_X$, $F1_X$, FPR_X, and FNR_X values. After similarly analyzing class Y, we can calculate the $Precision_Y$, $Recall_Y$, $F1_Y$, FPR_Y, and FNR_Y values. Finally, we can find the average model performance metrics as an arithmetic mean of individual values for class X and class Y. It must be noted that the accuracy value will be the same in both cases, because it is simply calculated as a ratio of correct predictions and all predictions.

Furthermore, for multi-class classification problems (n classes), the confusion matrix will be an $n \times n$ table, where each row represents one actual class and each column one predicted class. Along the main diagonal, each element is a correct prediction by the model, and the rest of the table is filled with incorrect predictions. Afterwards, we find TP, FN, FP, and TN values for each individual class and calculate its precision, recall, and F1-score values, as shown in Equations (2)–(4). To evaluate the model fully, we need to find the average of these metrics as an arithmetic mean (called macro-average) of individual values for each of the classes:

$$Precision_{macro-average} = \frac{\sum_{i=1}^{n} Precision_i}{n} \quad (7)$$

$$Recall_{macro-average} = \frac{\sum_{i=1}^{n} Recall_i}{n} \quad (8)$$

$$F1_{\ macro-average} = \frac{\sum_{i=1}^{n} F1_{\ i}}{n} \quad (9)$$

Again, the accuracy of the model can be calculated simply by dividing the correct predictions (main diagonal of the confusion matrix) by the total number of predictions.

4. Results and Discussion

4.1. Model Effectiveness

This section presents the results of the *robertaSentimentFT_Tripadvisor* model evaluation with the test dataset containing 770 randomly selected reviews from the augmented dataset with 7969 reviews in total. In the test dataset, there are 98 negative reviews, 220 neutral reviews, and 452 positive reviews. Figure 7 shows the confusion matrix for the model using data augmentation and random oversampling methods. The confusion matrix visually illustrates the effectiveness of the selected model for this multi-classification problem. Reviews can be classified by the model into one of three distinct classes: negative, neutral, and positive, denoted in the confusion matrix by 0, 1, and 2, respectively. Therefore, the confusion matrix in Figure 7 contains three rows (actual or true classes) and three columns (predicted classes). For example, by checking the first row of the confusion matrix, it can be seen that the vast majority of actual negative reviews from the test dataset (92/98) were classified by the trained model correctly, five were classified wrongly as neutral, and only one actual negative review was classified wrongly as a positive review. Similarly, in the second and third rows, there were only a handful of misclassifications of actual neutral and positive reviews. By observing the confusion matrix columns, it can be seen that the model classified 95/770 reviews as negative, 228/770 reviews as neutral, and 443/770 as positive, which is close to the actual distribution of reviews. For class 0 (negative reviews), we calculated the values of TP_0 = 92 (92 instances were correctly classified as class 0), FN_0 = 6 (5 + 1 class 0 instances were wrongly classified as class 1 or class 2), FP_0 = 3 (3 + 0 class 1 and class 2 instances were wrongly classified as class 0), and TN_0 = 669 (209 + 8 + 18 + 434 class 1 or class 2 instances were correctly classified as class 1 or class 2), which gave a false-negative rate of FNR_0 = 6.1% and a false-positive rate of FPR_0 = 0.44%. On the other hand, for class 1, we found the values of TP_1 = 209, FN_1 = 11, FP_1 = 23, and TN_1 = 527, resulting in the following values: FNR_1 = 5% and FPR_1 = 4.18%. Lastly, class 2 has TP_2 = 434, FN_2 = 18, FP_2 = 9, and TN_2 = 309, as well as FNR_2 = 3.98% and FPR_2 = 2.83%. Therefore, the false-negative rate was similar for all three classes, but the false-positive rate for class 1 and class 2 were much higher than that of class 0. Because of the nuances and ambiguities between the neutral and positive reviews, this model sometimes decided to classify an actual class 1 review into class 2 and vice versa.

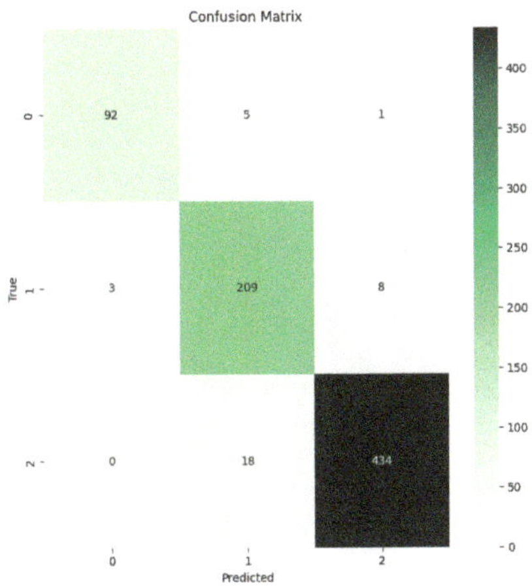

Figure 7. Confusion matrix.

Table 5 provides detailed performance metrics of the model, including the accuracy, precision, recall, and $F1$ measure. Because of the multi-classification problem, we first calculated the precision, recall, and $F1$ score for each of the three classes, and the values presented in Table 5 are their average values as arithmetic means. The performance of the model is given for both raw and preprocessed data using data augmentation and/or random oversampling methods. An analysis of the obtained results showed that the model performs excellently in recognizing sentiments in reviews when both random oversampling and data augmentation were applied. In this case, all four performance metrics had a high value of 95% (highlighted in bold in Table 5), which can be also verified from the confusion matrix presented in Figure 7. However, it must be noted that the individual precision values for classes 0, 1, and 2 vary between 90.09% for class 1, 96.84% for class 0, and 97.97% for class 2. On the other hand, the individual recall values for classes 0, 1, and 2 are quite similar—93.88% for class 0, 95% for class 1, and 96.02% for class 2.

Table 5. The results of the model evaluation.

Model	Method *	Accuracy	Precision	Recall	F1 Score
robertaSentimentFT_Tripadvisor	-	94%	74%	65%	68%
robertaSentimentFT_Tripadvisor	O	91%	72%	58%	63%
robertaSentimentFT_Tripadvisor	A	95%	94%	95%	95%
robertaSentimentFT_Tripadvisor	O + A	**95%**	**95%**	**95%**	**95%**

* O—random oversampling; A—data augmentation.

4.2. Sentiment Analysis of Reviews Written between 1 January 2022 and 31 December 2023

This section presents the results of the sentiment analysis of the previously excluded reviews, which were written in the period from 1 January 2022 to 31 December 2023. A total of 371 reviews were analyzed and classified. An exploratory data analysis was conducted to create a series of charts for a better understanding of the data.

Figure 8 shows a diagram with the distribution of sentiments in the reviews obtained by our model. The results show that the majority of visitors rated their experience in Dubrovnik as positive (92.7%), while neutral (4%) and negative (3.2%) reviews are rarer. This is in line with the rest of the initial dataset of reviews from 2017 to 2021, as presented in Figure 3.

The actual ratings play an important role in reflecting the opinions of visitors. The results in Figure 9 show that the majority of visitors rated their experience in Dubrovnik as excellent, with 265 reviews rated as 5. This is followed by 64 ratings of 4 and 28 reviews rated as 3. Ratings of 2 and 1 are less common, with only 8 and 6 reviews, respectively. It can be seen that 88.7% of the reviews (329/371) were rated, by users, as 4 or 5, and the model classified 92.7% of the reviews as positive. This means that the model also found positive sentiments in the texts of some reviews rated as 3, 2, or 1.

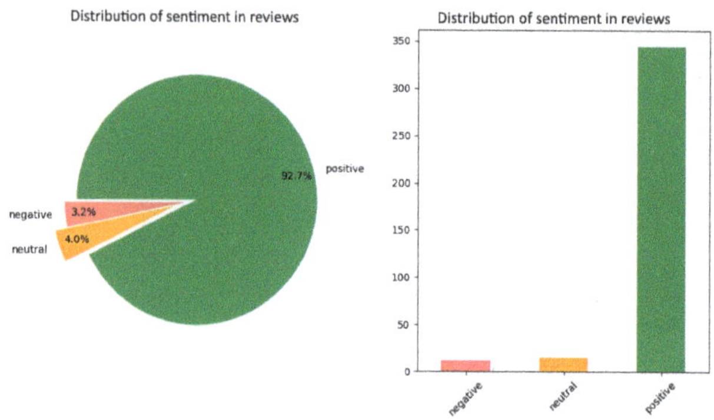

Figure 8. Distribution of sentiments in the reviews.

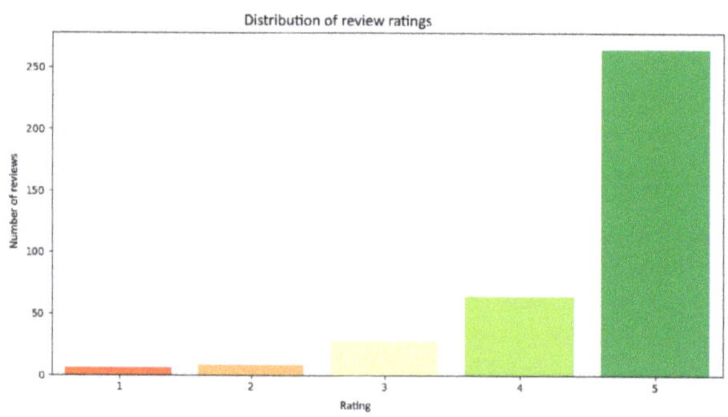

Figure 9. Distribution of ratings in the reviews.

The distribution of sentiments by ratings can be illustrated on the basis of user ratings and sentiments in more detail. Figure 10 shows how the sentiments detected by the model changes with the different ratings. As expected, only positive sentiments predominate for reviews with a score of 5. Positive sentiments also predominate in reviews with a rating of 4, with a lower number of neutral views. A rating of 3 shows a diversity between positive, neutral, and negative sentiments, but positive sentiments are still the most prevalent. Lower ratings (1 and 2) contain predominantly negative opinions, albeit in smaller numbers, but also sometimes positive and neutral sentiments.

Figure 11 shows the distribution of sentiments over time. In 2022, the positive sentiments remain stronger during the pre-season despite fewer reviews. There is a sharp increase in positive reviews at the start of the season, in late March and April, while the number of negative and neutral reviews remain relatively low. The positive sentiments continue to increase over the course of the season, even after a slight decline in August. The number of negative reviews reaches its peak in August, while September stands out with the most positive reviews. At the beginning of the post-season, in late September and October, there is a sudden drop in positive sentiments, as expected by the fewer visitors in Dubrovnik, which weakens by the end of the year but still remains higher compared to neutral and negative sentiments. In contrast to 2022, 2023 shows a larger increase in positive sentiments during the pre-season. However, a lower growth and a lower number of positive reviews were recorded at the start of the season. During the 2023 season, positive sentiments continue to rise slightly until July, after which they stagnate until August. It is important to note that June is characterized by the largest number of neutral reviews, July by the largest number of positive reviews, and September by the largest number of negative reviews. At the beginning of the post-season, the positive sentiments decrease sharply until the end of the year. Figure 12 shows the differences in sentiments between 2022 and 2023. The absolute number of reviews with a positive sentiment decreases by 45%, while neutral and negative sentiments increase by 100%. When comparing relative values, it can be seen that the proportion of reviews with positive sentiments decreased from 96.1% in 2022 to 87.1% in 2023, those with neutral sentiments increased from 2.1% in 2022 to 7.1% in 2023, and those with negative sentiments also increased from 1.7% in 2022 to 5.7% in 2023.

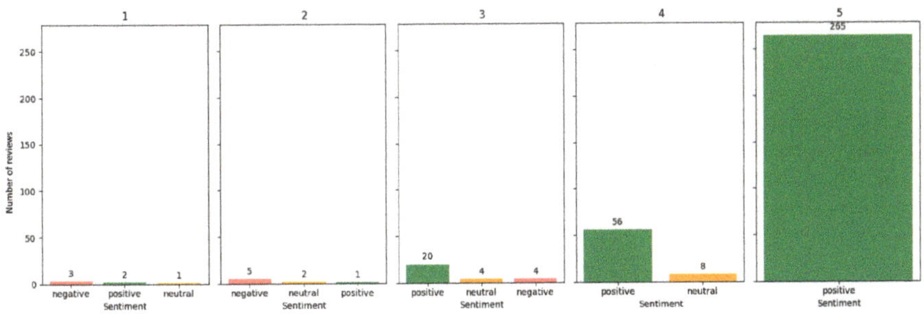

Figure 10. Distribution of sentiments according to ratings.

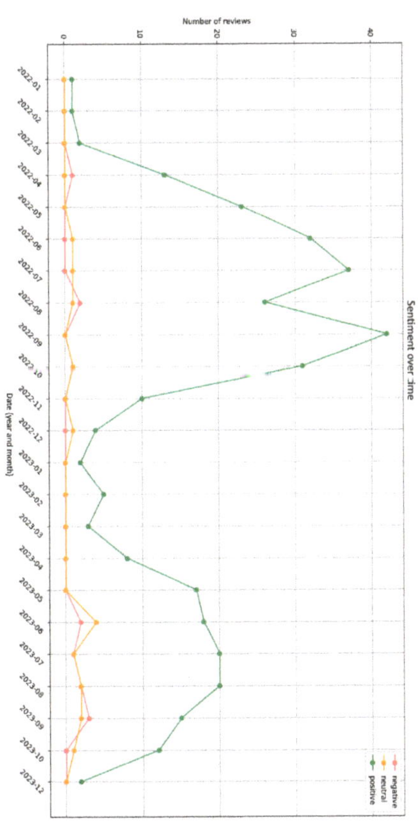

Figure 11. Distribution of sentiments over time.

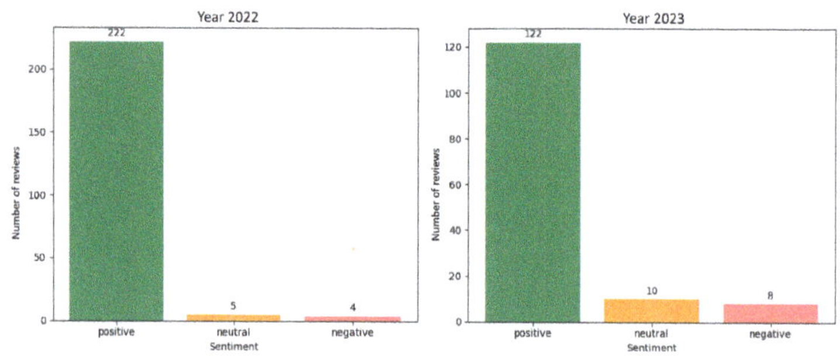

Figure 12. Distribution of sentiments in the reviews for the years of 2022 and 2023.

It was also important to examine how the length of the reviews differed according to sentiments. Figure 13 shows the distribution of sentiments according to the average character length within the reviews. In 2022, the longest reviews, on average, were negative (448.75 characters), while neutral (342.6 characters) and positive (304.5 characters) ones were quite shorter. In 2023, however, the length of reviews increased: reviews with negative sentiments increased by 12.77% (to 506 characters), reviews with neutral sentiments increased by 19.23% (to 408.5 characters), and reviews with positive sentiments recorded a significant increase of 49.01% (to 453.5 characters).

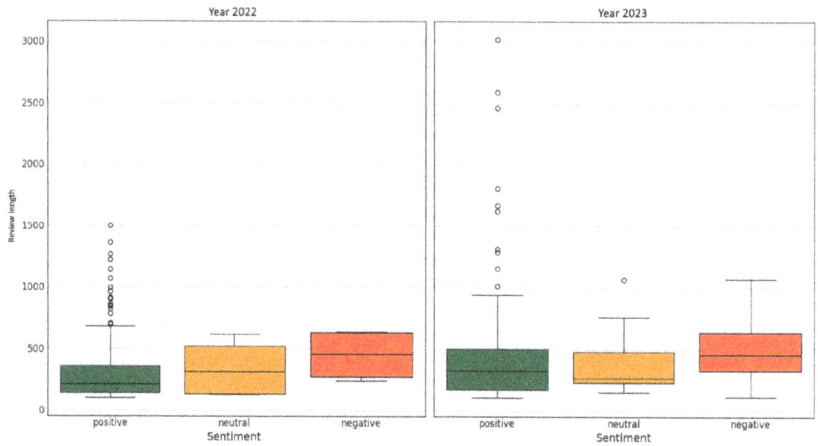

Figure 13. Distribution of sentiments according to average character length within the reviews. Data is presented in box-plots for years 2022 and 2023 that also include outliers as individual points.

In addition to the character length by sentiments, the average number of words in the reviews by sentiments were also examined in more detail, as presented in Figure 14. In 2022, the average number of words for reviews with a negative sentiment is 79.25 words; for neutral reviews, it is 59.6 words; and positive reviews contain an average of 55.84 words. In 2023, however, the average number of words for negative reviews increased by 17.75% (to 93.25 words); for neutral reviews, by 25.84% (to 74.90 words); and for positive reviews, by 48.93% (to 83.04 words). This increase in word count and review length indicates that reviews became more pronounced and detailed in 2023.

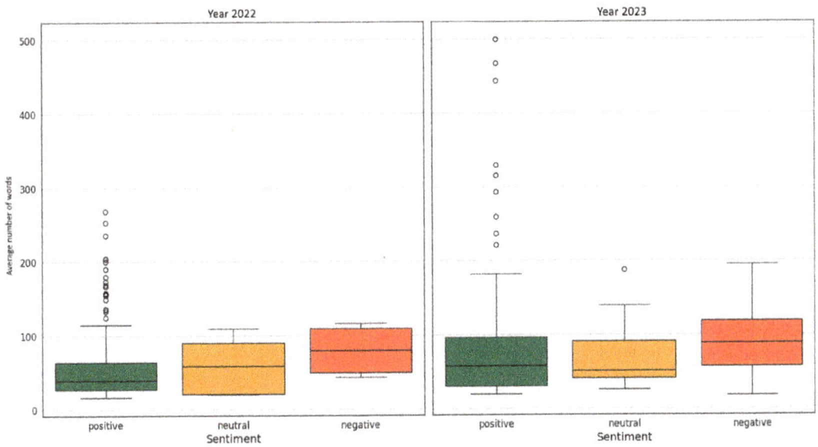

Figure 14. Distribution of sentiments according to the average number of words in the reviews. Data is presented in box-plots for years 2022 and 2023 that also include outliers as individual points.

A word cloud is a visual representation of the most frequently occurring words as a group of words that are displayed in different sizes. The larger and more emphasized a word is in the graphical representation, the more frequently it is repeated in the reviews. Figure 15 shows the word clouds for the positive, neutral, and negative sentiments.

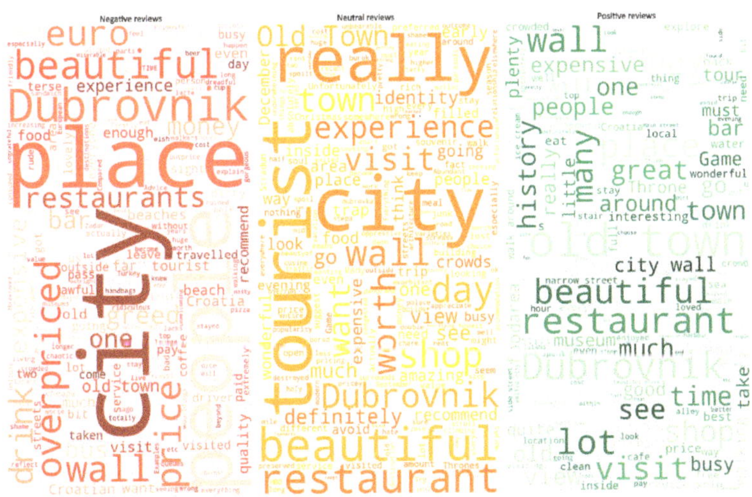

Figure 15. The word clouds for positive, neutral, and negative sentiments.

Data on the type of visitors were used to gain a deeper insight into the reviews. In 2022, the largest proportion of visitors were of the "unknown" type, with a share of 71.9%; while couples accounted for 16%; friends, 5.6%; families, 5.2%; and individuals, 1.3%. In 2023, the proportion of couples rose significantly to 40%, while the proportion of unknown visitors fell to 34.3%. Friends accounted for 11.4% of visitors; families, 8.6%; individuals, 5%; while the business segment had a share of 0.7%. Figure A1 shows the shares of visitor types in 2022 and 2023.

Regarding the distribution of sentiments by visitor type, in 2022, most positive reviews were given by unknown visitors (160 positive), while couples had 37 positive reviews. Friends had 12 positive and 1 negative review; family, 11 positive and 1 negative; and individuals,

2 positive and 1 neutral review. In 2023, couples had the most positive (46), neutral (5), and negative (5) reviews. Unknown visitors had 44 positive, 2 neutral, and 2 negative reviews. Friends had 14 positive, 1 neutral, and 1 negative reviews. Family had 11 positive and 1 neutral review, individuals had 6 positive and 1 neutral review, while the business segment had 1 positive review. Figure A2 shows the distribution of sentiments by visitor type.

Another feature that can be compared between 2022 and 2023 is the origin of the visitors. The differences between the sample and the population indicate a bias due to the language selection of the reviews, with English-speaking countries most strongly represented in the reviews. Figure A3 highlights the 10 most represented countries in the 2022 and 2023 reviews.

In 2022, most users came from the United Kingdom, for a 47.8% share of the total. The United States followed, with a share of 19.6%, while the proportion of users whose origin was unknown was 18.2%. Other countries include Ireland (3.8%), Canada (2.4%), Australia (1.9%), Germany (1.9%), the Netherlands (1.4%), Italy (1.4%), and Romania (1.4%). In 2023, the proportion of visitors from the United Kingdom fell to 39.7%, while the proportion of visitors of unknown origin rose to 23.1%. The United States also recorded a decline in its share to 15.7%. Increases were recorded by countries such as Australia (5%), Ireland (4.1%), the Netherlands (3.3%), and Canada (3.3%). The emergence of new countries should be highlighted, including, among others, Turkey (2.5%), France (1.7%), and Brazil (1.7%). Figure A4 provides the distribution of sentiments according to the users' countries of origin (a total of 584) in 2022 and 2023.

In 2022, users from the UK had the most positive reviews. In the United States of America, Ireland, Canada, Australia, and Romania, the majority of reviews were also positive, albeit in smaller numbers. In several European countries, including Germany, Italy, and the Netherlands, sentiments were mixed, with both neutral and negative reviews. However, there were some changes in the distribution of sentiments in 2023. In the UK, the number of positive reviews decreased, while the number of neutral and negative reviews increased. A similar trend can be observed in the US, where the number of positive reviews decreased and the number of neutral reviews increased. In Australia and Canada, the majority of positive reviews remained the same, while there was a change in neutral and negative reviews in Ireland. It is important to note that in new countries, such as Turkey and Brazil, positive sentiments predominate, while in France, the positive and negative sentiments are balanced. To present some of the results of the model, the most positive, the most neutral, and the most negative reviews are presented. The reviews are presented in Tables 6–8 along with the specific values of the model with the highest sentiment value highlighted in bold.

Table 6. The most positive reviews.

Review	Sentiment		
	Positive	Neutral	Negative
"Beautiful place but very hot, especially inside the old city. Drink plenty and definitely take a hat! Lots of places to eat and wonderful ice cream. We also went back the 2nd day (we pre booked our old city tickets online before we travelled from the UK, they are valid for 3 days but 2 days are enough) to go on a boat ride which was a welcome break from the heat. Recommend downloading the Uber app, very useful and quick. You can hail local taxis but they are more expensive. Also lots of buses, we didn't get any but they always looked crammed! Lots of fish restaurants, Recommend the Cave Bar; Sunset Beach, we walked from where we stayed which was Hotel Lapad".	**0.9999640**	0.0000184	0.0000175

Table 7. The most neutral reviews.

Review	Sentiment		
	Positive	Neutral	Negative
"With the exception of the overlooking walls and selected places, the city area is somewhat lifeless—like an open-air museum".	0.0000378	**0.9999399**	0.0000222

Table 8. The most negative reviews.

Review	Sentiment		
	Positive	Neutral	Negative
Nothing to write home about. Narrow streets and alleys, restaurants and bars but what a rip off. They want more than $30 to walk around the castle walls and people were paying it. Smuks! Plenty of much nicer and cheaper places to see in Croatia so my recommendation is avoid Dubrovnik".	0.0000687	0.0000340	**0.9998972**

We can see how the model made it possible to classify the reviews into different sentiments. The negative, neutral, and positive sentiment values depend on what the user wrote in the review. To better understand the model and its results, we compared the sentiments with the ratings of the individual reviews, as shown below. Table 9 shows the review that was rated 1 by the user and has the most positive value of the model. This is an example of a good prediction of the model as opposed to an incorrect rating by the user. This could be an unintentional error by the user, and the analysts can later decide how to evaluate such inconsistent reviews or exclude them from further analysis.

Table 9. The reviews with the most positive sentiments, rated 1.

Review	Sentiment			Rating
	Positive	Neutral	Negative	
Great place to visit. Loved all the alleyways, shops and restaurants/cafes. Walked the old wall of Dubrovnik. Quite an experience in the heat!"	**0.9999603**	0.0000165	0.0000231	1

5. Conclusions

Numerous studies analyzing sentiments of Dubrovnik focus mainly on hotel accommodations and restaurants, but no research study has yet been conducted that focuses exclusively on the attractions of the destination itself. With the aim of contributing to solving this problem, this paper analyzed the sentiments of the tourist attraction "Old Town" in Dubrovnik based on user experiences on the Tripadvisor platform. With the help of an implemented web-scraping script, a total of 5208 reviews of the mentioned attraction were collected between July 2017 and December 2023. We utilized ChatGPT as a very useful tool for dealing with the unbalanced dataset.

Together with the script, a sentiment analysis model was also implemented using the pre-trained RoBERTa model. The results of the model evaluation, which include metrics such as accuracy, precision, responsiveness, and F1 measure, indicate an excellent classification of the reviews by sentiment. A sentiment analysis was then performed on the previously excluded reviews from 2022 and 2023. A total of 371 reviews written from 1 January 2022 to 31 December 2023 were analyzed and classified. The results of the sentiment analysis are presented visually in various charts to explore unseen information and correlations. One of the most important findings is the distribution of sentiments by reviews. The majority of visitors rated their experience in Dubrovnik as positive (92.7%), while neutral (4%) and negative (3.2%) reviews are less common. The reviews play an important role in reflecting the opinion of visitors, and most reviews were rated highly. The sentiment analysis also showed how sentiments change with the different ratings. For example, reviews with a rating of 5 are dominated by exclusively positive sentiments, while reviews with a rating of 4 are also predominantly positive, but a smaller number also contain neutral views. A rating of 3 shows the diversity between positive, neutral, and negative sentiments, but the positive sentiment is still the most strongly represented. The lower levels (1 and 2) contain the most negative opinions, albeit in smaller numbers, but may also contain positive and neutral sentiments. The distribution of sentiments over time was also analyzed, and the results show interesting trends in the opinions of visitors in 2022 and 2023. In addition, the distribution of opinions by visitor type was analyzed, which further deepened the understanding of visitors' attitudes and experiences. In addition, the origin of visitors and their distribution by country were also examined, revealing changes in the composition of visitors over the years studied.

This research is not without limitations, and in particular, the use of a single platform, attractions, and reviews written in English may lead to biases. A larger number of tourist attractions should be considered in future studies. On the Tripadvisor platform, there are a number of tourist attractions in Dubrovnik and its surroundings, such as Dubrovnik's city walls, Lokrum, Elafiti, etc. Multiple data sources should also be included. In addition, a larger number of languages should be covered. For example, only reviews written in Croatian should be considered, and the opinion of the local population on certain tourist attractions should be analyzed. Finally, a facet-level sentiment analysis should be used to gain a more detailed insight into visitors' attitudes towards different elements of tourist attractions.

Taking into account all the advantages and disadvantages mentioned above, further studies should extend the problem areas and introduce new methods. We also plan to extend our research to other destinations to provide useful arguments for sustainability feasibility studies. We also see the possibility of applying our model to business process intelligence. Some preliminary experiments with various supporting tools have encouraged us to go in this direction.

Author Contributions: Conceptualization, I.Z. and F.Š.-M.; methodology, I.Z., F.Š.-M. and H.M.; software, H.M.; validation, I.Z., F.Š.-M. and H.M.; investigation, I.Z. and H.M.; data curation, H.M.; writing—original draft preparation, I.Z. and H.M.; writing—review and editing, I.Z., F.Š.-M., H.M. and B.B.; visualization, H.M.; supervision, I.Z.; project administration, I.Z. and B.B. All authors have read and agreed to the published version of the manuscript.

Funding: This research received no external funding.

Institutional Review Board Statement: Not applicable.

Informed Consent Statement: Not applicable.

Data Availability Statement: The raw data supporting the conclusions of this article will be made available by the authors on request.

Conflicts of Interest: The authors declare no conflicts of interest.

Appendix A

In this Appendix A, a deeper insight into the model is provided. We introduce some additional features in order to analyze the results of this paper. These features open the possibility of repeating experiments to gain a deeper insight into the reviews.

In addition to the representative data presented in the main text, Figure A1 shows the proportions of visitor types in 2022 and 2023, and Figure A2 illustrates the distribution of sentiments according to visitor type. Moreover, Figure A3 highlights the 10 most represented countries in the 2022 and 2023 reviews. Finally, Figure A4 provides the distribution of sentiments by users' countries of origin in 2022 and 2023.

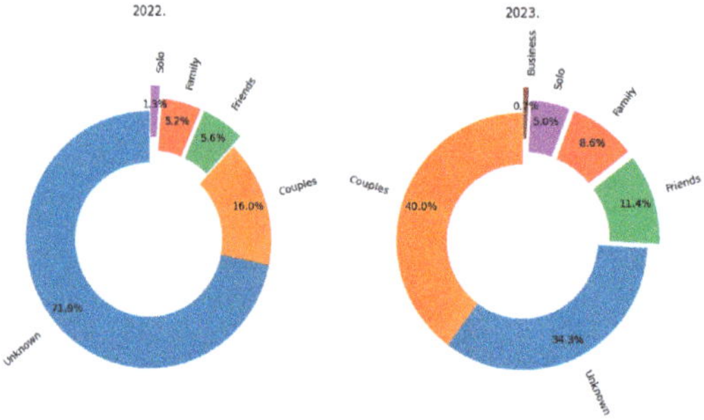

Figure A1. Visitor types of reviews.

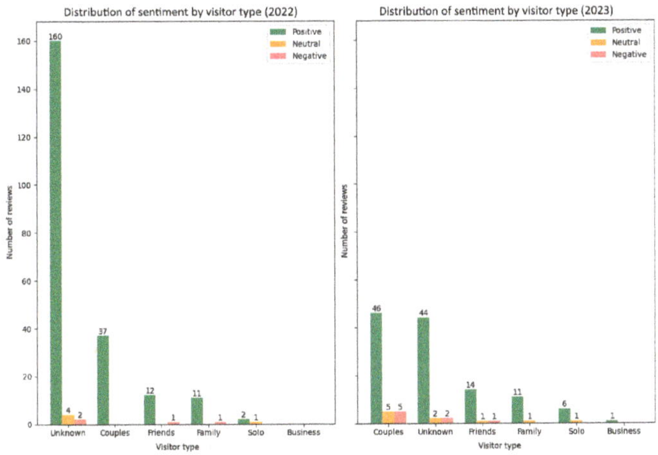

Figure A2. Distribution of sentiments by type of visitor in 2022 and 2023.

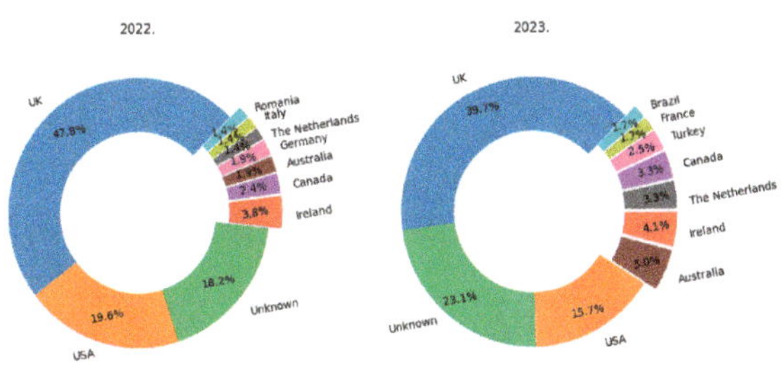

Figure A3. The 10 most represented countries in the reviews for 2022 and 2023 (percentages do not add up to 100 because of rounding to one decimal place).

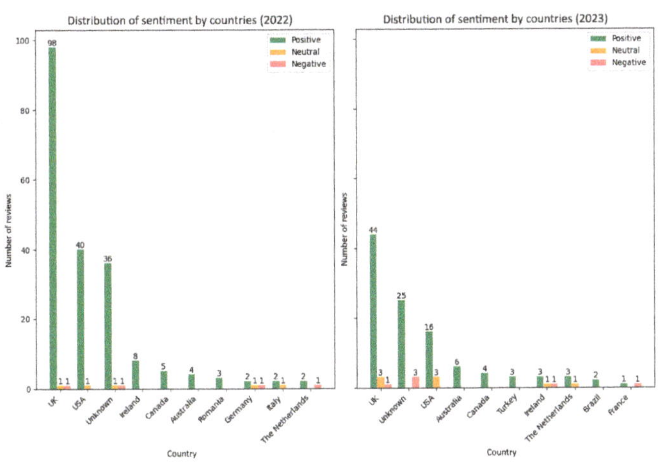

Figure A4. Distribution of sentiments by country in 2022 and 2023.

ferences

Rodríguez-Díaz, M.; Rodríguez-Díaz, R.; Rodríguez-Voltes, A.C.; Rodríguez-Voltes, C.I. A Model of Market Positioning of Destinations Based on Online Customer Reviews of Lodgings. *Sustainability* **2018**, *10*, 78. [CrossRef]

Ye, Q.; Zhang, Z.; Law, R. Sentiment Classification of Online Reviews to Travel Destinations by Supervised Machine Learning Approaches. *Expert Syst. Appl.* **2009**, *36*, 6527–6535. [CrossRef]

3. Filieri, R.; McLeay, F. E-WOM and Accommodation: An Analysis of the Factors That Influence Travelers' Adoption of Informati from Online Reviews. *J. Travel Res.* **2013**, *53*, 44–57. [CrossRef]
4. Rhee, H.T.; Yang, S.-B.; Kim, K. Exploring the Comparative Salience of Restaurant Attributes: A Conjoint Analysis Approach. *J. Inf. Manag.* **2016**, *36*, 1360–1370. [CrossRef]
5. Tripadvisor One Billion Reviews and Moments. Available online: https://www.onebillion.tripadvisor.com (accessed or September 2023).
6. Gour, A.; Aggarwal, S.; Erdem, M. Reading between the Lines: Analyzing Online Reviews by Using a Multi-Method W Analytics Approach. *Int. J. Contemp. Hosp. Manag.* **2021**, *33*, 490–512. [CrossRef]
7. Barbierato, E.; Bernetti, I.; Capecchi, I. Analyzing TripAdvisor Reviews of Wine Tours: An Approach Based on Text Mining a Sentiment Analysis. *Int. J. Wine Bus. Res.* **2022**, *34*, 212–236. [CrossRef]
8. Sulova, S.; Bankov, B. Approach for Social Media Content-Based Analysis for Vacation Resorts. *J. Commun. Softw. Syst.* **2019**, 262–271. [CrossRef]
9. Vignjević, M.; Car, T.; Šuman, S. Information Extraction and Sentiment Analysis of Hotel Reviews in Croatia. *Zb. Veleučilišta Rij* **2023**, *11*, 69–87. [CrossRef]
10. Jakopović, H. Detecting the Online Image of "Average" Restaurants on TripAdvisor. *Medijske Stud.* **2016**, *7*, 102–119. [CrossR
11. Simeon, M.I.; Buonincontri, P.; Cinquegrani, F.; Martone, A. Exploring Tourists' Cultural Experiences in Naples through Onli Reviews. *J. Hosp. Tour. Technol.* **2017**, *8*, 220–238. [CrossRef]
12. Bigne, E.; Ruiz, C.; Cuenca, A.; Perez, C.; Garcia, A. What Drives the Helpfulness of Online Reviews? A Deep Learning Study Sentiment Analysis, Pictorial Content and Reviewer Expertise for Mature Destinations. *J. Destin. Mark. Manag.* **2021**, *20*, 1005 [CrossRef]
13. Stojanovic, D. Mass Tourism Threatens Croatia's "Game of Thrones" Town. *AP News*, 21 September 2018.
14. Goodwin, H. The Challenge of Overtourism. Responsible Tourism Partnership. 2017. Available online: https://haroldgoodw info/wp-content/uploads/2020/08/rtpwp4overtourism012017.pdf (accessed on 1 September 2023).
15. Goodwin, H. *Responsible Tourism: Using Tourism for Sustainable Development*, 2nd ed.; Goodfellow Publishers Ltd.: Oxford, U 2016; ISBN 9781910158869.
16. Liu, B. *Sentiment Analysis and Opinion Mining*; Springer International Publishing: Cham, Switzerland, 2012; ISBN 97830310101
17. Das, S.R.; Chen, M.Y. Yahoo! For Amazon: Sentiment Parsing from Small Talk on the Web. *SSRN Electron. J.* **2001**. [CrossRef]
18. Pontiki, M.; Galanis, D.; Pavlopoulos, J.; Papageorgiou, H.; Androutsopoulos, I.; Manandhar, S. SemEval-2014 Task 4: Asp Based Sentiment Analysis. In Proceedings of the 8th International Workshop on Semantic Evaluation (SemEval 2014), Dubl Ireland, 23–24 August 2014; Nakov, P., Zesch, T., Eds.; Association for Computational Linguistics: Dublin, Ireland, 2014; pp. 27–
19. Cambria, E.; Das, D.; Bandyopadhyay, S.; Feraco, A. (Eds.) *A Practical Guide to Sentiment Analysis*; Springer Internatior Publishing: Cham, Switzerland, 2017; Volume 5, ISBN 9783319553924/9783319553948.
20. Agüero-Torales, M.M.; Cobo, M.J.; Herrera-Viedma, E.; López-Herrera, A.G. A Cloud-Based Tool for Sentiment Analysis Reviews about Restaurants on TripAdvisor. *Procedia Comput. Sci.* **2019**, *162*, 392–399. [CrossRef]
21. Asani, E.; Vahdat-Nejad, H.; Sadri, J. Restaurant Recommender System Based on Sentiment Analysis. *Mach. Learn. Appl.* **2021**, 100114. [CrossRef]
22. Consoli, S.; Barbaglia, L.; Manzan, S. Fine-Grained, Aspect-Based Sentiment Analysis on Economic and Financial Lexic *Knowl.-Based Syst.* **2022**, *247*, 108781. [CrossRef]
23. Wang, L.; Kirilenko, A.P. Do Tourists from Different Countries Interpret Travel Experience with the Same Feeling? Sentime Analysis of TripAdvisor Reviews. In *Information and Communication Technologies in Tourism 2021*; Wörndl, W., Koo, C., Stienme J.L., Eds.; Springer International Publishing: Cham, Switzerland, 2021; pp. 294–301.
24. Dilmegani, C.; Alp, E. Sentiment Analysis Methods in 2024: Overview, Pros & Cons. AIMultiple High Tech Use Cases & Tools to Gr Your Bus. 2024. Available online: https://research.aimultiple.com/sentiment-analysis-methods/ (accessed on 1 February 2024).
25. Maslej-Krešňáková, V.; Sarnovský, M.; Butka, P.; Machová, K. Comparison of Deep Learning Models and Various Text P Processing Techniques for the Toxic Comments Classification. *Appl. Sci.* **2020**, *10*, 8631. [CrossRef]
26. Soong, H.-C.; Ayyasamy, R.K.; Akbar, R. A Review towards Deep Learning for Sentiment Analysis. In Proceedings of the 20 International Conference on Computer & Information Sciences (ICCOINS), Kuching, Malaysia, 13–15 July 2021; pp. 238–243.
27. Murni; Handhika, T.; Fahrurozi, A.; Sari, I.; Lestari, D.P.; Zen, R.I.M. Hybrid Method for Sentiment Analysis Using Homogeneo Ensemble Classifier. In Proceedings of the 2019 2nd International Conference of Computer and Informatics Engineering (IC2I Banyuwangi, Indonesia, 10–11 September 2019; pp. 232–236.
28. Vázquez-Hernández, M.; Morales-Rosales, L.A.; Algredo-Badillo, I.; Fernández-Gregorio, S.I.; Rodríguez-Rangel, H.; Córdo Tlaxcalteco, M.-L. A Survey of Adversarial Attacks: An Open Issue for Deep Learning Sentiment Analysis Models. *Appl. S* **2024**, *14*, 4614. [CrossRef]
29. Valdivia, A.; Luzon, M.; Herrera, F. Sentiment Analysis in TripAdvisor. *IEEE Intell. Syst.* **2017**, *32*, 72–77. [CrossRef]
30. Hays, S.; Page, S.J.; Buhalis, D. Social Media as a Destination Marketing Tool: Its Use by National Tourism Organisations. *Cu Issues Tour.* **2013**, *16*, 211–239. [CrossRef]

Chang, Y.-C.; Ku, C.-H.; Chen, C.-H. Social Media Analytics: Extracting and Visualizing Hilton Hotel Ratings and Reviews from TripAdvisor. *Int. J. Inf. Manag.* **2019**, *48*, 263–279. [CrossRef]

Das, S.; Das, A. Fusion with Sentiment Scores for Market Research. In Proceedings of the 2016 19th International Conference on Information Fusion (FUSION), Heidelberg, Germany, 5–8 July 2016; pp. 1003–1010.

Luo, Q.; Zhai, X. "I Will Never Go to Hong Kong Again!" How the Secondary Crisis Communication of "Occupy Central" on Weibo Shifted to a Tourism Boycott. *Tour. Manag.* **2017**, *62*, 159–172. [CrossRef] [PubMed]

Kim, K.; Park, O.; Yun, S.; Yun, H. What Makes Tourists Feel Negatively about Tourism Destinations? Application of Hybrid Text Mining Methodology to Smart Destination Management. *Technol. Forecast. Soc. Chang.* **2017**, *123*, 362–369. [CrossRef]

Thelwall, M. Sentiment Analysis for Tourism BT. In *Big Data and Innovation in Tourism, Travel, and Hospitality: Managerial Approaches, Techniques, and Applications*; Sigala, M., Rahimi, R., Thelwall, M., Eds.; Springer: Singapore, 2019; pp. 87–104, ISBN 978-981-13-6339-9.

Schmunk, S.; Höpken, W.; Fuchs, M.; Lexhagen, M. Sentiment Analysis: Extracting Decision-Relevant Knowledge from UGC BT. In *Information and Communication Technologies in Tourism 2014*; Xiang, Z., Tussyadiah, I., Eds.; Springer International Publishing: Cham, Switzerland, 2013; pp. 253–265.

Cadeddu, A.; Chessa, A.; De Leo, V.; Fenu, G.; Motta, E.; Osborne, F.; Reforgiato Recupero, D.; Salatino, A.; Secchi, L. Optimizing Tourism Accommodation Offers by Integrating Language Models and Knowledge Graph Technologies. *Information* **2024**, *15*, 398. [CrossRef]

Yan, Q.; Zhou, S.; Wu, S. The Influences of Tourists' Emotions on the Selection of Electronic Word of Mouth Platforms. *Tour. Manag.* **2018**, *66*, 348–363. [CrossRef]

Anis, S.O.; Saad, S.; Aref, M. A Survey on Sentiment Analysis in Tourism. *Int. J. Intell. Comput. Inf. Sci.* **2020**, *20*, 1–15. [CrossRef]

Fu, M.; Pan, L. Sentiment Analysis of Tourist Scenic Spots Internet Comments Based on LSTM. *Math. Probl. Eng.* **2022**, *2022*, 5944954. [CrossRef]

Manosso, F.C.; Cristina, D.R.T. Using Sentiment Analysis in Tourism Research: A Systematic, Bibliometric, and Integrative Review. *J. Tour. Herit. Serv. Mark.* **2021**, *7*, 17–27. [CrossRef]

Ren, G.; Hong, T. Investigating Online Destination Images Using a Topic-Based Sentiment Analysis Approach. *Sustainability* **2017**, *9*, 1765. [CrossRef]

Mohri, M.; Rostamizadeh, A.; Talwalkar, A. *Foundations of Machine Learning*; MIT Press: Cambridge, MA, USA, 2018.

LeCun, Y.; Bengio, Y.; Hinton, G. Deep Learning. *Nature* **2015**, *521*, 436–444. [CrossRef]

Stojanovski, D.; Strezoski, G.; Madjarov, G.; Dimitrovski, I. Twitter Sentiment Analysis Using Deep Convolutional Neural Network BT. In *Hybrid Artificial Intelligent Systems*; Onieva, E., Santos, I., Osaba, E., Quintián, H., Corchado, E., Eds.; Springer International Publishing: Cham, Switzerland, 2015; pp. 726–737.

Jantan, H.; Ibrahim, P.I.S. Convolutional Neural Networks (CNN) Model for Mobile Brand Sentiment Analysis. In *Intelligent Systems Design and Applications*; Abraham, A., Gandhi, N., Hanne, T., Hong, T.-P., Nogueira Rios, T., Ding, W., Eds.; Springer International Publishing: Cham, Switzerland, 2022; Volume 418, pp. 624–636, ISBN 9783030963071/9783030963088.

Patel, P.; Patel, D.; Naik, C. Sentiment Analysis on Movie Review Using Deep Learning RNN Method BT. In *Intelligent Data Engineering and Analytics*; Satapathy, S.C., Zhang, Y.-D., Bhateja, V., Majhi, R., Eds.; Springer: Singapore, 2021; pp. 155–163.

Pagliarani, A.; Moro, G.; Pasolini, R.; Domeniconi, G. Transfer Learning in Sentiment Classification with Deep Neural Networks BT. In *Knowledge Discovery, Knowledge Engineering and Knowledge Management*; Fred, A., Aveiro, D., Dietz, J.L.G., Liu, K., Bernardino, J., Salgado, A., Filipe, J., Eds.; Springer International Publishing: Cham, Switzerland, 2019; pp. 3–25.

Qaisar, S.M. Sentiment Analysis of IMDb Movie Reviews Using Long Short-Term Memory. In Proceedings of the 2020 2nd International Conference on Computer and Information Sciences (ICCIS), Sakaka, Saudi Arabia, 13–15 October 2020; pp. 1–4.

Bommasani, R.; Hudson, D.A.; Adeli, E.; Altman, R.; Arora, S.; von Arx, S.; Bernstein, M.S.; Bohg, J.; Bosselut, A.; Brunskill, E.; et al. On the Opportunities and Risks of Foundation Models. *arXiv* **2021**, arXiv:2108.07258.

Vaswani, A.; Shazeer, N.; Parmar, N.; Uszkoreit, J.; Jones, L.; Gomez, A.N.; Kaiser, Ł.; Polosukhin, I. Attention Is All You Need. In *Advances in Neural Information Processing Systems 30, Proceedings of the Annual Conference on Neural Information Processing Systems 2017, Long Beach, CA, USA, 4–9 December 2017*; Guyon, I., Luxburg, U.V., Bengio, S., Wallach, H., Fergus, R., Vishwanathan, S., Garnett, R., Eds.; Curran Associates, Inc.: Red Hook, NY, USA, 2017; Volume 30.

Liu, Y.; Ott, M.; Goyal, N.; Du, J.; Joshi, M.; Chen, D.; Levy, O.; Lewis, M.; Zettlemoyer, L.; Stoyanov, V. RoBERTa: A Robustly Optimized BERT Pretraining Approach. *arXiv* **2019**, arXiv:1907.11692.

Facebook AI Research Sequence-to-Sequence Toolkit Written in Python. Available online: https://github.com/facebookresearch/fairseq (accessed on 1 February 2024).

OpenAI ChatGPT. Available online: https://openai.com/index/chatgpt/ (accessed on 10 September 2024).

What Is GPT? 2024. Available online: https://aws.amazon.com/what-is/gpt/ (accessed on 1 February 2024).

Zhuang, F.; Qi, Z.; Duan, K.; Xi, D.; Zhu, Y.; Zhu, H.; Xiong, H.; He, Q. A Comprehensive Survey on Transfer Learning. *Proc. IEEE* **2021**, *109*, 43–76. [CrossRef]

Baheti, P. Transfer Learning Guide: A Comprehensive Guide for Beginners. Available online: https://www.v7labs.com/blog/transfer-learning-guide (accessed on 1 February 2024).

58. Waskom, M. Seaborn: Statistical Data Visualization. *J. Open Source Softw.* **2021**, *6*, 3021. [CrossRef]
59. Oxford Economics Sizing Worldwide Tourism Spending (or "GTP") & TripAdvisor's Economic Impact. Available online: http //www.tourismeconomics.com/case-studies/sizing-worldwide-tourism-spending-or-gtp-tripadvisors-economic-impact/ (a cessed on 10 February 2024).
60. Bianchi, T. Global Travel & Tourism Websites by Visit Share 2023: Most Popular Travel and Tourism Websites Worldwide in Ap 2023, Based on Share of Visits. Available online: https://www.statista.com/statistics/459983/number-of-visits-to-travel-book g-sites-worldwide/ (accessed on 10 February 2024).
61. Statista Research Department Tripadvisor: Estimated Total Number of Visits to the Travel and Tourism Website Tripadvisor.Co Worldwide from August 2020 to June 2024. Available online: https://www.statista.com/statistics/1215473/total-visits-to-tripa visor-website/ (accessed on 10 February 2024).
62. Statista Research Department Most Visited Travel and Tourism Websites Worldwide as of July 2023. Available online: http //www.statista.com/statistics/1215457/most-visited-travel-and-tourism-websites-worldwide/ (accessed on 6 September 202
63. Boegershausen, J.; Datta, H.; Borah, A.; Stephen, A.T. Fields of Gold: Scraping Web Data for Marketing Insights. *J. Mark.* **2022**, 1–20. [CrossRef]
64. Golder, S.A.; Macy, M.W. Digital Footprints: Opportunities and Challenges for Online Social Research. *Annu. Rev. Sociol.* **2014**, 129–152. [CrossRef]
65. Mitchell, R.E. *Web Scraping with Python: Collecting More Data from the Modern Web*, 2nd ed.; O'Reilly Media: Sebastopol, CA, US 2018; ISBN 9781491985571.
66. Guo, X.; Yin, Y.; Dong, C.; Yang, G.; Zhou, G. On the Class Imbalance Problem. In Proceedings of the 2008 Fourth Internation Conference on Natural Computation, Jinan, China, 18–20 October 2008; Volume 4, pp. 192–201.
67. Henning, S.; Beluch, W.; Fraser, A.; Friedrich, A. A Survey of Methods for Addressing Class Imbalance in Deep-Learnir Based Natural Language Processing. In Proceedings of the 17th Conference of the European Chapter of the Association f Computational Linguistics, Dubrovnik, Croatia, 2–6 May 2023; Vlachos, A., Augenstein, I., Eds.; Association for Computation Linguistics: Dubrovnik, Croatia, 2023; pp. 523–540.
68. Wei, J.; Zou, K. EDA: Easy Data Augmentation Techniques for Boosting Performance on Text Classification Tasks. In Proceedin of the 2019 Conference on Empirical Methods in Natural Language Processing and the 9th International Joint Conference Natural Language Processing (EMNLP-IJCNLP), Hong Kong, 3–7 November 2019; Inui, K., Jiang, J., Ng, V., Wan, X., Ed Association for Computational Linguistics: Hong Kong, China, 2019; pp. 6382–6388.
69. Kobayashi, S. Contextual Augmentation: Data Augmentation by Words with Paradigmatic Relations. In *Proceedings of the 20 Conference of the North American Chapter of the Association for Computational Linguistics: Human Language Technologies, Volume 2 (Sho Papers)*; Walker, M., Ji, H., Stent, A., Eds.; Association for Computational Linguistics: New Orleans, LA, USA, 2018; pp. 452–4
70. Rizos, G.; Hemker, K.; Schuller, B. Augment to Prevent: Short-Text Data Augmentation in Deep Learning for Hate-Speec Classification. In Proceedings of the 28th ACM International Conference on Information and Knowledge Management, Beijin China, 3–7 November 2019; Association for Computing Machinery: New York, NY, USA, 2019; pp. 991–1000.
71. Gupta, A.; Agarwal, A.; Singh, P.; Rai, P. A Deep Generative Framework for Paraphrase Generation. *Proc. AAAI Conf. Artif. Inte* **2018**, 5149–5156. [CrossRef]
72. Feng, S.Y.; Gangal, V.; Wei, J.; Chandar, S.; Vosoughi, S.; Mitamura, T.; Hovy, E. A Survey of Data Augmentation Approaches f NLP. *arXiv* **2021**, arXiv:2105.03075. [CrossRef]
73. Bayer, M.; Kaufhold, M.-A.; Reuter, C. A Survey on Data Augmentation for Text Classification. *ACM Comput. Surv.* **2022**, *55*, 1– [CrossRef]
74. Zhang, D.; Li, T.; Zhang, H.; Yin, B. On Data Augmentation for Extreme Multi-Label Classification. *arXiv* **2020**, arXiv:2009.107 [CrossRef]
75. Fang, Y.; Li, X.; Thomas, S.; Zhu, X. ChatGPT as Data Augmentation for Compositional Generalization: A Case Study in Ope Intent Detection. In Proceedings of the Fifth Workshop on Financial Technology and Natural Language Processing and the Secor Multimodal AI for Financial Forecasting, Macao, China, 19–25 August 2023; Chen, C.-C., Takamura, H., Mathur, P., Sawhney, Huang, H.-H., Chen, H.-H., Eds.; pp. 13–33.
76. Chu, X.; Ilyas, I.F.; Krishnan, S.; Wang, J. Data Cleaning: Overview and Emerging Challenges. In Proceedings of the 20 International Conference on Management of Data, San Francisco, CA, USA, 26 June–1 July 2016; Association for Computir Machinery: New York, NY, USA, 2016; pp. 2201–2206.
77. Alzahrani, E.; Jololian, L. How Different Text-Preprocessing Techniques Using the Bert Model Affect the Gender Profiling Authors. In Proceedings of the 3rd International Conference on Machine Learning & Applications (CMLA 2021), Toronto, O Canada, 25–26 September 2021; Academy and Industry Research Collaboration Center (AIRCC): Chennai, India, 2021; pp. 1–
78. Ripley, B.D. *Pattern Recognition and Neural Networks*; Cambridge University Press: Cambridge, UK, 1996; ISBN 9780521717700
79. Baheti, P. Train, Validation, and Test Sets: How to Split Your Data. Available online: https://www.v7labs.com/blog/train-valic tion-test-set (accessed on 15 February 2024).
80. Brownlee, J. *Imbalanced Classification with Python: Better Metrics, Balance Skewed Classes, Cost-Sensitive Learning*; Machine Learnir Mastery: Melbourne, VIC, Australia, 2020.
81. Wang, Y.; Cang, S.; Yu, H. A Survey on Wearable Sensor Modality Centred Human Activity Recognition in Health Care. *Expe Syst. Appl.* **2019**, *137*, 167–190. [CrossRef]

Aravinda, C.V.; Arthur, R.; Chatterjee, M.; Dandıl, E.; Deperlioglu, O.; França, R.P.; Gaie, C.; Iano, Y.; Jayanthi, P.; Kaur, G.; et al. Contributors. In *Deep Learning for Medical Applications with Unique Data*; Gupta, D., Kose, U., Khanna, A., Balas, V.E., Eds.; Academic Press: Cambridge, MA, USA, 2022; ISBN 9780128241455.
Powers, D. Evaluation: From Precision, Recall and F-Factor to ROC, Informedness, Markedness & Correlation. *Mach. Learn. Technol.* **2011**, *2*, 37–63.

applied sciences

MDPI

Article

Detecting Offensive Language on Malay Social Media: A Zero-Shot, Cross-Language Transfer Approach Using Dual-Branch mBERT

Xingyi Guo *, Hamedi Mohd Adnan * and Muhammad Zaiamri Zainal Abidin

Department of Media and Communication Studies, University of Malaya, Kuala Lumpur 50603, Malaysia; zaiamrizainal@um.edu.my

* Correspondence: 22060166@siswa.um.edu.my (X.G.); hamedi@um.edu.my (H.M.A.)

Abstract: Social media serves as a platform for netizens to stay informed and express their opinions through the Internet. Currently, the social media discourse environment faces a significant security threat—offensive comments. A group of users posts comments that are provocative, discriminatory, and objectionable, intending to disrupt online discussions, provoke others, and incite intergroup conflict. These comments undermine citizens' legitimate rights, disrupt social order, and may even lead to real-world violent incidents. However, current automatic detection of offensive language primarily focuses on a few high-resource languages, leaving low-resource languages, such as Malay, with insufficient annotated corpora for effective detection. To address this, we propose a zero-shot, cross-language unsupervised offensive language detection (OLD) method using a dual-branch mBERT transfer approach. Firstly, using the multi-language BERT (mBERT) model as the foundational language model, the first network branch automatically extracts features from both source and target domain data. Subsequently, Sinkhorn distance is employed to measure the discrepancy between the source and target language feature representations. By estimating the Sinkhorn distance between the labeled source language (e.g., English) and the unlabeled target language (e.g., Malay) feature representations, the method minimizes the Sinkhorn distance adversarially to provide more stable gradients, thereby extracting effective domain-shared features. Finally, offensive pivot words from the source and target language training sets are identified. These pivot words are then removed from the training data in a second network branch, which employs the same architecture. This process constructs an auxiliary OLD task. By concealing offensive pivot words in the training data, the model reduces overfitting and enhances robustness to the target language. In the end-to-end framework training, the combination of cross-lingual shared features and independent features culminates in unsupervised detection of offensive speech in the target language. The experimental results demonstrate that employing cross-language model transfer learning can achieve unsupervised detection of offensive content in low-resource languages. The number of labeled samples in the source language is positively correlated with transfer performance, and a greater similarity between the source and target languages leads to better transfer effects. The proposed method achieves the best performance in OLD on the Malay dataset, achieving an F1 score of 80.7%. It accurately identifies features of offensive speech, such as sarcasm, mockery, and implicit expressions, and showcases strong generalization and excellent stability across different target languages.

Keywords: cross-language model; offensive language detection; mBERT; unsupervised methods; transfer learning

1. Introduction

With the rapid development of mobile network technology and the emergence of different social media platforms, Internet penetration rates continue to rise. The Internet has permeated people's daily lives and work, offering significant convenience through various applications for travel, shopping, communication, and more [1]. In the virtual society constructed by the Internet, netizens not only act as information recipients but also drive the widespread dissemination of information. Among these platforms, social media has experienced rapid growth in recent years, serving as a space for netizens to stay informed about current events, express opinions, and share snippets of their lives. However, on current social media platforms, some netizens exhibit a narrow perspective, hold extreme views, and are easily swayed by emotionally charged news reports, leading to the expression of offensive comments [2,3]. Offensive language is a broad concept encompassing various terms such as abusive language, cyber-bullying, hate speech, irony, profanity, and more, depending on the data source or viewpoint definition [4].

In recent years, numerous measures have been introduced to address hate speech and offensive language. On 25 February 2019, United Nations Secretary-General Guterres unveiled the "United Nations Strategy and Plan of Action on Hate Speech" to tackle the escalating global issues of xenophobia, racism, violence against women, anti-Semitism, and anti-Muslim hatred [5]. From Rwanda to Bosnia and Cambodia, offensive and hate speech has evolved into heinous crimes, including ominous signs of ethnic cleansing [6]. Amidst the recent COVID-19 pandemic, some extremists have utilized Twitter to disseminate racist remarks. Swift moderation by Twitter promptly eradicated these messages, underscoring the platform's commitment to combatting racial speech [7]. In Malaysia, social media has also witnessed instances of violent incidents triggered by offensive language. In 2020, a 20-year-old girl, Thivya Nayagi Rajendran, from Penang, tragically took her own life, leaving a note citing cyberbullying as the cause. The girl and her Bangladeshi male colleague faced online harassment after uploading a dance video online. In 2023, Malaysian actress Lee Yuan Ling survived a suicide attempt by hanging and courageously shared her experience on social media, highlighting the horrors of online violence. That same year, a 27-year-old Chinese–Malaysian singer, Yuki Koh, fell victim to a fatal stabbing by an obsessive male fan. The assailant, in his 40s, had relentlessly pursued the victim on social media for years, demonstrating the profound impact of such behaviors not only on individuals but on society as a whole.

Currently, research on offensive language detection (OLD) primarily focuses on high-resource languages, such as English, due to abundant dataset resources, monolingual dictionaries, and pre-trained language models [8,9]. However, on social media platforms, diverse languages are often used for offensive language, including different national languages, ethnic languages, and regional dialects [10]. Research on OLD in low-resource languages faces significant challenges due to the lack of labeled training data instances. Early methods for detecting offensive comments mainly employed dictionaries and traditional machine learning (ML) tools. Dictionary-based approaches recorded malicious vocabulary for detection, while traditional ML tools relied on manual feature engineering to extract text features, construct ML models, and perform offensive comment detection [11]. However, these methods struggled to promptly maintain and update dictionaries for large volumes of user comments. Traditional ML methods required labor-intensive feature engineering, resulting in time-consuming efforts and models with room for improved generalization. In recent years, due to the superior practical results of deep learning (DL) models, OLD methods have predominantly shifted towards DL-based methods [12]. In the English context, ample high-quality annotated data facilitates effective DL model training. However, in the Malay language scenario, there is a lack of publicly available large-scale datasets for offensive comments, posing challenges for training DL models.

Cross-lingual transfer (CLT) technique seeks to address the aforementioned challenge by transferring knowledge across languages, enabling models to accomplish tasks in a low-resourced target language with annotated samples from another source language [13]. The scenario of interest is zero-shot CLT, where the target language lacks any annotated samples [14]. This constitutes the most common and challenging issue in CLT research, and it is the focus of this paper. Specifically, our attention is on enhancing the performance of OLD task in zero-shot CLT scenarios. Recent findings highlight the remarkable CLT capabilities of Multilingual BERT (mBERT), a model pre-trained on Wikipedia data in 104 languages. Fine-tuning mBERT using annotated samples from the source language has emerged as a mainstream approach for cross-lingual text label prediction [15]. Given the practical scenario where unlabeled samples in the Malay language are easily obtainable and contain relevant information about the target distribution, we propose that jointly utilizing annotated samples from the source language (English) and unlabeled samples from the target language (Malay) for fine-tuning mBERT is an effective strategy to enhance cross-lingual OLD performance.

Detecting offensive speech in low-resource languages faces two primary challenges. Firstly, the limited availability of resources hampers the effective semantic encoding of text in these languages. Secondly, it impedes the effective training on offensive features inherent to these languages. Currently, most approaches to detecting offensive speech in low-resource languages rely on cross-lingual, pre-trained models. The foremost advantage of such methods lies in their ability to leverage unsupervised cross-lingual pre-training, thereby enabling detection in low-resource languages. However, previous methods have often overlooked the linguistic disparities between the source and target domains during transfer learning, consequently undermining detection performance in the target domain.

Building on the analysis above, this paper proposes a dual-branch CLT framework based on mBERT, designed to facilitate zero-shot transfer learning from high-resource languages (e.g., English) to low-resource languages (e.g., Malay), thereby enhancing the detection of offensive speech in low-resource languages. The main contributions of this paper include:

(1) Utilizing the first network branch of the mBERT model to extract features from both source and target domain data. By adversarially minimizing the Sinkhorn distance, effective domain-shared features are obtained.
(2) Identifying offensive pivot words through an unsupervised model and removing these pivots from the training data of the second network branch, thereby constructing an auxiliary offensive speech detection task. This encourages the model to rely on contextual information, enhancing detection performance in low-resource languages.
(3) Constructing a Malay offensive speech detection dataset, analyzing the knowledge graph of various offensive pivots, and introducing statements with or without pivot words to assess the model's understanding of deep semantics and its applicability in real-world scenarios.

The structure of the remainder of this paper is as follows. Section 2 reviews related research on OLD filed, including traditional manual feature detection methods, machine learning approaches, and deep learning techniques. Section 3 provides a detailed description of the proposed dual-branch zero-shot cross-lingual OLD framework based on Sinkhorn distance and pivots extraction. Section 4 validates the effectiveness of the proposed method through extensive experiments on low-resource Malay text for offensive speech detection. Finally, Section 5 concludes the paper and suggests directions for future research.

2. Related Works

In the early stages of social media development, platforms employed human moderators and encouraged users to report offensive content. Such manual approach was not only inefficient but also challenging to handle the vast number of online comments, exposing moderators to daily negative sentiments and potential psychological harm. Consequently, researchers sought to automate the OLD task. Traditional methods relied on manually designed grammar features and rule-based matching for identifying offensive comments. Razavi et al. [16] extracted features at different conceptual levels, enhancing multi-level classification accuracy with statistical models and rule-based pattern matching. Xu et al. [17] constructed a comment dataset from the English video platform YouTube. They proposed an automated sentence-level filtering method utilizing grammar relationships between words to create filtering rules for matching and removing offensive language.

Chen et al. [18] manually extracted lexical and syntactic features, combined with a designed syntax rule list to match and identify offensive content. Although these studies extensively analyzed rule patterns for offensive language, the definition of offensive statements remains ambiguous. Such methods heavily rely on rule lists, making them suitable for comments with specific keywords or distinct patterns. However, they face challenges in detecting more subtle forms of offensive language.

In order to better study the characteristics of offensive comments and enhance the accuracy of automated detection, researchers have constructed numerous large datasets from various social media scenarios for analysis. They have also begun utilizing ML-based methods for detection. Bassignana et al. [19] established the multilingual hate word lexicon, HurtLex, starting with a corpus of over 1000 harmful words in Italian, enriching the target language lexicon. Davidson et al. [20] gathered random tweets from Twitter, employing n-gram features, part-of-speech (PoS) features, and sentiment score features. These features were applied to various classifiers, including Linear Regression (LR), Naive Bayesian (NB), Decision Trees (DT), and linear Support Vector Machine (SVM). Experimental results demonstrated the superior performance of LR and linear SVM. Watanabe et al. [21] proposed an ML-based approach for detecting offensive language in Twitter based on writing patterns, unigrams, and sentimental features. The work refined various rules for extracting features, including rules for extracting sentiment features such as the total score of positive/negative words, the number of positive/negative slang words, and the number of positive/negative emoticons. Van Hee et al. [22] collected data from social media sites containing English and Dutch, refining label categories, including threats, curses, insults, defamation, and explicit content. SVM were used as classifiers in classification experiments, incorporating features such as character-based and word-based N-gram features, vocabulary features, and topic features. In OLD tasks, temporal information, contextual information, and sentiment information play crucial roles. However, ML-based methods might overlook sequential relationships in feature extraction, limiting their ability to fully utilize contextual information. In addition, such methods face challenges in extracting complex text features, and cannot handle the issue of data sparsity well [23].

In recent years, DL-based methods have started to be applied in the field of OLD. DL algorithms can automatically learn sample features and analyze the data accordingly. When employing DL-based methods in natural language processing (NLP), the text needs to be processed into suitable word representations as input for the network. The next step involves constructing an appropriate network to train and learn from the input data [24]. Badjatiya et al. [25] compared Convolutional Neural Network (CNN) and Long-Short Term Memory (LSTM) models with traditional ML tools for detecting hate speech on Twitter. The results demonstrated the superior performance of DL models over ML models. Pavloupos et al. [26] conducted a detection analysis of user comments on news portals and Wikipedia, identifying those containing abusive language. Leveraging a Greek news portal, they built a dataset of 1.6 million user comments, employing a Recurrent Neural Network (RNN) with an attention mechanism for classification. The attention mechanism automatically highlights potentially offensive words in comments. Park et al. [27] combined CharCNN and WordCNN to create a hybrid CNN model for OLD. Considering the uniqueness of Twitter tweets, the model simultaneously learned features at the character and word levels. Sigurbergsson et al. [28] built a Danish language dataset, employing an LSTM-based method to detect hate speech, cyberbullying, and other offensive language. Mishra et al. [29] applied Graph Convolutional Networks (GCN) in OLD tasks. By introducing additional information such as user personal data and social networks to address the limited features of short texts, they input data as graph nodes into GCN for learning. Through graph convolutional networks, the model could directly capture user language behavior and group structure features. Experimental results indicated that the combination of LR and GCN yielded the best results.

Recent studies have demonstrated the effectiveness of pre-trained language models like BERT in downstream tasks such as OLD [30]. Zhu et al. [31] utilized fine-tuned BERT for downstream classification tasks to identify offensive tweets. Howard et al. [32] successfully implemented transfer learning in offensive language detection using BERT and the ULMFiT (Universal Language Model Fine-tuning for Text Classification) method. Due to superior performance, such approaches have become mainstream for addressing OLD tasks. In the 2019 OffensEval competition, 7 out of the top 10 teams used BERT, differing mainly in parameter settings and preprocessing steps. As mBERT exhibits great CLT capabilities. it has gradually become the foundation for recent cross-lingual text detection and classification tasks. Kudugunta et al. [33] demonstrated the extraction of relevant features from cross-lingual pre-trained models for downstream tasks like part-of-speech tagging and named entity recognition, providing language-specific knowledge-based information. Wu et al. [34] employed a meta-learning approach to achieve improved cross-lingual transfer with M-BERT, particularly in named entity recognition. However, this method requires re-finetuning the model for each test sample during the inference stage, resulting in substantial computational costs. Keung et al. [35] used language adversarial training to encourage mBERT to generate more language-independent features. Zhang et al. [36] considered CLT tasks as domain adaptation problems, and utilized an unsupervised domain adaptation method based on adversarial training to reduce domain differences. Kumar et al. [37] achieved significant results in German and Hindi OLD tasks from social media by fine-tuning the mBERT pre-trained model. Libovický et al. [38] confirmed that context-based mBERT captures similarities between languages, clustering them by language, and cross-lingual fine-tuning does not disrupt this property. In other words, mBERT encodes part of the language information based on its position in the embedding space, concentrating the encoding of each language to achieve a degree of cross-lingual capability. Ayo et al. [39] proposed a method employing SVM and mBERT to construct a cross-lingual model for detecting offensive and misogynistic language on Twitter. Kapil et al. [40] enhanced mBERT with transfer learning strategy, transferring knowledge from a resource-rich language to low-resource languages, effectively improving the accuracy of OLD in low-resource languages. However, these methods overlook the differences between the source and target languages during the transfer learning process, impacting detection performance in the target domain. This oversight leads to negative transfer effects, which compromise detection performance in the target domain.

Negative transfer refers to the phenomenon in transfer learning where the transfer of knowledge or models from a source domain to a target domain not only fails to improve performance but may actually degrade it [41]. Significant linguistic differences exist between source and target languages, encompassing grammar, vocabulary usage habits, and more. These differences can hinder effective model transfer in zero-shot scenarios [42]. Variations in language usage backgrounds and cultural contexts across different languages can affect the model's understanding of text meaning, thereby impacting the effectiveness of transfer learning [43]. Disparities in data distribution between source and target languages, including differences in data volume, types, and quality, can also lead to poor model performance in the target language [44]. To mitigate the risks of negative transfer, this paper leverages the multilingual pre-training capability of mBERT. This enables the model to learn universal language representations. By minimizing the Sinkhorn distance, a stable feature alignment mechanism is established between source and target languages. This helps ensure the model effectively maintains consistency in the feature space during transfer, reducing negative transfer due to language differences. Furthermore, handling and masking pivot words during training enhances the model's robustness to the target language. Additionally, a joint domain-shared feature training strategy allows the model to simultaneously consider and utilize information from both source and target languages. This effectively addresses potential negative transfer issues in zero-shot CLT learning, enhancing the model's generalization capability and stability.

In the realm of cross-lingual OLD, ML models such as LR and SVM offer high interpretability, crucial for understanding how models make predictions and which features influence these predictions most significantly [45]. LR classifies by learning the weights of features, directly interpreting each feature's weight as its contribution to the final classification. This transparency makes LR intuitive and straightforward in terms of interpretability, as its linear decision boundary visibly shows which combinations of feature values lead to specific classification decisions. SVM's decisions hinge on support vectors—samples on the decision boundary—determining not only its location but also aiding in understanding the model's certainty and accuracy in delineating between different classes. When using kernel functions like the Radial Basis Function (RBF) kernel, SVM maps data into high-dimensional space to find the optimal decision hyperplane, where kernel choice affects model interpretability. In contrast, DL models are often dubbed "black box" models due to their complex internal structures and parameters, complicating direct explanations of decision processes and feature selection principles [46]. The interpretability of DL models tends to be more indirect, often relying on a deeper understanding of their internal mechanisms. For instance, models like mBERT, a pretrained language model, operate with intricate internal mechanisms learned via self-attention on vast text datasets. Consequently, the meanings of its features may not be as intuitively clear as those derived from traditional linear models like LR and SVM. Moreover, transfer learning emphasizes sharing knowledge across different tasks or domains, where interpretability hinges on effectively selecting and transferring knowledge from the source domain and adapting it to the target domain. Feature alignment and transfer rules play pivotal roles in this process. For example, our approach utilizes Sinkhorn distance minimization to enhance feature alignment between source and target languages, mitigating the risk of negative transfer caused by language disparities and thereby improving model generalization. To summarize, LR and SVM excel in interpretability due to their intuitive feature weight explanations and visualizable decision boundaries. In contrast, models like mBERT and transfer learning methods, leveraging large-scale pretrained models and complex transfer strategies, may offer interpretability that is more indirect or reliant on a deeper understanding of internal mechanisms. Therefore, a balance between interpretability and model performance must be struck when selecting the most suitable method to address specific task requirements.

3. Proposed Framework

In the realm of cross-language text processing, a prevalent challenge lies in the linguistic disparities between source and target languages. If common offensive features can be identified across different languages, and unique language-specific attributes are thoroughly considered in offensive determinations, it can play a pivotal role in cross-language OLD tasks. We propose a dual-branch zero-shot, cross-language OLD model based on mBERT combined with Sinkhorn distance and pivot extraction.

For a given set of monolingual offensive language instances, the first network branch trains on mBERT model with source language (e.g., English) offensive language samples to create a monolingual offensive language detector, then it is transferred to the given low-resource language (e.g., Malay). By estimating Sinkhorn distance between source and target language feature representations, adversarially minimizing the Sinkhorn distance provides more stable gradients, extracting more effective cross-domain shared features.

Subsequently, an auxiliary prediction task is constructed. In the input training data of source (labeled) and target (unlabeled) language for the second network branch, offensive pivot words are concealed to compel the model to rely more on contextual information for determining text offensiveness. This process yields domain-independent features, aiding the model in better understanding the context of the instance, thereby enhancing its capability to handle complex language structures and implicit information. Through joint training of the entire network, domain-shared features and domain-specific features are amalgamated to fulfill cross-language OLD tasks. Figure 1 illustrates the framework flowchart of the proposed method.

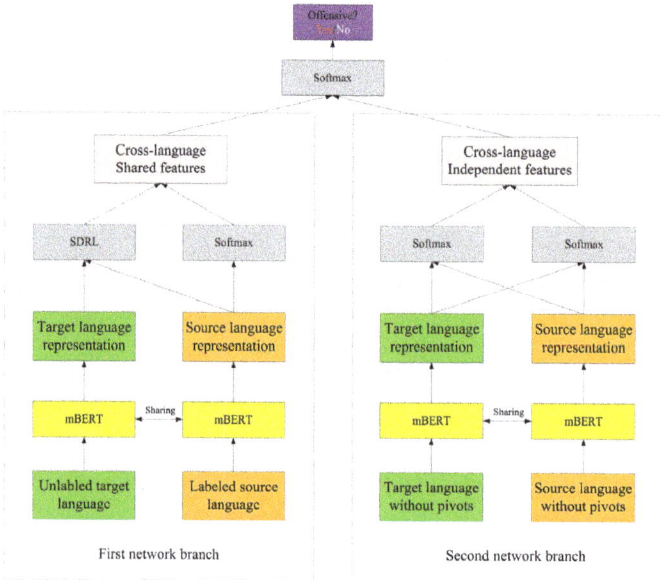

Figure 1. Illustration of the proposed dual-branch, zero-shot CLT framework for OLD tasks. In the first network branch on the left side, the labeled data from the source domain and the unlabeled data from the target domain are jointly used as inputs for feature extraction. mBERT transfer learning incorporates SDRL (Sinkhorn distance representation layer) to extract cross-language shared features. On the right side, the second network branch removes offensive pivot words from training data in both source and target languages, obtaining language-specific independent features. Ultimately, through end-to-end framework joint training of the two network branches, the OLD performance is enhanced for the unlabeled target language.

3.1. Problem Definition

In cross-language OLD tasks, let D_s and D_t be the training data of source and target languages, respectively. D_s contains labeled data $X_s^l = \{x_s^i, y_s^i\}_{i=1}^{N_s^l}$, where N_s^l denotes the quantity of annotated data in the source language, with y_s representing the labels for offensive detection in the source domain. D_t comprises unlabeled data $X_t = \{x_t^j\}_{j=1}^{N_t}$, where N_t is the quantity of unlabeled data in the target domain. The proposed method aims to leverage labeled samples from the source language to train a classifier for detecting offensive text in unlabeled samples X_t from the target domain.

3.2. BERT

The BERT model obtains semantically richer word embeddings through pre-training and fine-tuning, overcoming the limitations of traditional word embeddings' polysemy issue [47]. Fine-tuning allows the model to be applied to specific downstream tasks such as OLD, enhancing its generalization ability [48].

For pre-training, a base model is constructed by stacking the encoder part of Transformer models, as illustrated in Figure 2. Joint training of Masked Language Model (MLM) and Next Sentence Prediction (NSP) tasks captures semantic vector representations at both word and sentence levels. The MLM achieves the true bidirectional language modeling [49]. In the transfer to downstream tasks, BERT draws inspiration from OpenAI's Generative Pre-training (GPT) model and designs more versatile input and output layers, surpassing the generality of GPT [50].

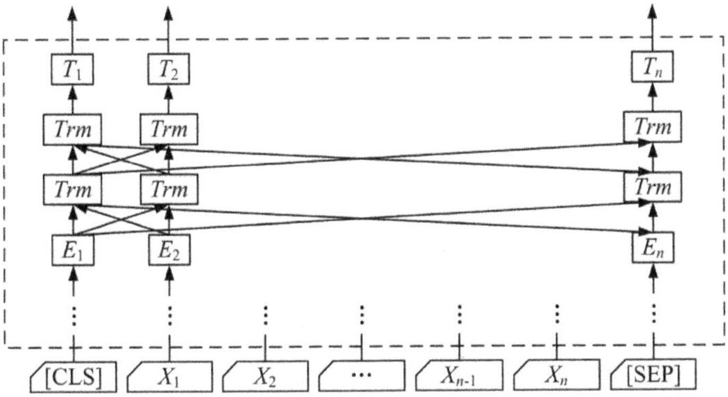

Figure 2. Model structure of BERT.

In BERT, text information is first transformed into word embeddings E, and then input into the Transformer structure, consisting of self-attention mechanisms and feedforward neural networks (FFN). The BERT pre-trained model undergoes extensive pre-training on large corpora, enabling it to convert semantically related words or characters into one-dimensional word vectors with close distances in the feature vector space. This retains more valuable information and emotional tendencies, facilitating the differentiation of offensive comments in subsequent tasks. In typical scenarios, the degree of association between words with negative sentiments and personal pronouns in a sentence largely determines its malicious intent. For instance, in the sentence written in Malay, "Kubur sudah sedia untukmu, kenapa kamu tidak masuk?" (The grave is ready for you, why do you not go in?), there are no explicit vulgar words. However, the word "kubur" (grave) carries strong negative connotations and is closely related to the personal pronoun "kamu" (you), demonstrating an offensive attitude. Therefore, inputting the transformed word vectors into the Transformer structure and calculating the closeness of their relationship aids in determining whether the statement is offensive.

The obtained word vectors E are used as input, passing through multiple layers of Transformer feature extractors, yielding feature information (T_1, T_2, ..., T_n). During the self-attention mechanism, an initial random matrix X is generated. The word embeddings multiplied by X produce three new vectors: Query Q, Key, and Value, denoted as Q, K, V. The corresponding Q, K, and V vectors for multiple word embeddings form matrices W^Q, W^K, and W^V. The use of matrices W simplifies the computation process. The Q of each input word embedding is computed with the K of other word embeddings, and both word vectors have an initial V. The operation result of Q and K generates a weight, merging the importance of the corresponding relationships between two words into the initial V, thereby preserving contextual semantic information. For example, to determine the relationship between "kubur" (grave) and "kamu" (you) in the sentence, the dot product of Q_{kubur} and K_{kamu} is calculated, resulting in a score S:

$$S = Q \cdot K \quad (1)$$

By extension, a set of scores $S = \{S_1, S_2, ..., S_n\}$ can be obtained, representing the closeness of relationships between specific words (e.g., "kubur") and all other words in the text. Dividing this score set by a constant and performing softmax operation, followed by multiplication with V, yields the feature T that encapsulate the relationships between words. The constant is typically the square root of the arithmetic dimensions of the initial random matrix:

$$T = softmax(\frac{S}{\sqrt{d_k}})V \quad (2)$$

where d_k represents the initial random matrix dimensions, V is the Value vector, and T is the output vector. The output vector encapsulates implicit features indicating the current word's association with other words. In subsequent training, these features assist in discerning offensive comments. The aforementioned computation calculates the relationship between one word and others. Multiple such computations are performed simultaneously to compute pairwise relationships between each pair of words. This calculation is crucial for recognizing offensive comments. After training with a substantial amount of offensive text, the model becomes adept at identifying offensive comments that do not necessarily contain explicit vulgar words.

Supervised learning methods typically require ample annotated data, which is available for English across various tasks. However, for languages with limited resources, acquiring abundant labeled data for supervised training poses challenges. Therefore, the transition from a well-trained high-resource language to a low-resource one, without the need for annotated data, becomes a new challenge. Unsupervised CLT methods, being domain-independent and not reliant on annotated data, are well-suited for languages with large-scale open and unstructured data.

3.3. *mBERT*

mBERT, a multilingual version of BERT, is trained on Wikipedia texts from 104 languages, allowing it to handle multilingual text within the same representation space, and a lot of studies have highlighted mBERT's excellent CLT performance [51]. Hence, this paper adopts mBERT as the base model.

A linear classification layer <W, b> can be directly added to the mBERT model f_θ to build the model ψ, $\psi = \{f_\theta, W, b\}$. Given a labeled dataset $X_s^l = \{x_s^i, y_s^i\}_{i=1}^{N_s^l}$ in the source language, the model is trained using the dataset X_s^l, resulting in the base model.

$$\psi_0 = \underset{\psi}{\operatorname{argmin}} \sum_{x_s^i \in X_s^l} CE(p(x_s^i, \psi), y_s^i) \tag{3}$$

where CE is the cross-entropy function. $p(x_s^i, \psi)$ represents the label distribution of model output samples. With mBERT, being a multilingual pre-trained model, ψ_0 can be directly applied to OLD task in the target language, and it generally offers some cross-language generalization. However, the direct transfer faces challenges and drawbacks:

(1) Language differences: Significant variations in syntax, vocabulary, and expressions exist across languages. Without labeled data in the target language, the model may struggle to adapt to specific language structures and cultural nuances, leading to performance degradation.
(2) Domain disparities: Even within the same language family, domain differences can persist. Applying a model trained in one domain directly to another may fail to capture specific features of the target domain, impacting performance.
(3) Task specifics: OLD is a task with unique challenges. Expression of offensive language can vary widely across languages and cultures. Models trained directly in the source language might not effectively capture offensive language features in the target language.
(4) Label bias: Offensive language in the source and target languages may have different label distributions. Without target language labels, the model may encounter label bias issues, resulting in unstable performance in the target language.
(5) Limitations of transfer learning: Despite mBERT's inherent transfer learning capabilities, without labeled data in the target language, the model's transfer ability may be restricted, making it challenging to fully adapt to the specific requirements of the target language.

3.4. Reducing Cross-Domain Discrepancy Based on Sinkhorn Distance

Similarity measurement is crucial for evaluating the degree of similarity between feature vectors. For feature vectors with ample representational capabilities, the choice of a similarity measurement algorithm directly impacts classification accuracy [52]. In metric learning, commonly used algorithms include Euclidean distance and cosine distance. Euclidean distance emphasizes absolute differences in numerical values between vectors, making it sensitive to outliers [53]. Cosine distance, on the other hand, focuses on the relative differences in the direction of vectors, remaining insensitive to absolute values [54]. However, cross-domain text features are prone to noise, category-independent feature points, and feature distribution that fails to meet the assumption of independent identical distribution. In such cases, using Euclidean or Cosine distance is inadequate. To address this, we employ the Box-Cox transformation to redistribute feature vectors extracted by mBERT into Gaussian or quasi-Gaussian distributions [55]. We then use the Sinkhorn distance as the similarity measurement for feature vectors [56].

Sinkhorn distance, proposed by Cuturi M, based on optimal transport, differs from traditional similarity measurement algorithms like Euclidean and cosine distances [57]. It calculates the work required to move from one vector to another, offering a unique perspective compared to direct physical distance calculations. The Sinkhorn distance can be seen as an optimal mapping from the source domain distribution to the target domain distribution, aiding in the understanding of inter-domain differences while offering greater stability compared to traditional metrics like Maximum Mean Discrepancy (MMD) that may be susceptible to local optima. It effectively handles high-dimensional, nonlinear data distribution disparities. This capability is particularly crucial in natural language processing, where text data often exhibit intricate semantic and syntactic structures, challenging for conventional distance measures to capture. Moreover, the Sinkhorn distance serves not only as a measure between domains but also supports domain adaptation learning. Minimizing the Sinkhorn distance between source and target domains facilitates learning more generalized feature representations, thereby enhancing model performance on the target domain. Importantly, grounded in optimal transport theory, the Sinkhorn distance provides robust theoretical underpinnings and mathematical guarantees. Under suitable conditions, it ensures convergence to genuine distribution disparities, a critical factor in several practical applications.

The computation process of Sinkhorn distance is illustrated in Figure 3, where $P(x)$ and $Q(x)$ represent two vectors, and the arrows depict the movement from $P(x)$ to $Q(x)$.

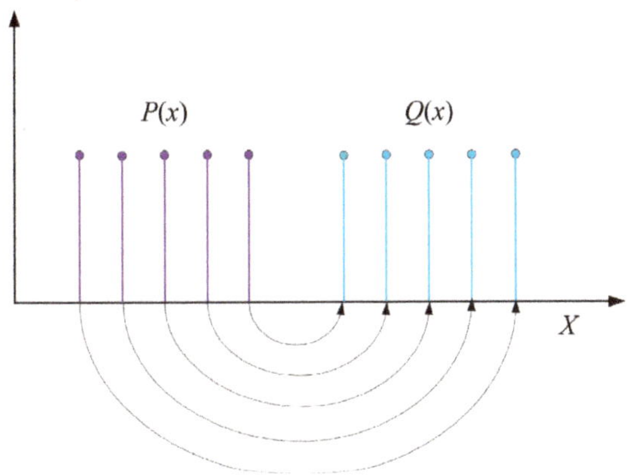

Figure 3. Illustration of Sinkhorn distance.

The aforementioned optimal transport process is defined as follows:

$$d(a,b) = \sum_{s \in U(a,b)} < S, L > = \sum_{i,j} S_{i,j} L_{i,j} \tag{4}$$

where S represents a coupling matrix. a and b are probability distributions of vectors P and Q, respectively, ensuring that the sums of elements in a and b are both 1. $U(a,b) = \{S \in R_+^{n \times m}\}$ denotes that U is an $n \times m$ matrix with rows summing to a and columns summing to b. L_{ij} signifies the cost of moving from point i to point j.

Since S is a probability distribution matrix, while Sinkhorn distance holds a natural advantage when the vector distributions are similar or approximately similar, complexities arise in computations, particularly with higher-dimensional vectors and extensive data. To address this, an entropy regularization term is added to the equation:

$$d(a,b) = \sum_{i,j} S_{i,j} L_{i,j} + \beta H(S) \tag{5}$$

where, β is the entropy regularization parameter, and $H(S)$ is the entropy function of S:

$$H(S) = -\sum_{i,j} S_{i,j} \log(S_{i,j}) \tag{6}$$

Approximating Sinkhorn distance typically involves maximizing a loss function L_{wd} concerning the parameter θ_w. This loss function is designed as a dual problem that minimizes Sinkhorn distance. Specifically, for the representation distributions P and Q of the source and target domains, along with their corresponding data X and Y, maximizing the Sinkhorn distance loss function with respect to the parameter θ_w can be expressed as:

$$L_{wd}(\theta_w) = \max_{u,v}(\sum_i u_i + \sum_j u_j - \varepsilon \sum_{i,j} u_i e^{-\varepsilon c_{i,j}} v_j) \tag{7}$$

where u and v are scaling coefficients. ϵ is the regularization parameter, and $c_{i,j}$ represents the cost or distance between samples X_i and Y_j. During the process of maximizing L_{wd}, the scaling coefficients u and v are iteratively updated to approximate the actual Sinkhorn distance.

Implementing a gradient penalty on the parameters is an effective approach to enforcing Lipschitz constraints [58]. This is particularly useful in DL-based models, controlling the model's Lipschitz constant through gradient clipping or regularization, enhancing stability, and mitigating issues like gradient explosion or vanishing during training [59].

In the context of Sinkhorn distance, enforcing Lipschitz constraints is typically achieved by adding a gradient penalty term to the loss function. The gradient penalty term can be in the form of parameter norms or other forms to ensure that the model's gradients do not become excessively large during training. To ensure the model's Lipschitz continuity, we choose the gradient penalty term $L_{grad}(\theta_w)$ as the L2 norm of the model parameters:

$$L_{grad}(\theta_w) = \frac{1}{2} |\theta_w|_2^2 \tag{8}$$

Due to the Sinkhorn distance being nearly continuously differentiable, the initial step involves training SDRL. After reaching optimal parameters for SDRL, these parameters are fixed, and the estimation of Sinkhorn distance is minimized. This process enables the mBERT network to learn domain-shared feature representations, accomplished by solving an optimization problem involving both maximization and minimization:

$$L_{adv} = \min_{\theta_{mBERT}} \max_{\theta_w} \{L_{wd} - \lambda L_{grad}\} \tag{9}$$

where θ_{mBERT} represents the parameters of the feature extraction layer. λ is the penalty coefficient, set to 0 during the minimization process, ensuring the gradient penalty does not guide the learning process. The optimization goal is to learn domain-shared feature representations by minimizing the Sinkhorn distance loss function L_{wd}. During training, the minimization of L_{wd} is achieved by adjusting the parameters θ_{mBERT} of the feature extractor network through solving a maximization-minimization problem. The estimation parameters θ_w for Sinkhorn distance are determined by maximizing L_{wd}. The overall optimization problem involves two components:

(1) Minimizing Sinkhorn distance: Adjusting the parameters θ_{mBERT} of the feature extractor network to reduce the loss of Sinkhorn distance.
(2) Maximizing gradient penalty: Tuning the estimated parameters θ_w for Sinkhorn distance to increase the gradient penalty term λL_{grad}. The ultimate optimization goal is to strike a balance between these two components, achieving a model with both domain-shared feature representation and compliance with Lipschitz constraints. This type of optimization problem is commonly referred to as adversarial training, where one network (m*BERT*) aims to minimize the loss, while the other network (*SDRL*) seeks to maximize it. This adversarial training process aids in learning more discriminative feature representations while satisfying predefined constraints.

Upon completing the training phase focused on reducing domain differences using Sinkhorn distance, the text representation d is mapped to label y through a softmax classifier for discerning offensive language. The loss L_{mBERT} of the $mBERT$ classifier employs the cross-entropy loss function. Combining this with the loss of the SDRL classifier yields the objective function for the first network branch:

$$L_1 = \min_{\theta_{mBERT}, \theta_{SDRL}} \{L_{mBERT} + \beta \max_{\theta_w}[L_{wd} - \lambda L_{grad}]\} \tag{10}$$

where β acts as the coefficient controlling the balance between offensive detection and learning domain-shared features.

3.5. Extracting Domain-Independent Features Based on Pivot Words

When there are fewer shared features between the source and target languages, the performance of cross-language OLD tends to decline. Effectively utilizing domain-specific features enhances detection capabilities. Typically, domain-specific pivot words in the dataset co-occur with domain-shared pivot words that exhibit similar offensive tendencies. To extract domain-specific features, it is essential to construct an auxiliary task closely related to the original task.

Firstly, the PERL method proposed in the paper [60] is employed to select domain-shared feature words, known as pivots. Words that meet the criteria of being adjectives, adverbs, or verbs with high attention weights are chosen as pivots for attack judgment. Subsequently, pivots are concealed in the training data of both the source and target languages, and a special UNK tag is used to replace all the pivots in the original data.

In BERT, the UNK (Unknown) label is employed to denote Out-Of-Vocabulary (OOV) terms, referring to words not encountered during the model's training, absent from the pre-trained vocabulary. Using the UNK label aids the model in better generalizing across different languages. Given BERT's capacity to grasp contextual information during pre-training, it is anticipated that the model can infer the semantic details of UNK-labeled words through context, thereby enhancing performance in tasks like cross-language text analysis. This approach also mitigates the model's reliance on pivot words for learning task labels, facilitating improved adaptation to new languages.

The CLT training of mBERT, concealing pivot words and training a model for detecting offensive text, offers several advantages:

(1) Enhanced Generalization: By concealing pivot words, the trained model avoids over-reliance on specific vocabulary, thereby improving its ability to generalize to a broader range of offensive text and increasing overall applicability.
(2) Reduced Overfitting: Over-dependence on pivot words during training may lead to overfitting, where the model performs well on training data but poorly on unseen data.

Hiding these crucial words diminishes overfitting tendencies, enhancing robustness to new data.

(3) Improved Contextual Understanding: Hiding pivot words compels the model to rely more on contextual information to discern text offensiveness. This fosters a better understanding of textual context, improving the model's capability to handle complex language structures and implicit information.

(4) Enhanced Model Robustness: Concealing pivot words during training increases the likelihood of the model learning more universal and general features of offensive text, bolstering its robustness across different contexts.

We introduce an auxiliary label, y_{off}, for each transformed data instance. If the original data instance contains at least one offensive pivot, label y_{off} as 1; otherwise, label it as 0. The transformed data serves as the input to the feature extraction layer of the second network branch to generate feature representations, predicting the auxiliary label y_{off}. The loss function is denoted as L_{off}. By training on the prediction task of auxiliary labels, the second network branch can extract domain-specific features coinciding with domain-shared features.

3.6. Incorporation of Both Domain-Shared and Domain-Specific Features

To better leverage domain-shared and domain-specific features, the two branches of the proposed framework undergo joint training. Source domain data and transformed data serve as inputs to the feature extraction layer, yielding feature representations d_s and $d_{s'}$. Concatenating both for OLD classification training with the loss function L_{joint}. The overall objective loss function combines the loss terms and regularization from both network branches:

$$L = L_{joint}(d_s \oplus d_{s'}) + L_{wd} + L_{off} + \vartheta L_{reg} \tag{11}$$

where ϑL_{reg} is an L2 regularization term applied to the parameters of mBERT, SDRL, and auxiliary label prediction to prevent overfitting. ϑ is a parameter used to balance the regularization term with other terms.

4. Experiment and Analysis

4.1. Data Collection

To assess model performance, a comprehensive analysis was conducted on the proposed method in executing zero-shot unsupervised detection of Malay offensive language. We collected a dataset of Malay offensive language from Twitter to support the training and evaluation of OLD models. The dataset was meticulously constructed to encompass tweets containing specific Malay offensive keywords, alongside contrasting tweets devoid of such keywords. This step aimed at creating a representative dataset covering various facets of offensive language.

Initially, a specific set of Malay offensive keywords was identified, addressing diverse aspects of offensive discourse, including but not limited to personal attacks, racial discrimination, or malicious statements. Examples include terms like "Bodoh" (Stupid/Foolish), "Mampus kau" (You are dead), "Lelaki jamban" (Men are unpleasant as a toilet), "Kafir" (Arabic term often used in Islamic contexts to refer to a non-believer or someone who rejects or disbelieves in Islam), and "Bapok" (Used to insult or demean transgender individuals or effeminate gay men). Leveraging Twitter's API and its keyword filtering functionality, we collected tweets containing these offensive keywords. To construct the comparative dataset, we utilized the Twitter API to gather tweets that did not include offensive keywords.

In the realm of cyberbullying, personal attacks emerge as its primary manifestation and a focal point in OLD tasks. Detecting discriminatory language proves challenging, relying on models to autonomously discover underlying patterns within the corpus. Subsequently, the collected tweets undergo data cleansing to eliminate duplicates, invalid information, and irrelevant content. Text preprocessing, encompassing tasks like tokenization and stop-word removal, enhances the efficacy of subsequent model training. The final dataset comprises approximately 625 offensive tweets and about 2200 non-offensive tweets.

It is crucial to note that the presence of offensive words in a tweet does not inherently classify it as offensive. Manual scrutiny of each tweet, considering the evolving connotations of specific terms within niche online cultures, is imperative. Comments with explicit vulgarities are directly categorized as offensive. As for texts with strong malicious intent but lacking explicit offensive terms, their classification often relies on subjective human perception. As of now, there are no universally quantifiable rules, and the majority sentiment determines the standard. Three individuals participated in the dataset annotation process, adopting a one-person labeling and two-person verification approach to ensure consistency in judgment criteria. In cases of differing opinions, a voting mechanism was employed to determine the classification outcome.

For the source language of model training, this paper utilizes the English annotated dataset from the 2019 OffensEval shared task 6, known as EN-OLID [61]. Previous efforts predominantly focused on detecting specific types of malicious content, neglecting to explore commonalities across different types of offenses (e.g., personal insults termed as cyberbullying and insults targeting groups termed as hate speech). This dataset takes a comprehensive approach, proposing the OLID (Offensive Language Identification Dataset) annotations. It employs a hierarchical modeling approach, discerning whether comments are malicious, identifying the type of malicious comments (non-targeted or targeted), and pinpointing the target of malicious comments (individuals or groups). These hierarchical annotations capture commonalities across diverse offensive text data, rendering it applicable to various OLD tasks.

To comprehensively assess the effectiveness and generality of the proposed method in cross-language OLD task, experiments also employed Danish and Arabic datasets released in the 2020 OffensEval shared task 12 [62]. Table 1 provides details on the sample distribution in the experimental datasets, while Table 2 presents examples of offensive texts in different languages.

Table 1. Data distribution of the experiment dataset.

Language	Training Set Offensive	Normal	Testing Set Offensive	Normal	Sum
English	4400	8840	240	620	14,100
Malay	500	1760	125	440	2825
Danish	344	2320	40	256	2960
Arabic	1395	5660	155	629	7839

Table 2. Offensive instances for different languages.

Language	Offensive Instances
English	You are really dumb, I cannot believe you made such a stupid comment. Seriously?
Malay	Kau benar-benar bodoh, tak boleh percaya kau buat komen bodoh macam tu. Seriuslah?
Danish	Du er virkelig dum, kan ikke tro, du sagde det.
Arabic	أنت غبي حقًا، لا أستطيع أن أصدق أنك قلت ذلك.

4.2. Parameter Configuration

This experiment was conducted using the PyTorch framework, with training performed on an NVIDIA GeForce RTX 2080 Ti GPU. Specific parameter settings are outlined as follows. For mBERT model, the word vector dimension is set at 768. This dimension is sufficient to capture rich semantic information and grammatical features, making it suitable for processing multilingual textual data. The mBERT pre-trained model utilizes a vocabulary of 104 languages, totaling 120,000 words. Through data analysis, it is observed that the majority of samples have lengths within 140 words; hence, the maximum sentence length was set to 140. The Softmax layer has hidden units corresponding to the 2 label (offensive/normal) categories. During model training, mBERT's word embedding layer remains fixed. Due to its pre-training on large-scale data, mBERT has learned rich semantic information in its word embedding layer. Therefore, in specific tasks such as cross-lingual OLD studied in this paper, the word embedding layer is typically frozen to prevent overfitting and expedite model convergence. The batch size is set to 32, with a total of 10 training epochs. The choice of batch size typically involves balancing computational resources and training efficiency. A smaller batch size, such as 32, can accelerate convergence and enhance the model's generalization ability. The number of epochs (10) signifies how many times the model will see the entire training dataset, which is usually sufficient for the model to converge to an appropriate state. The optimizer used is AdamW [63], with a weight decay of 0.01 and a learning rate of 3×10^{-5} to control the size of gradient updates. A linear warm-up of learning rate is applied for the first 10% of training steps, gradually increasing the learning rate during the initial stages to stabilize the model training process. Dropout rate is set to 0.1, this helps reduce the risk of overfitting the model while maintaining its generalization ability.

4.3. Evaluation Metrics

To evaluate the cyberbullying detection performance of the model, precision, recall, and F_1 score are used as the primary evaluation metrics:

$$Pre = \frac{TP}{TP + FP} \tag{12}$$

$$Rec = \frac{TP}{TP + FN} \tag{13}$$

$$F_1 = 2 \times \frac{Precision \cdot Recall}{Precision + Recall} \tag{14}$$

where TP denotes instances correctly identified as offensive, while TN signifies correctly identified normal instances. Conversely, FN refers to offensive instances mistakenly classified as normal, and FP represents normal instances incorrectly classified as offensive. The F_1 score, a holistic assessment metric, integrates precision and recall for a comprehensive evaluation.

Furthermore, to introduce error analysis metrics in OLD, we use the Brier Score (BS) to measure the accuracy of probability predictions. The calculation of BS for cross-lingual OLD is:

$$BS = \frac{1}{N}\sum_{i=1}^{N} (p_i - y_i)^2 \tag{15}$$

where N is the total number of samples. p_i represents the model's predicted probability that sample i is offensive. y_i is the ground truth label for sample i, where $y_i = 1$ indicates the text is offensive, and $y_i = 0$ indicates it is non-offensive. The BS measures the mean squared error between the model's predicted probabilities and the actual labels, evaluating the performance of the cross-lingual OLD model. BS ranges from 0 to 1, with lower values indicating more accurate probability predictions; 0 represents perfect predictions, and 1 represents the worst predictions.

Log Loss (LL) is used to measure the discrepancy between the predicted probabilities of a model and the actual labels. Although the BS focuses more on the accuracy of predicted probabilities, LL places greater emphasis on the divergence between predicted probability distributions and the true labels. LL is calculated as:

$$LL = -\frac{1}{N}\sum_{i=1}^{N} [y_i \log(p_i) + (1 - y_i)\log(1 - p_i)] \tag{16}$$

LL calculates the logarithmic loss between the predicted probability distribution of the model and the actual labels. A lower value indicates that the model's predictions are closer to the true labels, with 0 representing perfect prediction accuracy.

4.4. Comparison Methods

In the experimental validation of the proposed method for OLD in Malay, several comparison models are set up for comparison:

1. LR (Logistic Regression): Utilizing TF-IDF for text feature extraction, followed by LR detector for constructing an offensive language classifier. LR is a linear model, simple and interpretable. In specific parameter settings, feature extraction employs TF-IDF with a maximum of 5000 features and an n-gram range of (1, 2). The minimum document frequency (min_df) is set to 0.05, and the maximum document frequency (max_df) to 0.95. For LR, the penalty type is "l2" with a regularization strength of 1.0, using the solver "liblinear" with a maximum of 100 iterations [64].
2. SVM: Extracting features from ext using TF-IDF and feeding them into a SVM detector to learn text features. SVM classifies text by finding the optimal hyperplane in feature space. SVM classifies text by finding the optimal hyperplane in the feature space. The regularization parameter for SVM is set to 1.0, with a radial basis function kernel (rbf) and a gamma coefficient set to "scale" [65].
3. mBERT (Unsupervised): Training mBERT model on labeled source language dataset and leveraging mBERT's multilingual transfer capabilities for direct application in OLD task in the target language. However, limitations exist due to language differences, task specificity, label bias, and constraints of transfer learning.
4. MMSE [66]: Pretraining a multilingual neural translation model and transferring through the encoder for model transfer.
5. MDD-VAT [36]: Enhancing mBERT using unsupervised domain adaptation with target language unlabeled samples through virtual adversarial training.
6. mBERT (Supervised): Training mBERT model on labeled target language dataset for benchmark performance reference. In supervised settings, mBERT undergoes end-to-end training using labeled data for OLD tasks in the target language.

4.5. Results and Discussions

Table 3 presents the performance results on the Malay language test dataset using different models. Except for mBERT (Supervised), all other methods utilize Malay unlabeled samples as training data. Results show that LR and SVM methods, which directly extract features from target language unlabeled samples without employing transfer learning techniques, perform the worst. While ML-based classifiers have the advantages of simplicity, intuitiveness, and ease of implementation, they struggle to capture complex semantics and context relationships, lacking support for transfer learning and adaptability to language and task variations.

Table 3. OLD performance with different models (/%).

Models	Precision/%	Recall/%	F1/%	BS	LL
LR	52.1	40.2	33.6	0.49	0.82
SVM	62.1	50.9	44.9	0.44	0.78
mBERT (Unsupervised)	60.2	52.9	48.7	0.40	0.66
MMSE [66]	73.5	71.4	69.4	0.28	0.47
MDD-VAT [36]	76.7	74.4	72.3	0.25	0.42
Proposed method	81.5	80.5	80.7	0.14	0.23
mBERT (Supervised)	80.6	79.4	79.1	0.16	0.25

mBERT (Unsupervised), with its multilingual transfer capabilities and ability to train without target language labels, captures shared features to some extent. However, it fails to address issues such as language differences, domain disparities, and label bias.

The proposed method outperforms other unsupervised approaches in all metrics. This is attributed to using mBERT as the base language model in a dual-branch CLT framework. By minimizing Sinkhorn distance adversarially, the model extracts more effective domain-shared features, enhancing knowledge transfer in cross-language tasks. Additionally, constructing auxiliary OLD tasks aids the model in learning more universal and general offensive text features. The strategy of hiding offensive pivots in the training data forces the model to rely more on contextual information to determine text offensiveness. This approach helps the model better adapt to text features in the target language. The proposed method's superior performance stems from these considerations in addressing challenges like language differences and complex semantics.

In contrast to the supervised approach mBERT (Supervised), which excels in adapting to OLD tasks in the target language by utilizing labeled data, it requires a substantial amount of labeled data for effective training. This can be particularly challenging for low-resource languages where obtaining sufficient labeled data is a hurdle. Therefore, mBERT (Supervised) may struggle to adapt to the specific contexts and expressions of offensive language in low-resource languages when faced with insufficient labeled data. In contrast, our proposed method employs a transfer learning framework, performing zero-shot transfer from a high-resource language to a low-resource language, enabling unsupervised offensive text detection. This reduces the reliance on extensive labeled data. By hiding offensive pivots in the second branch of the model and constructing auxiliary OLD tasks, our method compels the model to depend more on contextual information to assess text offensiveness. This aids in learning more universal and general offensive text features. Results indicate that our method's performance in Malay OLD tasks is slightly superior to mBERT (Supervised).

In order to further assess the proposed model's zero-shot transfer learning capability for OLD tasks in different languages, we conducted experiments using English as the annotated source language and Danish and Arabic from the 2020 OffensEval shared task 12 dataset as unlabeled target languages. The results, illustrated in Figure 4, demonstrate the model's performance in unsupervised OLD across different languages. Compared to the results in Malay, it is evident that despite having the fewest unlabeled training samples in the target language and the most in Arabic, the proposed method performs best on the Danish dataset and least effectively on Arabic. This discrepancy arises due to the significant impact of semantic similarity on transfer learning efficacy. The closer the target language is to the source language, the better the knowledge transfer. Danish and English share some commonalities as they both belong to the Germanic language family, exhibiting certain similarities in grammar, vocabulary, and language structure. On the other hand, Arabic and Malay belong to different language families, showing greater differences from English in terms of grammar and structure. Additionally, Arabic is a right-to-left written language, while English is left-to-right, further increasing the dissimilarity between them. Malaysia, being a culturally diverse country with Malay, Chinese, Indian, and other ethnic groups, has a unique multicultural influence shaped by neighboring countries, history, and religion. In contrast, Arabic countries predominantly follow Islamic culture. The cultural disparities between Arabic-speaking countries and English-speaking ones may contribute to the decrease in model transfer learning performance.

The proposed method incorporates pivot extraction and hiding strategies in the training data, utilizing a second network branch for auxiliary label prediction tasks to assist the model in capturing language-specific features of offensive speech. Offensive pivots play a crucial role in OLD tasks. These pivots are key terms in the text that often carry malicious, insulting, or hostile semantics. By detecting and analyzing these pivot words, the model can more accurately identify and classify offensive speech. Therefore, the presence of pivot words can serve as one of the bases for text classification by the model. Figure 5 illustrates the distribution of offensive pivots in the Malay language dataset. Table 4 provides details on pivot extraction in the dataset along with some examples.

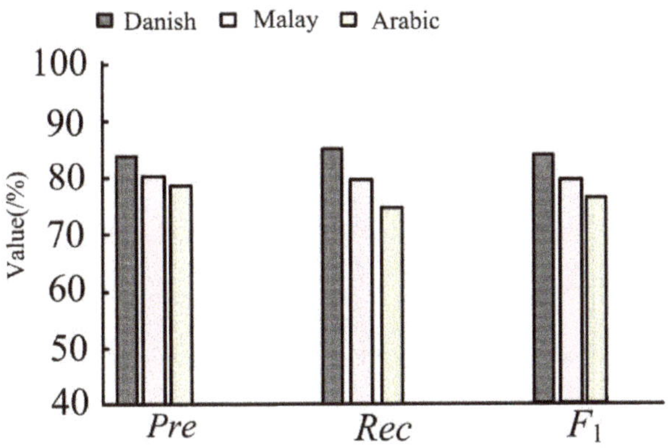

Figure 4. Zero-shot OLD results of the proposed method across different languages.

Figure 5. Visualization pivots distribution.

Table 4. Instances from the collected dataset and pivot extraction examples.

Sample Number	Sentence	Pivots	Offensive?
S1	Kau ni tak guna, macam bangsat. (You are useless, like scum.)	bangsat	yes
S2	Laman web anda adalah satu penipuan. Jangan percayakan penipu ini. (Your website is a scam. Do not trust this scammer.)	penipuan, penipu	yes
S3	Dia buat perkara yang agak bodoh tetapi sebenarnya dia punya hati yang baik. (He did something rather foolish, but actually he has a good heart.)	Bodoh	no
S4	Kebijaksanaanmu nampaknya hanya mencukupi untuk melakukan perkara-perkara mudah, seperti bernafas. (Your intelligence seems to be sufficient only for doing simple things, like breathing.)	/	yes

The presence of aggressive pivot words may indicate that the entire text is more likely to be offensive. For instance, in the examples S1 and S2 from Table 4, the model can determine both sentences as offensive using pivots like "bangsat", "penipuan", and "penipu". However, the appearance of aggressive pivot words might introduce noise, leading the model to misinterpret some sentences. Some texts contain aggressive pivot words, but the overall context is not offensive, resulting in false positives. Some offensive statements may lack common aggressive pivot words, causing the model to miss them. Additionally, some texts may not contain aggressive pivot words but still possess offensive content. Overreliance on pivot words may cause the model to overlook such cases. Moreover, in transfer learning, certain pivot words that are offensive in the source language may not carry the same meaning in the target language, leading to misjudgments. For example, in the instance S3 from Table 4: "Sejujurnya, saya baru mencuba resipi masakan baru, tetapi rasa yang dihasilkan agak bodoh. Mungkin saya perlu menambah lebih rempah pada masa akan datang!" ("To be honest, I just tried a new recipe, but the taste it produced was a bit bland. Maybe I need to add more spices in the future!"), the use of the word "Bodoh" is to express a bland taste rather than for offensive purposes. In Malay, "Bodoh" is sometimes used to describe something's underperformance but usually without insult. Similarly, some sentences may lack offensive words but still be aggressive using sarcasm or mockery, as seen in comment S4 from Table 4: "Intelek kamu nampaknya hanya mencukupi untuk melakukan perkara yang mudah, seperti bernafas". ("Your intelligence seems to be sufficient only for doing simple things, like breathing"). This statement is highly offensive as it includes derogatory remarks about the other person's intelligence. Aggression is not solely about specific words but also encompasses the overall tone and intent of the language. When constructing a model for detecting offensive text, one must consider such indirect forms of aggression. In our experiments, the comparative methods failed to correctly identify the offensiveness of the examples S3 and S4. In contrast, our proposed method successfully determined the offensiveness of these sentences through the joint training strategy of hiding pivot words and the domain-specific feature extraction capability in the auxiliary OLD task.

Finally, we analyze the impact of varying training resources on the transfer effect. We take different quantities of labeled training data from the source language (English), including 1000, 2000, 5000, and all (13,240) samples, and examine the performance of the proposed method on the Malay dataset. Figure 6 presents the F1 results, maintaining the training and testing data volume of non-tabled Malay samples consistent with the previous experiments. The results reveal that even with just 1000 source language training samples, the proposed method's performance surpasses the earlier experiment's direct transfer of the mBERT (Unsupervised) model. This demonstrates the method's high sample utilization efficiency. A larger quantity of labeled source language data implies a richer knowledge base for the model. This knowledge can be effectively transferred to the target language in transfer learning, providing a better starting point and helping the model adapt to the target language's context and expressions. Abundant source language data contributes to establishing more robust and universal feature representations, crucial for OLD models, as offensive language might exhibit similar features across different languages. In summary, the proposed model leveraging annotated samples from high-resource languages can achieve more robust and accurate OLD in the target language, providing substantial support for handling low-resource language data.

In order to further evaluate the effectiveness of each component module proposed in this study, we conducted ablation experiments. Figure 7 presents performance results on the Malay test dataset, where all models were trained using annotated English texts and unlabeled Malay texts, with Malay texts as the test data. Model 1 solely employed the unsupervised mBERT model, utilizing its multilingual transfer capabilities directly for detecting offensive text in the target language. Model 2 used only the first network branch of the proposed method (left branch in Figure 1), replacing the SDRL layer with a Gradient Reversal Layer (GRL), a common technique in domain adaptation aimed at reducing feature differences between different domains (such as source and target domains) to enhance model generalization in the target domain. The basic idea behind GRL is to force the network to learn feature representations that do not contain domain-specific information by reversing the direction of gradients. Model 3 employed only the first network branch of the proposed method. Model 4 represents the complete model of the proposed method, which constructs auxiliary tasks based on pivot words to extract domain-independent features and integrates cross-lingual shared features and independent features in an end-to-end training framework to achieve unsupervised detection of offensive speech in the target language. From the results, Model 1 performs the worst, indicating that the basic mBERT model struggles with effective cross-domain knowledge transfer. Model 2, by reversing gradient directions, forces the network to learn domain-invariant feature representations, enabling the model to learn more generalized feature representations in domain adaptation and thereby reducing domain discrepancies to some extent, resulting in improved performance. Model 3 achieves suboptimal performance through adversarial minimization of Sinkhorn distance, suggesting that methods based on Sinkhorn distance are more effective than those based on GRL for reducing domain discrepancies. Finally, the complete proposed model (Model 4) achieves the best performance, validating that the proposed method effectively aids in learning more universal and general offensive text features by constructing auxiliary OLD tasks, demonstrating its effectiveness in zero-shot cross-lingual OLD tasks.

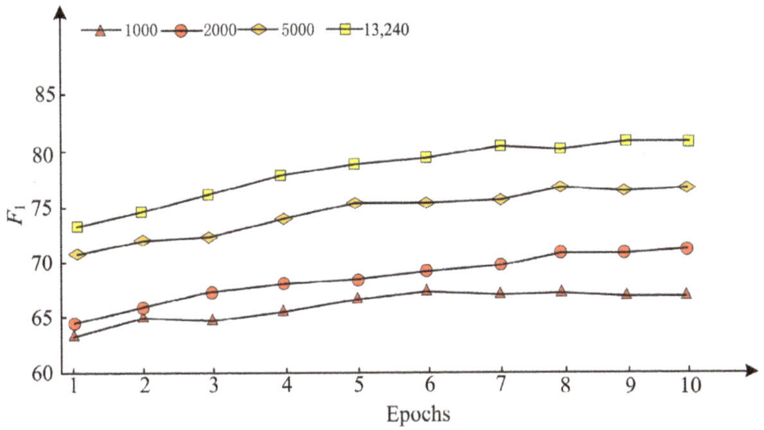

Figure 6. F_1 results for OLD task on the Malay dataset with varying amounts of source language training data.

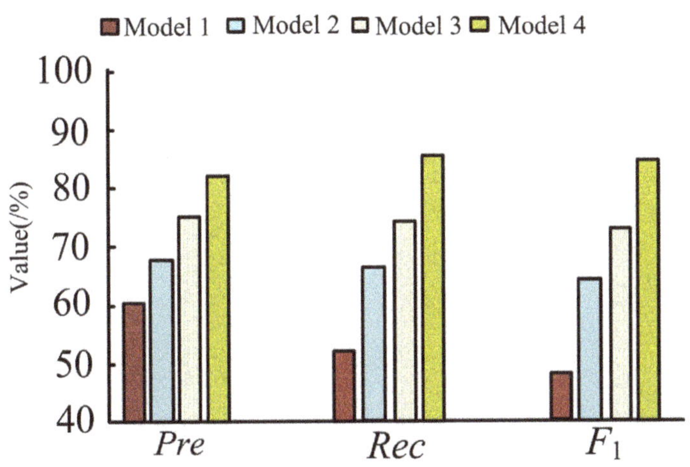

Figure 7. Results of the ablation experiments.

5. Conclusions

In addressing the shortcomings of existing methods in feature extraction for low-resource languages, such as Malay, in OLD tasks, this paper introduces a dual-branch zero-shot cross-lingual model based on mBERT. Effectively leveraging the Sinkhorn distance, the model acquires cross-lingual shared features with strong discriminatory power for detecting offensive content. Augmented with an auxiliary label prediction task, unique domain-specific features are extracted. The combination of these features facilitates robust training and achieves superior performance in offensive text detection compared to existing methods. The success of this approach can be attributed to the comprehensive utilization of the multilingual pre-trained model mBERT, efficient feature extraction strategies, adept adversarial training, and a thoughtful approach to handling offensive pivot words and dataset construction. Collectively, these factors contribute to the outstanding performance of this method in unsupervised CLT for offensive text detection.

Moreover, the proposed method may also face certain limitations. The interpretability of the adopted mBERT model is notably poor, restricting the model's credibility and explainability in specific scenarios. Despite employing unsupervised learning methods, the construction of datasets for OLD still relies on labeled data from high-resource languages such as English. The process of constructing and handling offensive pivot words could potentially render the model sensitive to specific attributes within the dataset. In our future research endeavors, we aim to explore the development and application of visualization tools such as LIME (Local Interpretable Model-agnostic Explanations) or SHAP (SHapley Additive exPlanations) to aid in elucidating the model's decision-making processes and feature importance. Additionally, we intend to investigate active learning strategies to automatically select the most informative samples for annotation, thereby reducing dependency on extensive annotated data from the source language. Furthermore, by introducing more variations and noise from real-world scenarios into our datasets, we seek to mitigate the model's reliance on specific data attributes.

In summary, the proposed approach demonstrates significant advancements in addressing OLD challenges in low-resource languages, providing valuable insights for the application of CLT learning in safeguarding security and order in social media environments. As further improvements in model performance and generalization are pursued, the potential impact of this method in practical applications is expected to grow. Future research endeavors will explore the application of this approach to various tasks, including machine translation, text generation, and other areas within the field of NLP.

Author Contributions: Conceptualization, X.G., H.M.A. and M.Z.Z.A.; Methodology, X.G., H.M.A. and M.Z.Z.A.; Software, X.G.; Validation, X.G., H.M.A. and M.Z.Z.A.; Investigation, X.G.; Resources, X.G. and M.Z.Z.A.; Writing—original draft, X.G.; Writing—review & editing, H.M.A. and M.Z.Z.A.; Supervision, H.M.A. All authors have read and agreed to the published version of the manuscript.

Funding: This research received no external funding.

Institutional Review Board Statement: Not applicable.

Informed Consent Statement: Not applicable.

Data Availability Statement: The data presented in this study are available on request from the corresponding author. The data are not publicly available due to the data are part of an ongoing study.

Conflicts of Interest: The authors declare no conflict of interest.

References

1. Aichner, T.; Grünfelder, M.; Maurer, O.; Jegeni, D. Twenty-five years of social media: A review of social media applications ar definitions from 1994 to 2019. *Cyberpsychol. Behav. Soc. Netw.* **2021**, *24*, 215–222. [CrossRef] [PubMed]
2. Meel, P.; Vishwakarma, D.K. Fake news, rumor, information pollution in social media and web: A contemporary survey state-of-the-arts, challenges and opportunities. *Expert Syst. Appl.* **2020**, *153*, 112986. [CrossRef]
3. Barrutia, L.; Vega-Gutiérrez, J.; Santamarina-Albertos, A. Benefits, drawbacks, and challenges of social media use in derma-tolo A systematic review. *J. Dermatol. Treat.* **2022**, *33*, 2738–2757. [CrossRef] [PubMed]

Risch, J.; Ruff, R.; Krestel, R. Offensive language detection explained. In Proceedings of the Second Workshop on Trolling, Aggression and Cyberbullying, Marseille, France, 11–16 May 2020; pp. 137–143.

Baider, F. Accountability Issues, Online Covert Hate Speech, and the Efficacy of Counter-Speech. *Politics Gov.* **2023**, *11*, 249–260. [CrossRef]

Marques, T. The expression of hate in hate speech. *J. Appl. Philos.* **2023**, *40*, 769–787. [CrossRef]

Awan, I.; Carter, P.; Sutch, H.; Lally, H. Online extremism and Islamophobic language and sentiment when discussing the COVID-19 pandemic and misinformation on Twitter. *Ethn. Racial Stud.* **2023**, *46*, 1407–1436. [CrossRef]

Jahan, M.S.; Oussalah, M. A systematic review of Hate Speech automatic detection using Natural Language Processing. *Neurocomputing* **2023**, *546*, 126232. [CrossRef]

Chinivar, S.; Roopa, M.S.; Arunalatha, J.S.; Venugopal, K.R. Online offensive behaviour in social media: Detection approaches, compre-hensive review and future directions. *Entertain. Comput.* **2023**, *45*, 100544. [CrossRef]

Mahmud, T.; Ptaszynski, M.; Eronen, J.; Masui, F. Cyberbullying detection for low-resource languages and dialects: Review of the state of the art. *Inf. Process. Manag.* **2023**, *60*, 103454. [CrossRef]

Akhter, M.P.; Zheng, J.; Naqvi, I.R.; AbdelMajeed, M.; Zia, T. Abusive language detection from social media comments using conventional machine learning and deep learning approaches. *Multimed. Syst.* **2022**, *28*, 1925–1940. [CrossRef]

Tontodimamma, A.; Nissi, E.; Sarra, A.; Fontanella, L. Thirty years of research into hate speech: Topics of interest and their evolu-tion. *Scientometrics* **2021**, *126*, 157–179. [CrossRef]

Pikuliak, M.; Šimko, M.; Bieliková, M. Cross-lingual learning for text processing: A survey. *Expert Syst. Appl.* **2021**, *165*, 113765. [CrossRef]

Martínez-García, A.; Badia, T.; Barnes, J. Evaluating morphological typology in zero-shot cross-lingual trans-fer. In Proceedings of the 59th Annual Meeting of the Association for Computational Linguistics and the 11th International Joint Conference on Natural Language Processing (Volume 1, Long Papers), Virtual, 1–6 August 2021; pp. 3136–3153.

Muller, B.; Elazar, Y.; Sagot, B.; Seddah, D. First align, then predict: Understanding the cross-lingual ability of multilingual BERT. *arXiv* **2021**, arXiv:2101.11109.

Razavi, A.H.; Inkpen, D.; Uritsky, S.; Matwin, S. Offensive language detection using multi-level classification. In *Advances in Artificial Intelligence, Proceedings of the 23rd Canadian Conference on Artificial Intelligence, Canadian AI 2010, Ottawa, ON, Canada, 31 May–2 June 2010*; Proceedings 23; Springer: Berlin/Heidelberg, Germany, 2010; pp. 16–27.

Xu, Z.; Zhu, S. Filtering offensive language in online communities using grammatical relations. In Proceedings of the Seventh Annual Collaboration, Electronic Messaging, Anti-Abuse and Spam Conference, Washington, DC, USA, 13–14 July 2010; pp. 1–10.

Chen, Y.; Zhou, Y.; Zhu, S.; Xu, H. Detecting offensive language in social media to protect adolescent online safety. In Proceedings of the 2012 International Conference on Privacy, Security, Risk and Trust and 2012 International Conference on Social Computing, Amsterdam, The Netherlands, 3–5 September 2012; IEEE: New York, NY, USA, 2012; pp. 71–80.

Bassignana, E.; Basile, V.; Patti, V. Hurtlex: A multilingual lexicon of words to hurt. In Proceedings of the CEUR Workshop Proceedings, CEUR-WS, Turin, Italy, 18 September 2018; Volume 2253, pp. 1–6.

Davidson, T.; Warmsley, D.; Macy, M.; Weber, I. Automated hate speech detection and the problem of offensive language. In Proceedings of the International AAAI Conference on Web and Social Media, Montreal, QC, Canada, 15–18 May 2017; Volume 11, pp. 512–515.

Watanabe, H.; Bouazizi, M.; Ohtsuki, T. Hate speech on twitter: A pragmatic approach to collect hateful and offensive ex-pressions and perform hate speech detection. *IEEE Access* **2018**, *6*, 13825–13835. [CrossRef]

Van Hee, C.; Jacobs, G.; Emmery, C.; Desmet, B.; Lefever, E.; Verhoeven, B.; De Pauw, G.; Daelemans, W.; Hoste, V. Automatic detection of cyberbullying in social media text. *PLoS ONE* **2018**, *13*, e0203794. [CrossRef] [PubMed]

Mahmud, T.; Das, S.; Ptaszynski, M.; Hossain, M.S.; Andersson, K.; Barua, K. Reason based machine learning approach to detect bangla abusive social media comments. In Proceedings of the International Conference on Intelligent Computing & Optimization, Hua Hin, Thailand, 27–28 October 2022; pp. 489–498.

Alrashidi, B.; Jamal, A.; Khan, I.; Alkhathlan, A. A review on abusive content automatic detection: Approaches, challenges and opportunities. *PeerJ Comput. Sci.* **2022**, *8*, e1142. [CrossRef] [PubMed]

Badjatiya, P.; Gupta, S.; Gupta, M.; Varma, V. Deep learning for hate speech detection in tweets. In Proceedings of the 26th Inter-national Conference on World Wide Web Companion, Perth, Australia, 3–7 April 2017; pp. 759–760.

Pavlopoulos, J.; Malakasiotis, P.; Androutsopoulos, I. Deeper attention to abusive user content moderation. In Proceedings of the 2017 Conference on Empirical Methods in Natural Language Processing, Copenhagen, Denmark, 7–11 September 2017; pp. 1125–1135.

Park, J.H.; Fung, P. One-step and two-step classification for abusive language detection on twitter. *arXiv* **2017**, arXiv:1706.01206.

Sigurbergsson, G.I.; Derczynski, L. Offensive language and hate speech detection for Danish. *arXiv* **2019**, arXiv:1908.04531.

Mishra, P.; Del Tredici, M.; Yannakoudakis, H.; Shutova, E. Abusive language detection with graph convolutional networks. *arXiv* **2019**, arXiv:1904.04073.

Chakkarwar, V.; Tamane, S.; Thombre, A. A Review on BERT and Its Implementation in Various NLP Tasks. In *International Conference on Applications of Machine Intelligence and Data Analytics (ICAMIDA 2022)*; Atlantis Press: Dordrecht, The Netherlands, 2023; pp. 112–121.

31. Zhu, J.; Tian, Z.; Kübler, S. UM-IU@ LING at SemEval-2019 task 6, Identifying offensive tweets using BERT and SVMs. *arXiv* 20 arXiv:1904.03450.
32. Howard, J.; Ruder, S. Universal Language Model Fine-tuning for Text Classification. In Proceedings of the 56th Annual Meeti of the Association for Computational Linguistics (Volume 1, Long Papers), Melbourne, Australia, 15–20 July 2018; Association Computational Linguistics: Stroudsburg, PA, USA, 2018.
33. Kudugunta, S.R.; Bapna, A.; Caswell, I.; Arivazhagan, N.; Firat, O. Investigating multilingual NMT representations at scale. *arX* **2019**, arXiv:1909.02197.
34. Wu, Q.; Lin, Z.; Wang, G.; Chen, H.; Karlsson, B.F.; Huang, B.; Lin, C.Y. Enhanced meta-learning for cross-lingual named enti recognition with minimal resources. In Proceedings of the AAAI Conference on Artificial Intelligence, New York, NY, USA, 7– February 2020; Volume 34, pp. 9274–9281.
35. Keung, P.; Lu, Y.; Bhardwaj, V. Adversarial learning with contextual embeddings for zero-resource cross-lingual classification an NER. *arXiv* **2019**, arXiv:1909.00153.
36. Zhang, D.; Nallapati, R.; Zhu, H.; Nan, F.; dos Santos,, C.N.; McKeown, K.; Xiang, B. Margin-aware unsupervised doma adaptation for cross-lingual text labeling. In Proceedings of the Findings of the Association for Computational Linguisti EMNLP 2020, Virtual, 16–20 November 2020; pp. 3527–3536.
37. Kumar, A.; Saumya, S.; Singh, J.P. NITP-AI-NLP@ HASOC-FIRE2020, Fine Tuned BERT for the Hate Speech and Offensi Content Identification from Social Media. In Proceedings of the FIRE (Working Notes), Hyderabad, India, 16–20 December 20 pp. 266–273.
38. Libovický, J.; Rosa, R.; Fraser, A. How language-neutral is multilingual BERT? *arXiv* **2019**, arXiv:1911.03310.
39. Ayo, F.E.; Folorunso, O.; Ibharalu, F.T.; Osinuga, I.A. Hate speech detection in Twitter using hybrid embeddings and improv cuck-oo search-based neural networks. *Int. J. Intell. Comput. Cybern.* **2020**, *13*, 485–525. [CrossRef]
40. Kapil, P.; Ekbal, A. A deep neural network based multi-task learning approach to hate speech detection. *Knowl.-Based Syst.* **20** *210*, 106458. [CrossRef]
41. Yu, Y.; Huang, J.; Liu, S.; Zhu, J.; Liang, S. Cross target attributes and sample types quantitative analysis modeling of near-infrar spectroscopy based on instance transfer learning. *Measurement* **2021**, *177*, 109340. [CrossRef]
42. Meftah, S.; Semmar, N.; Tamaazousti, Y.; Essafi, H.; Sadat, F. On the hidden negative transfer in sequential transfer learning f domain adaptation from news to tweets. In Proceedings of the Second Workshop on Domain Adaptation for NLP, Kiev, Ukrair 19–20 April 2021; pp. 140–145.
43. Alqahtani, Y.; Al-Twairesh, N.; Alsanad, A. A comparative study of effective domain adaptation approaches for arabic sentime classification. *Appl. Sci.* **2023**, *13*, 1387. [CrossRef]
44. Kanclerz, K.; Miłkowski, P.; Kocoń, J. Cross-lingual deep neural transfer learning in sentiment analysis. *Procedia Comput. S* **2020**, *176*, 128–137. [CrossRef]
45. Hasib, K.M.; Rahman, F.; Hasnat, R.; Alam, M.G.R. A machine learning and explainable ai approach for predicting seconda school student performance. In Proceedings of the 2022 IEEE 12th Annual Computing and Communication Workshop ar Conference (CCWC), Las Vegas, NV, USA, 26–29 January 2022; IEEE: New York, NY, USA, 2022; pp. 0399–0405.
46. Buhrmester, V.; Münch, D.; Arens, M. Analysis of explainers of black box deep neural networks for computer vision: A surv *Mach. Learn. Knowl. Extr.* **2021**, *3*, 966–989. [CrossRef]
47. Garí Soler, A.; Apidianaki, M. Let's play mono-poly: BERT can reveal words' polysemy level and partitionability into sens *Trans. Assoc. Comput. Linguist.* **2021**, *9*, 825–844. [CrossRef]
48. Merendi, F.; Dell'Orletta, F.; Venturi, G. On the Nature of BERT: Correlating Fine-Tuning and Linguistic Competence. Proceedings of the 29th International Conference on Computational Linguistics, Gyeongju, Republic of Korea, 12–17 Octob 2022; pp. 3109–3119.
49. Shah Jahan, M.; Khan, H.U.; Akbar, S.; Umar Farooq, M.; Gul, S.; Amjad, A. Bidirectional Language Modeling: A Systema Literature Review. *Sci. Program.* **2021**, *2021*, 1–15. [CrossRef]
50. Yang, B.; Luo, X.; Sun, K.; Luo, M.Y. Recent progress on text summarisation based on bert and gpt. In Proceedings of th International Conference on Knowledge Science, Engineering and Management, Guangzhou, China, 16–18 August 2023; Spring Nature: Cham, Switzerland, 2023; pp. 225–241.
51. Mabokela, K.R.; Celik, T.; Raborife, M. Multilingual Sentiment Analysis for Under-Resourced Languages: A Systematic Review the Landscape. *IEEE Access* **2022**, *11*, 15996–16020. [CrossRef]
52. Ge, L.; Parhi, K.K. Classification using hyperdimensional computing: A review. *IEEE Circuits Syst. Mag.* **2020**, *20*, 30–4 [CrossRef]
53. Dokmanic, I.; Parhizkar, R.; Ranieri, J.; Vetterli, M. Euclidean distance matrices: Essential theory, algorithms, and applicatio *IEEE Signal Process. Mag.* **2015**, *32*, 12–30. [CrossRef]
54. Usino, W.; Prabuwono, A.S.; Allehaibi KH, S.; Bramantoro, A.; Hasniaty, A.; Amaldi, W. Document similarity detection usin k-means and cosine distance. *Int. J. Adv. Comput. Sci. Appl.* **2019**, *10*, 165–170. [CrossRef]
55. Osborne, J. Improving your data transformations: Applying the Box-Cox transformation. *Pract. Assess. Res. Eval.* **2019**, *15*, 12.
56. Bhardwaj, R.; Vaidya, T.; Poria, S. KNOT: Knowledge Distillation using Optimal Transport for Solving NLP Tasks. *arXiv* **202** arXiv:2110.02432.
57. Cuturi, M. Sinkhorn distances: Lightspeed computation of optimal transport. *Adv. Neural Inf. Process. Syst.* **2013**, *26*, 2292–230

Genevay, A.; Cuturi, M.; Peyré, G.; Bach, F. Stochastic optimization for large-scale optimal transport. *Adv. Neural-Form. Process. Syst.* **2016**, *29*.
Lyu, J.; Zhang, S.; Qi, Y.; Xin, J. Autoshufflenet: Learning permutation matrices via an exact lipschitz continuous penalty in deep convolutional neural networks. In Proceedings of the 26th ACM SIGKDD International Conference on Knowledge Discovery & Data Mining, Virtual, 6–10 July 2020; pp. 608–616.
Ben-David, E.; Rabinovitz, C.; Reichart, R. PERL: Pivot-based domain adaptation for pre-trained deep contextualized embeding models. *Trans. Assoc. Comput. Linguist.* **2020**, *8*, 504–521. [CrossRef]
Zampieri, M.; Malmasi, S.; Nakov, P.; Rosenthal, S.; Farra, N.; Kumar, R. Semeval-2019 task 6, Identifying and categorizing offensive language in social media (offenseval). *arXiv* **2019**, arXiv:1903.08983.
Zampieri, M.; Nakov, P.; Rosenthal, S.; Atanasova, P.; Karadzhov, G.; Mubarak, H.; Derczynski, L.; Pitenis, Z.; Çöltekin, Ç. SemEval-2020 task 12, Multilingual offensive language identification in social media (OffensEval 2020). *arXiv* **2020**, arXiv:2006.07235.
Yao, Z.; Gholami, A.; Shen, S.; Mustafa, M.; Keutzer, K.; Mahoney, M. Adahessian: An adaptive second order optimizer for machine learning. In Proceedings of the AAAI Conference on Artificial Intelligence, Virtual, 9 February 2021; Volume 35, pp. 10665–10673.
Gnanavel, S.; Duraimurugan, N.; Jaeyalakshmi, M.; Rohith, M.; Rohith, B.; Sabarish, S. A live suspicious comments detection using TF-IDF and logistic regression. *Ann. Rom. Soc. Cell Biol.* **2021**, *25*, 4578–4586.
Gopi, A.P.; Jyothi, R.N.S.; Narayana, V.L.; Sandeep, K.S. Classification of tweets data based on polarity using improved RBF kernel of SVM. *Int. J. Inf. Technol.* **2023**, *15*, 965–980. [CrossRef]
Artetxe, M.; Schwenk, H. Massively multilingual sentence embeddings for zero-shot cross-lingual transfer and beyond. *Trans. Assoc. Comput. Linguist.* **2019**, *7*, 597–610. [CrossRef]

applied sciences

MDPI

Article

Adaptation of Augmentative and Alternative Communicators through the Study of Interactions with High-Tech Solution Users

Jaime González-González [1,*], Enrique Costa-Montenegro [1], Fátima María García-Doval [2], Cristina López-Bravo [1] and Francisco de Arriba-Pérez [1]

1 atlanTTic, Information Technologies Group, Telecommunication Engineering School, University of Vigo, Campus, 36310 Vigo, Spain; kike@gti.uvigo.es (E.C.-M.); clbravo@gti.uvigo.es (C.L.-B.); farriba@gti.uvigo.es (F.d.A.-P.)
2 Regional Ministry of Culture, Education, Vocational Training and University, Xunta de Galicia, San Caetano s/n, 15781 Santiago de Compostela, Spain; fmgdoval@edu.xunta.gal
* Correspondence: jaimegonzalez@gti.uvigo.es

Abstract: Augmentative and Alternative Communication (AAC) strategies ease communication tasks for people who require accessible solutions. These strategies are usually addressed by technological solutions such as mobile applications. This research seeks clues on the development of such applications by analyzing user interactions with Android application PictoDroid Lite, an AAC communicator. This study considered a data set containing more than 85,000 interactions of users from more than 50 countries. The goal was to identify the primary needs reflected in the users' behavior and how these applications handle them, providing other researchers and developers with relevant information about how users interact with these applications. We detected areas of improvement regarding the adaptation to users' needs in terms of profiling, smart suggestions, and time habits.

Keywords: augmentative and alternative communication; pictogram; mobile application; user interaction; sentiment analysis; large language models

1. Introduction

Augmentative and alternative communication (AAC) is a discipline that "studies and, when necessary, compensates for temporary or permanent impairments, activity limitations, and participation restrictions of persons with severe disorders of speech-language production and/or comprehension, including spoken and written modes of communication" [1]. Within the field of AAC, there exist multiple strategies to ease accessibility for those who need it.

One of the multiple solutions proposed to date is the use of specific software that assists in user communication [2]. In this context, in 2011, our research team published Android application PictoDroid Lite. It enables users to communicate using pictograms or images with their corresponding descriptions. The combination of multiple pictograms allows for the creation of different types of sentences. As we discuss later in this research, this solution is widely accepted and easily comparable with many other available applications.

The application offers two different modes of verbal expression. Punctual mode presents a group of indexed pictograms for easy, straightforward communication using simple sentences. Alternatively, the cumulative mode offers an evolved system of phrasal construction where users autonomously pick any pictograms needed to convey different pieces of information adapted to their communicative needs by means of more complex sentences.

We decided to carry out a wide-ranging exploratory analysis, studying interactions from hundreds of users representing a larger number of participants than the average for similar studies [3]. Unlike cited research, our study focuses on analyzing usage patterns from interactions of real users with communication impairments. This perspective differs from studies that directly evaluate user experiences via questionnaires, a matter which has already been proven positive for similar applications [4–6]. However, we value the significance of the user experience, as our particular app is endorsed by more than 50,000 downloads and plenty of positive feedback from users.

This novel study of usage patterns offers hints on how to best adapt applications to the needs of end users who require accessible solutions in their daily interactions by using data analysis and Artificial Intelligence (AI).

Therefore, the main objective of this research is to shed light on everyday habits of AAC application users by studying how they interact with a high-tech AAC solution. This can provide insights into how to offer better tailoring to their daily needs and a better and more profound comprehension of the intentions and purposes they attach to these applications. With these hints, we expect not only to foster the use of these AAC solutions but also to offer a better user experience. This will inform future developments in this area.

When reviewing previous works on AAC strategies, relevant research highlights that it is possible to classify them according to the following three main characteristics: purpose, autonomy, and use of technology [7]. We drafted this analysis of related works using a hierarchical vision to contextualize the application design that led to our study.

The purpose of AAC strategies depends on their desired effect on the preserved abilities of the user. Taking that into account, we can distinguish between rehabilitation and habilitation as follows:

- Rehabilitating solutions help users in the recovery of their communication capabilities [8,9].
- Habilitating solutions assist users in acquiring new communicative competencies [10].

Regarding autonomy, the literature defines a classification regarding the involvement of external assistance in AAC strategies. Figure 1 contains a graphic explaining the complete hierarchy of solutions in terms of autonomy. Thus, the more abstract levels that group them are unaided and aided solutions:.

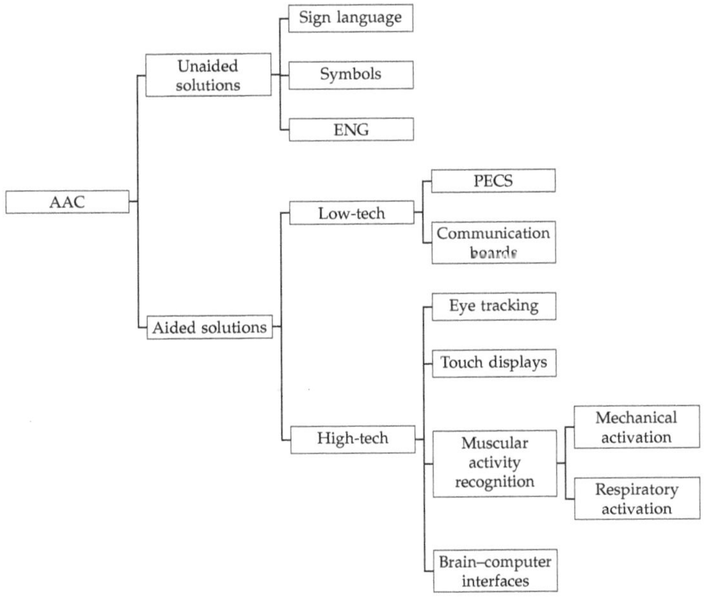

Figure 1. Hierarchy of AAC solutions.

- Unaided solutions include a wide variety of techniques that only depend on the user [11,12]. They usually involve symbols, sign language [13], or Enhanced Natural Gestures (ENG) [14].
- Aided solutions are strategies that require external devices or assistance during the communication process [3,15]. These solutions can be classified into low-technology and high-technology approaches.
  - Low-tech solutions include non-electronic strategies such as the Picture Exchange Communication System (PECS) [16] or alphabet and symbol boards [17,18].
  - High-tech solutions refer to any computer-based strategy [2,19], including mobile applications [20–23], artificial intelligence applications [24], and other technologies, for example, augmented reality [25].

Finally, it is important to add that high-tech solutions present multiple means of interaction depending on the patient's needs [26].

- Eye tracking: Scanning of eye movements and their position relative to a digital display [27,28].
- Touch displays: This is the most used input method nowadays. It requires the user to interact physically with a touch screen [20–23].
- Muscular activity recognition: Specific devices that capture voluntary or involuntary body actions. This can be achieved in the following different ways:
  - Mechanical activation: Detection of physical movements or gestures [29,30];
  - Respiratory activation: Detection of respiratory signals [31].
- Brain–computer interfaces: Scanning and modulation of electric brain signals [32].

PictoDroid Lite is an aided, high-tech solution. Although it can be used as a rehabilitating resource, its use is predominantly habilitating new communicative competencies. The application presents the user with a grid of pictograms to select from a touch screen. Pictogram communicators have been widely used and consistently proven useful in the literature [4–6]. It is important to point out that no dedicated device or specific training is required, and any Android mobile device will run the application effectively. Table 1 shows applications with methods similar to PictoDroid Lite.

Table 1. Android applications similar to PictoDroid Lite.

Application	Type	Graphics	Released on	Downloads
JABtalk [1]	Communicator	Others	October 2011	+100,000
PictoDroid Lite [2]	Communicator	Pictogram + Others	November 2011	+50,000
Dictapicto [3]	Translator	Pictogram	December 2016	+100,000
Card Talk [4]	Communicator	Pictogram + Others	April 2017	+100,000
SymboTalk [5]	Communicator	Pictogram + Others	January 2018	+100,000
Twinkl Symbols [6]	Communicator	Pictogram + Others	January 2021	+10,000
Click AAC [7]	Translator	Pictogram	June 2021	+5000
Search of Arasaac [8]	Translator	Pictogram	December 2021	+50,000

[1] Available at https://play.google.com/store/apps/details?id=com.jabstone.jabtalk.basic, 24 June 2024; [2] Available at https://play.google.com/store/apps/details?id=com.uvigo.gti.PictoDroidLite, 24 June 2024; [3] Available at https://play.google.com/store/apps/details?id=com.orange.dictapicto, 24 June 2024; [4] Available at https://play.google.com/store/apps/details?id=jp.co.litalico.cardtalk, 24 June 2024; [5] Available at https://play.google.com/store/apps/details?id=com.elelad.comboard, 24 June 2024; [6] Available at https://play.google.com/store/apps/details?id=co.uk.twinkl.symbolwriter, 24 June 2024; [7] Available at https://play.google.com/store/apps/details?id=com.clickAAC, 24 June 2024; [8] Available at https://play.google.com/store/apps/details?id=it.alessandrolarocca.searchonarasaac, 24 June 2024.

Communicators allow users to express themselves, while translators define a set of images or pictograms corresponding to an existing natural language expression. Applications typically use pictograms as their basic graphical representations, and many of them permit the use of external sources such as photographs or drawings.

After confirming it as a popular technological solution for AAC, the research team decided to conduct this study to offer relevant information for other researchers developing similar solutions. Any fully developed application has the potential for improvement, benefiting from the knowledge provided in this study.

Regarding previous research, we consider that this research cannot be compared qualitatively to others available in the literature. Many previous studies focus either on assessing usage experience by asking participants to fill out a questionnaire or evaluating their performance according to predefined metrics [5,33–35]. Nonetheless, this study observes how these users interact with the proposed AAC solution.

Our study implements a different approach, exploring usage patterns gathered from a larger audience with no need for additional interviews. With this technological perspective, we aim to analyze the possibilities of state-of-the-art AAC technologies to adapt to users' needs, preferences, and habits. The conclusions drawn from this paper could potentially encourage developers and researchers to undertake fundamental upgrades to their high-tech solutions, leading to a better AAC user experience.

The rest of this paper is structured as follows. Section 2 details the design and operation of PictoDroid Lite. Section 3 introduces the method of our study and the final data set and specifies how data were collected. Section 4 presents the conducted tests and their results. Finally, Section 5 concludes the paper and presents directions for future work in this field.

2. Materials

The main objective of this study is to offer an analysis of the most prevalent uses of an AAC application intended to facilitate communication through pictograms. PictoDroid Lite is a free Android application that allows users to communicate through pictograms or pictures and their corresponding text. The app has reached more than 50,000 downloads in more than 50 countries, predominantly in Spanish-speaking countries. In order to fully comprehend the data gathered for this project, we consider it necessary to briefly explain the main characteristics of the software that captured the interactions.

2.1. Functionality

PictoDroid Lite presents the user with a grid of different elements used to communicate in familiar environments. Each element includes a pictogram (or any other visual representation of a linguistic meaning) and its corresponding written text. The app also includes an oral form that can be identical to or different from the written text. This oral form might be played by a media player (when an audio file is included) or generated by the device's voice synthesizer. This functionality is comparable to other AAC applications listed in Table 1. There is also a resemblance with other low-tech solutions, such as symbol boards.

The pictograms can represent a semantic field or some other linguistic category (for example, food) or stand only for themselves (for example, apple). In the former case, selecting a pictogram implies accessing that category (a sublevel with similar display and distribution) to complete the message. This is what we refer to as pictogram indexation. With respect to the latter, the selection of a pictogram terminates the sentence itself. A final pictogram concludes the utterance, and when selected, the application automatically returns to the initial main screen after a few seconds.

The application has two modes of communication, namely punctual or cumulative communication, aimed clearly towards communication or language acquisition and development, respectively. These options are vital for the user's learning process, as they allow them to adjust the communication board to their cognitive, developmental, and social abilities at that time. They range from fewer to more pictograms on the screen, thus avoiding distraction or confusion with unnecessary ones. Punctual mode (see Figure 2) is intended for immediate, straightforward interaction. Cumulative mode (see Figure 3) presents a more complex functioning where the user must select the different pieces of information that form the final sentence before the voice synthesizer expresses it. Additionally, the cumulative mode may apply a layer of Natural Language Generation (NLG) that is currently only available for the Spanish language, which applies verb conjugations, as well as the introduction of determiners and connectors García-Méndez et al. [36]. This NLG layer provides the user with a socially appropriate utterance and a valid sentence model. As far as we know, no other AAC communicator includes an NLG layer in Spanish.

Figure 2. Punctual screen mode.

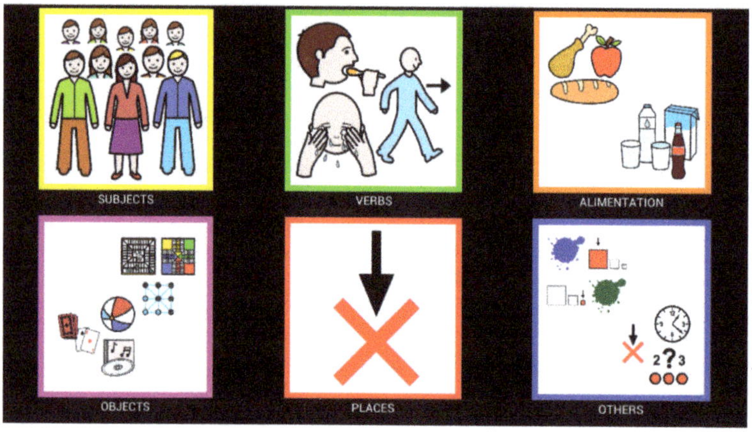

Figure 3. Cumulative screen mode.

2.2. *Configuration*

As previously stated, this app is fully configurable to meet each user's needs. Regarding verbal communication, the app is available in six languages (Spanish, French, Italian, German, English, and Swedish). The user can independently choose the language of the application and the language of the voice synthesizer, allowing for multilingual communication. As additional options, the user (or an assistant) may choose if the voice synthesizer is enabled; the modes previously presented; and, for the latter, the application of the NLG adaptation layer. Furthermore, the user can decide about the dimensions of the image grid presented on the different screens (to better adapt to their visual capabilities or preferences), among many other visual options.

Regarding pictogram administration, the application offers a manager that allows the user (or an assistant) to create new pictograms and categories; change meanings and representations; and modify the oral expressions, including recording voices and sounds, etc. All these features meet the vocabulary configuration need highlighted in previous research Caron et al. [37]. New pictograms or images can be registered using the device camera, loading an image from the gallery, or downloading a standardized pictogram from the ARASAAC repository (available at https://arasaac.org/pictograms/search, 24 June 2024).

Finally, the application includes a profile manager feature, which makes it possible to create, import, and export multiple profiles. This feature allows different people to use a single device still adapted to their specific needs. However, it also facilitates a single user in maintaining different profiles adapted to different contexts (e.g., family, school, or health care). By default, the application offers a basic profile for both modes (punctual and cumulative), including two additional profiles with masculine or feminine pronouns, a very relevant feature in languages with solid gender marks, such as Spanish or French.

3. Methodology and Implementation

This section presents the design of the study and the final data set for the research, along with the implementations that were necessary to carry it out.

3.1. Research Design

Figure 4 presents a general view of the research structure. The study's methodology is defined as follows.

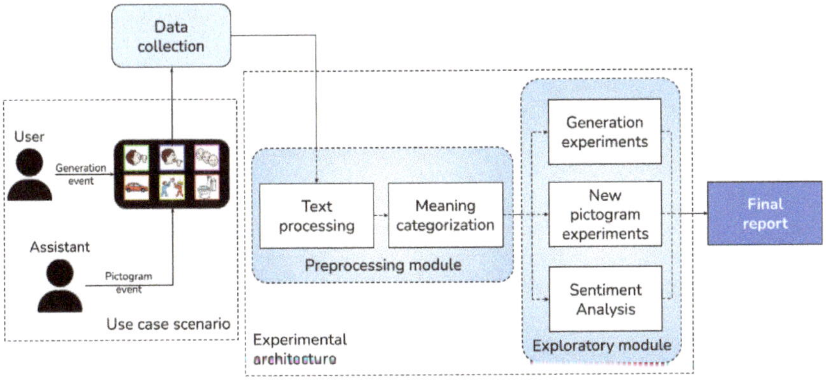

Figure 4. Architecture of the study.

The general architecture of the experiment consists of three parts, namely the use of an external platform for data collection, a preprocessing module, and an exploratory module. The final output of the research is a report containing all the insights studied later.

3.1.1. Data Collection

Our application is configured to collect anonymized usage data automatically. This data collection occurs each time a user performs any of the selected actions, namely (i) generation of sentences and (ii) creation, edition, or deletion of pictograms/images. For this purpose, it was necessary to establish a cloud storage system to collect this information in real time. In order to respect users' privacy, no personal data are collected, and all registered events are automatically anonymized.

Each user who generates at least one event with the application has a record in the database, with a unique identifier present in every registered action. The identifier, provided by the Android API, does not have any relation to the real information of the user, so no personal data are compromised. Additionally, we track the profile names registered by the application in order to sort different users. This allows us to distinguish between different people using the same device. Nonetheless, this field is equivalent to an identifier, and it is not used for the analysis. This record also contains the country from which such events are generated for statistical purposes. Depending on the type of action executed, the application provides different values. Every action is accompanied by its timestamp referencing local time.

For generation events, the app registers the final sentence, the mode of generation (punctual or cumulative) that was used, the language or languages chosen for the application, and the voice synthesizer (as they might be different). For the cumulative mode, the app registers the final sentence after the NLG phase, if available. For new pictograms or images, it records the item's name, the source of the image that represents it, the application's language and mode, and the categories to which the new picture belongs, if applicable. The latter also applies to deletion events, ignoring the source of the original image. Finally, the app registers the update of those elements whenever they change the associated written or oral text, as this is the meaningful part of the communication feature.

3.1.2. Preprocessing Module

First, data are retrieved from the cloud database and presented in a format suitable for processing. The data are divided into sets according to their nature, namely users, generation, new pictograms, updated pictograms, and deleted pictograms. The user table includes information related to the origin and the number of interactions from each type that the user has generated. The remaining tables include the data described in the previous subsection, adding the corresponding user identifier to each entry to guarantee its traceability.

For this research, only Spanish-speaking users are considered in the analysis, so the tables are filtered by language. We made this decision as Spanish is the only language represented in the data set with enough samples to conduct an exhaustive study (see Table 2). Free text fields (generated sentences, pictogram names, etc.) undergo minor modifications, like letter case change or graphic accent removal, to maximize coincidences. Major modifications such as lemmatization or stop-word removal are counterproductive, as the phrases' length and complexity are relevant to this research.

Table 2. Global and Spanish distribution of samples by event type.

Entry Type		Global	Spanish
Sentence generations	Punctual	79,793	72,308
	Cumulative	887	801
New pictograms	Punctual	2180	2096
	Cumulative	435	435
Deleted pictograms	Punctual	1939	1922
	Cumulative	157	157
Updated pictograms	Punctual	610	595
	Cumulative	20	20

Each entry is associated with a predefined category according to its meaning. The categorization requires manually labeled phrases in order to ensure consistency.

3.1.3. Exploratory Module

This research aims to extract relevant conclusions from the usage habits of an AAC application. When determining which tests to perform with the data, it is essential to keep in mind the depth and format of the data. Thus, the tests must be defined based on the preliminary observations made by the research team.

The tests are divided according to the type of event being analyzed (text generation or creation of new pictograms). Expert personnel should determine which are the most relevant aspects of the data to proceed with an exploratory analysis. A subsection of experiments involves sentiment analysis (SA) of the generated texts and the pictograms added by users in order to understand the main motivations for using the application.

3.2. Dataset Description

The data set contains 85,165 different entries in five languages (Spanish, French, English, Italian, and German, in descending order of prevalence). The data set contains the interactions generated by 2370 users from more than 50 different countries in the period between 18 November 2022 and 10 July 2023. Table 2 shows the distribution of entries by type of event. Table 3 presents the most represented countries in the data set.

Table 3. Eight most represented countries in the data set by number of entries.

Country	Users	Entries
Spain	38.80%	63.61%
Argentina	12.28%	7.46%
Chile	8.33%	5.51%
France	1.91%	4.57%
Mexico	7.69%	4.21%
Ecuador	2.34%	3.64%
Colombia	3.70%	2.13%
Peru	4.72%	1.11%

The predominant use of the application by Spanish-speaking users led to the decision to focus this research on the Spanish interactions of 1875 users. Additionally, we limited the scope of the study to interactions and pictograms generated with the punctual mode of the application, since the cumulative mode represent less than 2% of all the interactions. The highly adaptable nature of this mode adds an overwhelming amount of variability and makes it unsuitable for the methods and scope of this study. At this point, it is important to highlight the potential of these types of applications to reach Low- and Middle-Income Countries (LMICs) [38].

Regarding the accessibility of the devices used to run PictoDroid Lite, we studied the different formats of hardware used, as they condition how the screen is displayed. We know that 77% of users work with tablet devices, benefiting from larger displays that ease navigation through the pictogram grids, whereas 14% of the users work with smartphones, leaving the remaining 9% to unknown sources (devices that are not identified by Google).

3.3. Dataset Structure

Depending on the type of event, the number and type of retrieved parameters differ. The following subsection describes each set of data and their characteristics. Tables 4–7 present examples of the fields retrieved for each type of event contained in the data set.

All the events share a common group of parameters (index, user, event, mode, and language) that identify the entries, the user who generated them, the app mode used, and the language they are written in. Additionally, each event has some of the following particular fields adapted to its characteristics:

- Generation: The language synthesizer field contains the language of the text-to-speech tool used to pronounce the generated phrase . The **phrase** field contains the generated phrase.
- New and deleted pictograms: The **name** field contains the name of the new pictogram. The **category** field includes the indexation of the particular pictogram. For new pictograms, the **source** field contains the origin of the image used to represent it.
- Updated pictograms: The **old name** and **old voice** field represent the name and voice (the text read by the text-to-speech tool) that are being substituted, respectively, and the **new name** and **new voice** fields the new versions of them. As in new and deleted pictograms, the **category** field contains the indexation of the updated pictogram.

Table 4. Generation entry examples.

Index	User	Event	Language	Language Synth.	Mode	Phrase	Timestamp
1066	9	Generation	Español	es	PUNCTUAL	quiero leer una revista	2023-04-22 18:04:51.805
3976	105	Generation	Español	es	PUNCTUAL	me duele la garganta	2022-12-20 10:51:47.604
4235	115	Generation	Español	es	PUNCTUAL	quiero beber zumo	2023-04-08 08:47:25.255

Table 5. New pictogram entry examples.

Index	User	Event	Language	Mode	Name	Source	Timestamp	Category
1797	1335	NewPicto	Español	PUNTUAL	galletas	ARASAAC	2023-07-05 10:10:07.12	[Comer]
1832	1475	NewPicto	Español	PUNTUAL	futbol	PHOTO	2023-05-22 17:27:05.993	[deportes]
1891	1683	NewPicto	Español	PUNTUAL	Calmado	GALLERY	2023-04-18 15:01:33.666	[Emociones

Table 6. Deleted pictogram entry examples.

Index	User	Event	Language	Mode	Name	Timestamp	Category
68	11	DeletePicto	Español	PUNTUAL	coca-cola	2023-05-02 18:45:20.317	[quiero beber]
402	142	DeletePicto	Español	PUNTUAL	echar colonia	2023-02-27 09:54:03.585	[aseo]
589	194	DeletePicto	Español	PUNTUAL	verduras	2023-04-05 11:33:56.593	[Comer]

Table 7. Updated pictogram entry examples.

Index	User	Event	Language	Mode	New Name	New Voice	Old Name	Old Voice	Timestamp	Category
21	11	Update Picto	Español	PUNTUAL	jugo de manzana	jugo de manzana	zumo de manzana	zumo de manzana	2023-05-02 18:46:14.239	[quiero beber]
145	189	Update Picto	Español	PUNTUAL	Piano	tocando el Piano	Piano	Piano	2023-02-16 18:55:42.075	[Jugar]
191	264	Update Picto	Español	PUNTUAL	papas fritas	papas fritas	patatas fritas	patatas fritas	2023-02-06 10:44:12.679	[Comer, De picar]

3.4. Implementation

As introduced in Section 2, once the Android app was published, it was necessary to implement a system for data collection and processing.

3.4.1. Data Collection

The data collection takes advantage of the native implementation of the connection between Android applications and the Google Firebase real-time database (available at https://firebase.google.com/docs/database, 24 June 2024). The app packs the data into messages in JSON format and sends them to the database identified by the "app set id" provided by Android (available at https://developer.android.com/training/articles/app-set-id, 24 June 2024). This ensures the original user's privacy without compromising the data's traceability.

3.4.2. Data Processing

It is necessary to develop a program that downloads the data from the database and converts them to a table format for further analysis. Firebase Admin SDK for Python (available at https://firebase.google.com/docs/reference/admin/python/firebase_admin, 24 June 2024) offers the functionalities of authorization and access to the database. Once the data are downloaded in dictionaries, they is formatted as tables using Pandas Python library (available at https://pandas.pydata.org/, 24 June 2024).

After an initial observation of the data, we define a group of general categories that include generated sentences and pictograms created based on their meanings.

- Care: Pictures and sentences that refer to personal care (hygiene, rest, affection, or clothing), such as "*Lavar las manos*" (wash hands) or "*Ir al baño*" (go to the toilet).
- Emotions: Pictures and messages relative to the user's emotions or physical state, such as "*Yo estoy triste*" (I am sad) or "*Yo estoy cansado*" (I am tired).
- Social interaction: Pictures and utterances that help the user to perform basic daily interactions (greetings, interjections, questions, explanations, etc.), such as "*¡Hola amigos!*" (Hi friends!) or "*Ir a casa*" (go home).
- Nutrition: Pictures and messages relative to food and beverages such as "*Quiero comer*" (I want to eat) or "*Quiero agua*" (I want water).
- Leisure: Pictures and sentences involved in leisure and learning activities (board games, electronic devices, playtime, etc.), such as "*Ir al parque*" (go to the park) or "*Quiero dibujar*" (I want to draw).
- Health: Pictures and sentences that express health issues, such as "*Me duele el brazo*" (My arm hurts) or "*Dolor de cabeza*" (headache).
- Name: Only for new pictograms, including all personal names registered by users.

Additionally, we considered "incoherent" those sentences or pictograms that cannot be assigned to a single category (e.g., "*Quiero comer quiero jugar*", I want to eat I want to play) or misspelled words (e.g., "wwww"). A group of researchers manually labeled all the samples. The labeling process was later automated, taking advantage of the fact that many samples were repetitions of the same text.

The final distribution of samples by category is represented in Table 8.

Social interactions consistently concentrate a greater number of actions, either the formation of sentences or any other events linked to the administration of pictograms. It is interesting to note that all categories are consistent in their prevalence across the different events (sentences and new, deleted, or updated pictograms).

Table 8. Sample count for each defined category.

Category	Sentences		New Pictograms		Deleted Pictograms		Updated Pictograms	
Social interaction	20,394	28.20%	650	31.01%	359	18.68%	186	31.26%
Nutrition	20,340	28.13%	686	32.73%	797	41.47%	155	26.05%
Leisure	14,038	19.41%	419	19.99%	392	20.40%	140	23.53%
Care	9273	12.82%	110	5.25%	182	9.47%	47	7.90%
Emotions	4513	6.24%	61	2.91%	134	6.97%	22	3.70%
Health	2861	3.96%	31	1.48%	26	1.35%	18	3.03%
Incoherent	889	1.23%	23	1.10%	22	1.14%	21	3.53%
Names	-	-	116	5.53%	10	0.52%	6	1.01%

3.4.3. Exploratory Analysis

Having defined the categories, we propose a set of tests to perform an exploratory analysis. These tests study the frequencies of use and the complexity of the interactions and other routine habits that represent a relevant source of knowledge for future developments in this field.

We decided to study the events of sentence generation and pictogram creation, since these are the events that provide the greatest degree of new information about the use of the app and the needs of the users. All these tests were performed using the Pandas Python library (available at https://pandas.pydata.org/, 24 June 2024) for data processing and the Matplotlib Python library (available at https://matplotlib.org/, 24 June 2024) and Seaborn python library (available at https://seaborn.pydata.org/, 24 June 2024) for data representation.

For the SA, we tried two different approaches. The first approach involved using a basic lexicon-based approach such as the spaCy TextBlob Python library (available at https://spacy.io/universe/project/spacy-textblob, 24 June 2024) and the text2emotion Python library (available at https://pypi.org/project/text2emotion/, 24 June 2024). The second approach involved using a more complex Large Language Model (LLM) such as Llama 3 (available at https://llama.meta.com/llama3/, 24 June 2024) developed by META. We chose the Ollama Python library (available at https://ollama.com/, 24 June 2024) to run and interact with the LLM.

When testing the text2emotion Python library on generated phrases, we determined that only 6.23% of the phrases were non-neutral, presenting several inconsistencies considering neutral phrases like *"Yo estoy contento"* (I am happy) or *"Yo estoy enfadado"* (I am angry). On the other hand, the LLM method offered more reasonable results, with 60.62% of phrases identified as non-neutral and a reduced number of inconsistencies.

Considering both approaches, we decided to discard the lexicon-based technique as it offered inadequate results, failed to provide answers for basic sentences, and had inconsistent categories for similar phrases.

4. Results and Discussion

In this section, we discuss the results of the different tests proposed for this research. We divided these tests according to the type of events they study, namely phrase generation or new pictograms. All the tests include an explanation of their goal and the insights obtained from them.

4.1. Generation Events

We seek to evaluate fundamental aspects such as the average length, the time of day, or the frequency of repetition of sentences to observe users' behavior and needs regarding the PictoDroid Lite application. To provide more context, first, we studied user habits in terms of average number of sentences generated per day and how they distribute them throughout the day. Figure 5 presents a distribution of the users of the application regarding the average number of hours they use the application and the average number of phrases they generate daily. On the other hand, Figure 6 presents the total number of phrases generated by each group of users defined in Figure 5. As an example, in Figure 5, there are 1295 users who generate 1 to 10 phrases daily within 0 to 1 h of use. In Figure 6, we can see that those 1295 users generated 9506 phrases.

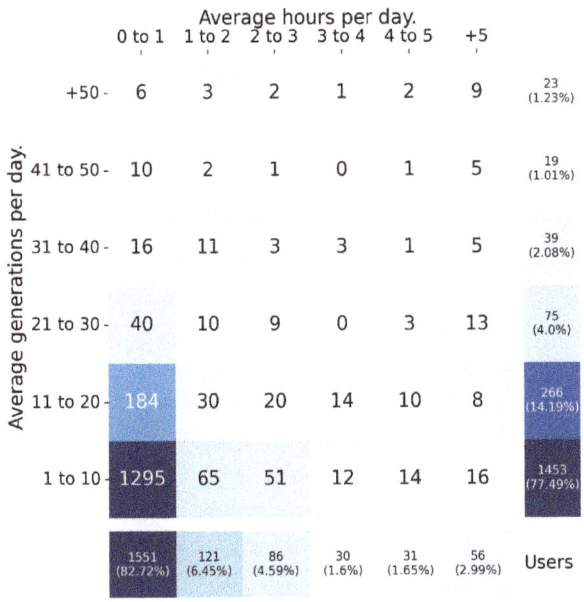

Figure 5. Distribution of users in terms of average number of generations and usage hour span.

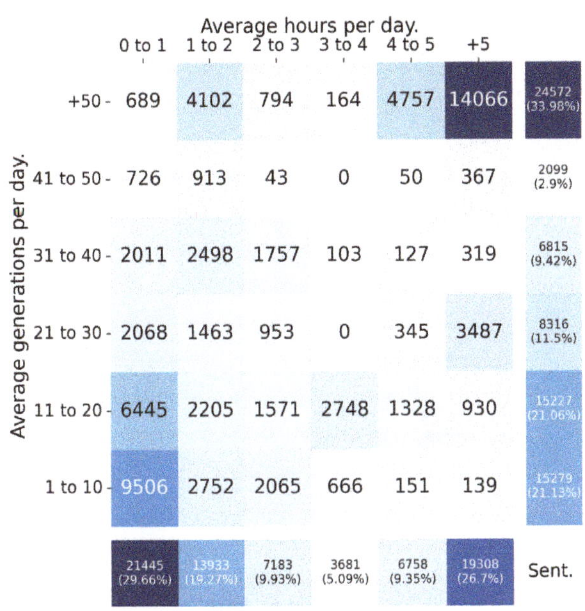

Figure 6. Distribution of sentences per average number of generations and usage hour span.

Figure 5 reveals that 77.49% of users generate 1 to 10 sentences in one day. Nonetheless, Figure 6 shows that only 21.13% of the sentences were generated by those users. On the other hand, 33.98% of sentences correspond to users who generate 50 or more per day. In terms of usage time, 29.66% of the sentences were generated by users who use the app one hour daily or less, while 26.70% were generated by users who use it five hours or more daily.

With this information, we can see that the majority of the users of the application generate, on average, just a few sentences in one day, but, in contrast, there are users who generate a lot of events each day. The even distribution according to the hour span indicates the existence of a smaller group of people who use the app intensively throughout the day, while a larger group uses it sporadically or for particular contexts (e.g., school, therapy, etc.). Both clues highlight how AAC communicators help users with very different needs and characteristics.

For a better understanding of this research, it is crucial to observe how frequently the users accessed the application, as many of them did not use the application during the complete data capture period. Table 9 presents the distribution of samples according to the frequency of access of the users that generated them.

Table 9. Distribution of users and samples by access frequency.

Frequency	Users	Phrases	New Pictograms
Daily	6.67%	4.64%	9.54%
Weekly	10.99%	44.65%	28.72%
Monthly	82.35%	50.71%	60.54%

A proportion of 6.67% of users generate a phrase at least once a day; almost double, the 10.99%, generate a phrase at least once a week, and the remaining 82.35% generate a phrase at least once a month. Daily and weekly generations are associated with people who use the app as an everyday tool for communication. On the other hand, monthly uses may correspond to context-specific cases (e.g., therapy or health care) or sporadic needs. The majority of both phrases and new pictograms are associated with users who use the app less than once a week. However, daily and weekly users represent half of the generated phrases and more than a third of the new pictograms.

4.1.1. What Is the Average Length of Generated Sentences for Each Category?

This analysis studies the characteristic complexity of interactions according to their meanings. Table 10 shows the number of sentences generated with the application according to their category and their average lengths in characters. We obtained the average length of the **phrase** field from Table 4.

Table 10. Test 1: Sentences in categories and their average lengths.

Category	Samples	Average Length
Social interaction	20,394	11.552
Nutrition	20,340	25.675
Leisure	14,038	17.811
Care	9273	19.083
Emotions	4513	13.293
Health	2861	13.852

Users tend to build longer sentences to communicate needs related to nutrition or care, where specificity prevails (e.g., *"Quiero comer para desayunar galletas de chocolate"*, I want to have chocolate cookies for breakfast). On the contrary, when interacting socially, they prefer to have shorter and more direct sentences (e.g., *"Hola"*, Hello, or *"Adiós"*, Good bye).

4.1.2. How Are Interactions Distributed throughout the Day?

We defined the day time slots in blocks of three hours, from midnight (00:00 to 02:59) to night (21:00 to 23:59). The **timestamp** field (see Table 4) captures time of day at which the interactions take place in local time; we can study how they are distributed over said time slots. Table 11 displays the overall distribution of interactions, and Table 12 shows how each category is distributed throughout the day.

Overall results show that users make the greatest use of the application in the mid-morning (09:00 to 11:59) and evening (18:00 to 20:59) slots.

This time distribution is coherent with time for activities (mid-morning) such as school, work, or therapy and social time at home (evening). It is relevant that the evening slot is the one with the most communicative activity.

Regarding the categories, we observe that emotions shift their interactions from the bands of greatest activity, with a very representative block in the afternoon (15:00 to 17:59). In the case of nutrition, care, and health, these are more distributed throughout the day. It is also important to point out that a significant percentage of social interaction, which more than doubles mid-morning activity and leisure, takes place in the evening slot, when most educational, occupational, and health activities take place, presumably with partners.

A plausible hypothesis that deserves further research is that for the users of these accessible tools, family is still the main source of social interaction despite inclusion efforts. It is also interesting that conversations on emotions are equally prevalent in mid-morning and evening. Usage during night hours results as expected, with few interactions mainly associated with well-being categories.

Table 11. Test 2: Percentage of usage in different time periods.

Day Slot	Hours	Samples
Midnight	00:00 to 02:59	1.75%
Dawn	03:00 to 05:59	0.55%
Morning	06:00 to 08:59	5.04%
Mid-morning	09:00 to 11:59	21.16%
Noon	12:00 to 14:59	17.37%
Afternoon	15:00 to 17:59	18.08%
Evening	18:00 to 20:59	25.89%
Night	21:00 to 23:59	10.17%

Table 12. Test 2: Usage of categories in different time periods.

Day Slot	Social Interaction	Nutrition	Leisure	Care	Emotions	Health
Midnight	0.51%	1.69%	1.45%	1.85%	3.11%	1.62%
Dawn	0.20%	0.77%	0.43%	0.49%	1.29%	0.55%
Morning	1.61%	5.64%	6.72%	4.01%	3.32%	2.99%
Mid-morning	18.30%	18.53%	21.69%	22.52%	17.58%	18.99%
Noon	10.30%	17.63%	15.09%	19.71%	17.76%	19.37%
Afternoon	11.01%	21.37%	15.20%	18.94%	26.25%	20.08%
Evening	52.12%	23.50%	30.82%	21.26%	19.33%	24.22%
Night	5.95%	10.87%	8.58%	11.23%	11.36%	12.19%

4.1.3. How Are Interactions Distributed throughout the Week?

Another relevant aspect of user habits regarding time refers to the distribution of their interactions throughout the week. Table 13 presents the global distribution of interactions. Table 14 shows the distribution of interactions depending on the category they belong to.

Table 13. Test 3: Percentage of usage on different weekdays.

Day	Total
Monday	14.76%
Tuesday	13.40%
Wednesday	18.18%
Thursday	21.69%
Friday	12.25%
Saturday	11.48%
Sunday	8.24%

Table 14. Test 3: Usage of categories on different weekdays.

Day	Social Interaction	Nutrition	Leisure	Care	Emotions	Health
Monday	20.69%	10.57%	15.52%	12.00%	12.52%	11.15%
Tuesday	10.36%	14.03%	13.90%	14.08%	15.67%	22.23%
Wednesday	23.26%	16.36%	15.36%	17.20%	16.53%	14.58%
Thursday	26.46%	18.30%	21.61%	20.16%	21.76%	17.02%
Friday	9.16%	13.25%	13.79%	13.68%	13.52%	13.00%
Saturday	5.82%	15.35%	11.87%	14.49%	11.26%	12.90%
Sunday	4.26%	12.13%	7.96%	8.38%	8.75%	9.12%

The general distribution shows that usage through the week is rather evenly distributed, peaking in the middle of the week and declining on Sundays. Category-wise, we observe that nutrition has the most consistent distribution over the week, while categories like social interaction, emotions, and leisure are mostly reserved for working days, when users may attend to school, their workplace, or therapy sessions.

4.1.4. What Is the Frequency of Sentence Repetition in Small Time Slots?

Data represent the characteristic behavior of certain users, tending to repeat sentences consecutively with a short time margin between them. This behavior might be a signal of urgency or necessity, or it might be a call for attention.

To study this phenomenon, we defined two different time margins in order to consider when one sentence is reiterated under 3 s and under 5 s. We calculated the time differences between the **timestamp** fields of consecutive iterations. Table 15 shows the percentage of sentences that were considered repetitions for each category.

Table 15. Test 4: Percentage of repetitions of sentences.

Category	Samples	3 s Reiteration	5 s Reiteration
Social interaction	20,394	11.03%	13.73%
Nutrition	20,340	15.08%	16.05%
Leisure	14,038	10.03%	12.10%
Care	9273	23.66%	34.45%
Emotions	4513	19.79%	21.58%
Health	2861	20.90%	23.31%

We observe a greater incidence for categories associated with personal well-being and care and health, accounting for 34% and 23% of repetitions in less than 5 s, respectively.

4.2. New Pictogram Events

Studying the general habits of users while registering new pictograms, we observed the distribution of image sources for the creation of pictograms with the **source** field (see Table 5). We could see that 55.87% of the pictograms were downloaded from the ARASAAC repository, 37.31% from the device's gallery, and the final 6.82% directly captured from the app. This indicates that users find it valuable to have an accessible source of standardized pictograms.

Another relevant behavior refers to how commonly pictograms of an equal category are created simultaneously. Table 16 shows the proportion of pictograms belonging to each category, which were created along with pictograms in the same category.

Table 16. Percentage of equal-category pictograms created together.

Category	Samples
Social interaction	56.90%
Nutrition	59.91%
Care	27.94%
Leisure	48.55%
Emotions	54.17%
Health	29.41%
Names	53.66%

These results suggest that for categories like nutrition or social interaction, users tend to create most of the pictograms they need at the same time, while for categories like care or health, they prefer to add new pictograms when they need them.

4.2.1. What Is the Indexing Level of Newly Created Pictograms Depending on Their Category?

Punctual mode offers a system of indexed pictograms. This way, "folder" pictograms can be established, serving as a container for related concepts that will be selected in the next level, adding extra precision to the sentence. We consider the level of indexation as the number of folders and subfolders in which a new pictogram is created. To illustrate this methodology, the default configuration of PictoDroid Lite contains the pictogram "apple" inside the pictogram subfolder "fruit", which is included in the pictogram folder "eat". This means that the pictogram "apple" presents a second level of indexation.

This analysis studies which categories show the highest degree of indexing. We know the level of indexation by observing the length of the list present in the **category** field (see Table 5). Figure 7 shows the distribution of new pictograms according to their level of indexing and the category they belong to.

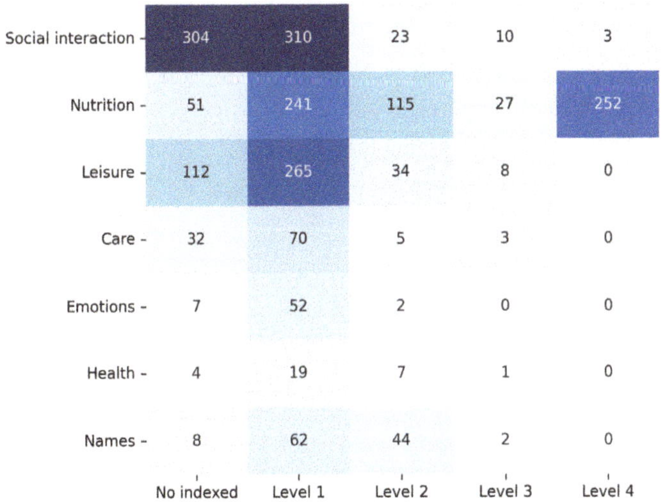

Figure 7. Distribution of pictograms regarding their indexation and the category they belong to.

Results clearly show that the nutrition category is the one that benefits the most from this indexing system, reaching up to four levels and with a broad representation of alternatives in each of them. Another relevant aspect is that the social interaction category tends to host all pictograms in an unindexed format, presumably for quick, straightforward access, in comparison with categories such as emotions, names, or health, with almost anecdotal representation of unindexed pictograms. In the case of names, they are created mostly in indexed form to be used as objects in the generated sentences (*"Quiero estar con profe María"*, I want to be with teacher María).

4.2.2. What Is the Average Length of Newly Created Pictograms for Each Category?

As with the generated sentences, by studying the average length of the **name** of the pictograms created for each category (see Table 5), we can deduce the complexity of the communication. Table 17 shows the average length, in characters, of the written texts of the created pictograms.

Table 17. Test 6: Average length of new pictograms in the different categories.

Category	Samples	Length
Social interaction	650	6.378
Nutrition	686	9.370
Leisure	419	8.795
Care	110	7.745
Emotions	61	7.639
Health	31	8.903
Names	116	5.405

Categories such as health, nutrition, and leisure opt for longer constructions (e.g., *"Dolor de garganta"*, sore throat), while categories like care and social interaction prefer more direct expressions (e.g., *"Dormir"*, sleep, or *"Hola"*, hello). It is noticeable that compared with the results obtained in Test 1 (see Section 4.1.1), there is not much difference in the average length of the sentences and the pictograms alone for categories like health, emotions, and social interaction (less than double the length). We see the opposite situation for categories such as care and nutrition, where the average length of sentences triples the length of their pictograms. This seems to back up the interpretation that categories such as health or social interaction prioritize immediacy, while nutrition and care communications prioritize specificity.

4.3. Sentiment Analysis

With a general perspective on data, we considered it necessary to perform an analysis of the prevalence of the most relevant emotions (happiness, sadness, fear, and anger) in the communications captured with the application. With this analysis, we can understand not only the way users communicate thanks to the application but also their main motivations for doing so. Table 18 shows the percentage of phrases that present any of the emotions previously listed for each category. We added a neutral column for those where no particular emotion stands out.

Table 18. Sentiment analysis of generation events.

Category	Happiness	Anger	Sadness	Fear	Neutral
Social interaction	46.46%	0.00%	0.01%	0.00%	53.53%
Nutrition	97.82%	0.00%	0.00%	0.00%	2.18%
Leisure	78.83%	0.00%	0.00%	0.00%	21.17%
Care	6.30%	0.00%	0.00%	0.00%	93.70%
Emotions	42.10%	2.57%	28.87%	0.60%	25.86%
Health	0.00%	0.00%	73.19%	0.00%	26.81%

For categories such as nutrition and leisure, we observe that an overwhelming majority of the interactions have an inherently positive emotion, as they mostly express desires for food or recreation. As expected, the emotions category presents the most wide range of emotions, being the only one where anger is expressed. Finally, health stands out, as the majority of entries express sadness, which is logical, given the fact that most the associated clauses are used to express discomfort. For care and social interaction, the majority of sentences are neutral.

We also considered conducting this analysis on newly added pictograms despite the limitation of the length of the added terms. Table 19 presents the results of this analysis.

Table 19. Sentiment analysis of new pictograms.

Category	Happiness	Anger	Sadness	Fear	Neutral
Social interaction	18.92%	0.00%	0.00%	0.00%	81.08%
Nutrition	37.46%	0.00%	0.00%	0.00%	62.54%
Leisure	27.68%	0.00%	0.00%	0.00%	72.32%
Care	10.00%	0.00%	0.00%	0.00%	90.00%
Emotions	34.43%	18.03%	14.75%	4.92%	27.87%
Health	0.00%	12.90%	0.00%	0.00%	87.10%

As the new pictograms are fractions of phrases, most of them lack complete meaning by themselves. This is why the majority are classified as neutral in all categories except emotions. We considered it interesting that the pictograms created under the latter are as evenly distributed as the generation events for the same category. In particular, the difference between the creation of new pictograms that represent anger and their use could mean that users identify a lack of predefined terms to express this emotion.

5. Conclusions

This research studies the usage habits of an AAC application, seeking a better understanding of the needs of its target users. This information is particularly useful in achieving better adaptation of AAC strategies to those needs. Adaptation is key for smarter, easier, and more efficient use, enabling more fluent interactions. An analysis of the state of the art revealed the singularity of the perspective of this research, prioritizing usage patterns over more clinic aspects of AAC and benefiting from a larger group of participants.

The data retrieved with PictoDroid Lite demonstrates that it is a useful tool reaching target users who demand accessible solutions, even from LMICs. Additionally, being distributed a platform as large as the Android operating system, applications such as PictoDroid Lite can offer their potential and services without cost restrictions or dedicated hardware specifications.

The tests conducted in this research revealed meaningful insights with respect to common usage of AAC applications. Our observations regarding the complexity of the generated phrases suggest that many users could benefit from using more complex methods like the cumulative mode, which offers greater versatility when building said sentences. Nevertheless, the immediacy and straightforwardness of the punctual mode have been proven useful and, by far, more appealing to the general public.

Furthermore, the conclusions drawn from the SA reinforce the idea that AAC communicators need to include default resources to express emotions besides the most functional or routine expressions. AAC users demand ways to express how they are feeling, including positive and negative emotions.

Limitations and Future Improvements

The tests and analysis performed in this study offer a privileged window into the everyday life of the people who need accessible communications. By this means and with due respect to privacy, we were allowed to observe their main concerns, how they adapt the application to their needs, and what their communication patterns are. From the test observations, we identified a series of limitations present in PictoDroid Lite (and many other communicators) and investigated how those limitations could be solved for any AAC application.

- **Specific profiles:** Observing the newly created pictograms and usage patterns, we conclude that the application could be offered alongside a set of predefined profiles adapted to specific contexts, such as school, health care, or playgrounds. This would reduce the time needed to navigate the pictogram grid and would make personalization faster and smarter.
- **Pictogram suggestion:** When creating a new pictogram on a predefined profile or when doing so in a given category, the application could suggest related concepts in order to make the creation process more dynamic.
- **Time-based sorting.** Test 2 (see Section 4.1.2) highlighted that users have different needs at different times of the day. The application could adapt to these changes by rearranging the grid, giving priority to those categories that are more likely to be needed at a particular time of the day. Test 3 (see Section 4.1.4) indicates that this could be useful for weekday adaption.
- **Repeat last action:** Test 4 (see Section 4.2.1) showed that users tend to repeat the same sentence one or many times. This process could be helped by introducing a button that allows one to repeat the last sentence without needing to navigate the grid again. This would be notably useful in urgent contexts.

Observing the applications cited in Table 1, almost all of them lack some or every point cited above. Apps like Card Talk, SymboTalk, and Twinkl Symbols include mechanics for category distinction, like communication boards. However, these boards do not constitute an entity similar to having a domain-specific profile, as our clues suggest.

On the edition and creation of new symbols, no application includes suggestions based on related concepts. The applications that include an online search of pictograms (ARASAAC being the most frequent source) only recommend other pictograms that also include the search query.

Regarding user experience, no application has previously considered time (time of the day, day of the week, etc.) as a relevant factor for adaption. Additionally, those applications that seek to provide fluent support for communication could consider introducing a shortcut for last-phrase reiteration.

We detected a set of strengths already implemented in PictoDroid Lite that would be positive for other existing applications. The method of pictogram indexation provides a straightforward method for sentence construction, SymboTalk being the only studied application that includes a similar technique. Moreover, developers should consider including access to an online source of predefined pictograms such as ARASAAC, as 55.87% of users find it useful.

The performed analysis led to relevant clues about the development of AAC mobile applications, highlighting the strengths of some methodologies implemented in PictoDroid Lite and noting some gaps that many applications present. These areas of improvement, if fixed, would result in more efficient communication and offer better service to AAC users. In other words, this research shows that communicators (and other AAC applications) like PictoDroid Lite have a margin for automated responsiveness that would serve the needs and preferences of most users well.

Author Contributions: J.G.-G.: Methodology, software, validation, formal analysis, investigation, data curation, and writing—original draft. E.C.-M.: conceptualization, methodology, investigation, formal analysis, writing—review and editing, and supervision. F.M.G.-D.: conceptualization, methodology, investigation, formal analysis, writing—review and editing, and supervision. C.L.-B.: methodology, formal analysis, writing—review and editing, and supervision. F.d.A.-P.: software, formal analysis, writing—review and editing, and supervision. All authors have read and agreed to the published version of the manuscript.

Funding: This work was partially supported by (*i*) Xunta de Galicia grant ED481A-2023-090, Spain; (*ii*) Xunta de Galicia grant ED481B-2022-093, Spain; (*iii*) Xunta de Galicia grant ED431C 2022/04, Spain; (*iv*) Ministerio de Ciencia e Innovación grant TED2021-130824B-C21, Spain; and (*v*) University of Vigo/CISUG for partial open access charge.

Institutional Review Board Statement: Not applicable.

Informed Consent Statement: Not applicable.

Data Availability Statement: The raw data supporting the conclusions of this article will be made available by the authors upon request.

Acknowledgments: The pictographic symbols used in this paper are the property of the Government of Aragón and were created by Sergio Palao for ARASAAC (http://www.arasaac.org, accessed on 24 June 2024), which distributes them under Creative Commons License BY-NC-SA. We wish to thank Jonathan Juncal Martínez and José María López Astáriz for their contribution in the development of the application.

Conflicts of Interest: The authors declare no conflicts of interest.

Abbreviations

The following abbreviations are used in this manuscript:

AAC	Augmentative and Alternative Communication
NLG	Natural Language Generation
LLM	Large Language Model
LMIC	Low and Middle-Income Country
SDK	Software Development Kit

ferences

Calculator, S. Roles and responsibilities of speech-language pathologists with respect to augmentative and alternative communication: Technical report. *ASHA Suppl.* **2004**, *17*, 48–59

Farzana, W.; Sarker, F.; Chau, T.; Mamun, K.A. Technological Evolvement in AAC Modalities to Foster Communications of Verbally Challenged ASD Children: A Systematic Review. *IEEE Access* **2021**, 2169–3536. [CrossRef]

Logan, K.; Iacono, T.; Trembath, D. A systematic review of research into aided AAC to increase social-communication functions in children with autism spectrum disorder. *AAC Augment. Altern. Commun.* **2017**, *33*, 1267795. [CrossRef] [PubMed]

Bautista, S.; Hervás, R.; Hernández-Gil, A.; Martínez-Díaz, C.; Pascua, S.; Gervás, P. Ara traductor: Text to pictogram translation using natural language processing techniques. In Proceedings of the XVIII International Conference on Human Computer Interaction, Cancun, Mexico, 25–27 September 2017; Volume Part F131194, pp. 1–8. [CrossRef]

Collette, D.; Brix, A.; Brennan, P.; DeRoma, N.; Muir, B.C. Proloquo2Go Enhances Classroom Performance in Children With Autism Spectrum Disorder. *OTJR Occup. Particip. Health* **2019**, *39*, 143–150. [CrossRef]

Hervás, R.; Bautista, S.; Méndez, G.; Galván, P.; Gervás, P. Predictive composition of pictogram messages for users with autism. *J. Ambient. Intell. Humaniz. Comput.* **2020**, *11*, 5649–5664. [CrossRef]

Beukelman, D.R.; Mirenda, P. *Augmentative & Alternative Communication. Supporting Children and Adults with Complex Communication Needs*; Paul Brookes Publishing Co.: Baltimore, MD, USA, 2005.

Dietz, A.; Wallace, S.E.; Weissling, K. Revisiting the role of augmentative and alternative communication in aphasia rehabilitation. *Am. J. Speech-Lang. Pathol.* **2020**, *29*, 909–913. [CrossRef]

Fager, S.K.; Burnfield, J.M.; Pfeifer, C.M.; Sorenson, T. Perceived importance of AAC messages to support communication in rehabilitation settings. *Disabil. Rehabil. Assist. Technol.* **2021**, *16*, 1736652. [CrossRef]

Babb, S.; Jung, S.; Ousley, C.; McNaughton, D.; Light, J. Personalized AAC Intervention to Increase Participation and Communication for a Young Adult with down Syndrome. *Top. Lang. Disord.* **2021**, *41*, 232–248. [CrossRef]

Moorcroft, A.; Scarinci, N.; Meyer, C. A systematic review of the barriers and facilitators to the provision and use of low-tech and unaided AAC systems for people with complex communication needs and their families. *Disabil. Rehabil. Assist. Technol.* **2019**, *14*, 1499135. [CrossRef] [PubMed]

Roche, L.; Sigafoos, J.; Trembath, D. Augmentative and Alternative Communication Intervention for People With Angelman Syndrome: A Systematic Review. *Curr. Dev. Disord. Rep.* **2020**, *7*, 28–34. [CrossRef]

Carbone, V.J.; Sweeney-Kerwin, E.J.; Attanasio, V.; Kasper, T. Increasing the vocal responses of children with autism and developmental disabilities using manual sign mand training and prompt delay. *J. Appl. Behav. Anal.* **2010**, *43*, 705–709. [CrossRef] [PubMed]

14. Calculator, S.N. Use of enhanced natural gestures to foster interactions between children with Angelman syndrome and th parents. *Am. J. Speech-Lang. Pathol.* **2002**, *11*, 340–355. [CrossRef]
15. Biggs, E.E.; Carter, E.W.; Gilson, C.B. A scoping review of the involvement of children's communication partners in aid augmentative and alternative communication modeling interventions. *Am. J. Speech-Lang. Pathol.* **2019**, *28*, 743–758. [CrossR [PubMed]
16. Bondy, A.S.; Frost, L.A. The Picture Exchange Communication System. *Focus Autism Other Dev. Disabil.* **1994**, *9*, 1–19. [CrossR
17. Balandin, S.; Hemsley, B.; Sigafoos, J.; Green, V.; Forbes, R.; Taylor, C.; Parmenter, T. Communicating with Nurses: The Experien of 10 Individuals with an Acquired Severe Communication Impairment. *Brain Impair.* **2001**, *2*, 109–118. [CrossRef]
18. Balandin, S.; Hemsley, B.; Sigafoos, J.; Green, V. Communicating with nurses: The experiences of 10 adults with cerebral pa and complex communication needs. *Appl. Nurs. Res.* **2007**, *20*, 56–62. [CrossRef] [PubMed]
19. Morin, K.L.; Ganz, J.B.; Gregori, E.V.; Foster, M.J.; Gerow, S.L.; Genç-Tosun, D.; Hong, E.R. A systematic quality review high-tech AAC interventions as an evidence-based practice. *AAC Augment. Altern. Commun.* **2018**, *34*, 104–117. [CrossR [PubMed]
20. Voon, N.H.; Bazilah, S.N.; Maidin, A.; Jumaat, H.; Ahmad, M.Z. Autisay: A mobile communication tool for autistic individu In Proceedings of the Computational Intelligence in Information Systems, Burgos, Spain, 15–17 June 2015; Volume 331, 349–359. [CrossRef]
21. Zaffke, A.; Jain, N.; Johnson, N.; Alam, M.A.U.; Magiera, M.; Ahamed, S.I. Icanlearn: A mobile application for creating flashca and social stories™ for children with autism. In Proceedings of the Smart Homes and Health Telematics, Geneva, Switzerla 10–12 June 2015; Volume 8456, pp. 225–230. [CrossRef]
22. Mohammad, H.; Abu-Amara, F. A mobile social and communication tool for autism. *Int. J. Emerg. Technol. Learn.* **2019**, 159–167. [CrossRef]
23. Sng, C.Y.; Carter, M.; Stephenson, J. Teaching on-Topic Conversational Responses to Students with Autism Spectrum Disord Using an iPad App. *Int. J. Disabil. Dev. Educ.* **2022**, *69*, 415–434. [CrossRef]
24. Sennott, S.C.; Akagi, L.; Lee, M.; Rhodes, A. AAC and Artificial Intelligence (AI). *Top. Lang. Disord.* **2019**, *39*, 389–403. [CrossR
25. Liu, R.; Salisbury, J.P.; Vahabzadeh, A.; Sahin, N.T. Feasibility of an autism-focused augmented reality smartglasses system social communication and behavioral coaching. *Front. Pediatr.* **2017**, *5*, 145. [CrossRef]
26. Elsahar, Y.; Hu, S.; Bouazza-Marouf, K.; Kerr, D.; Mansor, A. Augmentative and alternative communication (AAC) advances: review of configurations for individuals with a speech disability. *Sensors* **2019**, *19*, 1911. [CrossRef]
27. Kar, A.; Corcoran, P. A review and analysis of eye-gaze estimation systems, algorithms and performance evaluation methods consumer platforms. *IEEE Access* **2017**, *5*, 16495–16519. [CrossRef]
28. Chen, S.H.K.; O'Leary, M. Eye Gaze 101: What Speech-Language Pathologists Should Know About Selecting Eye Ga Augmentative and Alternative Communication Systems. *Perspect. ASHA Spec. Interest Groups* **2018**, *3*, 24–32. [CrossRef]
29. Ozioko, O.; Dahiya, R. Smart Tactile Gloves for Haptic Interaction, Communication, and Rehabilitation. *Adv. Intell. Syst.* **2022** 2100091. [CrossRef]
30. Gonçalves, C.W.P.; Richa, R.A.; Bo, A.P. Tracking and Classification of Head Movement for Augmentative and Alternati Communication Systems. *Sensors* **2022**, *22*, 435. [CrossRef]
31. Elsahar, Y.; Bouazza-Marouf, K.; Kerr, D.; Gaur, A.; Kaushik, V.; Hu, S. Breathing pattern interpretation as an alternative a effective voice communication solution. *Biosensors* **2018**, *8*, 48. [CrossRef]
32. Brumberg, J.S.; Pitt, K.M.; Mantie-Kozlowski, A.; Burnison, J.D. Brain—Computer interfaces for augmentative and alternati communication: A tutorial. *Am. J. Speech-Lang. Pathol.* **2018**, *27*, 1–12. [CrossRef]
33. Rodriguez, C.S.; Rowe, M.; Thomas, L.; Shuster, J.; Koeppel, B.; Cairns, P. Enhancing the communication of suddenly speechl critical care patients. *Am. J. Crit. Care* **2016**, *25*, e40–e47. [CrossRef] [PubMed]
34. Agius, M.M.; Vance, M. A Comparison of PECS and iPad to Teach Requesting to Pre-schoolers with Autistic Spectrum Disord *AAC Augment. Altern. Commun.* **2016**, *32*, 58–68. [CrossRef] [PubMed]
35. Broomfield, K.; Harrop, D.; Jones, G.L.; Sage, K.; Judge, S. A qualitative evidence synthesis of the experiences and perspectives communicating using augmentative and alternative communication (AAC). *Disabil. Rehabil. Assist. Technol.* **2022**, *2022*, 21059 [CrossRef]
36. García-Méndez, S.; Fernández-Gavilanes, M.; Costa-Montenegro, E.; Juncal-Martínez, J.; González-Castaño, F.J. A library automatic natural language generation of Spanish texts. *Expert Syst. Appl.* **2019**, *120*, 372–386. [CrossRef]
37. Caron, J.; Light, J.; Drager, K. Operational Demands of AAC Mobile Technology Applications on Programming Vocabulary a Engagement during Professional and Child Interactions. *AAC Augment. Altern. Commun.* **2016**, *32*, 12–24. [CrossRef]
38. Muttiah, N.; Gormley, J.; Drager, K.D. A scoping review of Augmentative and Alternative Communication (AAC) interventio in Low-and Middle-Income Countries (LMICs). *AAC Augment. Altern. Commun.* **2022**, *38*, 123–134. [CrossRef]

applied sciences

MDPI

ticle

Iate Speech Detection by Using Rationales for Judging Sarcasm

aliha Binte Mamun [1,*], Takashi Tsunakawa [1], Masafumi Nishida [1] and Masafumi Nishimura [2]

[1] Graduate School of Science and Technology, Shizuoka University, 3-5-1 Johoku, Chuo-ku, Hamamatsu 432-8011, Japan
[2] Department of Smart Design, Faculty of Architecture and Design, Aichi Sangyo University, 12-5 Harayama, Oka-machi, Okazaki 444-0005, Japan
* Correspondence: mamun.maliha.binte.19@shizuoka.ac.jp

Abstract: The growing number of social media users has impacted the rise in hate comments and posts. While extensive research in hate speech detection attempts to combat this phenomenon by developing new datasets and detection models, reconciling classification accuracy with broader decision-making metrics like plausibility and faithfulness remains challenging. As restrictions on social media tighten to stop the spread of hate and offensive content, users have adapted by finding new approaches, often camouflaged in the form of sarcasm. Therefore, dealing with new trends such as the increased use of emoticons (negative emoticons in positive sentences) and sarcastic comments is necessary. This paper introduces sarcasm-based rationale (emoticons or portions of text that indicate sarcasm) combined with hate/offensive rationale for better detection of hidden hate comments/posts. A dataset was created by labeling texts and selecting rationale based on sarcasm from the existing benchmark hate dataset, HateXplain. The newly formed dataset was then applied in the existing state-of-the-art model. The model's F1-score increased by 0.01 when using sarcasm rationale with hate/offensive rationale in a newly formed attention proposed in the data's preprocessing step. Also, with the new data, a significant improvement was observed in explainability metrics such as plausibility and faithfulness.

Keywords: hate speech; sarcasm; rationale

1. Introduction

Although half of the world's population uses social media for networking, many have encountered hostility in some form or another [1], such as those categorized under crimes against minorities [2]. Victims of online hate suffer from psychological and emotional distress like depression, anxiety, and in severe cases, physical harm, which potentially leads to suicide [3–6]. Over the years, continuous research has been conducted to develop hate speech detection methods that could effectively reduce online hate. In order to achieve such methods, understanding online hate and predicting hate crimes in their various manifestations are very important [7]. Therefore, to improve hate detection, hate speech datasets [8–13] have been developed over the years, which mostly focus on hate speech attributes closely related to hate expressions (e.g., abusive comment, hate speech, offensive, and disrespectful content), the target of hate (e.g., origin, gender, religion, and sex orientation), and retweets (now termed posts) or the like are made available for the purpose of progressive research and development.

A distinction is recognized between hate speech and offensive comments in this study. Hate speech is described as statements that incite violence or prejudice against specific groups based on protected attributes such as race, religion, or sexual orientation. These expressions typically aim to harm and marginalize, reflecting deep-seated prejudice.

Offensive comments, which are potentially hurtful or rude, are generally not directed to incite direct harm nor are they always targeted at specific groups. These may include profanity or derogatory remarks made in a general context without the intention to incite violence or discrimination against a group.

In this paper, a clear distinction between these two types of content is maintained to tailor the model's response appropriately. Not only is the presence of hate or offense identified, but also the context and the target, which are considered crucial for effective moderation on social platforms. This approach allows for more nuanced detection and response strategies, which are essential for maintaining the integrity and inclusivity of online communication spaces.

Some studies [14–17] have proposed models for improving automatic hate speech detection. However, these models often lack inductive reasoning due to an overestimation of state-of-the-art approaches for hate speech detection [18,19]. These advanced models typically rely on triggered vocabularies for predictions, leading to substantial evidence of racial bias in major published hate speech datasets [20,21]. Moreover, as hate speech detection models become more complex, it becomes increasingly challenging to clarify their decision-making process [22].

To address these concerns, a benchmark dataset named "HateXplain" [13] was introduced. This dataset is unique in that each data point is annotated with labels indicating whether the content is hate, offensive, or normal, along with details such as the mentioned target communities and text snippets known as rationales [23]. These rationales, which are identified by human annotators, provide context that is instrumental in teaching the model not only to recognize hate speech but also to understand the context that characterizes such language, enhancing both the robustness and interpretability of the model.

During the training phase, these rationales inform a specialized attention mechanism within a neural network architecture, focusing the model's attention more on words and phrases within these rationales. This targeted learning approach helps the model to prioritize the most critical attributes that indicate offensive/hate speech, leading to improved accuracy and reliability in classifications.

Furthermore, the use of rationales extends into the operational phase of the model. Here, the trained model applies the patterns it has learned to new, unseen texts. When it identifies words or phrases that mirror the rationales from the training dataset, the model scrutinizes these pieces of text with heightened attention. This method not only improves the accuracy of classification but also ensures that each decision made by the model can be traced back to clear, understandable linguistic evidence, thereby enhancing the transparency and accountability of automated hate speech detection systems.

Thus, incorporating rationales into the training and operational phases of model bridges the gap between traditional text analysis and a deep, contextual understanding of language used in hate speech. This not only enhances the model's performance but also ensures that each decision made by the model is transparent and explainable, which is crucial for applications in sensitive areas such as online content moderation.

While recent studies have highlighted flaws in previous hate speech detection methods, including issues with model performance and datasets, the evolving nature of language and the constant emergence of new ways social media users spread hate speech pose ongoing challenges. Platforms like Twitter or Facebook often inspire users to employ figurative language in conveying their opinions. This includes the concealment of hate comments under the guise of sarcasm [24], a common form of passive-aggressive speech.

Therefore, sarcasm represents a crucial aspect for enhancing hate speech detection. However, as far as the knowledge of this study extends, there has not been any previous research in this sector specifically addressing hate concealed under the pretext of sarcasm. As a solution to this problem, this research proposes a new dataset that also focuses on sarcasm alongside hate. For the study, 3199 data points were selected from the benchmark HateXplain dataset [13] and annotators were hired to label them based on sarcasm as well as choose the accompanying rationale. LIME [25] was utilized for generating important tokens as rationale to assist in the classification task. The BERT model, as documented in [26], gives significance to the HateXplain data rationales provided by human annotators, but it tends to misclassify the label (offensive speech—OF). Notably, for this study's data, BERT assigned the label (hate speech—HS).

This study aimed to enhance hate speech detection by incorporating a sarcasm-based rationale in addition to the conventional hate/offensive rationale. The main objectives were to develop a novel methodology for integrating these rationales into the existing model frameworks and to assess the impact of this integration on model performance, specifically in terms of classification accuracy and explainability.

The growing prevalence of online hate speech necessitates robust detection mechanisms that can effectively handle the nuances of language, including sarcasm, which is often used to disguise hateful intents. By addressing these challenges, the research seeks to contribute to safer online environments and more effective moderation tools.

The contributions of this research are as follows:

1. A new dataset for hate speech detection is presented, comprising two kinds of labeled categories: (i) sarcastic/non-sarcastic; and (ii) hate speech/offensive/normal. Rationale selection is based on whether it fits into the categories of sarcastic and hate/offensive;
2. The sarcasm rationale is incorporated in cases where the data are both sarcastic and hate speech/offensive. This involves preprocessing steps before utilizing it in the model's attention calculation;
3. The inclusion of sarcasm-based rationale alongside hate speech/offensive-based rationale improved both the classification and explainability metrics of the BERT model.

2. Related Works

The proliferation of online platforms has significantly increased incidents of hate speech, impacting vulnerable individuals and communities profoundly [3,5,6,27]. Comprehensive studies [4,28–30] have documented these effects, emphasizing the urgent need for effective detection mechanisms. Current research primarily focuses on developing computational models to detect explicit and implicit hate speech [11–13]. However, traditional methods often overlook nuanced expressions such as sarcasm and indirect speech that can mask hateful intentions [31–33], a critical gap highlighted in the literature. This study addresses this by enhancing model sensitivity to not only detect overt hate speech but also subtler, sarcastic expressions often overlooked by current methodologies [14–17,34,35].

Dataset: Previous datasets designed to detect hate speech primarily focus on expressions related to hate, encompassing abusive comments, hate speech, offensive language, and disrespectful content. A common issue in much of the preceding research is the tendency to conflate hate speech with abusive or offensive language [34]. Furthermore, some studies merged offensive and hate language into a single category, while only a limited number [34,36] made efforts to distinguish offensive from hate speech. In the published HateXplain dataset, subjectivity is recognized as a pivotal aspect, acknowledging that numerous messages may be offensive without qualifying as hate speech. For example, in the United States, the term "nigga" is commonly used in online language by the Black community in a manner that is not necessarily intended to be malevolent toward another individual [35]. Building on the categorization framework that separates hate from offensive language [34], the HateXplain dataset adopts three classes: hate, offensive, and normal. Moreover, HateXplain incorporates the concept of using rationales [23]. Since human annotators are required to highlight a span of text supporting their labeling decision, this enriches the rationale annotation process. As a result, HateXplain provides the first benchmark hate speech dataset with human-level explanations, enhancing interpretability and transparency.

Despite the progress made by HateXplain in addressing major issues related to hate speech, a contemporary challenge persists—the use of sarcasm as a disguise for spreading hate speech [24]. Given the non-physical and implicit nature of online violence, it often appears subtle. Social media platforms frequently host stereotypical, racial, and gender jokes, sometimes disguised as sarcasm. While seemingly harmless, the repetition of such jokes can lead to negative psychological effects, resembling a form of cyberbullying [37,38]. Despite existing research on sarcasm detection [39,40] and multi-modal detection [41], there is a noticeable gap—no research has explored the connection between hate and sarcasm for automatic hate speech detection. In our work, assuming hate is hidden under the guise of sarcasm, and rationale can provide human-level explanations, we collected data from HateXplain, which is already labeled with rationale based on hate/offensive/normal for new dataset creation. This new dataset is different from existing datasets in that it introduces two categories, and based on each category (sarcasm and hate/offensive), we provide rationale for human-level explanations.

Model: Despite numerous models claiming to achieve state-of-the-art performance on specific datasets, their ability to generalize is often questionable [18,19]. Challenges emerge when these models misclassify comments related to identities frequently under attack (e.g., gay, black, and/or Muslim) as toxic even when lacking any malicious intent [42]. The prevalence of biased predictions, stemming from an overemphasis on specific trigger vocabulary, can result in further discrimination against groups already targeted by online abuse [20,21]. Another pressing issue in current methodologies is the lack of decision-making transparency. As hate speech detection models grow in complexity, elucidating their decisions becomes increasingly challenging [22]. Therefore, it is important to focus on interpretable rather than performance-based models. HateXplain tackles the challenge of model explainability by concurrently learning target classification and the rationale behind human decisions. This dual learning approach aims to enhance both aspects. In this study, existing state-of-the-art models such as CNN-GRU [14], BERT [26] and BiRNN [43] were leveraged. Drawing insights from HateXplain, where BERT demonstrates slightly superior results in classification, bias, and a key explainability metric (faithfulness), as well as being the only model that can provide a vector representing the attention for each token, the study opted to employ BERT for a more comprehensive comparison with HateXplain.

3. Methods

This section explains the preprocessing steps and model employed in evaluating the dataset. The preprocessing steps encompass HateXplain dataset management, the data from the newly proposed dataset, and a novel preprocessing method designed for data exhibiting both sarcasm and hate/offensive characteristics. In the model details, the utilization of ground truth attention for training is clarified along with the model's requirement to produce a vector representing the attention for each token.

3.1. Dataset Selection

Among the various available hate speech datasets, HateXplain was selected for this research due to its unique features. HateXplain provides annotated rationales for each labeled instance, which is critical for developing models that not only predict hate speech but also offer insights into the reasons behind these classifications. This transparency is vital for the interpretability of models in sensitive applications like content moderation. Additionally, HateXplain's focus on both hate speech and offensive language, annotated in a real-world context, aligns well with the objectives of this study to handle nuanced expressions like sarcasm effectively.

3.2. Preprocessing

Conversion of text data: Essential preprocessing tasks are efficiently executed to ensure data uniformity and usability. Text normalization and cleaning involve converting all text to lowercase, removing HTML tags, and substituting URLs and other non-textual elements with placeholders to standardize data. The `Ekphrasis` tokenizer, designed for social media, segments and annotates text with emotional and stylistic cues critical for detecting sarcasm and hate speech. Advanced tokenization for the model input employs `BertTokenizer` to refine text into tokens suitable for BERT models, appending special tokens like '[CLS]' and

'[SEP]' to facilitate proper sequence formatting, while also preparing sequence input IDs and attention masks. Integration with SpaCy enhances the grammatical and semantic handling of the text, supporting accurate model training and effectiveness. These comprehensive preprocessing steps meticulously prepare the dataset, addressing language complexities and nuances vital for the effective detection of sarcasm and hate speech, thus enhancing model accuracy and interpretability.

Conversion of rationale to ground truth attention: Ground truth attention is established for posts identified as toxic (hatespeech/offensive) using a baseline method for scenario (i). Furthermore, for scenario (ii), where posts are classified as hatespeech/offensive in the first category and sarcasm in the second category, ground truth attention is derived from the annotator's rationales depicted in Figure 1. In this process, each rationale is transformed into an attention vector with values of 0 and 1. Tokens within the rationale are assigned a value of 1 in the attention vector, while the rest receive a 0. The average of these attention vectors is then calculated to obtain the ground truth attention for each post. Subsequently, a softmax function is applied to normalize the attention.

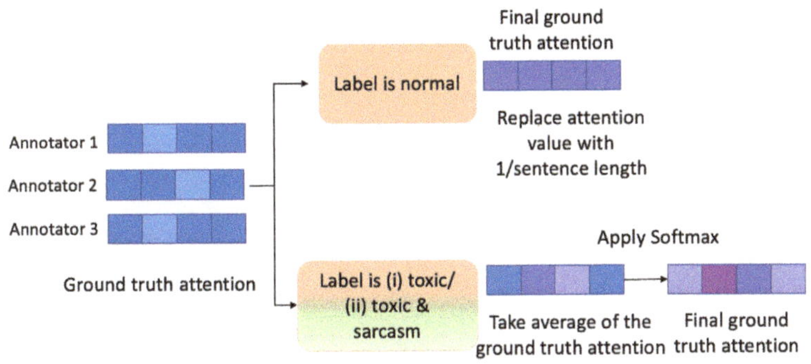

Figure 1. Ground truth attention algorithm is applied to (i) toxic data (hatespeech/offensive) and to data that is both (ii) sarcastic and toxic.

An inherent challenge in the ground truth attention vector arises from the potential proximity of values between rationale and non-rationale tokens. To address this, we utilize the temperature parameter (τ) within the softmax function. This strategic application of the temperature parameter facilitates an adjustment in the probability distribution, amplifying the emphasis on the rationales. The fine-tuning of this parameter is a meticulous process conducted through adjustments in the validation set.

In the conversion process of toxic (hatespeech/offensive) rationale, if at least two out of three annotators label the data as hatespeech/offensive, the rationale is considered. However, for sarcasm data, even if just one annotator labels the data as sarcasm, the rationale is converted. This distinction is made due to the subjective nature of understanding sarcasm in text data, which can vary significantly from person to person.

Proposed method for the conversion of rationale to ground truth attention: In this study, an innovative algorithm tailored for data exhibiting both hateful/offensive and sarcastic characteristics is introduced, see Algorithm 1. In this process, similar to the previous approach, each rationale is transformed into an attention vector with values of 0 and 1. Tokens within the rationale are assigned a value of 1 in the attention vector, while the rest receive a 0. Here, the attention vector for toxic (hate/offensive) after conversion is denoted as $H = (h_1, h_2, h_3, \ldots, h_n)$ in the 1st category, and the attention vector for sarcasm, denoted as $S = (s_1, s_2, s_3, \ldots, s_n)$, corresponds to the 2nd category. This procedure is applied to a sentence represented by tokens $t_1, t_2, t_3, \ldots, t_n$ and its corresponding rationale after vector conversion $r_1, r_2, r_3, \ldots, r_n$.

Algorithm 1 Calculate ground truth attention vector

procedure CALCULATE GROUND TRUTH ATTENTION Sentence tokens $t_1, t_2, t_3, \ldots, t_n$; Rationale vector after conversion $r_1, r_2, r_3, \ldots, r_n$; Hate/Offensive Attention Vector, $\mathbf{H} = (h_1, h_2, h_3, \ldots, h_n)$; Sarcasm Attention Vector, $\mathbf{S} = (s_1, s_2, s_3, \ldots, s_n)$
    for $i \leftarrow 1$ to n **do**
        Calculate combined attention score for token t_i:
        if $s_i > h_i$ **then**
            $r_i \leftarrow \frac{s_i + h_i}{2}$
        end if
        if $s_i < h_i$ **then**
            $r_i \leftarrow h_i$
        end if
        if $s_i = h_i$ **then**
            $r_i \leftarrow h_i + \frac{s_i + h_i}{2}$
        end if
    end for
    return Rationale Attention Vector r
end procedure

Drawing on the concept of an attention vector, a new attention vector is established for tokens within the rationale that simultaneously convey hateful/offensive and sarcastic elements. This new attention vector is utilized for the calculation of the ground truth attention. Specifically, if, in sarcasm rationale, a vector element s_i surpasses a hate rationale vector element h_i, the final newly assigned vector element is $r_i = 0.5$. When a sarcasm rationale vector element s_i is less than the hate rationale vector element h_i, the final new assigned vector element $r_i = 1$.

And lastly, when the sarcasm rationale vector element s_i is equal to the hate rationale vector element h_i and if both of them are 1, then the final new assigned vector element $r_i = 1.5$, as shown in Figure 2.

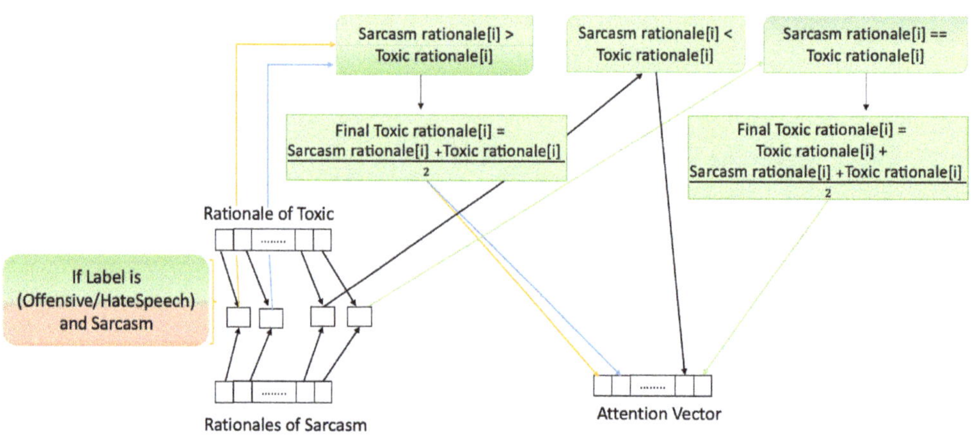

Figure 2. Attention vector calculation before the average of ground truth attention.

This approach refines the interpretation of attention dynamics in the context of sentences exhibiting both hatespeech/offensive and sarcasm. Following this, the average of the attention vectors is calculated to obtain the ground truth attention for each post, as in the previous process shown in Figure 1. Once the updated ground truth attention is obtained, a softmax function is applied to distribute the concentration of rationale, mirroring the final ground truth attention calculation as previously demonstrated.

3.3. Model

In this section, the details of the BERT model are provided. The model was trained on both HateXplain and the newly proposed dataset. Here, how the cross-entropy loss is calculated is explained for ground truth attention.

Bidirectional Encoder Representations from Transformers (BERT)

In the BERT model, there are approximately 12 layers, and each layer consists of 12 attention heads, resulting in a total of 144 attention heads. Typically, a subset of these heads, denoted as "supervised heads", is utilized in the last layer of BERT for attention supervision, Figure 3a. HateXplain [13] employs this term to describe the selected attention heads. For each supervised head, the attention weights corresponding to [CLS] are utilized, and the cross-entropy loss is calculated against the ground truth attention vector. This process ensures that the final weighted output corresponding to [CLS] focuses on words aligned with the ground truth attention vector. The same procedure is repeated for all supervised heads. The resultant loss from attention supervision is the average of the cross-entropy losses from each supervised head, further multiplied by the regularization parameter, denoted as λ. The utilization of attention weights associated with [CLS] in conjunction with the cross-entropy loss helps align the model's attention with the ground truth attention vector.

Following the computation of ground truth attention, the BERT model undergoes training using the preprocessed data and ground truth attention. Subsequently, a loss from attention supervision is computed, employing cross-entropy between attention values and the ground truth attention as the loss function for attention, Figure 3b. The total loss, denoted as L_{total}, is determined by the sum of the prediction loss ($L_{prediction}$) and the attention loss ($\lambda \cdot L_{attention}$). In this equation, λ acts as a weighting factor, regulating the influence of the attention loss on the overall loss.

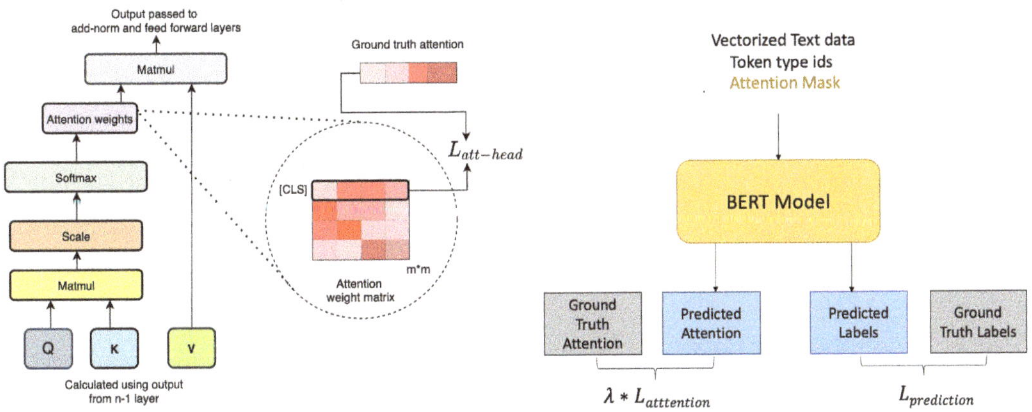

(**a**) Attention supervision for a particular head. (**b**) Training BERT with ground truth attention.

Figure 3. (**a**) Representation of the HateXplain [13] paper's model, showing the attention supervision for a particular head in the nth layer of the BERT model. (**b**) Representation of the BERT model showing how the attention of the model is trained using the ground truth attention and the total loss calculation.

4. Experimental Conditions

4.1. Dataset

This section is divided into two categories: Benchmark Dataset HateXplain [13] and New Dataset Creation.

Benchmark Dataset—HateXplain: This dataset was obtained from platforms like Twitter and Gab, which were previously explored in hate speech studies. The corpus, comprising tweets and Gab posts, was annotated with labels (hatespeech/offensive/normal), target communities, and text snippets marked by annotators supporting the labels. Each data point was evaluated by three independent annotators, and if there was a consensus among two or more annotators on a specific category, the data were officially categorized accordingly.

New Dataset Creation: From the benchmark dataset, HateXplain (which is publicly available in online), 3199 data points were randomly selected and each underwent manual scrutiny to determine its sarcastic nature, illustrated in Figure 4a. Three independent annotators meticulously labeled each data offering a nuanced perspective on the presence or absence of sarcasm, complemented by a detailed rationale for their labeling decisions, illustrated in Figure 4b.

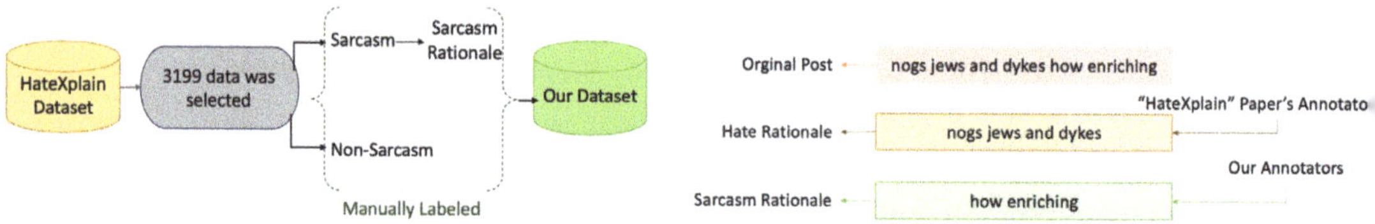

(**a**) Data selection and labeling. (**b**) Rationale selection by annotators.

Figure 4. (**a**) Description of how the data were selected and labeled. (**b**) Description of a certain data point that is labeled as both hate speech and sarcasm, the selected rationale of the benchmark dataset's annotators, and our annotators' rationale for the data point.

About 12 anonymous annotators, along with recruited volunteers, were engaged in the labeling task for this project. Exclusively provided with textual data (posts) from the selected entries in the HateXplain dataset, these annotators focused on identifying sarcasm. Drawing inspiration from the use of rationales in detecting hate/offensive comments, as observed in the benchmark dataset, our approach involved creating rationales [23] for sarcasm in comments. When an annotator labeled a data point as sarcasm, they highlighted a specific text span they believed conveyed the sarcastic nature of the comment/post. Given the subjective nature of sarcasm perception, even if just one annotator categorized a data point as sarcastic, it was officially placed into the sarcastic category.

4.2. Data Distribution

All 3199 data points were categorized into two groups: (i) toxic; and (ii) sarcasm. Within the first category, which comprises toxic (hatespeech/offensive) data, there were 1637 instances labeled as toxic, 1552 labeled as normal, and 10 labeled as undecided. The distribution of toxic data was visualized using a heatmap. Table 1 illustrates the distribution of toxic data, presenting two perspectives: (a) non-sarcasm and sarcasm data; and (b) other data and toxic data under sarcasm. In perspective (b), "other" encompasses sarcasm data not classified as toxic along with all non-sarcasm data.

Observing Figure 5, it is apparent that, while the total number of sarcasm data points was 1487, only 755 data points could be utilized under the proposed method as they fall under toxic data. Here, the last three data points from the undecided section could not be utilized as they do not conform to toxic data criteria. The heatmap depicted in the following figure illustrates the distribution of data from both perspectives.

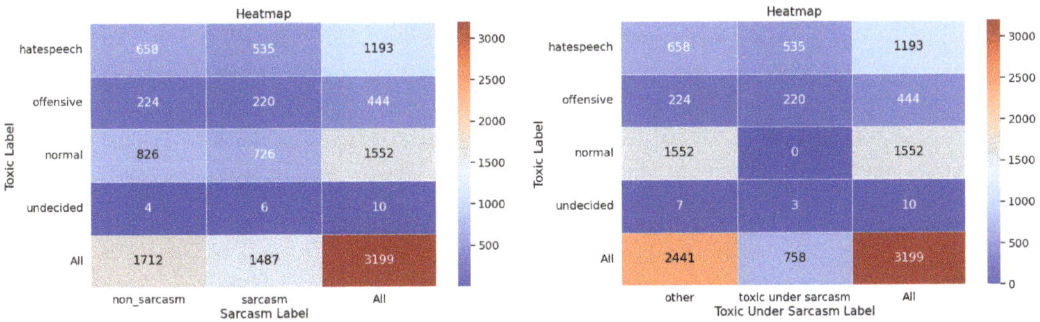

(**a**) Toxic and sarcasm data. (**b**) Toxic and toxic under sarcasm data.

Figure 5. (**a**) Heatmap chart of toxic and sarcasm data distribution. (**b**) Heatmap chart of toxic data and sarcasm data distribution, which effectively camouflaged and concealed the toxic data.

Table 1. Splitting of data into different sets.

Data Categories	Total Amount	Training	Validation	Testing
All category	3199	2599	300	300
Toxic (Hate + Offensive)	1637	1320	164	153
Sarcasm	1487	1198	145	144
Toxic under Sarcasm	755	608	79	68

Here, the table shows that data in both categories were not balanced and how they were distributed in different sets. Toxic under sarcasm shows which sarcasm data were used in the new method.

4.3. Dataset Splitting

The set of 3199 data points was divided into three subsets for training, validation, and testing. As the dataset was imbalanced, a stratified split was performed on the dataset to ensure a minimum class balance was maintained across all categories and the best performance was achieved. Table 1 shows the total amount of toxic data (hatespeech/offensive), sarcasm data, and data that are both sarcastic and toxic (toxic under sarcasm). Furthermore, the splitting of these data in different sets are shown here.

Through both criteria—(i) non-sarcasm and sarcasm data; and (ii) other data and toxic data under sarcasm—the data distribution can be observed for all subsets.

Figure 6 above illustrates the distribution of data across all subsets: training, validation, and testing. Each set exhibits two distinct criteria. Specifically, only criterion (ii) data were utilized in accordance with the proposed method. Furthermore, the graphs reveal that sarcasm comprises nearly half of the data for all labels within the first category (hatespeech, offensive, normal).

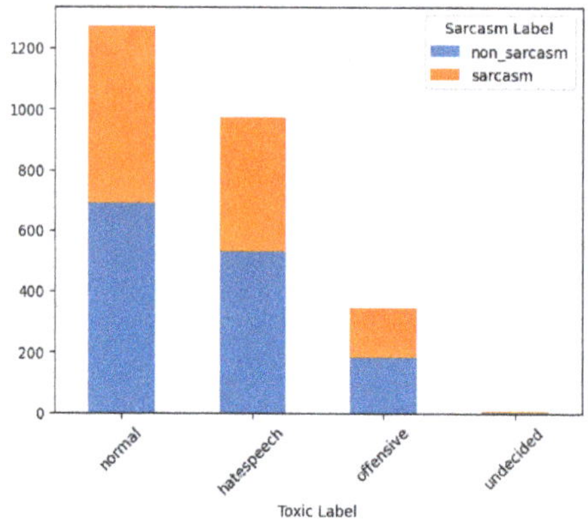

(**a**) Training data for criteria (i).

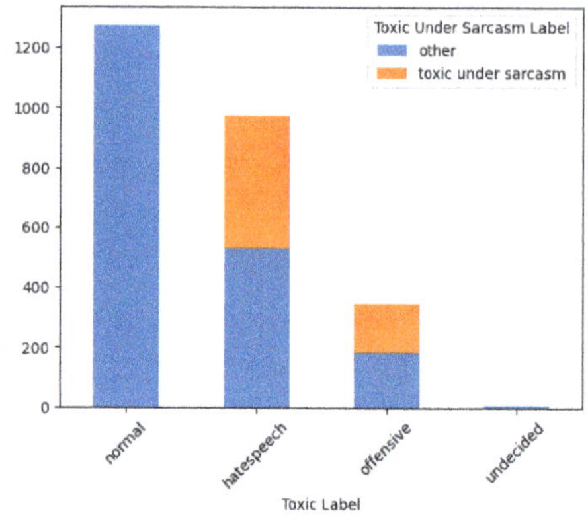

(**b**) Training data for criteria (ii).

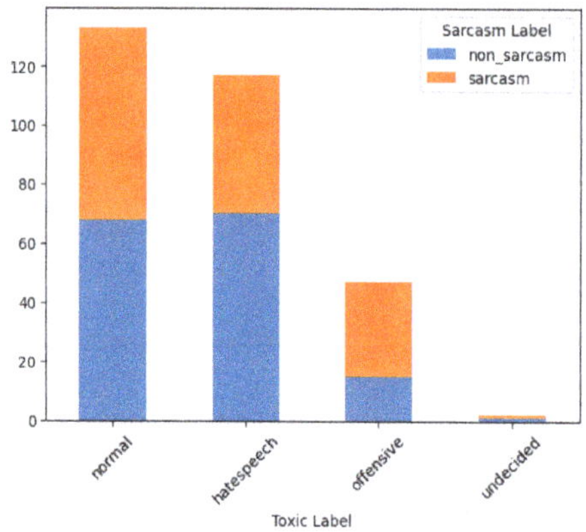

(**c**) Validation data for criteria (i).

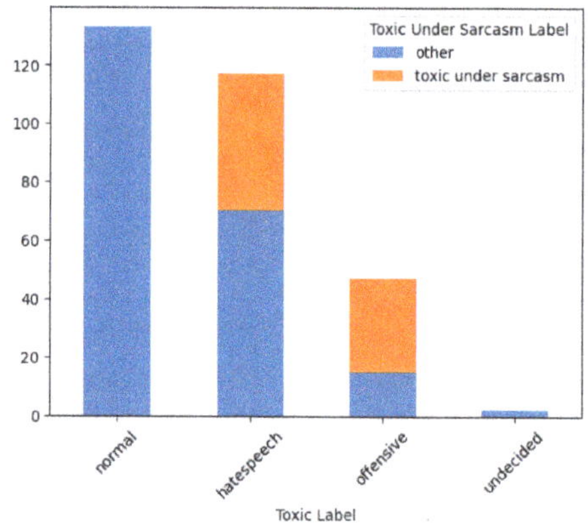

(**d**) Validation data for criteria (ii).

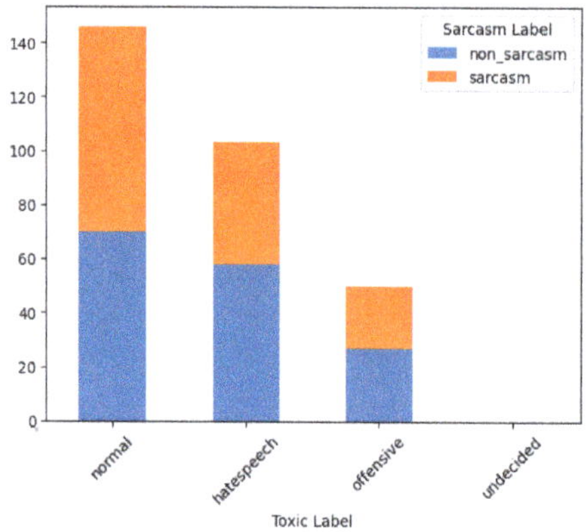

(**e**) Testing data for criteria (i).

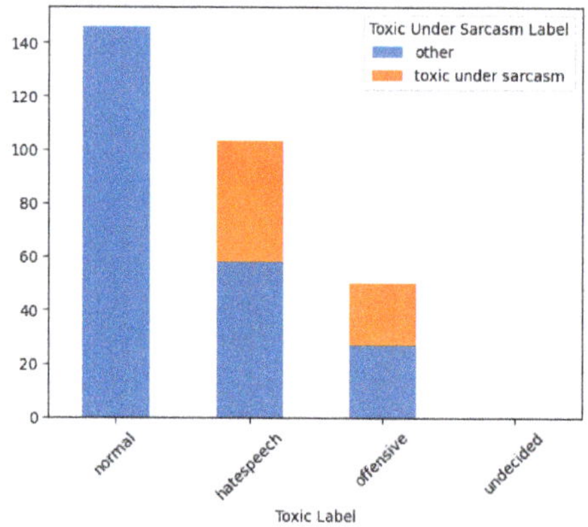

(**f**) Testing data for criteria (ii).

Figure 6. (**a**) Training data distribution for sarcasm data. (**b**) Training data distribution for toxic disguised under sarcasm data. (**c**) Validation data distribution for sarcasm data. (**d**) Validation data distribution for toxic disguised under sarcasm data. (**e**) Testing data distribution for sarcasm data. (**f**) Testing data distribution for toxic disguised under sarcasm data.

4.4. Hyperparameter Settings

In the hyperparameter tuning phase, our approach to training the BERT model involved the incorporation of specific settings. A dropout rate of 0.1 was applied after the fully connected layer, utilizing a batch size of 4 and adopting a learning rate of 2×10^{-5}. For the calculation of the ground truth attention, we opted for a configuration with six supervised heads, accompanied by an attention lambda (λ) value of 0.001. Notably, in the selection of rationale tokens, we adhered to the practice of choosing the top five tokens, aligning with the average length of annotation spans within the dataset. This careful calibration of hyperparameters contributes to the robustness and effectiveness of our model during training and attention calculation.

4.5. Metrics for Evaluation

In the quest to uncover hate speech masked within sarcasm, a range of metrics covering diverse dimensions of hate expression was considered. Taking cues from the HateXplain paper's approach to hate speech classification, emphasis was placed on two primary types of metrics: performance-based and explainability-based.

- *Performance-based metrics:* Priority was given to these metrics, with accuracy, macro F1-score, and AUROC score reported for both the baseline and proposed method in accordance with established standards. These metrics serve to assess the classifier's performance in distinguishing among the three classes: hate speech, offensive speech, and normal speech;
- *Explainability-based metrics:* We adhered to the framework outlined in the ERASER benchmark by to gauge the explainability aspect of the model. This assessment involved measuring the plausibility and faithfulness. Plausibility denotes the persuasiveness of the interpretation to humans, while faithfulness pertains to the accuracy with which it reflects the genuine reasoning process of the model [44,45].
    1. *Plausibility:* To assess plausibility, metrics for both discrete and soft selection were employed. Specifically, the Intersection-Over-Union (IOU) F1-score and token F1-score for the discrete case were reported, along with the Area Under the Precision-Recall curve (AUPRC) score for soft token selection [45]. The IOU metric was utilized for credit assignment in cases of partial matches. This metric, defined at the token-level, measures the overlap between two spans divided by the size of their union [45]. A prediction was considered a match if the overlap with any ground truth rationale exceeded 0.5. These partial matches were used to compute the IOU F1-score. Token-level precision and recall were also calculated, and these were used to derive token-level F1 scores (token F1). Additionally, to assess the plausibility of soft token scoring, the AUPRC was reported by sweeping a threshold over the token scores;
    2. *Faithfulness:* To assess faithfulness, two metrics were reported: comprehensiveness and sufficiency [45].
        - *Comprehensiveness:* This metric evaluates the extent to which the model's predictions are affected by the removal of predicted rationales. For each post x_i, a contrast example $\tilde{x}_i$ was created by removing the predicted rationales r_i from x_i. Let $m(x_i)_j$ be the original prediction probability provided by a model m for the predicted class j. Then, $m(x_i|r_i)_j$ represents the predicted probability of $\tilde{x}_i$ (i.e., x_i without r_i) by the model m for class j. Comprehensiveness was computed as $m(x_i)_j - m(x_i|r_i)_j$. A higher value of comprehensiveness suggested that the rationales significantly influenced the prediction;
        - *Sufficiency:* This metric measures the adequacy of the extracted rationales for the model to make a prediction. Sufficiency was calculated as $m(x_i)_j - m(r_i)_j$, where $m(r_i)_j$ represents the predicted probability of the rationales r_i by the model m for class j.

5. Results

In this section, the performance and explainability score of the BERT model for both the baseline and new method is shown. The tokens for the explainability calculation were chosen using the LIME method. Rationales were comprised of the top five tokens, consistent with the baseline methodology, reflecting the average length of annotation spans in the dataset.

Table 2 presents the outcomes derived from both the the baseline and proposed method. The proposed method was employed on the newly constructed proposed dataset, while the baseline approach was implemented on the HateXplain dataset [13] section of the proposed dataset. The performance metrics show an increase of 0.01 in the macro F1 score, 0.186 in the AUROC, and a slight increase in accuracy. In the explainability metrics, a significant increase was observed in two metrics (token F1 and AUPRC), from plausibility and on sufficiency from faithfulness. There is an increase of 0.04 in the token F1 and 0.17 in AUPRC. For sufficiency, it is understood that a lower value signifies better sufficiency, and a decrease of 0.08 was observed.

Table 2. Model's performance and explanability result.

Method	Performance			Explanability				
				Plausibility			Faithfulness	
	Acc. ↑	**Macro F1 ↑**	**AUROC ↑**	**IOU F1 ↑**	**Token F1 ↑**	**AUPRC ↑**	**Comp. ↑**	**Suff.**
Baseline	0.7425	0.6883	0.8264	0.0577	0.2799	0.3884	0.1789	0.1363
Proposed Method	**0.7492**	**0.6983**	**0.8450**	0.0429	**0.3232**	**0.5667**	−0.0655	**0.0546**

The symbol ↑ denotes improvement in metric values when there is an increase, whereas the symbol ↓ signifies enhancement when there is a decrease in metric values.

6. Discussion

The main results are reported in Table 2.

Performance: The results indicate a gradual enhancement in the performance metrics, with the macro F1 score exhibiting a marginal increment of 0.01 alongside improvements in other metrics when utilizing the proposed method in combination with sarcasm rationale. Figure 7 provides a detailed breakdown of the performance results via a confusion matrix.

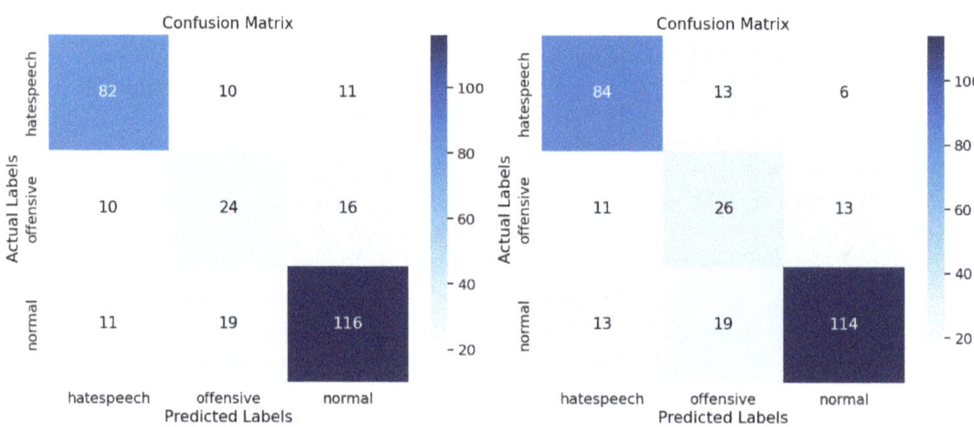

(**a**) Baseline. (**b**) Proposed method.

Figure 7. (**a**) Confusion matrix for baseline method's result. (**b**) Confusion matrix for proposed method's result.

Performance metrics from the confusion matrix are illustrated in Figure 7a,b for both the baseline and the proposed method using True Positives (TP), False Positives (FP), False Negatives (FN), and True Negatives (TN) for each class.

Baseline Performance Metrics Calculation

Precision:

$$\text{For hatespeech: } P = 0.796$$
$$\text{For offensive: } P = 0.533$$
$$\text{For normal: } P = 0.811$$

Recall:

$$\text{For hatespeech: } R = 0.796$$
$$\text{For offensive: } R = 0.480$$
$$\text{For normal: } R = 0.795$$

F1-Score:

$$\text{For hatespeech: } F1 = 0.796$$
$$\text{For offensive: } F1 = 0.506$$
$$\text{For normal } F1 = 0.803$$

Proposed Method Performance Metrics Calculation

Precision:

$$\text{For hatespeech: } P = 0.815$$
$$\text{For offensive: } P = 0.520$$
$$\text{For normal: } P = 0.814$$

Recall:

$$\text{For hatespeech: } R = 0.778$$
$$\text{For offensive: } R = 0.500$$
$$\text{For normal: } R = 0.781$$

F1-Score:

$$\text{For hatespeech: } F1 = 0.796$$
$$\text{For offensive: } F1 = 0.510$$
$$\text{For normal: } F1 = 0.797$$

The performance metrics from both the baseline and proposed method revealed a comparison in their effectiveness. The proposed method demonstrated improvements in precision for the hate speech and normal speech categories compared to the baseline. However, there was a slight decrease in precision for offensive language classification. The recall for all categories remained relatively similar between the baseline and proposed methods. Overall, the F1-scores for the hate speech and normal speech categories remained consistent, while there was a slight increase in the F1-score for offensive language classification with the proposed method.

Explainability: A significant improvement was evident in three out of five explainability metrics, encompassing both plausibility and faithfulness. Within the realm of explainability metrics, notable advancements were observed in two metrics (token F1 and AUPRC) under plausibility and sufficiency under faithfulness. The HateXplain [13] paper demonstrates that using rationale compared to not using it, alone, resulted in an increase in only one out of five explainability metrics for the BERT model, specifically in comprehensiveness within faithfulness. In contrast, our dataset and proposed method enhanced three metrics. Overall, it is evident that relying solely on a model's performance metric is inadequate. Models with slightly lower performance metrics but significantly higher scores for plausibility and faithfulness may be preferable depending on the specific task. Therefore, the presence of hate speech concealed within sarcasm could augment a model's ability to provide more interpretable outcomes.

LIME: LIME [25], or Local Interpretable Model-agnostic Explanations, enhances the interpretability of complex machine learning models, particularly for text data. It operates by generating new samples around the instance being explained through perturbation—slightly modifying the original data point to create a dataset of "synthetic" samples that are similar to the original instance. LIME then monitors how the predictions change with these modifications. Subsequently, LIME constructs a simpler, interpretable model that approximates the original model's behavior within a local region around the perturbed instance. This model identifies and highlights the words or phrases that significantly influence the model's decisions. By demonstrating how predictions shift when key text elements—termed rationales—are included or excluded, LIME helps in assessing the model's robustness and its reliance on specific features for decision-making. This methodology is crucial for applications requiring high interpretability, such as content moderation or hate speech detection, where understanding the basis of the model's decisions is essential for user trust and the validation of the model's effectiveness.

Figure 8 shows how LIME selected tokens for both baseline and proposed method along with the prediction probabilities for the toxic category, as evidenced by an example of hate speech data. For both the baseline and proposed method, the token selection was diverse, which led to distinct label predictions for each method. In Figure 8, the classification approaches of the baseline and proposed methods are compared using the BERT model, as illustrated by LIME. Figure 8a shows the baseline method utilizing BERT. Here, BERT marked tokens via LIME for a text example, demonstrating how each token influenced the classification, with the offensive category predicted with the highest probability. This highlights the baseline's sensitivity to specific trigger words, classifying them typically as offensive without deeper contextual analysis.

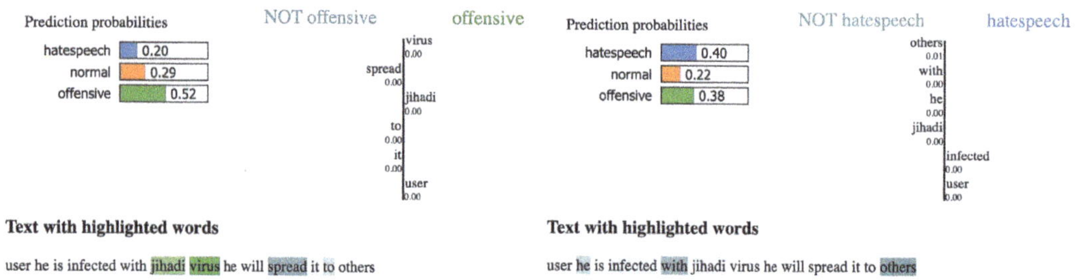

(**a**) Baseline. (**b**) Proposed method.

Figure 8. LIME-marked tokens that were deemed important for classification. (**a**) Baseline. (**b**) Proposed method.

Conversely, Figure 8b depicts the proposed method, also applying BERT with LIME to mark tokens. This method, however, assigned the highest prediction probability to the hate speech category, aligning more closely with the contextual use of the terms within the dialogue, hence providing a more accurate representation of the original label, which was hate speech. This contrast between the two figures illustrates the proposed method's enhanced ability to contextualize and accurately classify complex expressions of hate speech, leveraging the nuanced understanding capabilities of the BERT model.

The details of Figure 8 is explained in Table 3. The first two rows depict the "rationale" chosen by the annotators of the HateXplain paper [13] and our annotators, which they deemed essential for the classification task. The last two rows showcase significant tokens using LIME for the BERT model, encompassing both the baseline and proposed method. From Table 3, the details can be observed for the baseline ground truth attention calculation; therein, even though the BERT model marked the same "rationale" as the HateXplain human annotators, it assigned the wrong label (offensive speech—OF). But, for the proposed ground truth attention calculation, the BERT model marked almost the same "rationale" as that of our annotators and assigned the right label (hate speech—HS).

Table 3. Example of the rationales predicted by baseline and proposed method compared to human annotators.

Iodel	Text	Label
ateXplain Annotator	user he is infected with jihadi virus he will spread it to others	HS
ur Annotator	user he is infected with jihadi virus he will spread it to others	SARC
aseline	user he is infected with jihadi virus he will spread it to others	OF
roposed Method	user he is infected with jihadi virus he will spread it to others	HS

The orange highlight marks what the HateXplain [13] annotators found important for the prediction. The green highlight marks what our annotators found important for the prediction. The underlined words/tokens were identified by the model as important using LIME [25], and the lime highlight marks the highest probability tokens from this set for both the baseline and proposed method. (OF—offensive speech; HS—hatespeech; SARC—sarcasm).

7. Limitations

Several limitations are inherent in our work. Firstly, the absence of external context poses a significant challenge. Relying solely on the published dataset resulted in a lack of contextual information for each post, thereby complicating the annotation process for annotators. Providing additional context could facilitate a more accurate assignment of posts as sarcastic or non-sarcastic. Additionally, our work is limited to the English language, neglecting potential insights from other languages.

8. Conclusions and Future Work

This study introduces a novel dataset derived from the established HateXplain dataset, comprising 3199 posts extracted from Gab and Twitter. In the original HateXplain dataset, each post is annotated with labels such as normal, hate, or offensive, along with target communities (e.g., black, Muslim, LGBTQ+) and rationales marked by annotators. The data from HateXplain were re-labeled based on sarcasm by our annotators, with rationales selected based on their identification of sarcastic content. Additionally, a new methodology is proposed for calculating ground truth attention when the data exhibit both toxic (hate/offensive) content and sarcasm, aiming to enhance the decision-making process of models. This approach was tested on the BERT model, which incorporates sarcasm along with hate/offensive data to improve hate speech detection, particularly for toxic comments disguised within sarcasm. The results demonstrate that utilizing sarcasm to identify concealed toxic content led to a slight improvement in the performance metrics, while also providing plausible and faithful rationales that enhanced the model's decision-making capabilities.

Looking ahead, the plan is to explore the application of other Large Language Models (LLMs) to our methodology. Given the complexity and resource requirements of LLMs, this extension was not feasible within the current study's time frame. Future work will focus on comparing the efficacy and generalizability of our approach using a range of LLMs. This step is essential for verifying our model's robustness across various architectures and settings, providing deeper insights into its adaptability and performance. We also aim to incorporate context information into data annotation and utilize it in our model training process.

Author Contributions: Conceptualization, M.B.M.; methodology, M.B.M.; software, M.B.M.; validation, M.B.M.; formal analysis, M.B.M.; investigation, M.B.M.; resources, M.B.M.; data curation, M.B.M.; writing—original draft preparation, M.B.M., with suggestions from T.T., M.N. (Masafumi Nishida) and M.N. (Masafumi Nishimura); writing—review and editing, M.B.M., T.T., M.N. (Masafumi Nishida) and M.N. (Masafumi Nishimura); visualization, M.B.M.; supervision, T.T., M.N. (Masafumi Nishida) and M.N. (Masafumi Nishimura); project administration, M.B.M. All authors have read and agreed to the published version of the manuscript.

Funding: This research received no external funding.

Institutional Review Board Statement: Not applicable.

Informed Consent Statement: Not applicable.

Data Availability Statement: The data presented in this study are not publicly available due to privacy or ethical restrictions.

Conflicts of Interest: The authors declare no conflict of interest.

Appendix A. Examples of LIME

Figure A1 presents additional examples of how LIME highlights influential tokens for both the baseline and proposed methods, along with their prediction probabilities for hate speech data. Subfigures (a) and (b) show LIME's analysis for the same data point using the baseline and proposed methods, respectively. Similarly, subfigures (c) and (d) provide another comparative analysis for a different data point, following the same methodological contrast. These examples clearly demonstrate how token selection varies between the baseline and proposed methods, ultimately leading to different label predictions for each approach. This comparative visualization helps in understanding the impact of methodological changes on the model's interpretative outputs and decision-making process.

Hatespeech Data Example 1:

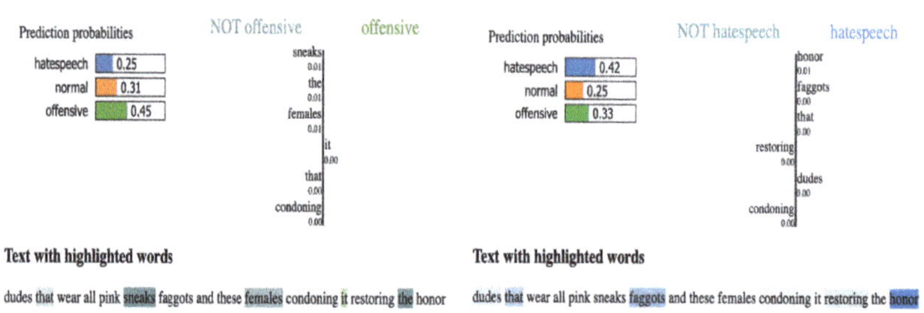

(**a**) Baseline. (**b**) Proposed method.

Hatespeech Data Example 2:

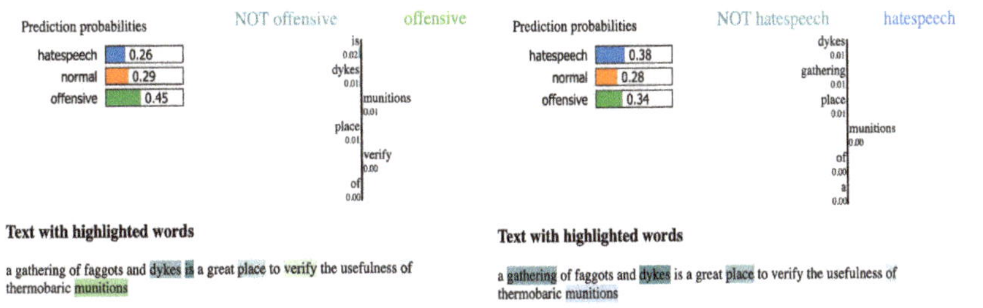

(**c**) Baseline. (**d**) Proposed method.

Figure A1. LIME-marked tokens that were deemed important for classification. (**a**) Baseline [Example 1]. (**b**) Proposed method [Example 1]. (**c**) Baseline [Example 2]. (**d**) Proposed method [Example 2].

ferences

Bozhidarova, M.; Chang, J.; Ale-rasool, A.; Liu, Y.; Ma, C.; Bertozzi, A.L.; Brantingham, P.J.; Lin, J.; Krishnagopal, S. Hate speech and hate crimes: A data-driven study of evolving discourse around marginalized groups. *arXiv* **2023**, arXiv:2311.11163.

Williams, M.L.; Burnap, P.; Javed, A.; Liu, H.; Ozalp, S. Hate in the machine: Anti-Black and anti-Muslim social media posts as predictors of offline racially and religiously aggravated crime. *Br. J. Criminol.* **2020**, *60*, 93–117. [CrossRef]

Gámez-Guadix, M.; Wachs, S.; Wright, M. "Haters back off!" psychometric properties of the coping with cyberhate questionnaire and relationship with well-being in Spanish adolescents. *Psicothema* **2020**, *32*, 567–574. [CrossRef] [PubMed]

Wachs, S.; Krause, N.; Wright, M.F.; Gámez-Guadix, M. Effects of the Prevention Program "HateLess. Together against Hatred" on Adolescents' Empathy, Self-efficacy, and Countering Hate Speech. *J. Youth Adolesc.* **2023**, *52*, 1115–1128. [CrossRef] [PubMed]

Saha, K.; Weber, I.; De Choudhury, M. A Social Media Based Examination of the Effects of Counseling Recommendations After Student Deaths on College Campuses. In Proceedings of the International AAAI Conference on Web and Social Media, Palo Alto, CA, USA, 25–28 June 2018; pp. 320–329.

Saha, K.; Chandrasekharan, E.; De Choudhury, M. Prevalence and Psychological Effects of Hateful Speech in Online College Communities. In Proceedings of the 10th ACM Conference on Web Science, Boston, MA, USA, 30 June–3 July 2019; pp. 255–264. [CrossRef]

Cahill, M.; Migacheva, K.; Taylor, J.; Williams, M.; Burnap, P.; Javed, A.; Liu, H.; Lu, H.; Sutherland, A. *Understanding Online Hate Speech as a Motivator and Predictor of Hate Crime, Los Angeles, California, 2017–2018*; ICPSR: Ann Arbor, MI, USA, 2021. [CrossRef]

de Gibert, O.; Perez, N.; García-Pablos, A.; Cuadros, M. Hate Speech Dataset from a White Supremacy Forum. In Proceedings of the 2nd Workshop on Abusive Language Online (ALW2): Association for Computational Linguistics, Brussels, Belgium, 31 October 2018; pp. 11–20.

Sanguinetti, M.; Poletto, F.; Bosco, C.; Patti, V.; Stranisci, M. An Italian Twitter Corpus of Hate Speech against Immigrants. In Proceedings of the Eleventh International Conference on Language Resources and Evaluation (LREC 2018), Miyazaki, Japan, 7–12 May 2018; European Language Resources Association (ELRA): Reykjavik, Iceland, 2018. Available online: https://aclanthology.org/L18-1443 (accessed on 7 April 2024).

Qian, J.; ElSherief, M.; Belding, E.M.; Wang, W.Y. Learning to Decipher Hate Symbols. In Proceedings of the 2019 Conference of the North American Chapter of the Association for Computational Linguistics: Human Language Technologies, Minneapolis, MN, USA, 4 June 2019; Association for Computational Linguistics: Stroudsburg, PA, USA, 2019; pp. 3006–3015.

Ousidhoum, N.; Lin, Z.; Zhang, H.; Song, Y.; Yeung, D.-Y. Multilingual and Multi-Aspect Hate Speech Analysis. In Proceedings of the 2019 Conference on Empirical Methods in Natural Language Processing and the 9th International Joint Conference on Natural Language Processing (EMNLP-IJCNLP), Hong Kong, China, 3–7 November 2019; Association for Computational Linguistics: Stroudsburg, PA, USA, 2019; pp. 4667–4676.

Albanyan, A.; Blanco, E. Pinpointing Fine-Grained Relationships between Hateful Tweets and Replies. In Proceedings of the AAAI Conference on Artificial Intelligence, Vancouver, BC, Canada, 28 February–1 March 2022; Volume 36, pp. 10418–10426. [CrossRef]

Mathew, B.; Saha, P.; Yimam, S.M.; Beimann, C.; Mukherjee, A. HateXplain: A Benchmark Dataset for Explainable Hate Speech Detection. In Proceedings of the AAAI Conference on Artificial Intelligence, Virtually, 2–9 February 2021; Volume 35, pp. 14867–14875. [CrossRef]

Zhang, Z.; Robinson, D.; Tepper, J.A. Detecting Hate Speech on Twitter Using a Convolution-GRU Based Deep Neural Network. In Proceedings of the Semantic Web—15th International Conference, Heraklion, Crete, Greece, 3–7 June 2018; pp. 745–760.

Mishra, P.; Del Tredici, M.; Yannakoudakis, H.; Shutova, E. Author profiling for abuse detection. In Proceedings of the 27th International Conference on Computational Linguistics, Santa Fe, NM, USA, 20–26 August 2018; Association for Computational Linguistics: Stroudsburg, PA, USA, 2018; pp. 1088–1098.

16. Qian, J.; ElSherief, M.; Belding, E.M.; Wang, W.Y. Hierarchical CVAE for Fine-Grained Hate Speech Classification. In Proceedin of the 2018 Conference on Empirical Methods in Natural Language Processing, Brussels, Belgium, 31 October–4 November 20 Association for Computational Linguistics: Stroudsburg, PA, USA, 2018; pp. 3550–3559.
17. Qian, J.; ElSherief, M.; Belding, E.M.; Wang, W.Y. Leveraging Intra-User and Inter-User Representation Learning for Automat Hate Speech Detection. In Proceedings of the 2018 Conference of the North American Chapter of the Association for Comp tational Linguistics: Human Language Technologies, New Orleans, LA, USA, 1–6 June 2018; Association for Computatior Linguistics: Stroudsburg, PA, USA, 2018; pp. 118–123.
18. Gröndahl, T.; Pajola, L.; Juuti, M.; Conti, M.; Asokan, N. All You Need is: Evading Hate Speech Detection. In Proceedings of t 11th ACM Workshop on Artificial Intelligence and Security, Toronto, ON, Canada, 15–19 October 2018; Association or Computi Machinery: New York, NY, USA, 2018; pp. 2–12.
19. Arango, A.; Pérez, J.; Poblete, B. Hate Speech Detection is Not as Easy as You May Think: A Closer Look at Model Validation. Proceedings of the 42nd International ACM SIGIR Conference on Research and Development in Information Retrieval, Par France, 21–25 July 2019; Association for Computing Machinery: New York, NY, USA, 2019; pp. 45–54.
20. Sap, M.; Card, D.; Gabriel, S.; Choi, Y.; Smith, N.A. The Risk of Racial Bias in Hate Speech Detection. In Proceedings the 57th Conference of the Association for Computational Linguistics, Florence, Italy, 28 July–2 August 2019; Association Computational Linguistics: Stroudsburg, PA, USA, 2019; pp. 1668–1678.
21. Davidson, T.; Bhattacharya, D.; Weber, I. Racial Bias in Hate Speech and Abusive Language Detection Datasets. In Proceedings the Third Workshop on Abusive Language Online, Florence, Italy, 1 August 2019; Association for Computational Linguisti Stroudsburg, PA, USA, 2019; pp. 25–35.
22. Goodfellow, I.; Bengio, Y.; Courville, A. *Deep Learning*; MIT Press: Cambridge, MA, USA, 2016.
23. Zaidan, O.; Eisner, J.; Piatko, C. *Using "Annotaor Rationales" to improve Machine Learning for Text Categorization*; NAACL: Rochest NY, USA, 2007; pp. 260–267.
24. Pasa, T.A.; Nuriadi; Lail, H. An Analysis of Sarcasm on Hate Speech Utterances on Just Jared Instagram Account. *J. Engl. Ed Forum (JEEF)* **2021**, *1*, 10–19.
25. Ribeiro, M.T.; Singh, S.; Guestrin, C. "Why Should I Trust You?": Explaining the Predictions of Any Classifier. In Proceedings the 22nd KDD, New York, NY, USA, 11 April 2016; pp. 1135–1144.
26. Devlin, J.; Chang, M.; Lee, K.; Toutanova, K. BERT: Pre-training of Deep Bidirectional Transformers for Language Understandir In Proceedings of the 2019 Conference of the North American Chapter of the Association for Computational Linguistics: Hum Language Technologies, Minneapolis, MN, USA, 2–7 June 2019; Volume 1 (Long and Short Papers), pp. 4171–4186.
27. Wachs, S.; Castellanos, M.; Wettstein, A.; Bilz, L.; Gámez-Guadix, M. Associations Between Classroom Climate, Empatl Self-Efficacy, and Countering Hate Speech Among Adolescents: A Multilevel Mediation Analysis. *J. Interpers. Violence* **2022**, 5067–5091. [CrossRef] [PubMed]
28. Bronfenbrenner, U. *The Ecology of Human Development: Experiments by Nature and Design*; Harvard University Press: Cambrid MA, USA, 1979.
29. Bandura, A. *Social Learning Theory*; General Learning Press: New York, NY, USA, 1977.
30. Kansok-Dusche, J.; Ballaschk, C.; Krause, N.; Zeißig, A.; Seemann-Herz, L.; Wachs, S.; Bilz, L. A systematic review on hate spee among children and adolescents: Definitions, prevalence, and overlap with related phenomena. *Trauma Violence Abus.* **2022**, 2598–2615. [CrossRef] [PubMed]
31. Ajzen, I. The theory of planned behavior. *Organ. Behav. Hum. Decis. Process.* **1991**, *50*, 179–211. [CrossRef]
32. Bandura, A.; Barbaranelli, C.; Caprara, G.V.; Pastorelli, C. Mechanisms of moral disengagement in the exercise of moral agency. *Personal. Soc. Psychol.* **1996**, *71*, 364–374. [CrossRef]
33. Olteanu, A.; Castillo, C.; Boy, J.; Varshney, K.R. The Effect of Extremist Violence on Hateful Speech Online. In Proceedings of t 12th ICWSM, Stanford, CA, USA, 25–28 June 2018; pp. 221–230.
34. Davidson, T.; Warmsley, D.; Macy, M.W.; Weber, I. Automated Hate Speech Detection and the Problem of Offensive Language. Proceedings of the Eleventh International Conference on Web and Social Media, Montréal, QC, Canada, 15–18 May 2017; AA Press: Menlo Park, CA, USA, 2017; pp. 512–515.
35. Vigna, F.D.; Cimino, A.; Dell'Orletta, F.; Petrocchi, M.; Tesconi, M. Hate Me, Hate Me Not: Hate Speech Detection on Facebook. Proceedings of the First Italian Conference on Cybersecurity, Venice, Italy, 17–20 January 2017; Volume 1816, pp. 86–95.
36. Founta, A.; Djouvas, C.; Chatzakou, D.; Leontiadis, I.; Blackburn, J.; Stringhini, G.; Vakali, A.; Sirivianos, M.; Kourtellis, N. Lar Scale Crowdsourcing and Characterization of Twitter Abusive Behavior. In Proceedings of the Twelfth International Conferen on Web and Social Media, Stanford, CA, USA, 25–28 June 2018; AAAI Press: Menlo Park, CA, USA, 2018; pp. 491–500.
37. Douglass, S.; Mirpuri, S.; English, D.; Yip, T. "They were just making jokes": Ethnic/racial teasing and discrimination amor adolescents. *Cult. Divers. Ethn. Minor. Psychol.* **2016**, *22*, 69–82. [CrossRef] [PubMed]
38. Hosseinmardi, H.; Mattson, S.A.; Rafiq, R.I.; Han, R.O.; Lv, Q.; Mishra, S. Detection of Cyberbullying Incidents on the Instagra Social Network. *arXiv* **2015**, arXiv:1503.03909.
39. Razali, M.S.; Halin, A.A.; Ye, L.; Doraisamy, S.; Norowi, N.M. Sarcasm Detection Using Deep Learning with Contextual Featur *IEEE Access* **2021**, *9*, 68609–68618. [CrossRef]
40. Ali, R.; Farhat, T.; Abdullah, S.; Akram, S.; Alhajlah, M.; Mahmood, A.; Iqbal, M.A. Deep Learning for Sarcasm Identification News Headlines. *Appl. Sci.* **2023**, *13*, 5586. [CrossRef]

Bharti, S.K.; Gupta, R.K.; Shukla, P.K.; Hatamleh, W.A.; Tarazi, H.; Nuagah, S.J. Multimodal Sarcasm Detection: A Deep Learning Approach. *Wirel. Commun. Mob. Comput.* **2022**, *2022*, 1653696. [CrossRef]
Dixon, L.; Li, J.; Sorensen, J.; Thain, N.; Vasserman, L. Measuring and Mitigating Unintended Bias in Text Classification. In Proceedings of the 2018 AAAI/ACM Conference on AI, Ethics, and Society, New Orleans, LA, USA, 2–3 February 2018; Association for Computing Machinery: New York, NY, USA, 2018; pp. 67–73.
Schuster, M.; Paliwal, K.K. Bidirectional recurrent neural networks. *IEEE Trans. Signal Process.* **1997**, *45*, 2673–2681. [CrossRef]
Jacovi, A.; Goldberg, Y. Towards Faithfully Interpretable NLP Systems: How Should We Define and Evaluate Faithfulness? In Proceedings of the 58th Annual Meeting of the Association for Computational Linguistics, Online, 5–10 July 2020; Association for Computational Linguistics: Stroudsburg, PA, USA, 2020; pp. 4198–4205.
DeYoung, J.; Jain, S.; Rajani, N.F.; Lehman, E.; Xiong, C.; Socher, R.; Wallace, B.C. ERASER: A Benchmark to Evaluate Rationalized NLP Models. In Proceedings of the 58th Annual Meeting of the Association for Computational Linguistics, Online, 5–10 July 2020; Association for Computational Linguistics: Stroudsburg, PA, USA, 2020; pp. 4443–4458.

applied sciences

MDPI

Article

A Survey of Adversarial Attacks: An Open Issue for Deep Learning Sentiment Analysis Models

Monserrat Vázquez-Hernández [1], Luis Alberto Morales-Rosales [2,*], Ignacio Algredo-Badillo [1,*], Sofía Isabel Fernández-Gregorio [3], Héctor Rodríguez-Rangel [4] and María-Luisa Córdoba-Tlaxcalteco [3]

1 Department of Computer Science, CONACYT-National Institute for Astrophysics, Optics and Electronics, Luis Enrique Erro #1, Sta María Tonanzintla, Puebla 72840, Puebla, Mexico; mvazquez@inaoe.mx

2 Facultad de Ingeniería Civil, CONACYT-Universidad Michoacana de San Nicolás de Hidalgo, C. de Santiago Tapia 403, Centro, Morelia 58000, Michoacan, Mexico

3 Facultad de Estadística e Informática, Univesidad Veracruzana, Av. Xalapa, Obrero Campesina, Xalapa 91020, Veracruz, Mexico; zs21000291@estudiantes.uv.mx (S.I.F.-G.); cmarluit@gmail.com (M.-L.C.-T.)

4 Tecnológico Nacional de México, Instituto Tecnológico de Culiacán, Juan de Dios Batiz No. 310pte., Culiacán 80220, Sinaloa, Mexico; hector.rr@culiacan.tecnm.mx

* Correspondence: lamorales@conacyt.mx (L.A.M.-R.); algredobadillo@inaoep.mx (I.A.-B.)

Abstract: In recent years, the use of deep learning models for deploying sentiment analysis systems has become a widespread topic due to their processing capacity and superior results on large volumes of information. However, after several years' research, previous works have demonstrated that deep learning models are vulnerable to strategically modified inputs called *adversarial examples*. Adversarial examples are generated by performing perturbations on data input that are imperceptible to humans but that can fool deep learning models' understanding of the inputs and lead to false predictions being generated. In this work, we collect, select, summarize, discuss, and comprehensively analyze research works to generate textual adversarial examples. There are already a number of reviews in the existing literature concerning attacks on deep learning models for text applications; in contrast to previous works, however, we review works mainly oriented to sentiment analysis tasks. Further, we cover the related information concerning generation of adversarial examples to make this work self-contained. Finally, we draw on the reviewed literature to discuss adversarial example design in the context of sentiment analysis tasks.

Keywords: adversarial attacks; sentiment analysis; deep learning; vulnerabilities

1. Introduction

User opinions allow researchers to identify the experience, either positive or negative, that actual consumers have had with a product, service, or topic of interest [1]. The opinions expressed by actual consumers play an influential role in the decision-making of new consumers and organizations. For example, potential consumers can take a look at the quality of a product or service through users' opinions and decide whether or not to select it. In the case of organizations, opinions allow them to determine necessary improvements to implement in their products or services to enhance their consumers' experience [2]. Lately, the volume of users' opinions has increased considerably, mainly due to the accessibility, anonymity, and free expression that digital media offer to users, becoming a comfortable space for users to express their opinions or feedback. Due to this large volume of information, tools are needed to facilitate simplified opinion analysis. In this context, sentiment analysis systems are an important tool for analyzing and providing summarized information concerning users' opinions to assist both users and organizations in the decision-making process.

Sentiment analysis (SA) is a Natural Language Processing (NLP) task that uses text analysis and machine-learning techniques to automatically extract and process users' opinions [3]. The purpose of sentiment analysis systems is to provide summarized information and assist potential users and organizations in evaluating their selections; popular sentiment analysis applications include social media monitoring, customer support management, and analyzing customer feedback, among others. Sentiment analysis has been predominantly applied to text analysis (analysis of user opinions). However, SA can be applied to different modalities as well, such as visual, speech, and text [4]. In recent years, multimodal sentiment analysis models have been proposed that combine different modalities to obtain more accurate results [5]. In this paper, we focus on sentiment analysis considering text modality.

In recent years, deep learning (DL) models have become a popular research topic for better handling large volumes of information on sentiment analysis [6]. Deep learning models are potent algorithms that achieve excellent performance, allowing previous results to be outperformed in different areas. In sentiment analysis systems, the aim of implementing deep learning models is to improve the precision of results obtained with traditional machine learning algorithms and raise the confidence of users; however, this does not always turn out to be true. Figure 1 presents the general operation of a sentiment analysis model.

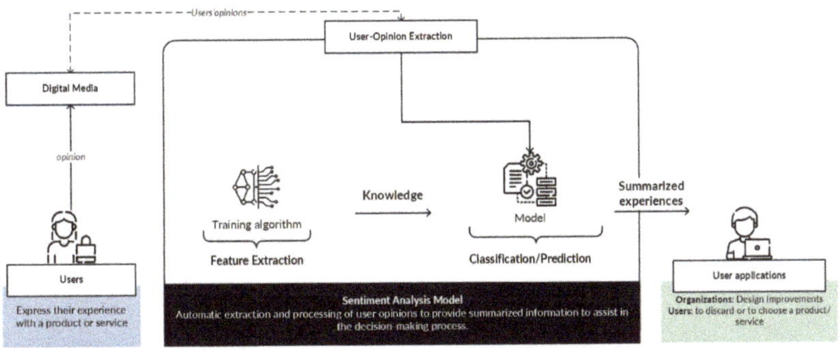

Figure 1. General operation of a deep learning-based sentiment analysis model.

After several years of research, it has been demonstrated both in theory and practice that DL models can be fooled with high probability by small modifications to the input data, causing incorrect results [7,8]. Research such as [7,8] has evaluated the robustness of deep learning models in face of small changes to the input data. Szegedy et al. [7] evaluated state-of-the-art deep neuronal network (DNN) models for image classification by making minor pixel-level modifications to inputs, identifying that DNN models can be fooled with a high probability by modified inputs causing classification errors even though people could not identify any change. The resulting images obtained after performing modifications called *adversarial examples*. Subsequently, this name has been applied to denote intentional modifications made to input data to fool models.

Based on the idea of adversarial examples, Jia and Liang [9] were the first to consider designing adversarial examples to fool DNN models for text applications (named textual deep neuronal networks). They generated short texts using words included in the training set of the neuronal network model. Then, the texts were added to the end of the original input data to generate the adversarial examples (also denominated adversarial texts), and it was observed that adversarial examples could also fool textual deep neuronal networks. Figure 2 shows an adversarial example designed in [9].

Led by [7], different approaches have been proposed that aim to: (1) design effective imperceptible modifications to confuse the DL models' understanding of inputs and cause incorrect results; (2) evaluate DL models against modified inputs; (3) propose defenses for potential modifications to input data; and (4) improve the robustness of DL models by adding new knowledge and capabilities via adversarial examples [10].

Since their introduction, adversarial examples have pointed to the limitations of deep learning models in correctly classifying modified inputs [11], which leads to the need to understand their current vulnerabilities (and continuously explore new vulnerabilities) when facing adversarial examples. This can help to propose defenses that effectively guarantee confidence in deep learning models' results. Due to the importance of sentiment analysis in the decision-making process, we survey adversarial attacks on textual deep neuronal networks in this work, specifically focusing on sentiment analysis. In this work, we aim to summarize efforts that expose the vulnerabilities presented by deep neuronal sentiment analysis models when facing adversarial examples. Considering the importance of sentiment analysis and the impact of adversarial examples, there is a need for this kind of work to provide successive researchers with an overview of extant efforts.

Article: Super Bowl 50
Paragraph: *"Peyton Manning became the first quarterback ever to lead two different teams to multiple Super Bowls. He is also the oldest quarterback ever to play in a Super Bowl at age 39. The past record was held by John Elway, who led the Broncos to victory in Super Bowl XXXIII at age 38 and is currently Denver's Executive Vice President of Football Operations and General Manager. Quarterback Jeff Dean had jersey number 37 in Champ Bowl XXXIV."*
Question: *"What is the name of the quarterback who was 38 in Super Bowl XXXIII?"*
Original Prediction: John Elway
Prediction under adversary: Jeff Dean

Figure 2. Adversarial example from [9]. The assembly model originally obtains the correct answer, but is fooled by the insertion of an adversarial text (in blue).

Related surveys and differences with this survey. Reviews of adversarial examples attacking deep learning models for text applications already exist in the literature, such as [10,12–14]; however, to the best of our knowledge, no comprehensive review has collected and summarized the efforts in this research direction while specifically focusing on sentiment analysis. This study attempts to cover this gap via three central questions: (1) How do adversarial attack methods fool sentiment analysis models? (2) What proposals exist to defend against these attacks? and (3) What are the open challenges and directions of text adversarial attacks within sentiment analysis?

Paper selection methodology. We performed a literature review on three primary data sources related to computer science and data security: IEEE, ScienceDirect, and SpringerLink. First, keywords related to the central topic of this paper, namely, adversarial examples, were defined: (Adversarial, Examples, and Attack). Subsequently, keywords to delimit the research to sentiment analysis and text applications were added: (Text, Sentiment Analysis (SA), and Sentiment). Through the set of keywords defined above (Adversarial, Examples, Attack, Text, SA, Sentiment), the following query string was integrated: (Adversarial Attacks in Sentiment Analysis, Adversarial Attacks in Text). Considering that the research topic for text applications has emerged only recently, we limited the search to papers published from 2017 to January of 2024. The executed query string was as follows: *("adversarial attack" or "adversarial texts") and ("text" or "sentiment" or "sentiment analysis").*

The inclusion and exclusion criteria for filtering and selecting papers were formally defined as follows:

- The inclusion criteria considered the following elements:
    1. The paper's contributions focus on the design of adversarial attack or defense mechanisms, particularly for the sentiment analysis task.
    2. Priority was given to papers published in the most recognized conferences on Natural Language Processing and Artificial Intelligence (ACL: Annual Meeting of the Association for Computational Linguistics; COLING: International Conference on Computational Linguistics; EMNLP: Empirical Methods in Natural Language Processing; IJCAI: International Joint Conference on Artificial Intelligence), although this was not a limitation.

- On the other hand, the following exclusion criteria were defined:
    1. Papers unrelated to text applications.
    2. The content and contributions of the papers were not related to the research subject, i.e., adversarial attacks and their application in sentiment analysis.
    3. Papers unrelated to sentiment analysis with deep neural network approaches.
    4. The method presented in the paper was largely derived from other work.

Through the search engines the selected information sources, the query string was executed for all metadata in the advanced search section. Figure 3 depicts the process of extracting and filtering works proposing adversarial attack designs for the study task. Figure 3a illustrates the amount of articles retrieved in the data extraction stage by executing the query string. We obtained a total of 1040 articles related to adversarial attacks for text applications, including articles for sentiment analysis. First, the retrieved works were manually filtered by checking the year of publication, title, and abstract to exclude those that did not align with the research objectives of this work. As a result, the number of retrieved works was reduced to 51 (refer to Figure 3b). As a final step, the inclusion and exclusion criteria were applied, resulting in 33 papers being selected for the initial review.

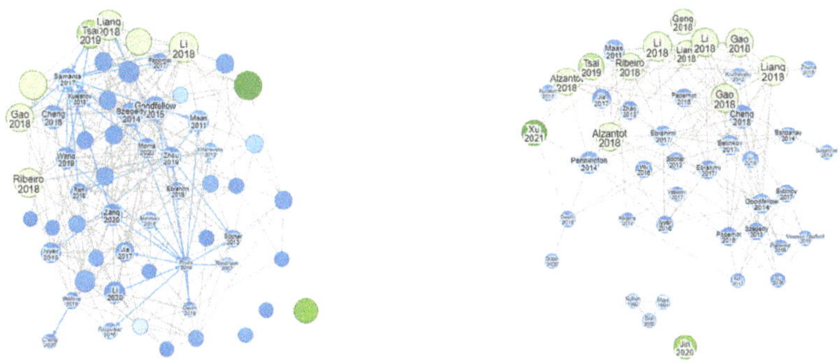

(**a**) (**b**)

Figure 3. Paper selection methodology. After applying the query string, a total of 1040 papers related to adversarial attacks for text applications and sentiment analysis were retrieved in the data extraction stage. These papers were filtered by reviewing the year, title, and abstract, then applying the inclusion and exclusion criteria after which the total number of papers for initial review was reduced to 33. (**a**) Papers retrieved during the data extraction stage. A total of 1040 works were obtained for text applications, including works addressing sentiment analysis attack. The green circles highlight the primary works from which others were derived according to our query string. (**b**) The papers obtained during data extraction were filtered by checking the year, title, and abstract to validate the period and determine whether they corresponded to the topics of adversarial attacks and sentiment analysis. A total of 51 papers remained after filtering. Application of the inclusion and exclusion criteria further reduced the total number of papers for initial review to 33.

Contributions of this survey. The objective of conducting this survey is to provide a comprehensive review of research efforts on adversarial example generation, specifically for deep neural networks used in sentiment analysis. In order to comprehend the importance of sentiment analysis in decision-making and knowing the scope that adversarial examples have on the results of deep learning models, it is necessary to understand the behavior of adversarial attacks with the aim of proposing defenses against them. We pursue this survey to serve researchers and practitioners interested in designing, attacking, and defending sentiment analysis deep neuronal networks. Although this work includes essential information concerning preliminary knowledge related to adversarial attacks, we expect that readers will have basic knowledge of sentiment analysis and deep neural network architectures, which are not the focus of this article. To summarize, the main contributions of this survey are:

- We collect, select, review, summarize, and discuss adversarial attacks, especially those suited to sentiment analysis models, with the objective of providing an information framework for current adversarial attacks methods that expose vulnerabilities of sentiment analysis models. This is the first survey to mainly focus on adversarial attacks for sentiment analysis. The aim is to assist researchers in addressing new vulnerabilities and developing defense methods to mitigate the negative consequences that can result from incorrect results produced by sentiment analysis models.
- We provide essential information concerning preliminary knowledge related to adversarial attacks, which allows this work to be self-contained.
- We draw on the reviewed literature to discuss open issues in adversarial example design for sentiment analysis deep neuronal network models, and identify possible new research directions concerning defenses for sentiment analysis models based on the issues and challenges identified during this review.

The rest of this document is organized as follows. Section 2 presents concepts related to the design of adversarial attacks for deep learning models in the sentiment analysis task, which allows for a better understanding of the primary state-of-the-art works regarding adversarial attacks presented in Section 3. The main works proposed for the sentiment analysis task involving defense against adversarial examples are presented in Section 4. Finally, a discussion of the current challenges in adversarial example design are described in Sections 5 and 6 presents the conclusions of this work.

2. Adversarial Examples and Deep Learning Models

Before introducing the reviewed works concerning adversarial examples and sentiment analysis models, we introduce some preliminary knowledge related to adversarial attacks and their application with regard to textual deep learning models, with the objective of providing an overview of how adversarial examples work in these types of applications.

2.1. Definitions

The principal definitions to consider when adversarial examples are studied are the following:

- **Deep Neuronal Network (DNN).** A deep learning model is a set of machine learning algorithms that attempts to model high-level abstractions using neural network architectures that support multiple and iterative nonlinear transformations of data expressed in matrix or tensor form [15].
- **Perturbation.** The perturbations η are small modifications intentionally made to input data in order to confuse the deep learning models.
- **Adversarial Example.** An adversarial example is a modified input created via a perturbation η of the input x of a deep learning model. The perturbation η is the minimal worst-case modification to input data that succeeds in confusing the model in its understanding and, as a consequence, in its classification. A robust model should continue to classify the correct class y to x', while a victim model will have a high probability of incorrectly classifying x'. Equation (1) presents the formalization of x':

$$\begin{gathered} f(x) = y,\ x \in X \\ x' = x + \eta,\ f(x') \neq y \\ or f(x') = y',\ y' \neq y \end{gathered} \tag{1}$$

where n is the worst-case perturbation. The goal of the adversarial examples is to cause the label to deviate to an incorrect label $f(x') \neq y$ or to a specific label $f(x') = y'$. Modifications to create adversarial examples should be as small as possible while being capable of fooling DL models without changing human perception.

2.2. Adversarial Examples for Text Applications

In recent years, the design of adversarial examples has attracted research interest with the aim of identifying the vulnerabilities of DNN models against modified inputs and thereby proposing defense mechanisms that guarantee the safety of the results. The original idea of adversarial examples was explained by Szegedy et al. [7] when evaluating the robustness of image classification DNN models by making minor pixel-level modifications. Nevertheless, when evaluating a textual DNN model, it is impossible to apply the same methods from evaluating image DNN due to three main differences:

1. **Input space.** Image inputs are continuous, while text data are symbolic, i.e., discrete. Thus, it is hard to define perturbations in texts that maintain the semantic and syntactical properties of the inputs.
2. **Perceptibility.** While small changes in image pixels are usually difficult to perceive, small changes in text, e.g., changing characters or words, can be much more easily perceived.
3. **Semantics.** In the case of images, small changes usually do not change the semantics of the image, while perturbation of text can easily change the semantics of words or sentences.

Considering these principal differences, works involving adversarial examples for textual DNNs have proposed novel methods using different techniques to carefully preserve the semantic inputs and the imperceptibility of modifications. Jia and Liang [9] were the first to consider designing adversarial examples for text applications with DNN models. In their work, they experimented by inserting small text fragments into the input data. These fragments were created synthetically based on observed terms in the training set (refer to Figure 2). Following Jia and Liang [9], different adversarial works oriented to text-based applications have shown that performing modifications at the character, term, or sentence level by inserting, deleting, substituting, or exchanging characters or terms can cause models to produce incorrect results [16–19]. When generating adversarial examples, the modifications should be as small as possible while remaining capable of fooling the model. For text-based tasks, the modifications should not make drastic changes to the text's semantics or syntax, and should maintain the readability of the input message.

2.3. Taxonomy of Adversarial Attacks

Generating adversarial examples is motivated by one of two objectives: (i) attacking by confusing the deep learning model's understanding of inputs to cause incorrect results; or (ii) defending by improving the robustness of the model through the addition of new knowledge and capabilities [10]. Adversarial example attacks attempt to identify and exploit model vulnerabilities when facing modified inputs, allowing effective defenses to subsequently be proposed to cover these vulnerabilities.

To identify the best criteria for designing adversarial examples, it is advisable to develop, test, and analyze different modifications to determine which will most effectively fool the target model while preserving the semantics and syntax of the text input. Zhang et al. [10] proposed a taxonomy of adversarial attacks on text application models based on the criteria established by Yuan et al. [20] for the design of a threat model or attack. According to [10,20], adversarial attacks can be classified as follows: (i) *model access*; this refers to the operational knowledge of the model under attack when the attack is performed; (ii) *semantic application*; while this can refer to different NLP applications, such as machine translation, machine comprehension, and speech recognition, among others, in this survey we focus on discussing the application of adversarial attacks to sentiment analysis; (iii) *target*; this refers to the objective of the attack, which may be to pursue an incorrect prediction or to direct the results to be specific to a class; (iv) *granularity*, which considers the level of text granularity at which the models are attacked; and (v) *attacked DNNs*, which indicates the DNN architecture used by the attacked model. We discuss the main models used in sentiment analysis in Section 2.6. In the following sections, we describe the different groups to which adversarial attacks can belong.

2.3.1. Model Access

According to the attacker's knowledge about the model to be fooled (or victim model), three types of attacks can be carried out: *black box*, *white box*, and *grey box*. A victim model can suffer attacks under different levels of knowledge at the same time, or the attacks can be generated independently.

- **Black box.** Black box attacks are applied when the architectures, parameters, activation, or loss functions are not accessible by the attacker. In this case, adversarial examples are generated by accessing the test dataset or querying the target model by making requests until a modification that allows for a change in the output is found.
- **White box.** Unlike black box attacks, white box attacks rely on knowledge of the complete details of the target model to be fooled.
- **Grey box.** Gray-box attacks occupy a middle ground between black box and white box attacks.

2.3.2. Target

The adversarial examples generated from an attack can be designed to change the model's output to make it incorrect $f(x') \neq y$, that is, an untargeted attack, or to change the output to a specific result $f(x') = y'$, that is, a targeted attack (as is indicated in Equation (1)). Targeted attacks are more strict compared to untargeted attacks, as they both change the prediction output and impose constraints on the output to produce a specific prediction [21].

2.3.3. Granularity

Different works oriented to text-based tasks have shown that it is possible to cause incorrect results by performing modifications at the character, term, or sentence level by inserting, deleting, substituting, or exchanging characters or terms [16–19]. To generate adversarial examples, the modifications must be as small as possible while being capable of fooling models. Furthermore, for text-based tasks, the modifications should not make drastic changes to the semantics and syntax, and should maintain the readability of the input message. In text inputs, modifications to generate adversarial examples can be performed at a different levels of detail, including character, term, sentence, and multilevel.

- **Character.** Modifications at the character level consist of modifying one or more characters within a term in an attempt to preserve its structure. Possible modifications include insertion, deletion, swapping, and replacing [22].
- **Term.** Modifications at the term-level consist of modifying a term (simple or n-gram) within a text while attempting to preserve the semantics and syntax. Modifications at this level include insertion, deletion, swapping, and replacing a term with a synonym or antonym [23].
- **Sentence.** Modifications at the sentence level mainly involve reordering terms by paraphrasing the sentence while maintaining the message's meaning [24]. Advanced methods aim to insert fragments of the text created based on the terms in the dataset.
- **Multilevel.** Multilevel modifications combine changes at the character/term/phrase levels with the aim of identifying the optimal change to be performed [25,26].

2.4. Strategies for Performing Modifications

Modifications can be performed through different strategies, such as modifying certain terms or a complete text in an original input according to the level of granularity. Text-based strategies for input modification include the following:

- **Concatenation.** Concatenation consists of adding a sentence called a distract text at the end of a text to confuse the model without changing the semantics of the message [9]. In this strategy, a distract text is added to the original inputs, then requests are made to the target model until the output is modified. When the target model is successfully confused and incorrect results are generated, the distract text is identified and added to the original input to create the adversarial example (Figure 4).

- **Editing.** The editing strategy (Figure 5 performs modifications to input data in two ways: (i) *synthetic*, in which a change in the order of the characters is made, which can be through *swapping*, *middle random* (random characters are exchanged except for the first and the last one), or *fully random* (all the characters are randomly rearranged and the keyboard type is changed); or (ii) *natural*, in which spelling errors in the original data are exploited. Advanced applications carry out modifications such as *random swap* by making an exchange of neighboring terms, *stop-word dropout* by randomly removing empty words, *paraphrasing* by substituting terms with paraphrased text, and *grammar errors* by modifying the conjugation of a verb, as well as *add negation* and *antonym* strategies.
- **Paraphrasing.** This strategy carefully produces a paraphrase of the original entry (Figure 6).
- **GAN-based strategies.** The purpose of adopting a generative adversarial network (GAN) architecture is to make adversarial examples seem more natural [10]. Generally, these attacks consist of two components: a GAN used to design adversarial examples, and an inverter that maps the input x to its representation within the latent space.
- **Substitution.** This strategy involves substituting terms with related terms, e.g., substitution by synonym.
- **Hybrid strategies.** The different strategies mentioned above can be hybridized to generate adversarial examples.

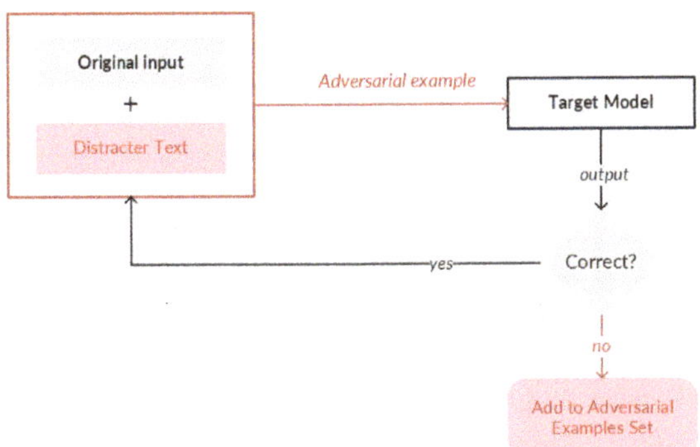

Figure 4. General principle for creating adversarial examples (or adversarial texts) by implementing concatenation.

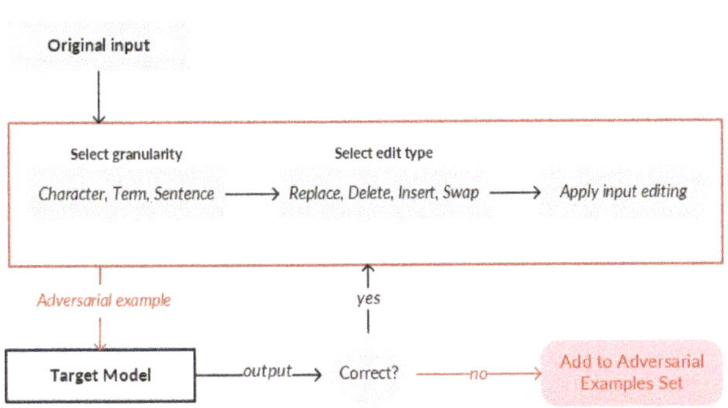

Figure 5. General principle for creating adversarial examples (or adversarial texts) by implementing editing. Modifications are made to sentences, terms, or characters by substitution, deletion, addition, or swapping.

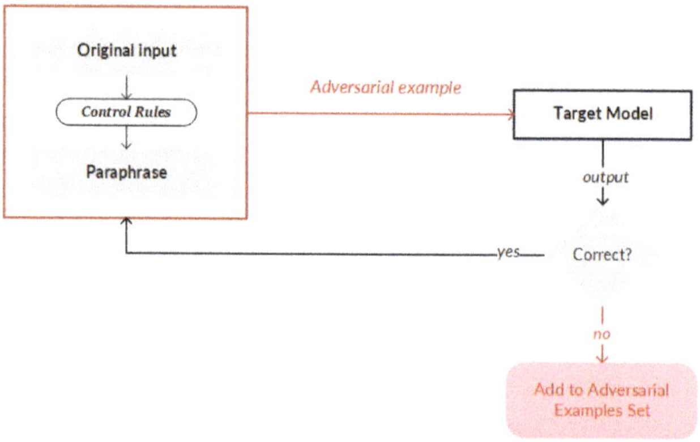

Figure 6. General principle for creating adversarial examples (or adversarial texts) by implementing paraphrases. Modifications are made carefully to ensure that the syntax and grammar of the input are not changed.

2.5. Measurement and Evaluation Metrics

During the development of an adversarial attack, it is necessary to measure and control the perturbations or modifications in order to keep their size to a minimum and ensure that they are imperceptible. Afterwards, the effectiveness of the attack in terms of the negative impact on model results and number of successfully misclassified modified inputs needs to be evaluated. The following measures are usually used to control modifications and measure the effectiveness of an attack.

2.5.1. Modification Control

After modifying the input data, it is necessary to measure the size of the modifications in orderto ensure that they are unnoticeable. Usually, the size of the modifications is measured based on the distance between the original data (or *clean data*) x and adversarial example x'. In the case of text data, the distance between x and x' must be measured. Correct grammar, syntax, and semantic preservation must be considered as well.

- **Grammar and syntax measurement.** Ensuring correct grammar and syntax is necessary to ensure that adversarial examples are undetectable. Strategies such as perplexity measure, paraphrase control, and grammar and syntax checkers have been proposed to measure grammar and syntax.
- **Semantic-preserving measurement.** The semantic similarity/distance measurement is performed on word vectors using measures of distances (such as the Euclidean distance) and similarity (such as the cosine similarity).
  - The Euclidean distance is the distance between two vectors in Euclidean space.

$$d(p,q) = \sqrt{(p_1 - q_1)^2 + (p_2 - q_2)^2 + ...(p_n - q_n)^2} \quad (2)$$

  - The cosine similarity computes the cosine value of the angle between the two vectors.

$$cos(p,q) = \frac{\sum_{i=1}^{n} p_i \times q_i}{\sqrt{\sum_{i=1}^{n}(p_i)^2} \times \sqrt{\sum_{i=1}^{n}(q_i)^2}} \quad (3)$$

- **Edit-based measurement.** Measuring the number of edits (modifications) quantifies the minimum changes from one text to the next. Different definitions of editing distances use different operations:

- Word Mover's Distance (WMD). The WMD measures the changes in the space of word embeddings. It measures the minimum distance from the word embeddings of an adversarial text to approach the *word embeddings* of an original text.
- Levenshtein distance. The Levenshtein distance is a string metric for measuring the difference between two sequences, i.e., the minimum number of single-character edits.
- Perturbation ratio. The ratio of perturbed words in the sentence to the total number of words in the sentence.
- Jaccard similarity coefficient. Used to measure the similarity of finite sets using the intersection and union of the sets:

$$J(A,B) = \frac{\mid A \cap B \mid}{\mid A \cup B \mid} \tag{4}$$

in two texts, A and B are the original and modified inputs, respectively, $\mid A \cap B \mid$ indicates the number of terms in both documents, and $\mid A \cup B \mid$ is the number of unique terms in both documents.

2.5.2. Attack Evaluation

During the development of an adversarial attack, it is necessary to measure and control the perturbations or modifications to keep their size to a minimum and ensure that they are imperceptible. Afterwards, the effectiveness of the attack must be evaluated.

- **Success rate.** The success rate is the most direct and effective evaluation criteria [27]. The attack success rate indicates the percentage of successful adversarial examples and the percentage of unsuccessfully attacked inputs. This measure provides insight into the susceptibility of a model to the designed adversarial examples.
- **Model Robustness.** Adversarial attacks are designed to affect the performance of models concerning the correct classifications. The robustness of DL models is related to the classification accuracy (*before-attack accuracy*, or BA) and how it is affected by adversarial examples (*after-attack accuracy*, or AA).

2.6. Deep Neural Networks

Deep learning models allow the characteristics of the input data to be learned at various abstraction layers, which in turn allows systems to learn the most complex functions to identify characteristics of the study domain. Feedforward, Convolutional Neural Network (CNN), and Recurrent/Recursive Neural Network (RNN) models and their variants have been the most widely implemented models for sentiment analysis tasks due to their natural ability to handle sequences and understand the relations between different elements. In particular, Long Short-Term Memory Network (LSTM) and Convolutional Neural Network (CNN) models are able to learn about sequences both locally and in the long term, preserving the most important and complex features to help the model understand the complete relationships. Recently, two major advances in deep learning have been popularized to address text-related tasks: (1) *sequence-to-sequence learning* [28] and (2) *attention mechanisms* [29].

- Recurrent Neural Networks. RNN models can handle input sequences with variable lengths. RNNs create and process arbitrary memory sequences of input patterns. Unlike traditional methods for automatic sequence synthesis, RNN models can process sequential and parallel information naturally and efficiently [30].
- Long Short-Term Memory Networks. LSTM models are a particular type of RNN composed of units of the same type. Conventional RNN models can encounter problems during training, as the gradients tend to grow enormously or fade over time due to their dependence on present and past errors. The accumulation of errors can cause difficulties when memorizing dependencies in long texts. LSTMs tackle these problems by incorporating decisions about which information will be stored and which will be discarded [31].

- Convolutional Neural Networks. CNN models consist of multiple layers of convolution filters of one or more dimensions. After each layer, a function is added to perform nonlinear causal mapping. At the beginning of the CNN, the feature extraction phase is composed of convolutional and downsampling neurons; as more data are processed, its dimensionality decreases, with the neurons in distant layers being much less sensitive to data perturbations while being activated by increasingly complex features (https://www.juanbarrios.com/redes-neurales-convolucionales/) (accessed on 12 April 2024).
  At the end of the network, perceptron neurons perform the final classification on the extracted features.

3. Adversarial Attacks on Sentiment Analysis

Sentiment analysis systems are an important tool that provides summarized information on users' opinions to assist potential users and organizations in the decision-making process. Sentiment analysis systems attempt to determine the user experience with respect to a product or service based on the positive or negative connotations of the words used by users to express their opinions [3]. In recent years, the use of deep learning models for deploying sentiment analysis systems has become a widespread topic due to their good processing capacity and superior results achieved on large volumes of information. However, as described above, deep learning models are vulnerable to modified inputs, making sentiment analysis models vulnerable to adversarial attacks. This issue leads us to study how adversarial attacks operate in order to propose defenses that minimize the negative impact that adversarial examples can have on the results of sentiment analysis models, which could potentially affect decision-making.

According to the characteristics of the reviewed works, and considering the discussed criteria in [20] for threat model design, we propose a new taxonomy specifically focused on adversarial attack methods for sentiment analysis models. Figure 7 presents the proposed taxonomy. In this taxonomy, six criteria are used to categorize the attack methods: (i) *model access* refers to the knowledge of the attacked model when the attack is performed; (ii) *analysis level* refers to the sentiment analysis level approached by the model under attack; (iii) *granularity* refers to the level of granularity at which the modifications are made; (iv) *element selection* refers to the way the methods select the element to be modified; (v) *strategy* indicates the strategy by which the modification is performed; and (vi) *DNN model* specifies the type of DNN being attacked. The main DNN architectures used for text applications are discussed in Section 2.6.

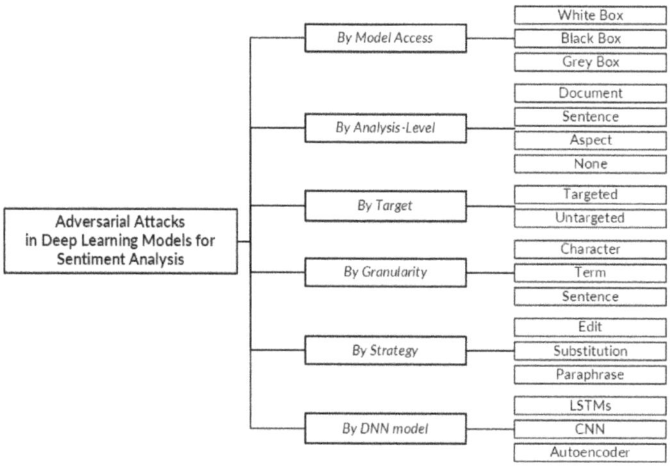

Figure 7. Taxonomy of adversarial attacks on deep learning models used for sentiment analysis.

3.1. Adversarial Attacks

The principal objective of sentiment analysis models is to obtain an effective set of terms that can uniquely identify different sentiments (positive, negative, or neutral), contributing to the classification of an opinion. Previous authors have referred to these terms as *valuable words* on account of their a crucial role in the final classification [32,33]. According to [34], to identify the most important terms in a text, it is necessary to consider two essential questions:

1. *Why is a text classified as positive or negative in a DNN model of sentiment analysis?*
2. *Do all words in an opinion contribute to the classification of an input to the same degree?*

The existing adversarial attacks seek to precisely determine those opinion terms that contribute to the correct input classification, then use them to perform modifications and create adversarial examples. However, when developing adversarial attacks, the ability to identify the most important terms in a text which impact the final classification of an input by a model is affected by the attacker's level of knowledge about the victim model.

Figure 8 illustrates that adversarial attacks on a sentiment analysis model may depend on the victim model's level of knowledge. In white box attacks, attackers have full knowledge of the target model to be attacked, including its data, architecture, and parameters, allowing adversarial examples to be created by using this knowledge directly. Typically, white box attacks modify the training data to make the model incorrectly learn features, producing incorrect results. On the other hand, in black box attacks the attackers do not know the target model's data or structure; thus, attackers can only consult the query output by the victim model to generate adversarial examples. In black box attacks, adversarial examples are generated by applying heuristics in a local model that represents the target model, which is trained until modifications that change the results are found. Usually, black box attacks collect representative data to generate adversarial examples; later, the adversarial examples generated by the substitute model are introduced to the victim model to cause incorrect results. Finally, in gray box attacks, the knowledge of the attackers is limited to the training data and general structure of the model to be attacked, and modifications are made using self-analysis methods to identify the most important parts of an input.

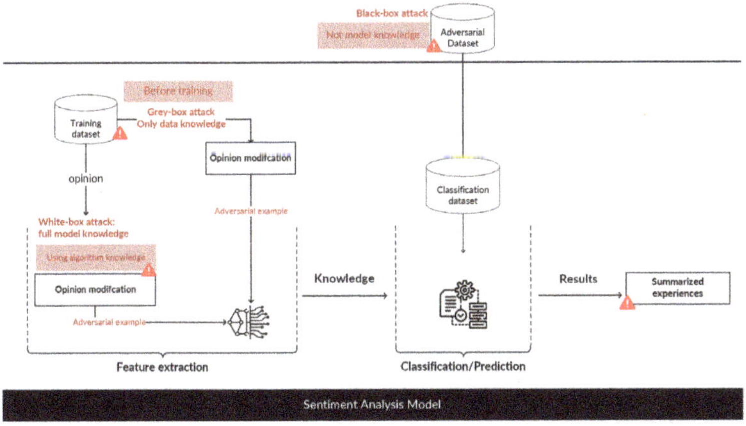

Figure 8. General overview of adversarial attacks on sentiment analysis models. Adversarial attacks can be classified as white box, black box, or gray box attacks depending on the attackers' level of knowledge about the data, architecture, and parameters of the victim model.

Table 1 summarizes the adversarial attacks reviewed in this paper. According to the proposed taxonomy (refer to Figure 7), we indicate each reviewed attack's principal criteria: model access, sentiment analysis level attacked, granularity, and strategy applied to perform input modifications. Additionally, we include the type of modification control used to perform the modifications. In the following sections, we present the reviewed methods separately based on the knowledge of the victim model. First, in Section 3.2, we discuss white box attacks, then, in Section 3.3, we introduce black box and gray box attacks.

Table 1. Reviewed adversarial attacks on sentiment analysis models.

Work	Sentiment Analysis Level	Model Knowledge	Modification Granularity	Select Elements to Be Modified via	Modification Strategy	Modification Control
[25]	-		Character/ Sentence	Word Importance on final prediction	Substitution	-
[16]	-	White-box	Term	-	Edit. Reconstruct the sentences via nearest semantic neighborby term	Word Mover's Distance
[18]	-		Term/ Character	Word Importance on final prediction	Edit. Synthetic	Edit distance, Jaccard similarity, Euclidean distance and Semantic similarity
[17]	-		Term	-	Substitution	Semantic Similarity
[19]	-		Term	-	Substitution	Euclidean Distance
[35]	-		Sentence	-	Edit. Paraphrases	Semantic similarity
[36]	-	Black-box	Term/ Character	Word Importance on final prediction	Edit. Eliminating one token at a time	-
[37]	-		Term	-	Substitution	Semantic Similarity
[38]	Aspect		Term	Word Importance on final prediction	Substitution	Semantic Similarity
[39]	-	Grey-box	Term	Word Importance on final prediction	Substitution	Semantic Similarity

3.2. White Box Adversarial Attacks

In white box attacks, the attack requires full access to the model's information, including its architecture, parameters, loss functions, activation functions, and input and output data. White box attacks typically approximate the worst-case attack scenario.

- Liang et al. [25] presented *TextFool*, a targeted attack that uses the FGSM (Fast Gradient Sign Method) concept to approximate the contribution of elements in a text in order to identify those that significantly impact the classification of the input text. Instead of using the sign of the cost gradient in FGSM, this work considers the magnitude. Specifically, the authors computed the cost gradient $\Delta_x J(f, x, c')$ of each instance in the training set by employing backpropagation, where f is the model function, x is the original data sample, and c' is the target text class. After that, *hot characters* were identified, which are the characters with the highest grand dimensions. The entries containing sufficient *hot characters* were denoted as *Hot Training Phrases* (HTP). Using HTP, the adversarial examples were created by implementing three types of modifications: (i) *insertion*, in which HTPs of the target class are inserted into c' nearby significant entries of the original class c; (ii) *modification*, in which some characters in the HTPs are replaced and *Hot Sample Phrases* (HSPs) are created; and (iii) *deletion*, in which unnecessary adjectives or adverbs in the HSPs are eliminated. These three strategies and their combinations were evaluated using a CNN architecture.
- Gong et al. [16] proposed an untargeted attack to perturb text inputs in the word embedding space of a CNN model. The proposed method addresses two main problems when performing text modifications, namely, the input space and the quality of adversarial examples. The main difficulties in generating adversarial texts are: (i) the text input's discrete space, which makes it difficult to accumulate small noise samples; and (ii) measuring the quality of adversarial texts. To deal with the input space issue, the authors perturbed the text inputs in the space of *embeddings* against a CNN model. Specifically, they applied FGSM and DeepFool. However, applying methods from computer vision would generate meaningless adversarial texts. To address this, the authors rounded the adversarial examples to the nearest meaningful word vectors, using the word mover's distance measure (WMD) as the distance measurement. Their evaluation on sentiment analysis and text classification datasets showed WMD to be a qualified metric for controlling perturbations.
- Li et al. [18] presented an untargeted attack method called TextBugger, which provides a perturbation constraint by using similarity measures such as edit distance,

Jaccard similarity coefficient, Euclidean distance, and cosine similarity. To generate adversarial examples, the proposed method first finds important words by computing the Jacobian matrix for the given input text to find the confidence value of each word, then finds the important words that have a significant impact on the classifier's outputs. By finding the most significant words, adversarial examples are generated by five kinds of modifications at the character or word level: (i) inserting a space into the word; (ii) deleting a random character of the word (except for the first and the last character); (iii) randomly swapping two adjacent letters; (iv) Substitute-C (Sub-C), in which characters are replaced with visually similar characters; and (v) Substitute-W (Sub-W), in which a word is replaced with its top_k nearest neighbors. For character-level perturbations, the authors deliberately misspelled important words to convert these important words to "unknown" words. For word-level perturbations, they used a semantic-preserving technique, i.e., replacing the word with its top_k nearest neighbors in a context-aware word vector space. In addition, the authors presented the application of their method under a black box setting while making word-level modifications. The process of generating adversarial examples contained three steps: (i) finding important sentences that contribute most to the final prediction results; (ii) using a scoring function to determine the importance of each word to the classification result and ranking the words based on their scores; and (iii) making modifications to selected words, similar to the white box approach. The attack methods were evaluated on CNN and LSTM architectures.

- Tsai et al. [17] presented an untargeted method called *Greedy Search*. Given a text input, this method considers the k nearest neighbors of each word in the space of *embeddings*. The greedy approach forms adversarial examples by replacing the original word w with each candidate w' among the k neighbors and determining whether the sigmoid value of the adversary x' is less than the value σ, which indicates whether replacing w with w' can contribute to change the prediction result. In addition, a more sophisticated approach called *Global Search* was proposed, in which simple modifications are performed by adding spelling error noise. *Global Search* by computes small perturbations δ to the original word embeddings. To learn the perturbations δ, an objective function $J(\delta)$ is defined to maximize the difference between the sigmoid values of the original input x and the perturbed input $x + \delta$:

$$J(\delta) = (f_{sigmoid}(E_x) - f_{sigmoid}(E_x + \delta)^2 \\ +\lambda_1 \cdot ||\delta||_2 \\ +\lambda_2 \cdot ||(E_x - (E_x + \delta))||_2 \tag{5}$$

where λ_1 penalizes large perturbations and λ_2 penalizes large distances between the original and perturbed word embeddings. The two regularization terms are added to help maintain the semantics of the chosen words. The perturbed embedding $E'_x = Ex + \delta$ usually does not have an actual word that it can be mapped back to; thus, the attack algorithm finds the candidate words w in the embedding space that are the closest to the perturbed word embedding. After computing the perturbed embedding and recording the candidate words, the algorithm checks whether the current perturbed embedding changes the prediction result. The algorithm continues to compute new samples E' until it fools the model. Both attacks were evaluated on a CNN using the IMDB movie reviews dataset.

- Alzantot et al. [19] used a population-based optimization algorithm to generate semantically and syntactically similar adversarial examples that fool sentiment analysis and textual entailment models. The proposed attack algorithm exploits population-based gradient-free optimization via genetic algorithms. Given an input sentence x, the algorithm randomly selects a word w in x and then selects a suitable replacement word that has similar semantic meaning, fits within the surrounding context, and increases the target label prediction score. To select the replacement word, for each w in x, the nearest N neighbors in the space of *embeddings* are determined by computing the Euclidean distance and selecting words greater than δ that are synonyms of the term to be replaced. Then, using the *Google one billion words language model*, the identified synonyms that are less frequent in the context of the text are discarded, keeping only the top K words. Finally, from the K remaining terms, those that contributes most to the classification when substituting the original term are selected. The attack algorithm was evaluated on an LSTM architecture and a textual entailment model trained on the Stanford Natural Language Inference (SNLI) corpus using the IMDB movie reviews dataset.

3.3. Black Box and Gray Box Adversarial Attacks

Black box attacks do not require the details of the neural networks, although they can access the input and output. This type of attack often relies on heuristics to generate adversarial examples, and is more practical in real-world applications.

- Ribeiro et al. [35] exploited the paraphrasing strategy to create semantically equivalent adversarial examples (SEA). They generated paraphrases of an input text x and observed the model predictions from $f(x')$ until the original prediction was modified. To control the generation of paraphrases, the authors defined an indicator function $SemEq(x, x')$ that is 1 if x is semantically equivalent to x' and 0 otherwise. They defined a semantically equivalent adversary (SEA) as a semantically equivalent instance that changes the model prediction:

$$SEA(x, x') = 1[SemEq(x, x') \wedge f(x) \neq f(x')]. \tag{6}$$

  To generate adversarial samples, a set of paraphrases Πx around x was generated via beam search to obtain predictions on Πx using the victim model until an adversary was found or until $S(x, x0) < \tau$. Additionally, a semantic equivalent rule-based method was proposed to generalize adversarial examples to understand and correct the failures when generating paraphrases. The rule takes the form $r = (a \rightarrow c)$, where the first instance of the antecedent a is replaced by the consequent c for every instance x that includes a. The authors generated SEAs and proposed rules for every $x \in X$.
- Gao et al. [36] proposed the DeepWordBug method for generating small text perturbations in a black box environment. In this method, the *Replace-1 Score (R1S)*, *Temporal Head Score (THS)*, *Temporal Tail Score (TTS)*, and *Combined Score (CS)* punctuation strategies are used to identify key terms that cause the classifier to make an incorrect prediction when modified. Character-level transformations can then be performed on the most relevant terms to minimize the edit distance of the perturbation from the original input.
- Jin et al. [37] presented the TextFooler method, which uses the fundamental NLP tasks of text classification and textual entailment to generate adversarial examples. When provided with a sentence, the proposed approach selects the words that most significantly influence the final prediction results through a selection mechanism that measures the influence of a word $w_i \in X$ on the classification result $F(X) = Y$. Each word is removed from the sentence one at a time in order to calculate the word importance, then the prediction score for label Y is measured. The importance score I_{wi} is then calculated as the prediction change before and after deleting the word w_i. When the words with a high importance score have been obtained, they are replaced by the closest synonyms according to the cosine similarity between w_i and every other word. The proposed attack was evaluated on CNN and LSTM architectures, including pretrained BERT.
- Xu et al. [39] presented a gray box adversarial attack and defense framework which consists of a generator ς (updated) and two copies of a pretrained target classifier: a static classifier C and an updated/augmented classifier C*. During the training phase, the output of ς is directly fed to C and C* to form a joint architecture. Post-training, the generator ς is used independently to generate adversarial examples (adversarial attack), while the augmented classifier C* is an improved classifier with increased

robustness (adversarial defense). The training phase is divided into attack and defense, where the former updates only the generator ς and learns to introduce slight perturbations to the input by maximizing the objective function of the target model and the latter updates C* and ς by feeding both original examples and adversarial examples generated by ς. Here, the adversarial examples are assumed to share the same label as their original examples. The defending steps consist of training an improved classifier with data augmented by adversarial examples. The generator ς is implemented as an autoencoder or a paraphrase generator. The proposed attacks were evaluated on CNN and Bi-LSTM architectures and a C-BERT model obtained by fine-tuning the BERT-Base model.

4. Defense against Adversarial Attacks on Sentiment Analysis

In recent years, different studies and researchers have proposed several methods for dealing with the new threats of adversarial examples for text applications models. Such defenses aim to deal with modified inputs, seeking to identify and discard them in order to mitigate their negative impact on the model's results. Until now, defensive methods have focused mainly on implementing techniques such as data augmentation and adversarial training or incorporating methods that identify changes in the inputs; these approaches use knowledge of the attack process to intentionally generate adversarial examples that models can learn from to identify and discard possible modifications. Figure 9 illustrates the general operation of actual defenses against adversarial examples.

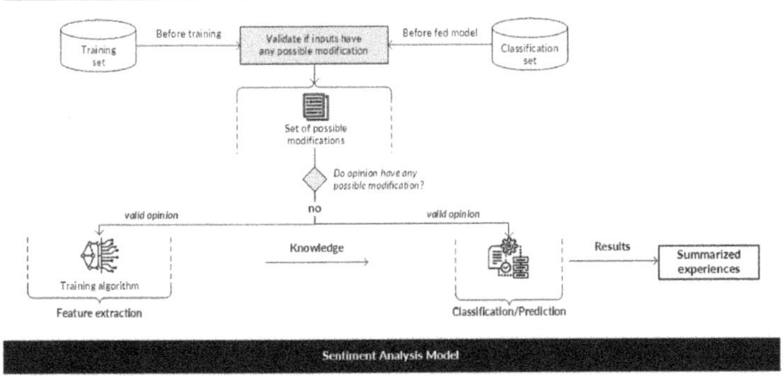

Figure 9. General defense mechanism within a sentiment analysis model. The aim of the defense mechanism is to identify and discard modified inputs in order to mitigate their negative impact on model results.

General functioning of defenses against adversarial examples consists of the following:

1. **Modification control investigates the differences between legitimate and adversarial texts.** Frequently, textual adversarial examples present notable differences compared to the original input texts. For example, adversarial texts may use character-level modifications, in many cases consisting of misspelled words. Consequently, researchers have used spell checkers to identify modified text inputs as a means of detecting this type of adversarial text [40,41]. However, modifications made by substitution with synonyms cannot be detected by these types of defenses.
2. **DNN models can be improved to strengthen them against adversarial attacks.** This defense includes modifying architectures to improve security and working with a training set with known parameters [42].

One fundamental purpose of generating effective adversarial examples is to use them to improve the robustness of existing models [8]. There are two principal strategies in text applications models to achieve this goal, namely, adversarial training and distillation.

These strategies are briefly described in the following sections. For more comprehensive reviews of defense strategies for text applications, please refer to [43,44].

4.1. Adversarial Training Strategy

In [7], the authors proposed the adversarial training strategy. This strategy consists of training a neural network to correctly classify both legitimate inputs (inputs without modifications) and adversarial examples. The adversarial strategy includes techniques such as data augmentation, model regularization, and robust optimization, which are explained below.

- **Data augmentation.** This process augments the original training set with the generated adversarial examples and attempts to teach the model to discard them during the training phase.
- **Model regularization.** The model's regularization imposes the adversary examples generated as a form of regularization.

$$min(J(f(x),y)) + \lambda J(f(x'),y)) \tag{7}$$

  where λ is a hyperparameter.
- **Robust Optimization.** Madry et al. [45] proposed DNN-model learning as a robustness optimization with a min–max formulation, which is the composition of a non-concave internal maximization problem (attack) and a non-convex external minimization problem (defense).

4.2. Distillation Strategy

Papernot et al. [42] proposed distillation as another defense against adversarial examples. The objective is to use the softmax output of the original neural network (for example, the class probabilities when classification is made) to train a second model with the same structure as the original. The softmax of the original DNN is modified by introducing a *temperature* parameter T:

$$q_i = \frac{exp\ (z_i/T)}{\sum_k exp\ (z_k/T)} \tag{8}$$

where z_i is an input of softmax layer and T controls the level of knowledge distillation. When $T = 1$ (refer to Equation (8)) returns to the normal softmax function, if T is *large*, then q_i is close to a uniform distribution; when it is small, the function will output more extreme values. Grosse et al. [46] adopted distillation defense for discrete data and applied a high temperature T, as a high-temperature softmax has been proven to reduce models' sensitivity to small perturbations.

4.3. Adversarial Defense

In this section, we present the main reviewed defense works proposed against adversarial examples, particularly for sentiment analysis models. These works have been used as a reference for the design of other proposals. Table 2 summarizes the reviewed defenses according to their main characteristics.

Table 2. Reviewed adversarial defenses for sentiment analysis models.

Work	Defense Strategy	Granularity	Defense Evaluation	DNN Model Defended
[47]	Modification control	Character	Accuracy in recognizing misspelled words, Sensitivity to adversarial pertubations on a input	BERT fine-tuned
[40]	Modification control	Term	Model robustnes	CNN, RNN and BERT
[48]	Modification control	Character/Term	Model robustnes	BERT
[34]	Modification control	Term	Model robustnes	CNN, BiLSTM, RNN
[39]	Data augmentation	Term	Model robustnes	CNN, BiLSTM, BERT-Base

- Pruthi et al. [47] proposed designing and implementing a model for word validation and recognition before the classifier. The method is trained to recognize words modified by dropping, adding, and swapping internal characters within words. This defense proposes a two-stage solution to deal with character-level adversarial attacks, placing a word recognition model W before the downstream classifier C. This recognition model is based on a semi-character architecture of RNNs, introducing various feedback strategies for handling uncommon or unseen words. The proposed defense method is inspired by psycholinguistic studies that proposed a semi-character-based RNN (ScRNN) that processes a sentence of words with misspelled characters and predicts the correct words. ScRNN treats the first and the last characters individually and is agnostic about the ordering of the internal characters. At each sequence step, the training target is the correct corresponding word (output dimension equal to vocabulary size), and the model is optimized using the cross-entropy loss.
- Wang et al. [40] proposed a defense mechanism called the Synonym Encoding Method (SEM). This mechanism inserts an encoder before the input layer of the model and then trains the model to remove adversary perturbations. Using an encoder, the defense method substitutes the words in the original sentence with their close synonyms. To define the encoder E that encodes a set of synonyms, the authors clustered the synonyms in the embedding space and allocated a unique token for each cluster, obtaining the same cluster for different words.
- Zhou et al. [48] proposed the DIScriminate Perturbations (DISP) mechanism for identifying and adjusting malicious modifications and blocking attacks. To identify adversarial examples, the discriminator validates the probability of a term in the text being modified, based on which it provides a set of potential modifications. For each potential modification, an insertion estimator learns to restore modified terms by selecting a replacement token based on a search of the k nearest neighbors. The proposed mechanism tries to block adversarial attacks on some models for texts without modifying their structure or the training process.
- Wang et al. [34] proposed a general defense mechanism called TextFirewall for different attacks with different strategies. Given a text input x, TextFirewall analyzes and quantifies each word's impact in the text to distinguish the polarity instead of directly detecting the difference between adversarial text and legitimate input (inputs without any modification). With x feeding the model the *top-k* items that impact the classification results, if the *loss* is greater than zero, then y^* is set to 1; otherwise, y^* is 0. The defense mechanism compares y^* and y' to judge the role of x. If y^* is the same as y', then x is predicted as a legitimate input (input without modification); otherwise, x is an adversarial example.
- Xu et al. [39] presented a gray box adversarial attack and defense framework consisting of a generator ς (updated) and two copies of a pretrained target classifier: a static

classifier C and an updated/augmented classifier C^*. The operation of this method is described above in Section 3.3.

5. Discussion of Adversarial Attacks and Open Challenges for Sentiment Analysis

The design of adversarial example attacks in text applications has become popular in recent years. The volume and depth of contributions regarding defenses for text applications such as sentiment analysis has been less than for other tasks. Therefore, effective attack strategies and defense mechanisms must be explored to ensure the correct functioning of sentiment analysis systems. At present, two critical and significant challenges are present when designing textual adversarial examples: preserving syntax, and validating correct grammar and semantics. Additionally, there are challenges within text applications that inherently need to be addressed within the sentiment analysis task, for example, making modifications that are both imperceptible to humans and effective in confusing models. This might be one of the most challenging problems, as changes within a text are easy to detect even when unintentional, such as orthographic errors. Another remaining challenge is to ensure the generality of the methods used to create adversarial examples in order to preserve their effectiveness and make them easy to use in other models.
Based on the reviewed literature, this section includes the current challenges in designing adversarial examples:

- **Perceptibility.** While image modifications are often imperceptible to humans, modifications in texts are readily identifiable. Invalid words and syntactical errors can be identified relatively easily using a grammar checking process, allowing them to be discarded. From the point of view of semantic preservation, changing a word in a sentence can drastically change the semantics; thus, without additional processing, the modified inputs can be easily identified and dismissed. To ensure an effective attack, successful approaches must make the modifications imperceptible while preserving correct grammar and semantics [10]. In [49], the authors presented a white box attack method against a word-level CNN text classifier. The proposed approach uses the Euclidean and cosine distances as a combined metric to find the most semantically similar substitution when generating perturbations. In addition, the dispersion of the location of the modified words in the adversarial examples is controlled by introducing a coefficient of variation (CV) factor. Combining these two methods increases the attack success rate and makes the modification positions in the generated examples more dispersed. Recent research seeks to precisely determine the terms that contribute to the correct classification of input and use them to create adversarial examples [32–34]. For sentiment analysis applications, adversarial examples must be carefully designed to consider an effective set of terms that uniquely identify different sentiments (positive, negative, or neutral) that contribute to classifying an opinion.
- **Transferability.** Transferability is a desirable property in adversarial examples, reflecting the generalization of attack methods by ensuring that the adversarial instances created for one model and on one dataset can be used on another model or dataset while remaining effective [10]. In Reference [50], the authors proposed that transferability between seemingly different models is due to a high linear correlation between the feature sets extracted by different networks. In Reference [51], a systematic investigation of factors affecting adversarial examples' transferability for text classification models was explored. The authors contemplated several factors, including network architectures, tokenization schemes, word embedding, and model capacity. On this basis, they proposed a genetic algorithm to find an ensemble of models that can be used to induce adversarial examples to fool different existing models. We remark that to achieve transferability between sentiment analysis models, adversarial examples should be designed under modifications that consider disrupting the characteristics of the task, thereby confounding the model understanding and management of the sentiment analysis task over the understanding of text input.

- **Task-oriented.** Most current works address different tasks by applying global strategies to modify inputs. This does not necessarily provide a correct solution, as specific challenges in each task must be handled to ensure a correct modification process. Although previous adversarial example attacks focusing on sentiment analysis have fooled models and reduced the precision of the results, these works have focused on addressing the sentiment analysis at the document level, and have not modeled the problem to deal with aspect-level natural characteristics. An ideal adversarial example design for sentiment analysis models should combine sentiment analysis and adversarial example characteristics to perform modifications on inputs to achieve task-oriented adversarial examples. In this design, two main issues are encountered. First, to construct task-oriented adversarial examples, it is necessary to correctly determine a set of terms that uniquely identify different sentiments (positive, negative, or neutral) contributing to classifying an opinion. Second, it is necessary to establish the set of possible perturbations N for each term while evaluating and controlling them so that each perturbation can be performed while both preserving the correct semantics and syntax and fooling the model.
- **New architectures.** Several architectures that are widely used in sentiment analysis have not yet been effectively attacked, for example, generative models (Generative Adversarial Networks (GAN)) and Variational Auto-Encoders (VAE). These models require a great deal of experience for model training, which may explain why they have not been effectively attacked. Other architectures that have attracted attention involve attention mechanisms, which are becoming a prevalent component in sequential models. However, as there are few studies examining the functioning of these attention mechanisms, there is a lack of models that can be used to generate modified inputs that are effectively against them. Nevertheless, adversarial examples do not have to identify and exploit DNN vulnerabilities. Instead, the design of adversarial examples should approach the modifications to be performed based on the input elements that support the task. In this way, adversarial attacks could be transferred among different DNN models, at least for the same task.
- **Attack-dependent defenses.** Current defenses against adversarial examples rely on knowledge of the generation process by which the model's inputs were modified, an approach that is not appropriate due to the increasing performance of adversarial examples. More effective defenses must be attack-independent, meaning that they do not require knowledge of the generation process to identify modifications and discard adversarial examples. Notably, such defense mechanisms should be more preventive than reactive.

6. Conclusions

Since their introduction, adversarial examples have pointed out the limitations of deep learning models in correctly classifying intentionally modified inputs. The negative impact of adversarial examples on the deep learning models compels the exploration of new vulnerabilities and defense mechanisms that can effectively cover them to guarantee the model's results.

This work has presented an informative framework in which key concepts concerning the design of adversarial examples are outlined, and has summarized the principal works on attack and defense for deep neural network models performing sentiment analysis tasks. This knowledge is expected to help researchers develop new approaches for designing attacks using adversarial examples and propose new defenses specific to the sentiment analysis task.

At present, designing and implementing adversarial texts remains challenging, as the nature of the data makes it relatively easy to identify modifications in a text. Currently, the main challenge in text applications is to design adversarial examples with imperceptible modifications that preserve the correct semantics and grammar. For effective adversarial examples, design methods must create effectively modified inputs capable of being transferred to other models that can successfully affect the model's results. In addition, it is necessary to explore recent architectures to find vulnerabilities and carry out experiments to find weaknesses in them. On the other hand, due to the effectiveness that adversarial examples have already demonstrated in breaking the safety of deep learning models in the text area, it is necessary to propose effective defense mechanisms to guarantee the reliability of the results. Thus far, the existing defense mechanisms depend primarily on knowledge of the attack process; however, in a real scenario it is not always possible to know this process. Therefore, future defense mechanisms should be independent of the attack mechanism in order to prevent future attacks. We suggest that sentiment analysis models should incorporate defense mechanisms in their design in order to safeguard their data and avoid their results being disturbed.

Author Contributions: Conceptualization, M.V.-H., L.A.M.-R. and I.A.-B.; Data curation, M.-L.C.-T.; Formal analysis, I.A.-B. and H.R.-R.; Investigation, M.V.-H., S.I.F.-G., H.R.-R. and M.-L.C.-T.; Methodology, M.V.-H. and L.A.M.-R.; Software, M.V.-H.; Supervision, L.A.M.-R. and I.A.-B.; Validation, L.A.M.-R., I.A.-B. and H.R.-R.; Visualization, S.I.F.-G.; Writing—original draft, M.V.-H., L.A.M.-R. and I.A.-B.; Writing—review and editing, S.I.F.-G., H.R.-R. and M.-L.C.-T. All authors have read and agreed to the published version of the manuscript.

Funding: This research was funded by the Mexican National Council of Humanities Science and Technology (CONAHCYT) through scholarships 814461 and 478112 and research projects 882 and 613.

Institutional Review Board Statement: Not applicable.

Informed Consent Statement: Not applicable.

Data Availability Statement: The original contributions presented in the study are included in the article, further inquiries can be directed to the corresponding authors.

Conflicts of Interest: The authors declare no conflicts of interest. The funders had no role in the study's design, in the collection, analysis, and interpretation of data, in the writing of the manuscript, or in the decision to publish the results.

Abbreviations

The following abbreviations are used in this manuscript:

AA	After-attack Accuracy
BA	Before-attack Accuracy
BERT	Bidirectional Encoder Representations from Transformers
CNN	Convolutional Neuronal Network
DL	Deep Learning
DNN	Deep Neuronal Network
GAN	Generative Adversarial Network
IEEE	Institute of Electrical and Electronics Engineers
LSTM	Long Short-Term Memory
BiLSTM	Bidirectional Long Short-Term Memory
NLP	Natural Language Processing
RNN	Recurrent Neuronal Network
SA	Sentiment Analysis
SNLI	Stanford Natural Language Inference
WMD	Word Mover's Distance

References

1. Shaba, M. A Real-Time Sentimental Analysis on E-Commerce Sites in Nigeria Using Machine Learning. In Proceedings of t Hybrid Intelligent Systems: 21st International Conference on Hybrid Intelligent Systems (HIS 2021), Online, 14–16 December 20 p. 452.
2. Liu, B.; Zhang, L. A survey of opinion mining and sentiment analysis. In *Mining Text Data*; Springer: Boston, MA, USA, 20 pp. 415–463.
3. Liu, B. *Web Data Mining: Exploring Hyperlinks, Contents, and Usage Data*; Springer: Berlin/Heidelberg, Germany, 2011; Volume

Chandrasekaran, G.; Nguyen, T.N.; Hemanth D, J. Multimodal sentimental analysis for social media applications: A comprehensive review. *Wiley Interdiscip. Rev. Data Min. Knowl. Discov.* **2021**, *11*, e1415. [CrossRef]
Zhu, L.; Zhu, Z.; Zhang, C.; Xu, Y.; Kong, X. Multimodal sentiment analysis based on fusion methods: A survey. *Inf. Fusion* **2023**, *95*, 306–325. [CrossRef]
Sarker, I.H. Deep learning: A comprehensive overview on techniques, taxonomy, applications and research directions. *Comput. Sci.* **2021**, *2*, 420. [CrossRef] [PubMed]
Szegedy, C.; Zaremba, W.; Sutskever, I.; Bruna, J.; Erhan, D.; Goodfellow, I.; Fergus, R. Intriguing properties of neural networks. *arXiv* **2013**, arXiv:1312.6199.
Goodfellow, I.J.; Shlens, J.; Szegedy, C. Explaining and Harnessing Adversarial Examples. *arXiv* **2014**, arXiv:1412.6572.
Jia, R.; Liang, P. Adversarial Examples for Evaluating Reading Comprehension Systems. In Proceedings of the 2017 Conference on Empirical Methods in Natural Language Processing, Copenhagen, Denmark, 9–11 September 2017; pp. 2021–2031. [CrossRef]
Zhang, W.E.; Sheng, Q.Z.; Alhazmi, A.; Li, C. Adversarial attacks on deep-learning models in natural language processing: A survey. *ACM Trans. Intell. Syst. Technol.* **2020**, *11*, 1–41. [CrossRef]
Meng, D.; Chen, H. Magnet: A two-pronged defense against adversarial examples. In Proceedings of the 2017 ACM SIGSAC Conference on Computer and Communications Security, Dallas, TX, USA, 30 October–3 November 2017; pp. 135–147.
Alsmadi, I.; Ahmad, K.; Nazzal, M.; Alam, F.; Al-Fuqaha, A.; Khreishah, A.; Algosaibi, A. Adversarial attacks and defenses for social network text processing applications: Techniques, challenges and future research directions. *arXiv* **2021**, arXiv:2110.13980.
Xu, H.; Ma, Y.; Liu, H.C.; Deb, D.; Liu, H.; Tang, J.L.; Jain, A.K. Adversarial attacks and defenses in images, graphs and text: A review. *Int. J. Autom. Comput.* **2020**, *17*, 151–178. [CrossRef]
Han, X.; Zhang, Y.; Wang, W.; Wang, B. Text Adversarial Attacks and Defenses: Issues, Taxonomy, and Perspectives. *Secur. Commun. Netw.* **2022**, *2022*, 6458488. [CrossRef]
Bengio, Y.; Courville, A.; Vincent, P. Representation learning: A review and new perspectives. *IEEE Trans. Pattern Anal. Mach. Intell.* **2013**, *35*, 1798–1828. [CrossRef]
Gong, Z.; Wang, W.; Li, B.; Song, D.; Ku, W.S. Adversarial Texts with Gradient Methods. *arXiv* **2018**, arXiv:1801.07175.
Tsai, Y.T.; Yang, M.C.; Chen, H.Y. Adversarial Attack on Sentiment Classification. In Proceedings of the 2019 ACL Workshop BlackboxNLP: Analyzing and Interpreting Neural Networks for NLP, Florence, Italy, 1 August 2019; pp. 233–240. [CrossRef]
Li, J.; Ji, S.; Du, T.; Li, B.; Wang, T. TextBugger: Generating Adversarial Text Against Real-world Applications. In Proceedings of the 2019 Network and Distributed System Security Symposium, San Diego, CA, USA, 24–27 February 2019. [CrossRef]
Alzantot, M.; Sharma, Y.; Elgohary, A.; Ho, B.J.; Srivastava, M.; Chang, K.W. Generating Natural Language Adversarial Examples. In Proceedings of the 2018 Conference on Empirical Methods in Natural Language Processing, Brussels, Belgium, 31 October–4 November 2018; pp. 2890–2896. [CrossRef]
Yuan, X.; He, P.; Zhu, Q.; Li, X. Adversarial examples: Attacks and defenses for deep learning. *IEEE Trans. Neural Netw. Learn. Syst.* **2019**, *30*, 2805–2824. [CrossRef] [PubMed]
Wang, T.; Zhu, L.; Zhang, Z.; Zhang, H.; Han, J. Targeted Adversarial Attack Against Deep Cross-Modal Hashing Retrieval. *IEEE Trans. Circuits Syst. Video Technol.* **2023**, *33*, 6159–6172. [CrossRef]
Eger, S.; Şahin, G.G.; Rücklé, A.; Lee, J.U.; Schulz, C.; Mesgar, M.; Swarnkar, K.; Simpson, E.; Gurevych, I. Text Processing Like Humans Do: Visually Attacking and Shielding NLP Systems. In Proceedings of the 2019 Conference of the North American Chapter of the Association for Computational Linguistics: Human Language Technologies, Minneapolis, MN, USA, 2–7 June 2019; Long and Short Papers, Volume 1, pp. 1634–1647. [CrossRef]
Zang, Y.; Qi, F.; Yang, C.; Liu, Z.; Zhang, M.; Liu, Q.; Sun, M. Word-level Textual Adversarial Attacking as Combinatorial Optimization. In Proceedings of the 58th Annual Meeting of the Association for Computational Linguistics, Online, 5–10 July 2020; pp. 6066–6080. [CrossRef]
Gan, W.C.; Ng, H.T. Improving the Robustness of Question Answering Systems to Question Paraphrasing. In Proceedings of the 57th Annual Meeting of the Association for Computational Linguistics, Florence, Italy, 28 July–2August 2019; pp. 6065–6075. [CrossRef]
Liang, B.; Li, H.; Su, M.; Bian, P.; Li, X.; Shi, W. Deep Text Classification Can be Fooled. In Proceedings of the Twenty-Seventh International Joint Conference on Artificial Intelligence, IJCAI-18. International Joint Conferences on Artificial Intelligence Organization, Stockholm, Sweden, 13–19 July 2018; Volume 7, pp. 4208–4215. [CrossRef]
Vijayaraghavan, P.; Roy, D. Generating Black-Box Adversarial Examples for Text Classifiers Using a Deep Reinforced Model. In *Machine Learning and Knowledge Discovery in Databases*; Springer International Publishing: Cham, Switzerland, 2020; pp. 711–726. [CrossRef]
Zhang, J.; Li, C. Adversarial examples: Opportunities and challenges. *IEEE Trans. Neural Netw. Learn. Syst.* **2019**, *31*, 2578–2593. [CrossRef] [PubMed]
Sutskever, I.; Vinyals, O.; Le, Q.V. Sequence to sequence learning with neural networks. In *Advances in Neural Information Processing Systems*; Curran Associates, Inc.: Glasgow, UK, 2014; pp. 3104–3112.
Bahdanau, D.; Cho, K.; Bengio, Y. Neural Machine Translation by Jointly Learning to Align and Translate. *arXiv* **2014**, arXiv:1409.0473.
Quintero, Y.C.; Garcia, L.A. Estudio del análisis de sentimentos basado en espectos. In Proceedings of the "IV Conferencia Internacional en Ciencias Computacionales e Informáticas", Havana, Cuba, 26–30 November 2018.

31. Graves, A. Long short-term memory. In *Supervised Sequence Labelling with Recurrent Neural Networks*; Springer: Berlin/Heidelbe Germany, 2012; pp. 37–45.
32. Ma, Y.; Peng, H.; Cambria, E. Targeted aspect-based sentiment analysis via embedding commonsense knowledge into an attenti LSTM. In Proceedings of the Thirty-Second AAAI Conference on Artificial Intelligence, New Orleans, LA, USA, 2–7 February 201
33. Xiao, Y.; Zhou, G. Syntactic edge-enhanced graph convolutional networks for aspect-level sentiment classification with interacti attention. *IEEE Access* **2020**, *8*, 157068–157080. [CrossRef]
34. Wang, W.; Wang, R.; Ke, J.; Wang, L. TextFirewall: Omni-Defending Against Adversarial Texts in Sentiment Classification. *IEE Access* **2021**, *9*, 27467–27475. [CrossRef]
35. Ribeiro, M.T.; Singh, S.; Guestrin, C. Semantically Equivalent Adversarial Rules for Debugging NLP models. In Proceedings the 56th Annual Meeting of the Association for Computational Linguistics, Melbourne, Australia, 15–20 July 2018; Long Pape Volume 1, pp. 856–865. [CrossRef]
36. Gao, J.; Lanchantin, J.; Soffa, M.L.; Qi, Y. Black-box generation of adversarial text sequences to evade deep learning classifiers. Proceedings of the 2018 IEEE Security and Privacy Workshops (SPW), San Francisco, CA, USA, 24 May 2018; pp. 50–56.
37. Jin, D.; Jin, Z.; Zhou, J.T.; Szolovits, P. Is bert really robust? A strong baseline for natural language attack on text classificatic and entailment. In Proceedings of the AAAI Conference on Artificial Intelligence, New York, NY, USA, 7–12 February 202 Volume 34; pp. 8018–8025.
38. Ekbal, A. Adversarial Sample Generation for Aspect based Sentiment Classification. In Proceedings of the Findings of tl Association for Computational Linguistics: AACL-IJCNLP 2022, Online, 20–23 November 2022; pp. 478–492.
39. Xu, Y.; Zhong, X.; Jimeno Yepes, A.; Lau, J.H. Grey-box Adversarial Attack and Defence For Sentiment Classification. Proceedings of the 2021 Conference of the North American Chapter of the Association for Computational Linguistics: Huma Language Technologies, Online, 6–11 June 2021; pp. 4078–4087. [CrossRef]
40. Wang, X.; Jin, H.; Yang, Y.; He, K. Natural Language Adversarial Defense through Synonym Encoding. In Proceedings of tl Conference on Uncertainty in Artificial Intelligence, Online, 27–30 July 2021.
41. Wang, Z.; Wang, H. Defense of word-level adversarial attacks via random substitution encoding. In Proceedings of the Intern tional Conference on Knowledge Science, Engineering and Management, Hangzhou, China, 28–30 August 2020; pp. 312–324.
42. Papernot, N.; McDaniel, P.; Wu, X.; Jha, S.; Swami, A. Distillation as a defense to adversarial perturbations against deep neur networks. In Proceedings of the 2016 IEEE Symposium on Security and Privacy (SP), San Jose, CA, USA, 22–26 May 201 pp. 582–597.
43. Goyal, S.; Doddapaneni, S.; Khapra, M.M.; Ravindran, B. A survey of adversarial defenses and robustness in nlp. *ACM Comp Surv.* **2023**, *55*, 1–39. [CrossRef]
44. Zhou, Y.; Zheng, X.; Hsieh, C.J.; Chang, K.w.; Huang, X. Defense against adversarial attacks in nlp via dirichlet neighborhoc ensemble. *arXiv* **2020**, arXiv:2006.11627.
45. Mądry, A.; Makelov, A.; Schmidt, L.; Tsipras, D.; Vladu, A. Towards deep learning models resistant to adversarial attacl *Stat* **2017**, *1050*, 9.
46. Grosse, K.; Papernot, N.; Manoharan, P.; Backes, M.; McDaniel, P. Adversarial examples for malware detection. In Proceedin of the Computer Security—ESORICS 2017: 22nd European Symposium on Research in Computer Security, Oslo, Norwa 11–15 September 2017; Part II 22; Springer: Cham, Switzerland, 2017; pp. 62–79.
47. Pruthi, D.; Dhingra, B.; Lipton, Z.C. Combating Adversarial Misspellings with Robust Word Recognition. In Proceedings of tl 57th Annual Meeting of the Association for Computational Linguistics, Florence, Italy, 28 July–2 August 2019. [CrossRef]
48. Zhou, Y.; Jiang, J.Y.; Chang, K.W.; Wang, W. Learning to Discriminate Perturbations for Blocking Adversarial Attacks in Te Classification. *arXiv* **2019**, arXiv:1909.03084.
49. Du, X.; Yi, Z.; Li, S.; Ma, J.; Yu, J.; Tan, Y.; Wu, Q. Generating More Effective and Imperceptible Adversarial Text Examples f Sentiment Classification. In Proceedings of the International Conference on Artificial Intelligence and Security, Dublin, Irelan 19–23 July 2020; pp. 422–433.
50. Wiedeman, C.; Wang, G. Disrupting adversarial transferability in deep neural networks. *Patterns* **2022**, *3*, 100472. [CrossRe [PubMed]
51. Yuan, L.; Zheng, X.; Zhou, Y.; Hsieh, C.J.; Chang, K.W. On the Transferability of Adversarial Attacks against Neural Text Classifi In Proceedings of the Empirical Methods in Natural Language Processing, Punta Cana, Dominican Republic, 7–11 November 202

applied sciences

MDPI

ticle

nowledge Graph Completion Using a Pre-Trained Language lodel Based on Categorical Information and Multi-Layer esidual Attention

ang Rao [1], Tiejun Wang [2,*], Xiaoran Guo [2], Kaijie Wang [1] and Yue Yan [1]

1 Key Laboratory of China's Ethnic Languages and Information Technology of Ministry of Education, Northwest Minzu University, Lanzhou 730030, China; rao2581444@163.com (Q.R.); foxnotail@foxmail.com (K.W.); yy1054270233@gmail.com (Y.Y.)

2 School of Mathematics and Computer Science, Northwest Minzu Univsersity, Lanzhou 730030, China; wguoxr1982@163.com

* Correspondence: wtj@mail.lzjtu.cn

Abstract: Knowledge graph completion (KGC) utilizes known knowledge graph triples to infer and predict missing knowledge, making it one of the research hotspots in the field of knowledge graphs. There are still limitations in generating high-quality entity embeddings and fully understanding the contextual information of entities and relationships. To overcome these challenges, this paper introduces a novel pre-trained language model-based method for knowledge graph completion that significantly enhances the quality of entity embeddings by integrating entity categorical information with textual descriptions. Additionally, this method employs an innovative multi-layer residual attention network in combination with PLMs, deepening the understanding of the joint contextual information of entities and relationships. Experimental results on the FB15k-237 and WN18RR datasets demonstrate that our proposed model significantly outperforms existing baseline models in link prediction tasks.

Keywords: knowledge graph completion; pre-trained language models (PLMs); textual information; categorical information; multi-layer residual attention

1. Introduction

The goal of knowledge graph completion (KGC) is to find missing entities or relation links in an existing knowledge graph, thereby enhancing and expanding the knowledge graph by predicting missing information from known triplets. Currently, there are two main approaches in this field. The first approach is structure-based KGC, where entities and relations are represented as embedding vectors, and the matching scores for each triplet are computed by modeling their interactions. Typical models include TransE [1] and RotatE [2]. Although structure-based methods have made some progress, they perform poorly in predicting long-tail entities and struggle to obtain effective embedding representations for entities that appear infrequently during training. Additionally, these methods only use entity and relation embeddings for link prediction, without fully leveraging the semantic information of entities and relations to enrich their embedding representations. The second approach is text-based KGC, with notable models such as KG-BERT [3], StAR [4], and C-LMKE [5]. This approach combines textual descriptions of entities and relations with pre-trained language models to enrich the representation of entities and relations in the knowledge graph, thereby alleviating the performance issues of structure-based methods in handling long-tail entities and relations. However, this approach has two main problems. (1) The issue of entity embedding quality: Existing methods rely solely on combining textual descriptions with pre-trained language models to generate entity embeddings, which may not fully capture the semantic information of entities. (2) Insufficient understanding of context information between entities and relations: Current text-based methods typically transform the textual descriptions of entities and relations into their contextual embeddings using language models. However, these methods employ different strategies to enhance the embedding representations of entities and relations, overlooking the complex interactions between entities and relations, thereby struggling to capture the complex semantic correlations between entities and relations.

To address these issues, this paper proposes a knowledge graph completion method that combines entity category information with an attention mechanism. The main contributions can be summarized as follows:

(1) Proposing a novel text-based contrastive learning model called CAKGC, which incorporates both entity category semantic information and textual descriptions to more accurately model entity embedding representations.
(2) Design a new attention network called Multi-layer Residual Attention Network (MRAN), which combines MRAN with pre-trained language models. The multi-layer self-attention mechanism allows the model to iterate and propagate information between entities, better capturing the complex relationships between entities. By simultaneously learning multiple attention heads, the model can model different types of relationships in parallel, enhancing the representation capability for diverse relationships. Each attention head can focus on different relationship patterns, capturing finer-grained features of relationships.

2. Related Works

2.1. Structure-Based Approach

Existing structure-based knowledge graph completion methods can be classified into two main categories: (1) distance-based methods and (2) tensor-decomposition-based methods.

In distance-based methods, TransE [1] is one of the earliest proposed models. It projects entities and relations into a vector space and treats relations as translation operations from head entities to tail entities. However, TransE's scoring function is too simplistic to effectively represent the semantic differences between different entities under the same relation. To address this issue, TransH [6] introduces the concept of relation hyperplanes, which allow for different representations of the same entity under different relations. TransR [7] defines different mapping matrices for different relation categories, but this leads to a large number of model parameters. To tackle the parameter explosion problem, TransD [8] decomposes the relation mapping matrix. Addressing the inability of TransE to handle symmetric relations, RotatE [2] represents relations as rotational operations in the complex space, enabling better learning and differentiation of symmetric relations. PairRE [9] projects relations into the embeddings of head and tail entities and further models sub-relations based on RotatE while simplifying the complexity of extending the complex space.

Tensor-decomposition-based methods were initially proposed by RESCAL [10]. They optimize the product of head entity vector v_h, relation matrix M_r, and tail entity vector v_t to satisfy the equation $v_h^T M_r v_t = T_{hrt}$, and the loss function is optimized to maximize the scoring function $v_h^T M_r v_t$. The drawback of the RESCAL algorithm is that it sets a separate matrix for each relation, resulting in a large number of parameters. To address this parameter issue, DistMult [11] constrains the relation matrix to be a diagonal matrix, reducing the model parameters and significantly improving computational efficiency. To handle asymmetric relations, ComplEx [12] introduces complex operations in matrix multiplication. HolE [13] computes circular correlation values between head and tail entities, where circular correlation operations provide advantages in computational efficiency and space utilization. SimplE [14] addresses the inability of DistMult to model asymmetric relations by introducing separate distributed representations for entities and relations, resulting in fewer parameters compared to RESCAL. Inspired by automated machine learning, Zhang et al. propose an algorithm called AutoBLM [15] for automatically designing and discovering better scoring functions in knowledge graph embeddings.

As shown in Table 1, both methods only learn some structural information in the knowledge graph through triples. For long-tail entities and relations, embedding representations learned through structure-based methods often produce poor completion results.

Table 1. Comparison of distance-based and tensor-decomposition-based methods.

Method Category	Key Innovations
Distance-based methods	Introduce various improvements to manage the semantic representation of relations, including translation operations, relation hyperplanes, relation-specific mapping matrices, and complex rotational operations to better handle symmetrical relationships.
Tensor decomposition-based methods	Focus on matrix factorization techniques that optimize computational efficiency and parameter count, addressing asymmetry in relations and automating the design of scoring functions.

2.2. Text-Description-Based Approach

Research has shown that pre-trained language models, such as the Transformer [16]-based bidirectional encoder BERT [17], can significantly improve the performance of natural language processing tasks with limited data. Calderón-Suárez R [18] introduced a novel data augmentation method that utilizes lyrics to improve the generalization ability of the method and enhance its performance. For long-tail entities and relations in knowledge graphs, traditional methods that utilize structural information often yield randomly initialized entity and relation representations, which leads to a sharp decline in reasoning performance on long-tail entities. To better leverage the rich semantic knowledge in pre-trained language models to represent long-tail data, KG-BERT [3] was proposed as the first model to fine-tune pre-trained language models for knowledge graph completion tasks. This model treats triplets as textual sequences and uses the output probabilities from BERT to judge the truthfulness of triplets. Building upon KG-BERT, Pretrain-KGE [19] introduces a general training framework consisting of three stages: semantic-based fine-tuning, knowledge extraction, and KG training. It learns the structural information of triplets while retaining some of the knowledge from BERT to learn better knowledge graph embeddings. Inspired by masked language modeling (MLM), MEM-KGC [20] is proposed by BONGGEUN CHOI et al. This method first masks the tail entity and treats the head entity and relation as the context for the tail entity. Then, it predicts the masked entity from all entities, effectively capturing the characteristics of unseen entities. KG-BERT only encodes the textual descriptions of entities and relations, overlooking the structural information in the knowledge graph. To address this, StAR [4] by Bo Wang et al. combines text and structure information. This model adopts a Siamese network structure with a pre-trained language model as the encoder to fully utilize the textual information of entities and relations. To overcome the limited number of negative samples and the issue of some entities lacking textual descriptions, LMKE [5] by Xintao Wang et al. introduces contrastive learning into text-based reasoning methods. The embeddings of entities within a batch are used as negative samples for each other, avoiding the extra cost of encoding negative samples. For entities without textual descriptions, LMKE jointly uses entity names, relation names, relation textual descriptions, and other information to represent their embeddings, enriching the representation of entities with missing information. SimKGC [21] argues that the key to model performance lies in an efficient negative sampling method for contrastive learning. Therefore, this method designs three types of negative sampling: within-batch negative sampling, batch-level negative sampling, and a simplified form of self-negative sampling for hard negatives. These methods have brought new ideas and performance improvements to knowledge graph embedding and completion tasks.

3. CAKGC

In this section, we elaborate on the proposed knowledge graph completion method using a pre-trained language model based on categorical information and multi-layer residual attention (CAKGC). The overall architecture is depicted in Figure 1. The model consists of two main components: an encoder and a decoder. The encoder takes the textual descriptions and category information about entities and relations as input and encodes them using a dual encoder. The decoder takes the encoded sequences and feeds them into the improved attention network MRAN, which dynamically adjusts the attention focus based on different contextual information. Finally, the triplet's score indicating its truthfulness is computed using a two-layer MLP.

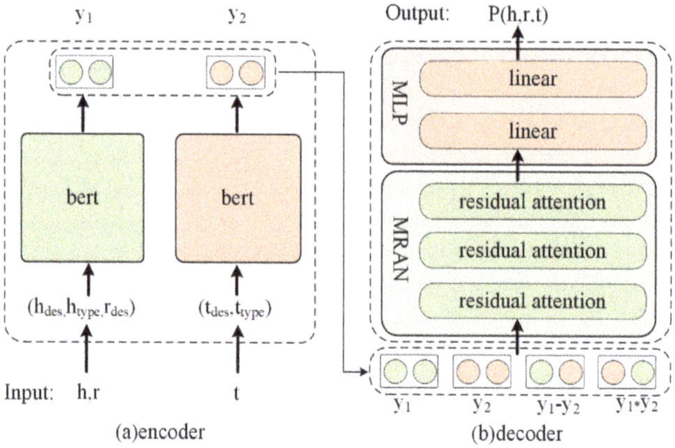

Figure 1. Overview of CAKGC.

3.1. Encoder

The CAKGC model employs a dual encoder architecture. The two encoders are initialized using the same pre-trained language model, BERT, but they do not share parameters. Given a triplet (h, r, t), we consider the case of predicting the tail entity. Specifically, the input of the first encoder is defined as follows in Equation (1):

$$x_1 = hh_{des}[CLS]h_{type}rr_{des}[MASK] \tag{1}$$

where h and r represent the head entity and relation of a triplet and h_{des}, r_{des}, h_{type} denote the textual descriptions of the head entity, textual description of the relation, and the category information of the head entity, respectively. Compared to the textual description sequences, category information sequences are typically much shorter. In the context of modeling long sequences, the shorter category information sequences may not provide sufficient contextual information as the model needs to process a large amount of information. In such cases, the model may tend to prioritize processing the textual description information while neglecting the category information, leading to a performance decline.

To assist the model in better understanding long sequences and guide the model to pay more attention to the category information, we prepend a special token $[CLS]$ before the category information. Additionally, we adopt the Masked Entity Modeling (MEM) approach by replacing the tail entity with a special token $[MASK]$. The input sequence x1 is then fed into the pre-trained language model BERT to obtain the output $y_1 \in \mathbb{R}^H$ for the first encoder, which represents the embedding of the masked tail entity. This is formally represented as Equation (2).

$$y_1 = BERT_1(x_1)_{mask} \tag{2}$$

Similarly, for the second encoder, we introduce the input of entity category information, which is represented as Equation (3):

$$x_2 = tt_{des}[CLS]t_{type} \quad (3)$$

where t, t_{des}, and t_{type} represent the tail entity, textual description of the tail entity, and the category of the tail entity, respectively. To emphasize the importance of category information, we also prepend a special token $[CLS]$ before the category information. The input sequence x_2 is fed into BERT, and the output $y_2 \in \mathbb{R}^H$ from the second encoder is obtained. It represents the embedded representation of the tail entity encoded by the pre-trained language model BERT, as shown in Equation (4).

$$y_2 = BERT_2(x_2)_t \quad (4)$$

For a given triplet (h, r, t), we utilize two encoders to obtain the embedding representations of the head entity and tail entity. The first encoder encodes the textual description of the head entity, its category information, and the textual description of the relation, resulting in the embedding representation, y_1, for the head entity–relation pair. The second encoder jointly encodes the textual description and category information of the tail entity, obtaining the embedding representation, y_2, for the tail entity. Thus, y_1 and y_2 can be regarded as positive sample pairs for the entities. Additionally, we can replace the tail entity, t, with other entities from the same batch and encode them using the second encoder, obtaining multiple negative sample pairs. We aim to maximize the similarity between positive sample pairs and minimize the similarity between negative sample pairs. Through contrastive learning between positive and negative sample pairs, the model can learn more accurate representations of entities and relations. Furthermore, by jointly encoding the textual description and category information, we can significantly enrich the representation of entities, especially for entities with shorter textual descriptions.

3.2. Decoder

In the decoder part, the embedding representations y_1 from the first encoder, which encodes the masked tail entity, and y_2 from the second encoder, which encodes the tail entity, are concatenated and expanded for similarity calculation. This calculation aims to determine the probability that the current triplet is a positive triplet (i.e., the probability that the candidate entity or relation is the true entity or relation). Specifically, given the inputs $y_1, y_2 \in \mathbb{R}^H$, they are expanded to form the input sequence $z_1 \in \mathbb{R}^{4 \times H}$ as shown in Equation (5).

$$z_1 = [y_1, y_2, y_1 - y_2, y_1 * y_2] \quad (5)$$

The similarity calculation consists of two parts: (1) MRAN and (2) MLP. The MRAN component is utilized to capture complex relationships between entities, resulting in improved entity and relation embeddings. Subsequently, two linear layers are employed to obtain the similarity scores between the current entity pairs.

MRAN. To effectively capture key information from the context of entities and relations, inspired by ResiDual, a novel attention mechanism called Multi-Layer Residual Attention Network (MRAN) is designed, as shown in Figure 2. Specifically, each layer consists of a residual attention module. The initial inputs for MRAN are $u_0 = z_1$ and $v_0 = z_1$. For the k-th layer of MRAN, the output is given by

$$u^k = \text{LayerNorm}(u^{k-1} + \text{Attn}(u^{k-1})) \quad (6)$$

$$v^k = v^{k-1} + \text{Attn}(u^{k-1}) \quad (7)$$

where u_{k-1} and v_{k-1} are the outputs of the $k-1$th layer, representing the inputs to the kth layer. Attn refers to the attention mechanism. To better capture complex relationships within the input sequence, we employ a variant of multi-head self-attention that utilizes learnable transformations. Specifically, for the attention part of the kth layer of MRAN, linear transformations are applied to the input u_{k-1}.

$$Q^k = Linear_1^k(u^{k-1}) \tag{8}$$

$$K^k = Linear_2^k(u^{k-1}) \tag{9}$$

$$K^k = Linear_3^k(u^{k-1}) \tag{10}$$

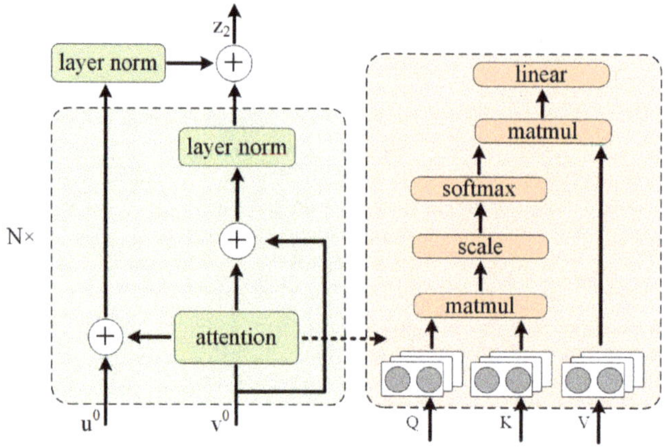

Figure 2. Structure of MRAN.

The Q^k, K^k, V^k are divided into h heads. For the i head, where $Q_i^k, K_i^k, V_i^k \in \mathbb{R}^{4\times hs}$, the weighted output $out_{attn_i^k} \in \mathbb{R}^{4\times hs}$ is calculated as follows:

$$attn_i^k = Softmax\left(\frac{Q_i^k {K_i^k}^T}{\sqrt{hs}}\right) \tag{11}$$

$$out_{attn_i^k} = attn_i^k \cdot V_i^k \tag{12}$$

where $attn_i^k$ represents the normalized attention scores for the i head and hs denotes the dimensionality of the i head. The final weighted output $out^k \in \mathbb{R}^{4\times H}$ is obtained by concatenating the weighted outputs from all h heads and applying a linear transformation as follows:

$$out_{attn^k} = \left[out_{attn_1^k}; out_{attn_2^k}; \cdots out_{attn_h^k}\right] \tag{13}$$

$$out^k = Linear_4^k(out_{attn^k}) \tag{14}$$

To alleviate the issues of gradient vanishing or exploding during network training, MRAN incorporates residual connections. Additionally, to accelerate model training and facilitate convergence, MRAN introduces layer normalization. For the final layer of MRAN, the outputs are denoted as u^N and v^N. The output v^N is layer-normalized and added to u^N to obtain the final output $z_2 \in \mathbb{R}^{4\times H}$.

$$z_2 = u^N + LayerNorm\left(v^N\right) \tag{15}$$

MLP. For computational convenience, $z_2 \in \mathbb{R}^{4\times H}$ is reshaped into $z_3 \in \mathbb{R}^{4H}$, and the RELU activation function is applied to introduce non-linearity to the model. To further enhance the model's performance, the degree information of the head entity d_h and tail entity d_t is incorporated. After passing through two layers of MLP, the probability $p(h,r,t)$ of the input triplet being true is obtained.

$$z_4 = RELU(Linear_5([z_3; d_h; d_t])) \tag{16}$$

$$p(h,r,t) = Linear_6(z_4) \tag{17}$$

Loss. To reduce the time complexity of the model, we adopt the negative sample construction technique from LMKE. Within the same batch, we replace the tail entity of the current triplet with other entities within that batch to form a set of negative triplets. For a single triplet (h,r,t) within the current batch, when predicting the tail entity, we utilize a self-adversarial negative sampling loss function as shown in Equation (18):

$$L(h,r,t) = -\log(p(h,r,t^+)) - \frac{exp(p(h,r,t^-))}{\sum_{t\in T^-} exp(p(h,r,t))} \cdot \log(1 - p(h,r,t^-)) \tag{18}$$

Here, t^+, t^- represent the positive and negative samples of the tail entity, respectively, and T^- denotes the set of negative samples for the tail entity.

4. Experiment

4.1. Datasets

To evaluate the effectiveness of the proposed method in this paper, we employed two public datasets, FB15k-237 and WN18RR, as well as a Tibetan Thangka dataset specifically constructed for Thangka knowledge graph completion.

FB15k-237 is a dataset based on the Freebase knowledge graph, containing 14,951 entities, 237 relations, and 310,116 triplets. It is a subset of FB15k and is designed to achieve a more balanced dataset by removing some low-frequency relations. The dataset provides three parts: a training set with 272,115 triplets, a validation set with 17,535 triplets, and a test set with 20,466 triplets.

WN18RR is a dataset based on the WordNet knowledge graph, consisting of 40,943 entities, 11 relations, and a total of 90,343 triplets. The triplets are divided into training, validation, and test sets. The training set contains 86,835 triplets, the validation set contains 3034 triplets, and the test set contains 3134 triplets. This dataset is commonly used to evaluate the performance of knowledge graph completion algorithms. WN18RR is a simplified and revised version of the WN18 dataset, designed to increase the difficulty of training models and better reflect real-world applications.

The Thangka domain knowledge graph, constructed by our project team, describes the history, figures, events, era, style, genre, material, and craftsmanship of Thangka, a special form of painting art. Due to the semi-automatic and manual construction process, there are issues such as incomplete entities, insufficient relationships, and limited knowledge. Therefore, we propose the CAKGC knowledge completion method and validate it on the Thangka dataset. The dataset consists of 3491 triplets, including 1399 entities and 13 relations. It is divided into a training set (2793 triplets), a validation set (349 triplets), and a test set (349 triplets) in a ratio of 8:1:1.

4.2. Experimental Setup and Evaluation Metrics

During the training process, we utilized BERT-base [17] and BERT-tiny [22] as pre-trained language models. BERT-base is a pre-trained deep bidirectional Transformer model with 110 million parameters, consisting of 12 Transformer encoder layers and 768 hidden units. On the other hand, BERT-tiny is a smaller-scale pre-trained bidirectional Transformer model. Compared to BERT-base, BERT-tiny has a smaller model size with only two Transformer encoder layers and 10 million parameters, making it suitable for resource-constrained environments. We trained the CAKGC model with the BERT-base version on an NVIDIA GeForce RTX 3090 GPU (NVIDIA, Santa Clara, CA, USA) and the BERT-tiny version on an NVIDIA Tesla K80 GPU (NVIDIA, Santa Clara, CA, USA).

In the entity prediction task of knowledge graph completion, MRR, Hits@1, Hits@3, and Hits@10 are commonly used evaluation metrics to measure the performance of models. They are defined as follows:

MRR: MRR is calculated by sorting the candidate entity list for each query entity in descending order based on the predicted probabilities from the model. Then, the reciprocal rank of the correct entity for each query entity in the candidate entity list is computed.

$$MRR = \frac{1}{|S|}\sum_{i=1}^{|S|}\frac{1}{rank_i} \tag{19}$$

where N is the number of candidate entities and $rank_i$ represents the rank of the correct entity in the candidate entity list based on the descending order of probabilities.

Hits@k: Hits@k is calculated by sorting the candidate entity list for each query entity in descending order based on the predicted probabilities from the model. Then, it checks if the correct entity is present within the top k predicted entities for each query entity. Hits@k focuses solely on whether the correct entity is among the top k predicted entities.

$$Hits@k = \frac{1}{|S|}\sum_{i=1}^{|S|}\Gamma(rank_i \leq k) \tag{20}$$

where N represents the number of candidate entities, and $I(x)$ takes values from the set $\{0,1\}$. Specifically, when $rank_i \leq k$, I takes the value of 1; otherwise, I takes the value of 0.

4.3. Comparison with Baseline Model Performance

CAKGC (BERT-tiny) and CAKGC (BERT-base) were compared with existing structurally based and textually based methods in the link prediction task. The structurally based methods included TransE, RotatE, DistMult, and AutoBLM. The textually based methods included Pretrain-KGE, KG-BERT, StAR, MEM-KGC, C-LMKE, and SimKGC.

Two versions of the CAKGC model, based on BERT-tiny with 10 million parameters and BERT-base with 110 million parameters, were employed for link prediction on two popular publicly available datasets, FB15k-237 and WN18RR. Tables 2 and 3 present the results, showing that both versions of the CAKGC model achieved state-of-the-art performance on the FB15k-237 dataset and demonstrated competitive performance on the WN18RR dataset. Specifically, the CAKGC (BERT-tiny) model achieved MRR, Hits@1, Hits@3, and Hits@10 scores of 0.416, 0.335, 0.451, and 0.571, respectively, on the FB15k-237 dataset. Compared to the previous best-performing model C-LMKE (BERT-tiny), the CAKGC (BERT-tiny) model improved the scores by 1%, 1.6%, and 0.6%, respectively. On the WN18RR dataset, the CAKGC (BERT-base) model performed second best, trailing the SOTA model SimKGC. Compared to the C-LMKE (BERT-base) model, the CAKGC (BERT-base) model achieved improvements of 3.8%, 6.4%, and 2.3% in MRR, Hits@1, and Hits@3, respectively. Furthermore, compared to C-LMKE (BERT-tiny), the CAKGC (BERT-base) model demonstrated improvements of 3.4%, 3.5%, 2.7%, and 1.2% in MRR, Hits@1, Hits@3, and Hits@10, respectively.

Table 2. Dataset statistics.

Dataset	Entities	Relations	Train	Valid	Test
FB15k-237	14,151	237	272,115	17,535	20,466
WN18RR	40,943	11	86,835	3034	3134
Thangka	1399	13	2793	399	399

From the results presented in Table 3, it can be observed that the performance improvement of our model on the FB15k-237 dataset is not as significant as that on the WN18RR dataset. We attribute this to two main reasons. (1) Compared to the WN18RR dataset, the FB15k-237 dataset has a higher average degree for each entity, indicating richer neighborhood information for entities in the FB15k-237 dataset. We can see that even advanced structure-based methods like AutoBLM achieve good performance on FB15k-237, indicating that modeling only textual descriptions is insufficient, and the internal structural information of the knowledge graph is equally important. (2) The FB15k-237 dataset contains a large number of two-hop relations, while the WN18RR dataset only consists of one-hop relations. Therefore, link prediction on FB15k-237 is more challenging, as the information obtained solely from textual descriptions is limited and cannot support better reasoning for two-hop or even multi-hop relations.

Table 3. Link prediction experiments on the FB15k-237 and WN18RR datasets.

Method	FB15k-237				WN18RR			
	MRR	**Hits@1**	**Hits@3**	**Hits@10**	**MRR**	**Hits@1**	**Hits@3**	**Hits@10**
TransE	0.279	0.198	0.376	0.441	0.243	0.043	0.441	0.532
RotatE	0.338	0.241	0.375	0.533	0.476	0.428	0.492	0.571
DistMult	0.241	0.155	0.263	0.419	0.430	0.390	0.440	0.490
AutoBLM	0.364	0.270	-	0.553	0.492	0.452	-	0.567
Pretrain-KGE	0.332	-	-	0.529	0.235	0.263	0.423	0.557
KG-BERT	-	-	-	0.420	0.216	0.041	0.302	0.524
StAR	0.296	0.205	0.322	0.482	0.401	0.243	0.491	0.709
ΛEM-KGC$_{(BERT_{base})}$	0.346	0.253	0.381	0.531	0.557	0.475	0.604	0.704
C-LMKE$_{(BERT_{tiny})}$	0.406	0.319	0.445	0.571	0.545	0.467	0.587	0.692
C-LMKE$_{(BERT_{base})}$	0.404	0.324	0.439	0.556	0.598	0.480	0.675	0.806
SimKGC	0.336	0.249	0.362	0.511	0.666	0.587	0.717	0.800
CAKGC$_{(BERT_{tiny})}$	0.416	0.335	0.451	0.571	0.579	0.512	0.614	0.704
CAKGC$_{(BERT_{base})}$	-	-	-	-	0.636	0.544	0.698	0.795

In the link prediction experiments conducted on the Tangka dataset we constructed, we compared our model with C-LMKE (BERT-base). According to Table 4, our model achieved MRR, Hits@1, Hits@3, and Hits@10 scores of 0.612, 0.566, 0.635, and 0.713, respectively, on the Tangka knowledge graph completion dataset. Compared to C-LMKE (BERT-base), our model demonstrated improvements of 1.9%, 3.2%, 1.2%, and 2% in MRR, Hits@1, Hits@3, and Hits@10, respectively.

Table 4. Link prediction experiments on the Thangka dataset.

Model	MRR	Hits@1	Hits@3	Hits@10
C-LMKE$_{(BERT_{base})}$	0.593	0.534	0.623	0.683
CAKGC$_{(BERT_{base})}$	0.612	0.566	0.635	0.703

4.4. Ablation Experiment

To demonstrate the effectiveness of incorporating entity category information and the Multi-Relation-aware Multi-hop Attention Network (MRAN), we conducted ablation experiments, as shown in Table 5. The experiments consisted of four groups: (1) CAKGC model, (2) CAKGC model without entity category information, (3) CAKGC model without MRAN, and (4) CAKGC model without both entity category information and MRAN. The results in Table 5 indicate that the model's performance decreased when MRAN and entity category information were removed separately. This demonstrates the effectiveness of incorporating entity category information and the MRAN in improving the model's performance.

Table 5. Ablation experiments of the CAKGC (BERT-tiny) model on the WN18RR dataset.

Model	MRR	Hits@1	Hits@3	Hits@10
CAKGC	0.579	0.512	0.614	0.704
CAKGC (w/o type)	0.571	0.502	0.606	0.698
CAKGC (w/o attn)	0.550	0.482	0.580	0.681
CAKGC (w/o type and attn)	0.545	0.467	0.587	0.692

5. Discussion

5.1. Entity Visualization

To qualitatively assess the effectiveness of the addition of category information in our proposed model, we focused specifically on the three categories with a higher number of instances in the WN18RR dataset. We randomly selected 100 entities from each category and used the second encoder in our model, which incorporates category information (the CAKGC model), to obtain embeddings for these entities. In Figure 3, it is clearly observable that entities from different categories are well separated in the space. This result not only demonstrates the high quality of the entity embeddings learned by our model, but, more importantly, it proves that the addition of category information significantly enhances the model's performance capabilities.

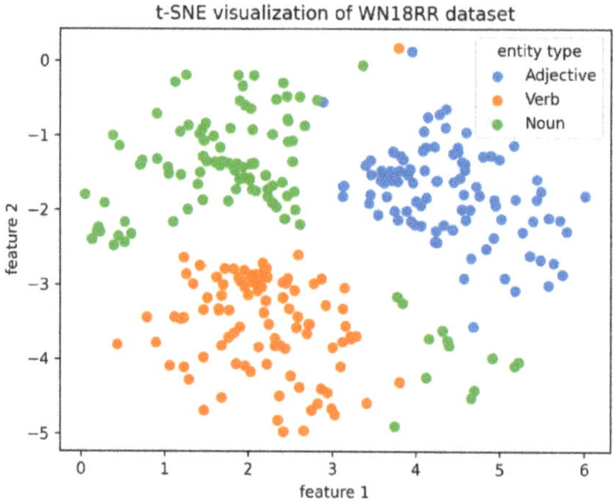

Figure 3. Entity embedding t-SNE two-dimensional visualization on the WN18RR dataset.

5.2. Sparse Entity Prediction

For entity prediction on the sparse knowledge graph of WN18RR, we utilized the BERT-tiny pre-trained language model. The test set entities were divided into ten groups based on their degree values. Specifically, the ith group, denoted as $both_i$, consisted of entities with degree values ranging from 2^i to $2^{(i+1)} - 1$. From Figure 4, it can be observed that CAKGC outperforms C-LMKE in terms of Hits@1 for sparse entity prediction, demonstrating a significant improvement.

5.3. Attention Mechanism

For the attention component in MRAN, we explored three attention mechanisms: Pre-Layer Normalization attention (Pre-LN), Post-Layer Normalization attention (Post-LN), and Residual Bi-directional Layer Normalization attention (ResiDual), as illustrated in Figure 5. The attention layers were stacked three times (N = 3).

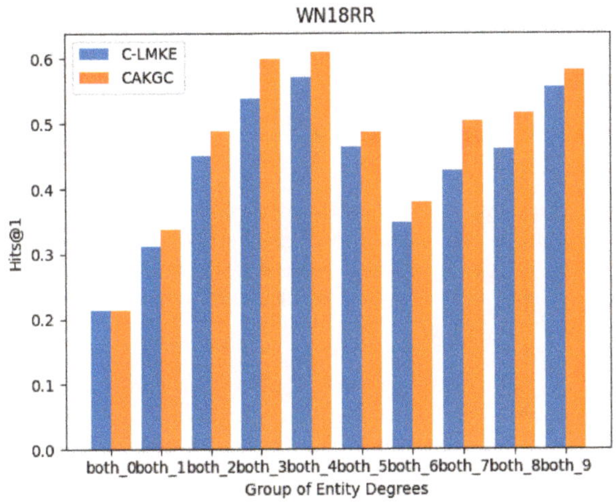

Figure 4. Entity prediction of different degrees on the WN18RR dataset.

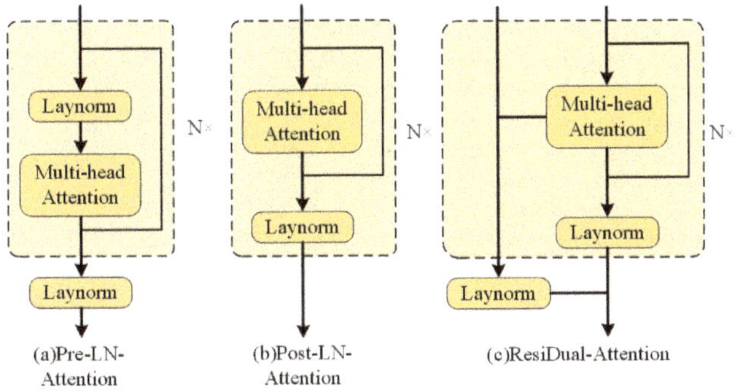

Figure 5. Different attention mechanisms.

From Table 6, it can be observed that ResiDual outperforms the traditional Pre-LN and Post-LN attention mechanisms. In Pre-LN, the normalization is performed before the self-attention, which means that the normalization heavily depends on the input. In Post-LN, the input of each sub-layer is the sum of the outputs from all preceding sub-layers. Therefore, any errors in the preceding sub-layers can accumulate and propagate to subsequent sub-layers, potentially leading to error accumulation. ResiDual, with its bidirectional attention mechanism, effectively addresses both of these issues, resulting in further performance improvement.

Table 6. Comparison of entity prediction performance of the WN18RR data set under different attention mechanisms. The model uses CAKGC (BERT-tiny).

Model	MRR	Hits@1	Hits@3	Hits@10
CAKGC (Pre-LN-Attention)	0.568	0.499	0.602	0.693
CAKGC (Post-LN-Attention)	0.573	0.504	0.609	0.701
CAKGC (ResiDual-Attention)	0.579	0.512	0.614	0.704

6. Conclusions

In order to overcome the limitations of text-based methods in understanding the contextual information between entities and relations and improving the quality of entity embeddings in knowledge graph completion, this paper proposes a novel contrastive learning method called CAKGC. CAKGC significantly improves the representation quality of entity embeddings by introducing the category of semantic information of entities. In addition, we also designed a novel attention mechanism called a multi-relation-aware multi-hop attention network (MRAN) to more accurately capture the contextual information between entities and relations. Experimental results on the FB15k-237 and WN18RR datasets show that our model is one of the best-performing models. Nevertheless, the generalization ability of the model when processing a wider range of datasets and its dependence on advanced hardware still need further study. Future work will explore optimizing computational efficiency and extending the model to adapt to more diverse knowledge graphs. In summary, the CAKGC method provides an effective solution for the field of knowledge graph completion, promoting the depth and accuracy of entity and relation understanding.

6.1. Future Work

(1) SimKGC achieves the best performance on the WN18RR dataset, mainly due to the design of a high-quality negative sampling strategy. In future work, we will focus on constructing high-quality negative samples to further improve the performance of CAKGC on WN18RR. (2) Recent studies have shown that MLP architectures perform comparably to attention architectures in the field of image processing, while attention mechanisms have significantly higher time complexity than MLP. To reduce the model's time complexity, future work will explore designing an MLP architecture to replace the attention mechanism in MRAN, with the expectation of achieving comparable or even better performance. (3) The performance improvement of CAKGC on FB15k-237 is not as significant as on WN18RR, possibly due to its text-based nature, which fails to consider the rich contextual information of entities. In future work, we plan to incorporate graph neural networks to capture the neighborhood information of entities and further enhance the model's performance by effectively integrating the entity's neighborhood information with text descriptions and category information.

6.2. Limitations of the Research

(1) Model complexity: Our method CAKGC has two versions, BERT-base and BERT-tiny. CAKGC (BERT-base) uses NVIDIA RTX 3090, which has high video memory requirements. This reliance on high-end hardware may limit the deployment of the model in environments with limited computing resources and may increase the cost of research and practice. (2) Dependence on the quality of text descriptions: The performance of the model may rely heavily on the quality of the text descriptions of entities and relations. If these descriptions are uninformative or biased, it may affect the quality of the embedding and the predictive power of the model. (3) Limitations of the attention mechanism: Although multiple layers of residual attention networks are used, the attention mechanism may still have difficulty capturing all key contextual information, especially in large-scale graphs with complex relations or a large number of entities. (4) Completeness and accuracy of entity category information: The performance of the model depends in part on the completeness and accuracy of the entity classification information. If the category information is incomplete or wrong, it may affect the performance of the model.

Author Contributions: Conceptualization, Q.R. and Y.Y.; Methodology, Q.R.; Validation, Q.R. and K.W.; Writing—original draft, Q.R.; Writing—review & editing, T.W. and X.G. All authors have read and agreed to the published version of the manuscript.

Funding: This research was funded by the 2023 Basic Research Operating Expenses of Central Universities (No. 31920230175), National Natural Science Foundation of China (No. 62166035), Natural Science Foundation of Gansu Province (No. 21JR7RA163).

Institutional Review Board Statement: Not applicable.

Informed Consent Statement: Not applicable.

Data Availability Statement: The original contributions presented in the study are included in the article, further inquiries can be directed to the corresponding author.

Conflicts of Interest: The authors declare no conflict of interest.

ferences

Bordes, A.; Usunier, N.; Garcia-Duran, A.; Weston, J.; Yakhnenko, O. Translating Embeddings for Modeling Multi-relational Data. In *Advances in Neural Information Processing Systems 26, Proceedings of the 27th Annual Conference on Neural Information Processing Systems 2013, Lake Tahoe, NV, USA, 5–10 December 2013*; Curran Associates, Inc.: Red Hook, NY, USA, 2013.

Sun, Z.; Deng, Z.H.; Nie, J.Y.; Tang, J. Rotate: Knowledge graph embedding by relational rotation in complex space. *arXiv* **2019**, arXiv:1902.10197.

Yao, L.; Mao, C.; Luo, Y. KG-BERT: BERT for knowledge graph completion. *arXiv* **2019**, arXiv:1909.03193.

Wang, B.; Shen, T.; Long, G.; Zhou, T.; Wang, Y.; Chang, Y. Structure-Augmented Text Representation Learning for Efficient Knowledge Graph Completion. *Proc. Web Conf.* **2021**, *2021*, 1737–1748.

Wang, X.; He, Q.; Liang, J.; Xiao, Y. Language Models as Knowledge Embeddings. In Proceedings of the International Joint Conference on Artificial Intelligence, Vienna, Austria, 23–29 July 2022.

Wang, Z.; Zhang, J.; Feng, J.; Chen, Z. Knowledge Graph Embedding by Translating on Hyperplanes. In Proceedings of the Twenty-Eighth AAAI Conference on Artificial Intelligence, Québec, QC, Canada, 27–31 July 2014.

Lin, Y.; Liu, Z.; Sun, M.; Liu, Y.; Zhu, X. Learning Entity and Relation Embeddings for Knowledge Graph Completion. In Proceedings of the Twenty-Ninth AAAI Conference on Artificial Intelligence, Austin, TX, USA, 25–30 January 2015.

Ji, G.; Liu, K.; He, S.; Zhao, J. Knowledge Graph Completion with Adaptive Sparse Transfer Matrix. In Proceedings of the Thirtieth AAAI Conference on Artificial Intelligence, Phoenix, AZ, USA, 12–17 February 2016.

Chao, L.; He, J.; Wang, T.; Chu, W. PairRE: Knowledge graph embeddings via paired relation vectors. *arXiv* **2020**, arXiv:2011.03798.

Nickel, M.; Volker, T.; Hans-Peter, K. A Three-Way Model for Collective Learning on Multi-Relational Data. In Proceedings of the 28th International Conference on Machine Learning, Bellevue, DC, USA, 28 June–2 July 2011.

Yang, B.; Yih, W.; He, X.; Gao, J.; Deng, L. Embedding Entities and Relations for Learning and Inference in Knowledge Bases. *arXiv* **2014**, arXiv:1412.6575.

Théo, T.; Johannes, W.; Sebastian, R.; Éric, G.; Guillaume, B. Complex Embeddings for Simple Link Prediction. In Proceedings of the 33rd International Conference on International Conference on Machine Learning, New York, NY, USA, 19–24 June 2016.

Nickel, M.; Rosasco, L.; Poggio, T. Holographic Embeddings of Knowledge Graphs. In Proceedings of the Thirtieth AAAI Conference on Artificial Intelligence, Phoenix, AZ, USA, 12–17 February 2016.

Kazemi, S.; Poole, N. Simple embedding for link prediction in knowledge graphs. In *Advances in Neural Information Processing Systems 31, Proceedings of the Annual Conference on Neural Information Processing Systems 2018, Montréal, QC, Canada, 3–8 December 2018*; Curran Associates, Inc.: Red Hook, NY, USA, 2018.

Zhang, Y.; Yao, Q.; Kwok, J.T. Bilinear Scoring Function Search for Knowledge Graph Learning. *IEEE Trans. Pattern Anal. Mach. Intell.* **2022**, *45*, 1458–1473. [CrossRef] [PubMed]

Vaswani, A.; Shazeer, N.; Parmar, N.; Uszkoreit, J.; Jones, L.; Gomez, A.N.; Kaiser, Ł.; Polosukhin, I. Attention is all you need. In *Advances in Neural Information Processing Systems, Proceedings of the 31st Conference on Neural Information Processing Systems, Long Beach, CA, USA, 4–9 December 2017*; Curran Associates, Inc.: Red Hook, NY, USA, 2017.

Devlin, J.; Chang, M.; Lee, K.; Toutanova, K. BERT: Pre-training of Deep Bidirectional Transformers for Language Understanding. In Proceedings of the naacL-HLT, Minneapolis, MN, USA, 6–7 June 2019.

Calderón-Suárez, R.; Ortega-Mendoza, R.M.; Montes-Gómez, M.; Toxqui-Quitl, C.; Márquez-Vera, M.A. Enhancing the Detection of Misogynistic Content in Social Media by Transferring Knowledge from Song Phrases. *IEEE Access* **2023**, *11*, 13179–13190. [CrossRef]

Zhang, Z.; Liu, X.; Zhang Y.; Su, Q.; Sun, X.; He, B. Pretrain-KGE: Learning knowledge representation from pretrained language models. In *Findings of the Association for Computational Linguistics*; Association for Computational Linguistics: Baltimore, MD, USA, 2020.

Choi, B.; Jang, D.; Ko, Y. MEM-KGC: Masked entity model for knowledge graph completion with pre-trained language model. *IEEE Access* **2021**, *9*, 132025–132032. [CrossRef]

Wang, L.; Zhao, W.; Wei, Z.; Liu, J. SimKGC: Simple Contrastive Knowledge Graph Completion with Pre-trained Language Models. In Proceedings of the 60th Annual Meeting of the Association for Computational Linguistics, Dublin, Ireland, 22–27 May 2022.

Iulia Turc, T. Well-read students learn better: On the importance of pre-training compact models. *arXiv* **2019**, arXiv:1908.08962.

applied sciences

MDPI

Article

REACT: Relation Extraction Method Based on Entity Attention Network and Cascade Binary Tagging Framework

Lingqi Kong and Shengquau Liu *

School of Information Science and Engineering, Xinjiang University, Urumqi 830017, China; 107552101311@stu.xju.edu.cn

* Correspondence: liu@xju.edu.cn

Abstract: With the development of the Internet, vast amounts of text information are being generated constantly. Methods for extracting the valuable parts from this information have become an important research field. Relation extraction aims to identify entities and the relations between them from text, helping computers better understand textual information. Currently, the field of relation extraction faces various challenges, particularly in addressing the relation overlapping problem. The main difficulties are as follows: (1) Traditional methods of relation extraction have limitations and lack the ability to handle the relation overlapping problem, requiring a redesign. (2) Relation extraction models are easily disturbed by noise from words with weak relevance to the relation extraction task, leading to difficulties in correctly identifying entities and their relations. In this paper, we propose the Relation extraction method based on the Entity Attention network and Cascade binary Tagging framework (REACT). We decompose the relation extraction task into two subtasks: head entity identification and tail entity and relation identification. REACT first identifies the head entity and then identifies all possible tail entities that can be paired with the head entity, as well as all possible relations. With this architecture, the model can handle the relation overlapping problem. In order to reduce the interference of words in the text that are not related to the head entity or relation extraction task and improve the accuracy of identifying the tail entities and relations, we designed an entity attention network. To demonstrate the effectiveness of REACT, we construct a high-quality Chinese dataset and conduct a large number of experiments on this dataset. The experimental results fully confirm the effectiveness of REACT, showing its significant advantages in handling the relation overlapping problem compared to current other methods.

Keywords: relation extraction; relation overlapping problem; attention mechanism; gate mechanism

1. Introduction

Relation extraction, an important research direction [1,2] in the field of information extraction [3], aims to automatically extract entities and their relations from massive text data, providing support for downstream tasks such as intelligent recommendation, semantic search, and deep question answering [4,5]. Relation extraction is usually divided into two subtasks: entity identification [6,7] and relation identification [8,9]. The main goal of entity identification is to identify entities with specific meanings from text, such as names of people, places, dates, organizations, and so on. Entity identification technology has a wide range of applications in the field of natural language processing, including the tasks of question-and-answer systems, public opinion analysis, entity linking, and so on. The main goal of relation identification is to identify the relations between entities from text. By automatically extracting relations between entities from large amounts of textual data, relation identification can help build applications such as knowledge graphs, recommendation systems, and sentiment analysis.

With the increasing complexity of information, the relation overlapping problem has begun to emerge [10]. The relation overlapping problem refers to the situation where there are shared entities among the entity-relation triad in the text. According to the types of overlapping, the relation overlapping problem can be further divided into three subcategories: Normal, Single Entity Overlap (SEO), and Entity Pair Overlap (EPO), as illustrated in the examples in Figure 1.

	Texts	Triplets
Normal	The **US** president **Trump** will visit **Beijing, China**	(Trump, *President_of*, US) (China, *Contains*, Beijing)
SEO	The **US** president **Trump** was born in **New York City**.	(**Trump**, *President_of*, US) (**Trump**, *Born_in*, New York City)
EPO	Trump will visit **Beijing**, which is the capital of **China**.	(**China**, *Contains*, **Beijing**) (**China**, *Capital*, **Beijing**)

Figure 1. Examples of cases of Normal, Single Entity Overlap (SEO), and Entity Pair Overlap (EPO). The overlapping entities are marked in bold. The first example belongs to the Normal class, which has no overlapping entities. The second one, with triplets sharing one single head entity "Trump", belongs to the SEO class. The last one with triplets, with the overlapping entity pair "{China, Beijing}", belongs to the EPO class.

Most existing relation extraction methods cannot effectively deal with the relation overlapping problem for two main reasons: (1) The model design is flawed and does not consider the situation where one entity in the text may have relations with multiple entities (Zheng et al. [4]), or it does not consider the existence of multiple relations between a particular head and tail entity situation (Miwa et al. [11]). (2) When the relation overlapping problem arises, there are always numerous entities in the text, and most of these entities do not have relations with each other. The noise interference from these irrelevant entities may mislead the model, causing it to incorrectly identify these irrelevant entities as part of the tail entity or relation. Additionally, the model needs to accurately understand the context around the head entity in order to correctly identify the tail entity and relation. The presence of irrelevant entities increases the difficulty of understanding the context. As shown in Figure 2, the head entity "Zhang Fansheng" in the text is only able to form the entity-relation triad "{Zhang Fansheng, Founder, Jinghai Enterprises}" with the tail entity "Jinghai Enterprises", and there are no relations with other entities. Due to the interference of entities unrelated to "Zhang Fansheng", it is difficult for the model to identify the tail entities related to the head entity "Zhang Fansheng" and the relations between them.

Text: In 1994, Zhang Fansheng established Jinghai Enterprises in Shanghai, which has been in operation for 25 years. As a renowned local enterprise, Jinghai Enterprises comprises two major subsidiaries: Jinghai Entertainment and Jinghai Football, both of which generate substantial profits

Figure 2. "Zhang Fansheng" is only able to form an entity-relation triad with "Jinghai Enterprises" and has no relations with any other entities.

In order to solve the above problems, we have designed the Entity Attention network, and we propose the Relation extraction method based on the Entity Attention network and Cascade binary Tagging framework (REACT). To address problem (1), we divide the relation extraction task into two subtasks: head entity identification and tail entity and relation identification. REACT first identifies the head entities present in the text and then identifies the tail entities that can be paired with the head entities and all possible relations between them. With this architecture, REACT is able to handle the relation overlapping problem. Please note that in this paper, entity pairs specifically refer to combinations of head and tail entities that have at least one type of relation. To address problem (2), we introduce the Entity Attention network. The Entity Attention network includes two parts: an Entity Attention Mechanism and an Entity Gated Mechanism. Words in the text have different degrees of importance for different head entities, and by introducing head entity information into the Entity Attention Mechanism, REACT is able to assign attention weights to words according to the head entities and reduce the word noise accordingly. After reducing the word noise according to the head entity, it is also necessary to consider the relevance of the words to the relation extraction task. The Entity Gated Mechanism calculates the degree of association of the words with the relation extraction task and diminishes the noise from words noise less associated with the task. By reducing the word noise through the above operations, REACT is able to focus on words with higher relevance to the head entity and the relation extraction task, thus increasing the accuracy of identifying the tail entity and relation and improving the performance of relation extraction.

Our main contributions are as follows:

1. Due to the current lack of Chinese datasets, we constructed a high-quality Chinese dataset with a high number of data with relation overlapping problems by optimizing the public Duie 2.0 entity-relation dataset;
2. For the relation overlapping problem, we propose the Relation extraction method based on the Entity Attention network and Cascade binary Tagging framework;
3. We conducted extensive experiments on a high-quality Chinese dataset to evaluate REACT and compared it with other baselines. The results demonstrate that REACT outperforms other baselines in handling relation overlapping problems.

2. Related Works

Early works on relation extraction adopted a pipeline approach (Zelenko et al. [8], Zhou et al. [12], Chan et al. [13], Mintz et al. [14], and Gormley et al. [15]). It first identifies all the entities in a sentence and then performs relation classification for each entity pair. This approach often faces the problem of error propagation because errors in the early stages cannot be corrected in later stages. To address this problem, subsequent works proposed joint learning of entities and relations, which includes feature-based models (Yu et al. [16]; Li et al. [17]; and Ren et al. [18]), as well as more recent neural network models (Gupta et al. [19]; Katiyar et al. [20]; Zhou et al. [21]; and Fu et al. [22]). By replacing manually constructed features with learned representations, neural network-based models have achieved considerable success in the relation extraction task.

As research has progressed, the relation overlapping problem has been increasingly emphasized. The relation overlapping problem refers to the situation where there are shared entities among the entity-relation triad in the text. To address this problem, many neural network-based joint models have been proposed [23].

Zeng et al. [24] were among the first to consider the relation overlapping problem. They first divided the relation overlapping problem into Normal, SEO, and EPO, and proposed a sequence-to-sequence (Seq2Seq) model with a copying mechanism. To address the relation overlapping problem, they allowed entities to participate freely in multiple triples. Building upon the Seq2Seq model, Zeng et al. [25] further investigated the impact of triple extraction order on relation extraction performance, transforming the relation extraction task into a reinforcement learning process, resulting in significant improvements.

Yuan et al. [26] redesigned the relation extraction method and successfully enabled the model to handle the relation overlapping problem. They first identified all entity pairs in the text and then individually determined whether each relation existed, rather than extracting only the most probable relation. Additionally, they pointed out that previous relation extraction methods ignored the connections between relations and independently predicted each possible relation. For example, if an entity pair has the "liveIn" relation, the "dieIn" relation is almost impossible to establish. Therefore, when determining the existence of a certain relation between entities, it is necessary to not only consider the target relation but also calculate the probability scores with respect to other relations. Inspired by the aforementioned research, Yuan et al. [27] assumed that the importance of words in text varies across different relations. They constructed a joint model based on a specific attention mechanism, which first identifies the relation existing in the text, then incorporates the relation into the attention mechanism, and finally identifies entity pairs containing the relation based on attention scores.

Although the above research was able to address the relation overlapping problem, they still regarded the identification of head and tail entities as independent processes, ignoring the semantic and logical connections between them. For example, organizational entities usually have relations with human entities (leaders, founders, members, etc.), but do not always have relations with entities such as songs, animals, movies, etc. Yu et al. [28] re-designed the method to first identify the head entity, then identify the potential tail entities based on the head entity, and finally determine all possible relations that may exist between the head entity and the tail entities. This approach not only addressed the relation overlapping problem but also achieved outstanding performance by utilizing head entity information in the tail entity identification process. Building upon this research, Li et al. [29] proposed an HBT framework, where they regarded the relation extraction task as a multi-turn question-answering task, incorporating external knowledge to introduce entities and relations. However, generating appropriate questions remains a challenge and is not suitable for most complex scenarios [30]. Inspired by the work of Yuan et al. [26] and Yu et al. [28], Fu et al. [22] introduced graphical convolutional networks, which are widely used in the field of logical reasoning [31], into the task of relation extraction. After identifying the relation between entity pairs, graph convolutional networks are used to infer the possibility of the existence of other relations. For example, "{Trump, LiveIn, United States}" can be inferred from "{Trump, LiveIn, Florida}". Prior to this, Zheng et al. [4] proposed a strong neural end-to-end joint model based on an LSTM sequence tagger for entities and relations, which helped infer unidentified relations based on identified relations. However, they were unable to address the relation overlapping problem.

Although current research has achieved joint extraction of entities and relations and developed models to address the relation overlapping problem, relations are still treated as discrete labels for entity pairs. This makes it difficult for models to correctly extract overlapping triples. Wei et al. [32] proposed a new cascaded binary labeling framework (CasRel), which uses BERT [33] as the feature extraction method and maps the tail entities through the head entities conditioned on the relations. As shown in the equation, r stands for relation, S stands for head entity, and O stands for tail entity. Relations are modeled as functions that map the head entity to the tail entity:

$$F_r(S) \to O \tag{1}$$

In natural language, the relations between entities are often closely related to their context. By introducing information about the head entity, the model can better understand the semantic structure of the sentence, thus predicting the tail entity and relations more accurately. Additionally, entities in a sentence may have multiple roles or meanings, but when paired with a specific head entity, their roles or meanings become clearer, reducing ambiguity in the tail entity and relations and improving the accuracy of identifying them. Therefore, CasRel has achieved good results. However, Wei et al. [32] were still unable to effectively utilize head entity information. Specifically, they only used head entity information as a parametric feature when identifying tail entities and relations, ignoring the potential role of head entity information in reducing word noise. When the problem of overlapping relations occurs, especially in cases of multiple overlapping relations, numerous entities typically emerge in the text. However, most of these entities do not participate in forming effective relations. This situation leads to the generation of a large number of potential invalid entity pairs, making it difficult for the model to accurately identify truly effective entity pairs among numerous possibilities, ultimately affecting the overall accuracy of relation extraction tasks.

In order to utilize the head entity information to reduce text noise and minimize interference from other irrelevant entities, we propose the Relation extraction method based on the Entity Attention network and Cascade binary Tagging framework (REACT). We utilize Entity Attention networks to help the model focus on words that are highly relevant to the head entity and the relation extraction task, thereby reducing the likelihood of identifying errors in tail entities and relations and improving the accuracy of extracting entity relation triplets.

3. Methodology

In this section, we propose the Relation extraction method based on the Entity Attention network and Cascade binary Tagging framework (REACT). A diagram outlining REACT is shown in Figure 3, and its detailed structure is shown in Figure 4. REACT consists of four main parts: the Encoding layer, the Head Entity Identification layer, the Entity Attention network layer (feature fusion layer), and the Tail Entity and Relation Identification layer. Our main contribution is in the Entity Attention network layer. In the following sections, each of these four parts is introduced.

3.1. Formalization of the Task

The input is a text $X = \{x_1, x_2, \ldots, x_n\}$ with n words. The desired output is an entity-relation triad, such as $T(X) = \{(h,r,t)|h,t \in E, r \in R\}$, where E and R are the set of entities and the set of relations, respectively. For example, in Figure 5, given a text containing 35 words, the goal is to extract the entity-relation triad "{United States, Contains, Los Angeles}", where "United States" is h, "Los Angeles" is t, and "Contains" is r in the entity-relation triad.

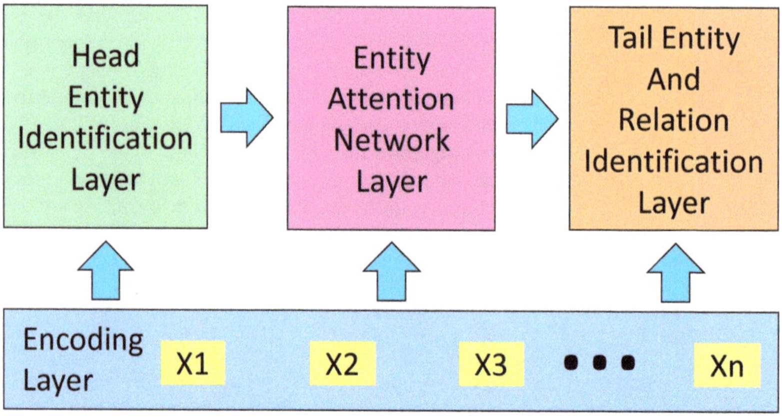

Figure 3. Diagram outlining REACT.

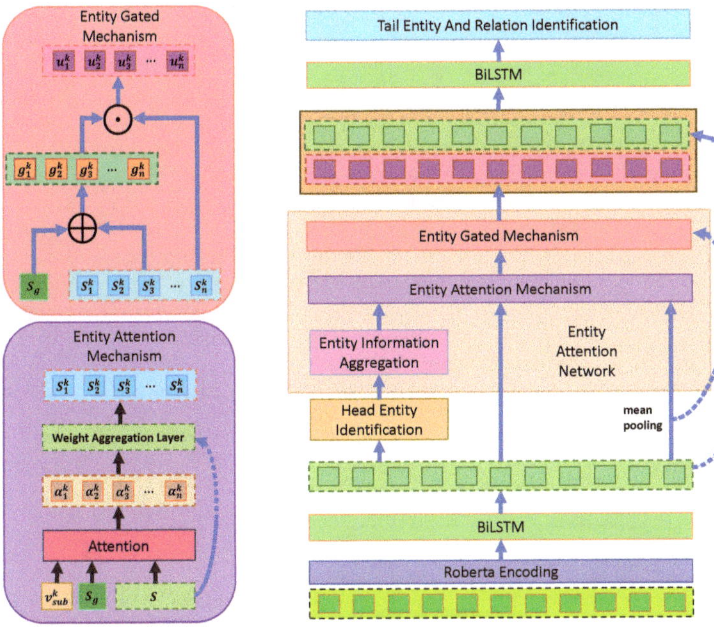

Figure 4. Detailed structure of REACT.

> Los Angeles, the second largest city in the United States, is also the largest city in the western United States and is often referred to as the "City of Angels".

Figure 5. Example of a relation extraction task. Blue part represents the head entity, and the green part represents the tail entity.

3.2. Encoding Layer

3.2.1. Roberta Layer

In order to convert text into information that can be understood by computers and capture the semantic features of the text to improve the model's understanding of the text, we use *Roberta* [34] to encode the input text. Roberta is an improved version of Bert [34], and it is currently the mainstream method for encoding text features [35].

Here, we briefly review *Roberta*, a multi-layer bidirectional Transformer-based language representation model. It is designed to learn deep representations by jointly conditioning on both the left and right contexts of each word. Specifically, it is composed of a stack of N identical Transformer blocks. We denote the Transformer block as $Trans(h)$, in which h represents the input vector. The detailed operations are as follows:

$$h_0 = DW_d + W_p \tag{2}$$

$$h_\alpha = Trans(h_{\alpha-1}), \alpha \in [1, N] \tag{3}$$

where D is the matrix of one-hot vectors of subword indices in the input sentence. W_d is the subword embedding matrix. W_p is the positional embedding matrix, where p represents the position index in the input sequence. h_α is the hidden state vector, i.e., the context representation of the input sentence at the α_{th} layer, and N is the number of Transformer blocks. For a more comprehensive description of the Transformer structure, we refer readers to Liu et al. [34] and Vaswani et al. [36].

Using *Roberta*, we obtain the text encoding $H = \{h_1, h_2, \ldots, h_n\}$ for the text X.

3.2.2. BiLSTM Layer

Due to the complexity of the relation overlapping problem, we desire to exploit the interaction information among the words in the textual data. *BiLSTM* consists of two independent *LSTM* networks: one responsible for the forward sequence and the other responsible for the backward sequence. During the forward pass, the first *LSTM* gradually processes the input data from the beginning to the end of the sequence. During the backward pass, the second *LSTM* processes the input data from the end of the sequence to the beginning. By combining the hidden states of these two *LSTM* networks, a comprehensive sequence representation can be obtained that considers the contextual interaction information throughout the entire sequence.

The detailed network architecture is shown in Figure 6, which mainly consists of an update gate and a forget gate [11].

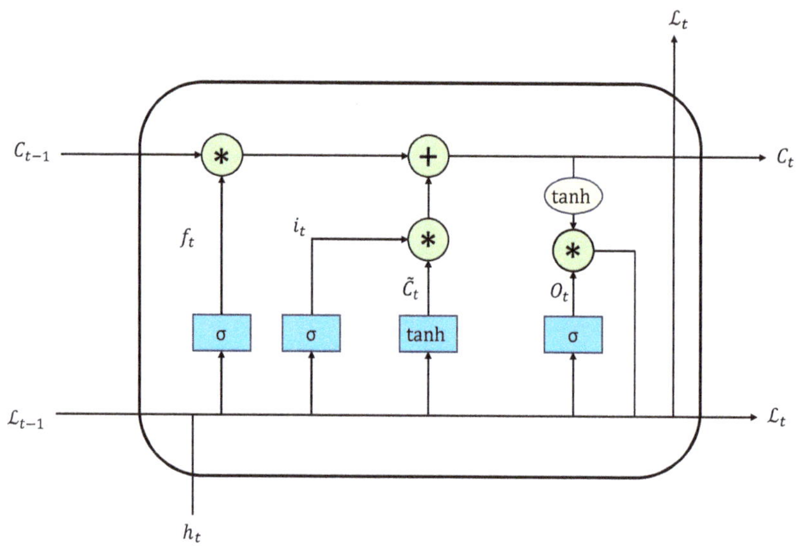

Figure 6. Detailed structure of LSTM. "*" denotes the dot product operation.

The update gate mainly controls the retention or deletion of some information from the forward state. The forget gate is used to control whether the calculation of the candidate state depends on the previous state.

The forget gate is calculated using the following formula:

$$f_t = \sigma(W_f \cdot [\mathcal{L}_{t-1}, h_t] + b_f) \tag{4}$$

The update gate is calculated using the following formula:

$$i_t = \sigma(W_i \cdot [\mathcal{L}_{t-1}, h_t] + b_i) \tag{5}$$

$$\widetilde{C}_t = tanh(W_c \cdot [\mathcal{L}_{t-1}, h_t] + b_c) \tag{6}$$

The output state is calculated using the following formula:

$$O_t = \sigma(W_o\, [\mathcal{L}_{t-1}, h_t] + b_o) \tag{7}$$

$$C_t = f_t * C_{t-1} + i_t * \widetilde{C}_t \tag{8}$$

$$\mathcal{L}_t = O_t * tanh(C_t) \tag{9}$$

where h_t represents the current input data, $\mathcal{L}_{t-1}$ represents the input at the previous time, and $\mathcal{L}_t$ represents the current output. σ is the sigmoid function with a value ranging from 0 to 1; W_f, W_i, W_c, W_o, b_f, b_i, and b_c represent the weight matrix; and *tanh* is the activation function.

Use text encoding H as the input for the *BiLSTM*, and obtain the output s_i.

$$s_i = [\overrightarrow{LSTM}(h_i); \overleftarrow{LSTM}(h_i)], i \in [1, n] \tag{10}$$

$S = \{s_1, s_2, \ldots, s_n\}$ denotes the contextual features.

3.3. Head Entity Identification

Since the problem of entity nesting may occur in the text, the decoder separately predicts all possible head entity start and end positions. In Figure 7, the start and end positions are predicted for the head entity "Stephen King". The specific operation is shown below:

$$P_i^{H-start} = W_{start} s_i + b_{start} \tag{11}$$

$$P_i^{H-end} = W_{end} s_i + b_{end} \tag{12}$$

where $P_i^{H-start}$ and P_i^{H-end} represent the probabilities that the i_{th} word in the text denotes the start and end positions of the head entity, respectively, which are set to 1 if they exceed a set threshold during the experiment, and 0 otherwise. W_{start} and W_{end} denote trainable weights.

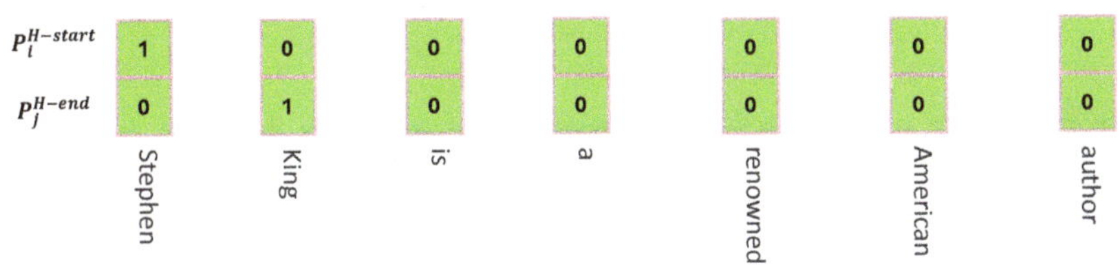

Figure 7. Head entity prediction example.

3.4. Entity Attention Network

3.4.1. Entity Information Aggregation

Assuming that the head entity k in the text has already been predicted, we cannot directly input the words comprising the head entity k into the Entity Attention Mechanism because the computer cannot understand them. Therefore, it is necessary to convert them into an appropriate form.

We take the average of the word feature s_i from the contextual features S that comprise the head entity k, obtaining the head entity feature v_{sub}^k. The specific calculation process is as follows:

$$v_{sub}^k = \sum_{i=start}^{end} \frac{s_i}{end - start + 1} \tag{13}$$

where s_i denotes the contextual features of the i_{th} word in the text and *start* and *end* indicate the start and end positions of the head entity, respectively. For example, the head entity "United States" in Figure 5 has a start position of 10 and an end position of 11.

3.4.2. Entity Attention Mechanism

The main reason for the occurrence of the relation overlapping problem is the presence of a large number of entities in the text. Even worse, most of these entities do not have relations with each other, which poses a significant challenge for the model in extracting entity pairs.

Therefore, in order to allow the model to focus on words and entities related to the head entity and improve the accuracy of entity pair extraction, we have designed the Entity Attention Mechanism. By introducing the head entity information into the Entity Attention Mechanism, the model can allocate attention weights to words based on the head entity, reducing the interference of words unrelated to the head entity. Using the head entity k as an example, the specific calculation method is as follows:

$$S_g = avg\{s_1, s_2, \ldots, s_n\} \tag{14}$$

$$e_i^k = V^T tanh(W_v v_{sub}^k + W_g S_g + W_s s_i) \tag{15}$$

$$\alpha_i^k = \frac{\exp\left(e_i^k\right)}{\sum_{j=1}^{n} \exp\left(e_j^k\right)} \tag{16}$$

where V, W_v, W_g, and W_s are trainable weights; avg refers to the averaging operation applied to vectors in the context features S; S_g denotes the global features; $tanh$ represents the activation function; and $\sum_{j=1}^{n} \exp\left(e_j^k\right)$ denotes the summation of attention weights for each word. After calculating the attention weight e_i^k for each word based on the head entity k using Equation (15), we then use Equation (16) to calculate the proportion α_i^k of each word's attention weight relative to the total weight.

Using the above operation, the attention score α_i^k not only measures the importance of each word to the head entity but also quantifies the contribution of each word to the entire sentence.

After obtaining the attention scores, we need to reduce the features of words with low relevance to the head entity k. This helps reduce text noise. The specific calculation process is as follows:

$$s_i^k = \alpha_i^k s_i \tag{17}$$

$$S^k = (s_1^k, s_2^k, \ldots, s_n^k) \tag{18}$$

where s_i^k represents the word feature of the i_{th} word based on the head entity k.

3.4.3. Entity Gated Mechanism

The Entity Attention Mechanism is primarily used to attenuate the noise interference of words with weak associations to the head entity. However, in the text, there may exist some words that have strong associations with the head entity but are almost irrelevant to the relation extraction task. This is also a form of noise.

In order to attenuate the text word noise that is weakly associated with the relation extraction task, we propose the Entity Gated Mechanism. Still using the head entity k as an example, the operation is as follows:

$$g_i^k = \sigma((W_1 S_g + b_1) \oplus (W_2 s_i^k + b_2)) \tag{19}$$

$$u_i^k = g_i^k \odot tanh(W_3 s_i^k + b_3) \tag{20}$$

$$U^k = \{u_1^k, u_2^k, \ldots, u_n^k\} \tag{21}$$

where W_1, W_2, W_3, b_1, b_2, and b_3 are trainable weights, $\oplus$ is the cascade operation, $\odot$ is the dot-product operation, and σ denotes the shape activation function, which returns a value from 0 to 1.

The above formula compares S_g and s_i^k to calculate the degree of association g_i^k between the i_{th} word and the relation extraction task. Subsequently, based on the degree of association, the text noise is attenuated to obtain the associated feature u_i^k.

3.5. Tail Entity and Relation Identification

After deep noise attenuation, there may be a loss of fine-grained information [37]. We connect the noise-weakened U^k and the non-noise-weakened S to provide fine-grained features. After that, in order to learn the interaction information of the two granularity features, we feed them into *BiLSTM* to obtain the final representation O^k. The specific calculation is as follows:

$$h_i^k = u_i^k \oplus s_i \tag{22}$$

$$o_i^k = [\overrightarrow{LSTM}(h_i^k); \overleftarrow{LSTM}(h_i^k)], i \in [1, n] \tag{23}$$

$$O^k = \{o_1^k, o_2^k, \ldots, o_n^k\} \tag{24}$$

Finally, we extract the tail entities for each relation based on the head entity k. An example of *SEO* is given in Figure 8. For the head entity "Tim Robbins", we first identify the tail entity "United States" based on the relation "LiveIn" and then identify the tail entity "The Shawshank Redemption" based on the relation "leadActor". Through the above steps, two entity-relation triples "{Tim Robbins, LiveIn, United States}" and "{Tim Robbins, leadActor, The Shawshank Redemption}" are extracted from the text.

```
Tim Robbins currently lives in the United States and played the
leading role in "The Shawshank Redemption".
```

Figure 8. Specific case of identifying the tail entity and relation based on the head entity.

The specific calculation process is as follows:

$$p_i^{T-start} = W_r^{start} o_i^k + b_r^{start} \tag{25}$$

$$p_i^{T-end} = W_r^{end} o_i^k + b_r^{end} \tag{26}$$

$p_i^{T-start}$ and p_i^{T-end} represent the probabilities that the i_{th} word denotes the start and end positions of the tail entity, respectively. W_r^{start} and W_r^{end} denote the weight matrices for relation r. b_r^{start} and b_r^{end} denote the biases for relation r.

4. Experimental Section

4.1. Balanced Chinese Dataset Construction

DuIE2.0 [38] is the largest Chinese entity-relation extraction dataset, with 173,109 rows in the training set and 15,475 rows in the test set, including 49 entity-relation types. However, the number of occurrences of each relation in DuIE2.0 is uneven and varies greatly, making it unsuitable for relation extraction experiments [39]. At the same time, the two special scenarios of SEO and EPO also account for a small percentage, making it unsuitable for demonstrating the advantages of REACT. For this reason, We optimized DuIE2.0 by setting the threshold for the maximum number of occurrences of each relation in the training set to 230 and the threshold for each relation in the test set to 46. Table 1 shows some examples of sampling results where a few relation types fail to reach the threshold. To increase the number of data in the dataset containing EPO or SEO issues, we carefully collected over 1000 pieces of data, with each piece containing at least one type of overlapping problem. Figure 9 shows some of the data.

Table 1. Comparison between the optimized DuIE2.0 dataset and the original version.

Relation Number	DuIE2.0 Training Set	Uniform Sampling Training Set	DuIE2.0 Test Set	Uniform Sampling Test Set
1	984	230	101	46
2	3159	230	302	46
3	1807	230	170	46
4	7188	230	639	46
5	8345	230	718	46
6	593	230	46	46
7	937	230	87	46
8	1849	230	101	46
...	...	...	...	...
31	22	51	1	29
...	...	...	...	46
49	395	230	32	46
Total number	173,109	10,423	15,475	2012

	Texts	Triplets
Normal	Princess **Pingyang Zhao** was born during the late Sui Dynasty and early Tang Dynasty. Her **father** was none other than Emperor Gaozu of Tang, **Li Yuan**, and she was his third daughter.	(**Pingyang Zhao**, *Father*, Li Yuan)
SEO	According to reports from Japanese media citing Deadline, renowned Japanese horror film director **Hideo Nakata** will serve as the producer of the movie "**The Suicide Forest.**" Nakata is best known for his direction of the classic horror film "**The Grudge.**"	(**Hideo Nakata**, *Producer*, The Suicide Forest) (**Hideo Nakata**, *Director*, The Grudge)
EPO	**Jay Chou** finally returned to the stage of the Spring Festival Gala this year, performing a magic trick and singing the song "**Love Confession Balloon**" with magician Cai Weize.	(**Jay Chou**, *Singer*, **Love Confession Balloon**) (**Jay Chou**, *Composer*, **Love Confession Balloon**)

Figure 9. Data of Normal, SEO, and EPO classes in the high-quality Chinese dataset.

Finally, the high-quality Chinese dataset we constructed consists of 10,423 rows of training data, 2012 rows of test data, and 49 relation types. After optimization, the frequencies of various relations in the dataset were relatively uniform, covering multiple fields such as education, healthcare, finance, and law. The average length of all sentences is 56.28, with a total of 8043 different Chinese characters. Among the sentences in the dataset, 67% come from the Baidu Baike corpus, whereas 33% come from the Baidu News Push corpus. The distribution of different entity types is shown in Figure 10, with the most common types in the dataset being person, audiovisual work, song, and book. In the Chinese high-quality dataset we constructed, data with relation overlapping problems account for 32% of the total data.

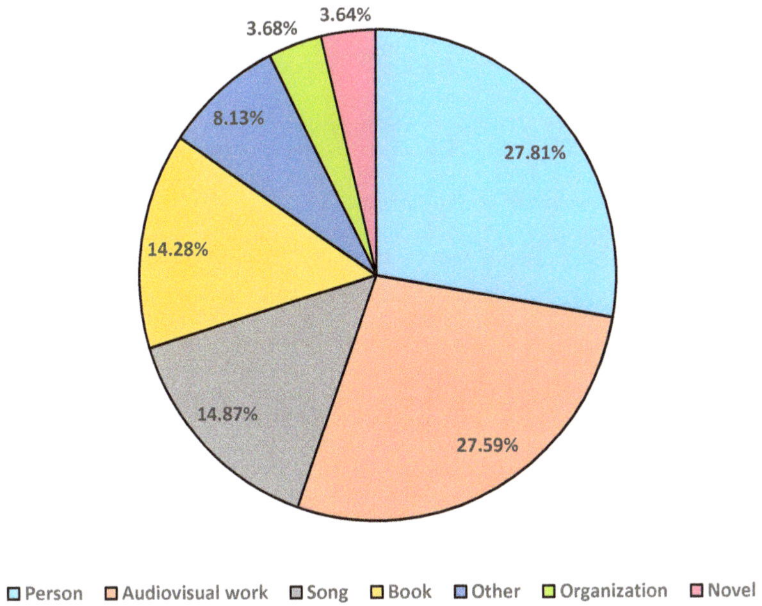

Figure 10. Proportions of different entity types in the high-quality Chinese dataset.

4.2. Baseline Comparison Experiment

To demonstrate the performance of REACT, we compared it with RSAN proposed by Yuan et al. [27], CasRel proposed by Wei et al. [32], and TPLinker proposed by Wang et al. [40] on the high-quality Chinese dataset we constructed. For the parameter settings of *Roberta*, we referred to the work of Cui et al. [41]. For Roberta, Cui et al. [41] conducted a large number of experiments in the field of Chinese natural language processing, achieving excellent results. Therefore, the parameter settings are relatively reliable, and the performance of the model can be guaranteed. As for *BiLSTM*, we conducted experiments for fine-tuning and selected the optimal parameters. The parameter settings for REACT are shown in Table 2.

Table 2. Settings for various parameters in REACT.

Module	Parameter	Value
Roberta	hidden_size	768
	max_position_embedding	512
	num_attention_heads	12
	num_hidden_layers	12
	pooler_fc_size	768
	pooler_num_attention_heads	12
	pooler_num_fc_layers	3
	pooler_size_per_head	128
	vocab_size	21,128
	input_size	768
BiLSTM	hidden_size	64
LSTM	hidden_size	64
	dropout	0.4
CNN	in_channels	768
	out_channels	128
	kernel_size	3

RSAN: Yuan et al. [27] hypothesized that words in a text have different degrees of importance under different relations. For this reason, they proposed a relation-based attention model, RSAN, which assigns different weights to contextual words under each relation. The reason for choosing this baseline for comparison is that the Relation Attention Mechanism in RSAN has some similarities with our proposed Entity Attention Mechanism.

CasRel: Wei et al. [32] adopted a new perspective instead of the previous classification mechanism, modeling the relation as a mapping from the head entity to the tail entity, and proposed a new cascading binary labeling framework (CaeRel). Excellent results were achieved due to the introduction of header entity information when identifying tail entities and relations. Since our model is an improvement on CasRel, a comparison with CasRel is necessary.

TPLinker: In order to alleviate the exposure bias and error propagation issues in CasRel, Wang et al. [40] proposed TPLinker. Joint extraction was described as a token-pair linking problem, and a new handshake labeling scheme was proposed to align entity pairs under each type of relation with boundary marking. This model ultimately achieved SOTA performance. Because our model is also an improvement on CasRel, it is necessary to compare REACT with TPLinker.

The experimental results for this section are shown in Table 3 and Figure 11. It can be seen that CasRel, TPLinker, and REACT outperformed RSAN in the relation extraction task, with an improvement of about 10% in the F1-score. REACT outperformed CasRel and TPLinker. Therefore, we can conclude that by utilizing head entity information to reduce word noise instead of treating head entity information as a parameter for identifying tail entities and relations, we can achieve better performance.

Table 3. The experimental data for REACT and the baselines on the high-quality Chinese dataset.

Model	Precision	Recall	F1-Score
RSAN	59.7	57.6	58.6
CasRel	65.7	64.2	64.9
TPLinker	65.3	66.4	65.8
REACT	68.5	66.0	67.2

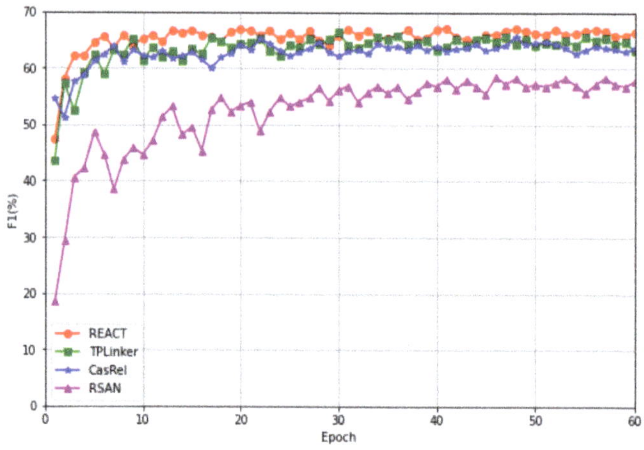

Figure 11. Comparison of convergence rates between REACT and the baselines.

4.3. Model Variants and Ablation Experiments

In order to comprehensively evaluate the performance of REACT and the effects of the proposed Entity Attention Mechanism (EAM) and Entity Gated Mechanism (EGM), we compared it with 14 variants, as shown in Table 4. We employed *Dictionary Encoding (DE),*

BERT, and *Roberta* as feature extraction methods, and replaced the *BiLSTM* in the Encoding layer with a *CNN* and *LSTM*. The parameter settings for the Dictionary Encoding in the experiments were based on the work of Liu et al. [42]. The parameter settings for *BERT* were based on the work of Wei et al. [32]. Liu et al. [42] conducted a large number of experiments in the field of Chinese relation extraction, and their proposed model achieved good results. The CasRel model proposed by Wei et al. [32] achieved state-of-the-art performance in 2020. Therefore, by referring to the above research to set model parameters, we can ensure the performance of the model. For *LSTM* and *CNN*, we conducted experiments and fine-tuned them to select the optimal parameters, as shown in Table 2.

Table 4. The fourteen variant models used as baselines. DE stands for Dictionary Encoding, EAM stands for Entity Attention Mechanism, and EGM stands for Entity Gated Mechanism.

No.	Encoding Layer	Additional Modules
1	DE+CNN	EAM+EGM
2	DE+LSTM	EAM+EGM
3	DE+BiLSTM	EAM+EGM
4	BERT+CNN	EAM+EGM
5	BERT+LSTM	EAM+EGM
6	BERT+BiLSTM	NULL
7	BERT+BiLSTM	EAM+EGM
8	Roberta+CNN	EAM+EGM
9	Roberta+LSTM	NULL
10	Roberta+LSTM	EAM
11	Roberta+LSTM	EAM+EGM
12	Roberta+BiLSTM	NULL
13	Roberta+BiLSTM	EAM
14	Roberta+BiLSTM	EGM
15 (REACT)	Roberta+BiLSTM	EAM+EGM

As shown in Table 5, the best performance was achieved using the *BiLSTM*, and the worst performance was achieved using the *CNN*, regardless of which encoding method was used. The relation extraction task usually requires the analysis of the whole sentence and needs to be inferred in context. The *BiLSTM* was able to perform forward and backward processing along the sentence sequence, thus capturing the long-term dependencies and context in the sentence, helping to better understand the semantics of the sentence and the relations between sentence components. *CNNs* are mainly used to process fixed-size local features and have a relatively low ability to model long-distance dependencies in sentences. Furthermore, *CNNs* are usually locally aware and do not have an explicit memory mechanism, thus may not be able to handle long-term dependencies and complex semantics in sentences.

Based on the overall results, compared to using *Dictionary Encoding* as the feature extraction method, using *BERT* and *Roberta* as the encoder was more effective, with their F1-scores both above 63%. Both *BERT* and *Roberta* are based on pre-trained language models that learn rich linguistic representations from large amounts of textual data through large-scale unsupervised learning. *BERT* and *Roberta* utilize the mechanism of parameter sharing to encode the individual words of an entire sentence at the same time. In contrast, *Dictionary Encoding* usually only extracts features based on independent words and lacks modeling of the sentence as a whole. In addition, *BERT* and *Roberta* employ the Transformer, which is capable of bidirectional context modeling to better capture the semantics and context of words in a sentence or text. This synthesis of contextual information is essential for understanding and expressing the meaning of a text. *Dictionary Encoding* usually performs feature extraction based on independent words or phrases and cannot capture the contextual information between words.

Table 5. Comparison of experimental results between REACT and the 14 model variants.

No.	Models	Precision	Recall	F1-Score
1	DE+CNN+EAM+EGM	70.7	40.5	51.5
2	DE+LSTM+EAM+EGM	74.3	44.7	55.8
3	DE+BiLSTM+EAM+EGM	74.6	46.7	57.4
4	BERT+CNN+EAM+EGM	67.5	62.0	64.6
5	BERT+LSTM+EAM+EGM	68.3	63.7	65.9
6	BERT+BiLSTM	64.8	63.8	64.1
7	BERT+BiLSTM+EAM+EGM	69.0	64.3	66.5
8	Roberta+CNN+EAM+EGM	69.2	60.1	64.3
9	Roberta+LSTM	65.7	62.2	63.9
10	Roberta+LSTM+EAM	66.4	65.1	65.7
11	Roberta+LSTM+EAM+EGM	68.1	64.8	66.4
12	Roberta+BiLSTM	66.2	63.9	65.0
13	Roberta+BiLSTM+EAM	67.6	65.3	66.4
14	Roberta+BiLSTM+EGM	67.8	64.7	66.2
15	(REACT) Roberta+BiLSTM+EAM+EGM	68.5	66.0	67.2

As can be seen from the 9th, 10th, 12th, and 13th data in Table 5, when the Entity Attention Mechanism was used, there was an increase of more than 1.4% in the F1-score, demonstrating that our designed Entity Attention Mechanism indeed enhanced model performance. The main purpose of an attention mechanism [36] is to enable the model to assign different attention weights to different words when processing input data in order to better understand and process the data. Therefore, the Entity Attention Mechanism can assist the model in focusing on words strongly associated with the head entity, which are typically crucial components in forming a correct entity-relation triad. This enables the model to encounter fewer disturbances from irrelevant words during prediction, thereby reducing the probability of misidentifying the tail entity or relation. Precision is the ratio of correctly identified entity-relation triads to the total number of identified entity-relation triads. Through the Entity Attention Mechanism, the model reduced instances of incorrectly pairing unrelated or erroneous tail entities with the head entity, thereby reducing false positives and directly enhancing precision. Consequently, compared to recall, the enhancement in precision was more pronounced.

From the 12th and 14th data in Table 5, we can observe that the F1-score improved by 1.2% when the Entity Gated Mechanism was used. A gated mechanism [43] can learn which information is more important for the current task and selectively retain or discard input information. The improvements in the F1-score demonstrate that our designed Entity Gated Mechanism indeed enhanced model performance.

As can be seen from the 6th, 7th, 9th, 11th, 12th, and 15th data in Table 5, when the Entity Attention network was used, the F1-scores improved by an average of about 2.5%. Therefore, the Entity Attention Mechanism and the Entity Gated Mechanism can be used together to improve the performance of the model.

4.4. Detailed Results on Different Types of Sentences

To further validate the capability of REACT in extracting overlapping relational triples, we conducted two extended experiments on different types of sentences and compared the performance of REACT with that of the baselines.

The detailed experimental results on three different datasets are shown in Figure 12. It can be seen that REACT achieved the best results in all three cases, proving that it has some advantages in addressing the relation overlapping problem.

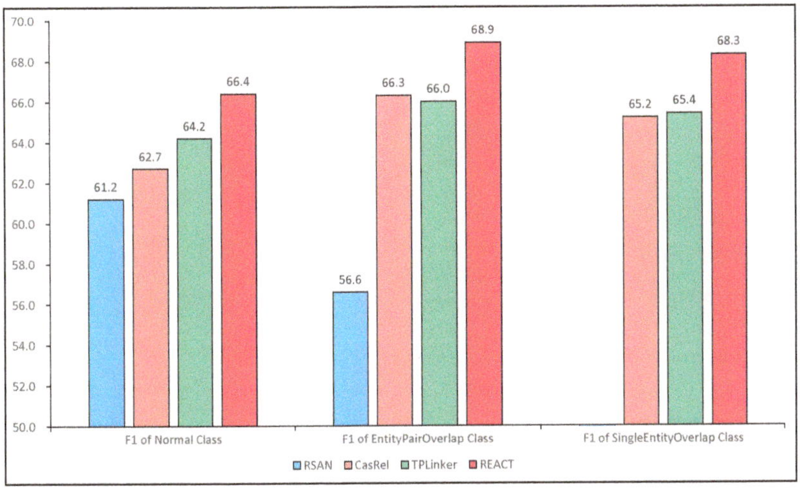

Figure 12. F1-score for extracting relational triples from sentences with different overlapping patterns.

We validated REACT's ability to extract relational triples from data containing different numbers of relational triples. Sentences were categorized into four classes, and the results are shown in Table 6. Again, REACT achieved excellent performance across all four classes. Although it is not surprising that the performance of most baselines decreased as the number of relational triples in a sentence increased, there are still some details that can be observed in the variation of the models' performance. Compared to these baselines, which are dedicated to addressing the relation overlapping problem, REACT exhibited the least degradation and achieved the best performance when confronted with complex situations.

Table 6. F1-score for extracting relational triples from sentences with different numbers (denoted as N) of triples.

Model	N = 1	N = 2	N = 3	N ≥ 4
RSAN	64.5	61.3	58.7	51.2
CasRel	62.9	65.0	68.6	63.4
TPLinker	65.7	67.6	68.4	61.5
RANGE	66.0	68.3	71.4	65.8

5. Conclusions

Regarding the problem of relation overlapping, we analyzed the current mainstream methods and proposed the Relation extraction method based on the Entity Attention network and Cascade binary Tagging framework (REACT). To demonstrate the effectiveness of REACT, we constructed a high-quality Chinese dataset. Experiments on this dataset showed that compared to the baselines, REACT achieved higher F1-scores, even when faced with complex situations, maintaining a certain advantage. In future work, we plan to integrate REACT with recently popular large language models. After identifying the head entity, we will use the large model to provide additional prior knowledge about the head entity. By introducing prior knowledge, the model can better understand the specific meaning and characteristics of the head entity, allocate attention weights more accurately, and improve the performance of identifying tail entities and relations.

Author Contributions: Conceptualization, L.K.; methodology, L.K.; software, L.K.; validation, L.K. and S.L.; formal analysis, L.K.; investigation, L.K.; resources, L.K.; data curation, L.K.; writing—original draft preparation, L.K.; writing—review and editing, L.K.; visualization, L.K.; supervision, L.K.; project administration, L.K.; funding acquisition, S.L. All authors have read and agreed to the published version of the manuscript.

Funding: This research was funded by the Major Science and Technology Projects in Xinjiang Uygur Autonomous Region (No. 2022A02012-1); National Natural Science Foundation of China (61966034).

Institutional Review Board Statement: Not applicable.

Informed Consent Statement: Not applicable.

Data Availability Statement: The data presented in this study are available on request from the first author.

Conflicts of Interest: The authors declare no conflicts of interest.

References

1. Golshan, P.N.; Dashti, H.R.; Azizi, S.; Safari, L. A study of recent contributions on information extraction. *arXiv* **2018**, arXiv:1803.056
2. Freitag, D. Machine learning for information extraction in informal domains. *Mach. Learn.* **2000**, *39*, 169–202. [CrossRef]
3. Hahn, U.; Oleynik, M. Medical information extraction in the age of deep learning. *Yearb. Med. Inform.* **2020**, *29*, 208–2 [CrossRef] [PubMed]
4. Zheng, S.; Hao, Y.; Lu, D.; Bao, H.; Xu, J.; Hao, H.; Xu, B. Joint entity and relation extraction based on a hybrid neural netwo *Neurocomputing* **2017**, *257*, 59–66. [CrossRef]
5. Li, C.; Tian, Y. Downstream model design of pre-trained language model for relation extraction task. *arXiv* **2020**, arXiv:2004.037
6. Ratinov, L.; Roth, D. Design challenges and misconceptions in named entity recognition. In Proceedings of the CoNLL '(Proceedings of the Thirteenth Conference on Computational Natural Language Learning, Boulder, CO, USA, 4–5 June 2009.
7. Sang, E.F.; De Meulder, F. Introduction to the CoNLL-2003 shared task: Language-independent named entity recognition. *arX* **2003**, arXiv:cs/0306050.
8. Zelenko, D.; Aone, C.; Richardella, A. Kernel methods for relation extraction. *J. Mach. Learn. Res.* **2003**, *3*, 1083–1106.
9. Bunescu, R.; Mooney, R. A shortest path dependency kernel for relation extraction. In Proceedings of the Human Langua Technology Conference and Conference on Empirical Methods in Natural Language Processing, Vancouver, BC, Cana 6–8 October 2005; pp. 724–731.
10. Zhou, Y.; Huang, L.; Guo, T.; Hu, S.; Han, J. An attention-based model for joint extraction of entities and relations with impli entity features. In Proceedings of the Companion Proceedings of the 2019 World Wide Web Conference, Montreal, QC, Cana 25–31 May 2019; pp. 729–737.
11. Miwa, M.; Bansal, M. End-to-end relation extraction using lstms on sequences and tree structures. *arXiv* **2016**, arXiv:1601.007
12. Zhou, G.; Su, J.; Zhang, J.; Zhang, M. Exploring various knowledge in relation extraction. In Proceedings of the 43rd Annu Meeting of the Association for Computational Linguistics (acl'05), Ann Arbor, MI, USA, 25–30 June 2005; pp. 427–434.
13. Chan, Y.S.; Roth, D. Exploiting syntactico-semantic structures for relation extraction. In Proceedings of the 49th Annu Meeting of the Association for Computational Linguistics: Human Language Technologies, Portland, OR, USA, 19–24 June 20 pp. 551–560.
14. Mintz, M.; Bills, S.; Snow, R.; Jurafsky, D. Distant supervision for relation extraction without labeled data. In Proceedings the Joint Conference of the 47th Annual Meeting of the ACL and the 4th International Joint Conference on Natural Langua Processing of the AFNLP, Suntec, Singapore, 2–7 August 2009; pp. 1003–1011.
15. Gormley, M.R.; Yu, M.; Dredze, M. Improved relation extraction with feature-rich compositional embedding models. *arXiv* **20** arXiv:1505.02419.
16. Yu, X.; Lam, W. Jointly identifying entities and extracting relations in encyclopedia text via a graphical model approach. Proceedings of the Coling 2010: Posters, Beijing, China, 23–27 August 2010; pp. 1399–1407.
17. Li, Q.; Ji, H. Incremental joint extraction of entity mentions and relations. In Proceedings of the 52nd Annual Meeting of t Association for Computational Linguistics (Volume 1: Long Papers), Baltimore, MD, USA, 23–25 June 2014; pp. 402–412.
18. Ren, X.; Wu, Z.; He, W.; Qu, M.; Voss, C.R.; Ji, H.; Abdelzaher, T.F.; Han, J. Cotype: Joint extraction of typed entities and relatio with knowledge bases. In Proceedings of the 26th International Conference on World Wide Web, Perth, Australia, 3–7 April 20 pp. 1015–1024.
19. Gupta, P.; Schütze, H.; Andrassy, B. Table filling multi-task recurrent neural network for joint entity and relation extraction. Proceedings of the COLING 2016, the 26th International Conference on Computational Linguistics: Technical Papers, Osal Japan, 11–17 December 2016; pp. 2537–2547.
20. Katiyar, A.; Cardie, C. Going out on a limb: Joint extraction of entity mentions and relations without dependency trees. Proceedings of the 55th Annual Meeting of the Association for Computational Linguistics (Volume 1: Long Papers), Vancouv BC, Canada, 30 July–4 August 2017; pp. 917–928.

Zhou, P.; Zheng, S.; Xu, J.; Qi, Z.; Bao, H.; Xu, B. Joint extraction of multiple relations and entities by using a hybrid neural network. In Proceedings of the Chinese Computational Linguistics and Natural Language Processing Based on Naturally Annotated Big Data: 16th China National Conference, CCL 2017, and 5th International Symposium, NLP-NABD 2017, Nanjing, China, 13–15 October 2017; Proceedings 16; Springer: Berlin/Heidelberg, Germany, 2017; pp. 135–146.
Fu, T.J.; Li, P.H.; Ma, W.Y. Graphrel: Modeling text as relational graphs for joint entity and relation extraction. In Proceedings of the 57th Annual Meeting of the Association for Computational Linguistics, Florence, Italy, 28 July–2 August 2019; pp. 1409–1418.
Bai, F.; Ritter, A. Structured minimally supervised learning for neural relation extraction. *arXiv* **2019**, arXiv:1904.00118.
Zeng, X.; Zeng, D.; He, S.; Liu, K.; Zhao, J. Extracting relational facts by an end-to-end neural model with copy mechanism. In Proceedings of the 56th Annual Meeting of the Association for Computational Linguistics (Volume 1: Long Papers), Melbourne, Australia, 15–20 July 2018; pp. 506–514.
Zeng, X.; He, S.; Zeng, D.; Liu, K.; Liu, S.; Zhao, J. Learning the extraction order of multiple relational facts in a sentence with reinforcement learning. In Proceedings of the 2019 Conference on Empirical Methods in Natural Language Processing and the 9th International Joint Conference on Natural Language Processing (EMNLP-IJCNLP), Hong Kong, China, 3–7 November 2019; pp. 367–377.
Yuan, Y.; Liu, L.; Tang, S.; Zhang, Z.; Zhuang, Y.; Pu, S.; Wu, F.; Ren, X. Cross-relation cross-bag attention for distantly-supervised relation extraction. In Proceedings of the AAAI Conference on Artificial Intelligence, Honolulu, HI, USA, 27 Januray–1 February 2019; Volume 33, pp. 419–426.
Yuan, Y.; Zhou, X.; Pan, S.; Zhu, Q.; Song, Z.; Guo, L. A Relation-Specific Attention Network for Joint Entity and Relation Extraction. In Proceedings of the IJCAI, Yokohama, Janpan, 11–17 July 2020; Volume 2020, pp. 4054–4060.
Yu, B.; Zhang, Z.; Shu, X.; Wang, Y.; Liu, T.; Wang, B.; Li, S. Joint extraction of entities and relations based on a novel decomposition strategy. *arXiv* **2019**, arXiv:1909.04273.
Li, X.; Yin, F.; Sun, Z.; Li, X.; Yuan, A.; Chai, D.; Zhou, M.; Li, J. Entity-relation extraction as multi-turn question answering. *arXiv* **2019**, arXiv:1905.05529.
Li, X.; Feng, J.; Meng, Y.; Han, Q.; Wu, F.; Li, J. A unified MRC framework for named entity recognition. *arXiv* **2019**, arXiv:1910.11476.
Yao, L.; Mao, C.; Luo, Y. Graph convolutional networks for text classification. In Proceedings of the AAAI Conference on Artificial Intelligence, Honolulu, HI, USA, 27 January–1 February 2019; Volume 33, pp. 7370–7377.
Wei, Z.; Su, J.; Wang, Y.; Tian, Y.; Chang, Y. A novel cascade binary tagging framework for relational triple extraction. *arXiv* **2019**, arXiv:1909.03227.
Devlin, J.; Chang, M.W.; Lee, K.; Toutanova, K. Bert: Pre-training of deep bidirectional transformers for language understanding. *arXiv* **2018**, arXiv:1810.04805.
Liu, Y.; Ott, M.; Goyal, N.; Du, J.; Joshi, M.; Chen, D.; Levy, O.; Lewis, M.; Zettlemoyer, L.; Stoyanov, V. Roberta: A robustly optimized bert pretraining approach. *arXiv* **2019**, arXiv:1907.11692.
Zhong, P.; Wang, D.; Miao, C. Knowledge-enriched transformer for emotion detection in textual conversations. *arXiv* **2019**, arXiv:1909.10681.
Vaswani, A.; Shazeer, N.; Parmar, N.; Uszkoreit, J.; Jones, L.; Gomez, A.N.; Kaiser, L.; Polosukhin, I. Attention is all you need. *Adv. Neural Inf. Process. Syst.* **2017**, *30*.
Chen, N.; Liu, F.; You, C.; Zhou, P.; Zou, Y. Adaptive bi-directional attention: Exploring multi-granularity representations for machine reading comprehension. In Proceedings of the ICASSP 2021–2021 IEEE International Conference on Acoustics, Speech and Signal Processing (ICASSP), Toronto, ON, Canada, 6–11 June 2021; pp. 7833–7837.
Li, S.; He, W.; Shi, Y.; Jiang, W.; Liang, H.; Jiang, Y.; Zhang, Y.; Lyu, Y.; Zhu, Y. Duie: A large-scale chinese dataset for information extraction. In Proceedings of the Natural Language Processing and Chinese Computing: 8th CCF International Conference, NLPCC 2019, Dunhuang, China, 9–14 October 2019; Proceedings, Part II 8; Springer: Berlin/Heidelberg, Germany, 2019; pp. 791–800.
Feng, J.; Huang, M.; Zhao, L.; Yang, Y.; Zhu, X. Reinforcement learning for relation classification from noisy data. In Proceedings of the AAAI Conference on Artificial Intelligence, New Orleans, LA, USA, 2–7 February 2018; Volume 32.
Wang, Y.; Yu, B.; Zhang, Y.; Liu, T.; Zhu, H.; Sun, L. TPLinker: Single-stage joint extraction of entities and relations through token pair linking. *arXiv* **2020**, arXiv:2010.13415.
Cui, Y.; Che, W.; Liu, T.; Qin, B.; Wang, S.; Hu, G. Revisiting pre-trained models for Chinese natural language processing. *arXiv* **2020**, arXiv:2004.13922.
Liu, Y.; Wen, F.; Zong, T.; Li, T. Research on joint extraction method of entity and relation triples based on hierarchical cascade labeling. *IEEE Access* **2022**, *11*, 9789–9798. [CrossRef]
Dey, R.; Salem, F.M. Gate-variants of gated recurrent unit (GRU) neural networks. In Proceedings of the 2017 IEEE 60th International Midwest Symposium on Circuits and Systems (MWSCAS), Boston, MA, USA, 6–9 August 2017; pp. 1597–1600.

applied sciences

MDPI

Article

Prefix Data Augmentation for Contrastive Learning of Unsupervised Sentence Embedding

Chunchun Wang and Shu Lv *

School of Mathematical Sciences, University of Electronic Science and Technology of China, Chengdu 611731, China; 202221110310@std.uestc.edu.cn
* Correspondence: lvshu@uestc.edu.cn

Abstract: This paper presents prefix data augmentation (Prd) as an innovative method for enhancing sentence embedding learning through unsupervised contrastive learning. The framework, dubbed PrdSimCSE, uses Prd to create both positive and negative sample pairs. By appending positive and negative prefixes to a sentence, the basis for contrastive learning is formed, outperforming the baseline unsupervised SimCSE. PrdSimCSE is positioned within a probabilistic framework that expands the semantic similarity event space and generates superior negative samples, contributing to more accurate semantic similarity estimations. The model's efficacy is validated on standard semantic similarity tasks, showing a notable improvement over that of existing unsupervised models, specifically a 1.08% enhancement in performance on BERTbase. Through detailed experiments, the effectiveness of positive and negative prefixes in data augmentation and their impact on the learning model are explored, and the broader implications of prefix data augmentation are discussed for unsupervised sentence embedding learning.

Keywords: contrastive learning; sentence embedding; prefix data augmentation

1. Introduction

Sentence embedding learning has long been a core focus within the field of natural language processing, serving as a critical component in a wide array of downstream applications [1–6]. Researchers have been constructing sentence vector models through text-matching annotated datasets, where each sample is formatted as (Sentence A, Sentence B, Label). When comparing or ranking pairs of sentences for semantic similarity, we typically rely on the cosine value of the angle between sentence vectors for judgment, as shown in Equation (1). Here, A and B represent sentence vectors, and cos(A, B) denotes the cosine value of the angle between them. This equation is based on a standard coordinate basis, where the cosine value of the angle between different basis vectors is 0. Due to the high-dimensional nature of sentence vectors, using the cosine value of the angle between vectors to measure semantic similarity offers the following advantages: (1) it is unaffected by scale; (2) it effectively captures angular information; (3) it exhibits high computational efficiency; and (4) it remains effective in high-dimensional spaces (whereas metrics based on vector norms are susceptible to the curse of dimensionality in high-dimensional spaces). Gao et al. [7] discovered that the sentence vectors learned via Transformers exhibit anisotropy, a characteristic similarly identified in BERT and GPT-2 by Ethayarajh [8]. "Anisotropy" refers to the phenomenon where word embeddings occupy a narrow conical region in the vector space, implying that the coordinate system of the sentence vectors is not a standard coordinate basis, rendering the equality in Equation (1) invalid. Methods such as Bert-flow [9], Bert-whitening [10], IS-Bert [11], CT-Bert [12], and Simcse [13] aim to eliminate or mitigate the anisotropy of the learned sentence vectors, thereby enabling more accurate semantic similarity judgments between sentence pairs.

$$\cos(A, B) = \frac{\mathbf{A} \cdot \mathbf{B}}{||\mathbf{A}|| ||\mathbf{B}||} \tag{1}$$

In recent years, contrastive learning has seen successfully applied in sentence embedding learning [13–15]. The goal of contrastive learning is to bring positive sample pairs closer together in the encoding space, while pushing negative samples further apart. Wang et al. [16] introduced two key concepts for measuring the quality of contrastive learning: alignment and uniformity. For alignment, two samples forming a positive pair should be mapped to nearby features and thus be (mostly) invariant to unneeded noise factors. For uniformity, feature vectors should be roughly uniformly distributed on the unit hypersphere, preserving as much information from the data as possible. Therefore, constructing positive samples and selecting negative samples are crucial for enhancing the effectiveness of contrastive learning, among which SimCSE [13] stands out as a representative method. SimCSE's unsupervised model uses dropout [17] as a form of data augmentation to construct positive samples with minimal noise. Specifically, SimCSE processes N sentences as a batch, where each sentence undergoes two independent rounds of dropout masking before being input into a pretrained BERT model. The resulting embeddings from the same sentence serve as positive pairs, whereas embeddings from different sentences are treated as negative pairs.

SimCSE assumes that dropout serves as the "minimal" form of data augmentation, but a crucial weakness is overlooked. Because dropout aims to retain as much information from the original sentence as possible, including the positional information of each token, this approach inadvertently leads to a misunderstanding: sentences of the same length are perceived to have a higher probability of being semantically similar. Conversely, the unsupervised version of SimCSE does not effectively differentiate between various negative examples. The supervised version of SimCSE, which uses a supervised natural language inference (NLI) dataset, constructs hard negative samples to further enhance the effect of contrastive learning. Wang et al. [18] proposed SNCSE, which acquires word vectors through cue learning and syntactic parsing using spacy and constructs soft negative examples. Nishikawa et al. [19] proposed Ease, which generates positive sample pairs by associating entities sourced from Wikipedia. Negative entities are constrained to be the same type as the positive ones and are excluded if they appear on the same Wikipedia page. Randomly selected candidate entities that meet these criteria are used as hard negative data to construct triplet data. However, these methods for distinguishing negative samples are limited to annotated datasets and are not applicable in unsupervised learning scenarios.

To address these aforementioned issues, we propose PrdSimCSE, an unsupervised contrastive learning framework based on prefix data augmentation. As illustrated in Figure 1, PrdSimCSE uses prefix data augmentation (Prd) to construct positive samples and differentiate negative samples. Next, Section 2 introduces the background knowledge on text augmentation, including the basic concepts of sentence embedding and contrastive learning. Section 3 details the prefix data augmentation method, including how to determine positive and negative prefixes and their impact on the model. Section 4 outlines the unsupervised PrdSimCSE, covering algorithm design, experimental environment setup, parameter settings, datasets, and baseline comparisons. Section 5 describes the progress of prefix data augmentation determined through ablation studies, where we further discuss how to determine positive and negative prefixes and the semantic bias caused by prefix data augmentation. Section 6 discusses the relationship between semantic similarity events and prefix data augmentation, including the advantages and roles of positive and negative prefixes. Section 7 concludes the paper by providing the contributions of prefix data augmentation to unsupervised sentence embedding learning and directions for future research.

The contributions of this paper can be summarized as follows:

- This paper introduces a novel text data augmentation method, prefix data augmentation. Positive samples are constructed using modal particle prefixes combined with dropout, thus preserving the original semantics as much as possible while altering the positional information of each token. This approach enhances and facilitates contrastive learning.

- Prefix data augmentation can also be used to modify the original semantics. By constructing prompts that reverse the semantics and using them as prefixes, the modified sentences can serve as negative samples. This method allows for the creation of a richer set of negative samples from unsupervised corpora, thereby increasing the discriminability between different negative samples.
- We developed a novel unsupervised sentence embedding learning approach, PrdSimCSE, which we used to construct both positive and negative samples through prefix data augmentation. Additionally, the approach treats other sentences within the same batch as negative samples.
- We evaluated PrdSimCSE across various datasets, and the experimental results demonstrated that our proposed PrdSimCSE achieves superior performance in sentence representation compared with prior approaches. Furthermore, through ablation studies, we further examined the effectiveness of PrdSimCSE and discussed the advantages and limitations of our method in detail.

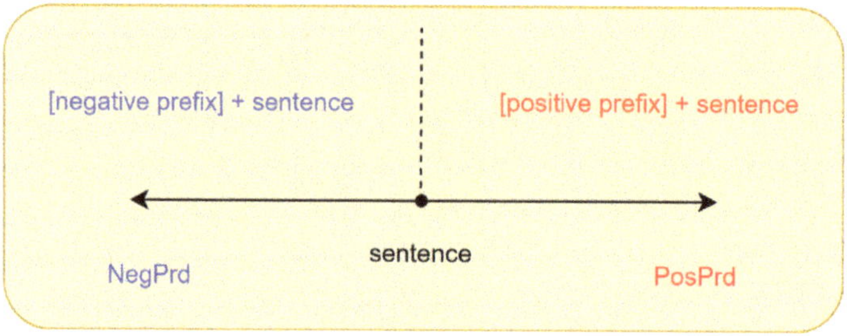

Figure 1. Prefix data augmentation. PosPrd: positive prefix. NegPrd: negative prefix.

2. Background

Text Augmentation Text augmentation can be categorized into two main types based on the generation method: back-translation and adding noise. Back-translation is a simple and efficient text augmentation technique that generates more high-quality samples on the basis of existing datasets by translating and then retranslating the text in scenarios with few samples [20,21]. However, back-translation carries an implicit prior, whereas the model is presented with input texts that, despite having different linguistic expressions, share the same semantics. Adding noise involves directly performing operations such as the addition, deletion, or replacement of sentences. The easy data augmentation (EDA) technique proposed by Wei et al. [22] is a compilation of such methods. EDA consists of four strategies: (1) synonym replacement (SR): randomly select nonstop words from a sentence and replace them with randomly chosen synonyms; (2) random insertion (RI): randomly identify a nonstop word in a sentence, find a synonym for it, and insert that synonym into a random position in the sentence; then, repeat this process n times; (3) in random swap (RS), two words in the sentence are randomly chosen, and their positions are swapped, repeating this process n times; and (4) random deletion (RD): each word in the sentence is randomly deleted with a probability p. Given that these methods involve random operations, a question arises: can the text's label remain unchanged after EDA operations? To address this concern, Xie et al. [23] proposed unsupervised data augmentation (UDA), where the core idea involves replacing a certain proportion of nonessential words in the text with unimportant words from a dictionary, thereby generating new texts. However, in the context of contrastive learning for sentence representation, using such text augmentation methods to construct positive samples for unsupervised learning typically results in lower performance compared with supervised models. SimCSE has achieved notable success in unsupervised learning, also demonstrating that dropout can serve as a "minimal" form of text data augmentation, offering an alternative to other text augmentation methods. However, dropout augmentation does not alter the positional information of words within a sentence, which can introduce new biases to the model. Inspired by

SimCSE, we developed a text augmentation technique suitable for unsupervised learning: prefix data augmentation.

Sentence Embedding Sentence embedding learning aims to convert natural language text sequences into numerical sequences that machines can comprehend. Depending on whether the training corpus is labeled, sentence embedding learning processes can be categorized into supervised and unsupervised approaches. In this study, we primarily focused on unsupervised sentence embedding learning. Word2Vec [24] was one of the earlier models developed for the unsupervised learning of semantic knowledge from large text corpora. Word2Vec proposed the CBOW and skip-gram methods. In CBOW, surrounding words are predicted based on the center word; in skip-gram, the center word is predicted based on surrounding words. BERT [25] introduced the masked language model (MLM) and next sentence prediction (NSP) training methods, but the training data must be at the document level. Subsequent models such as CrossThought [26] and CMLM [27] face similar issues. SimCSE [13] is an unsupervised contrastive learning framework, enabling direct sentence embedding learning using widely available short texts. SimCSE also adapts well to downstream tasks that primarily involve short texts.

Contrastive Learning In the context of sentence embedding learning, the aim of contrastive learning is to train an encoder that produces similar encodings for sentences of the same class within the same dataset, while ensuring the encoding results for sentences of different classes are as dissimilar as possible. Suppose we have a set of samples to be learned, $x_0, x_+^1, \ldots, x_+^m, x_-^1, \ldots x_-^n$, where x_0 serves as the anchor sample, x_+ serves as the positive sample for x_0, and x_- serves as the negative sample for x_0. We drew inspiration from the infoNCE used in MoCo [28] and adopted the SimCSE approach, using other samples within the same batch as negative samples. In a single batch, the contrastive learning objective for the anchor sample x_0 is

$$loss = -\log \frac{\sum_{i=1}^{m} e^{\mathrm{sim}(x_0, x_+^i)/t}}{\sum_{i=1}^{m} e^{\mathrm{sim}(x_0, x_+^i)/t} + \sum_{j=1}^{n} e^{\mathrm{sim}(x_0, x_+^j)/t}} \tag{2}$$

where the batch size is denoted as $N = 1 + m + n$, where t is the temperature hyperparameter, and sim is the function used to compute the cosine similarity between two vectors. In our experiments, positive samples were generated only using PosPrd (positive prefix), represented as m = 1 in the formula. For the selection of negative samples, in addition to using other samples within the batch as negative samples, we employed NegPrd (negative prefix). Subsequently, we used pretrained models such as BERT and RoBERTa [29] and fine-tuned all parameters using the contrastive learning objective.

3. Prefix Data Augmentation

As the name suggests, prefix data augmentation involves changing text data by adding prefixes to augment the dataset. In theory, any text can serve as a prefix for other texts. However, from the perspective of constructing positive samples, we aimed for prefixes that did not alter the original sentence's semantics. When constructing negative samples, we preferred prefixes that reversed or disrupted the semantics of the original sentence as much as possible. Through multiple experiments and trials, we found that modal particle prefixes are excellent positive prefixes, whereas prompts that reverse the semantics are effective as negative prefixes.

In the field of computer vision, various effective data augmentation methods are employed to construct positive examples for contrastive learning, such as cropping, rotation, and color adjustments. These methods are employed because the information in images is continuous [30], and partial pixel blocks of an image can convey information. However, in natural language processing (NLP), the semantic information embedded in text data is discrete. As shown in Table 1, text augmentation methods such as Random deletion, Word substitution, and Rearrangement substantially alter the semantics of the original sentence, resulting in decreased similarity between the modified and original sentences.

However, the positive prefix preserves the original semantic information. SimCSE applies dropout as a method that effectively addresses the challenge posed by the discrete nature of semantics in text data. When using contrastive learning for sentence embeddings, dropout can serve as a "minimal" positive data augmentation method for constructing positive examples. However, the dropout method only deactivates certain positions in the sentence embeddings. Does constructing positive samples using this approach ensure the encoder is sensitive to the length and structure of sentences? To mitigate this issue, we introduced a simple meaningless prefix in PosPrd.

Table 1. An example of different data augmentation techniques for changing the semantic meaning of a sentence.

Data Augmentation	Sentence	Similarity
Origin	I love natural language processing.	1
Positive prefix	Um, I love natural language processing.	0.99
Random deletion	I natural language processing.	0.65
Word substitution	I love artificial language processing.	0.51
Rearrangement	natural language processing love I.	0.32

We found that specific semantic reversal prefixes can serve as negative data augmentation, used for constructing negative samples in contrastive learning. In the contrastive learning of sentence embeddings, a common approach involves using other sentences within the same batch as negative samples for the anchor sentence. This method is based on the assumption that in a rich training corpus, each sentence belongs to two semantically different categories. However, text data often contain a considerable amount of repetition. For instance, in restaurant reviews, many sentences may belong to the positive semantic category, whereas others belong to the negative semantic category. Consequently, during training, many negative samples may be "problematic", where two semantically similar sentences are treated as negative pairs, which is detrimental to contrastive learning. By introducing manually crafted negative prefixes, we ensure the original sentence is augmented into a category with the opposite semantic meaning, thereby constructing higher-quality negative samples. This approach contributes to increasing the effectiveness of contrastive learning, enabling the model to more accurately capture semantic distinctions.

4. Unsupervised PrdSimcse

4.1. Algorithm Design

PrdSimCSE uses a pretrained BERT (uncased) or RoBERTa as the starting point for training, with all data sharing the same encoder. As illustrated in Figure 2, the model receives three inputs: the original sample, a positive sample that has undergone prefix data augmentation, and a negative sample also enhanced with prefix data augmentation. The output generated from the original sample is used to calculate the contrastive learning loss according to Equation (2), after which gradients are back-propagated to update the parameters of the entire model.

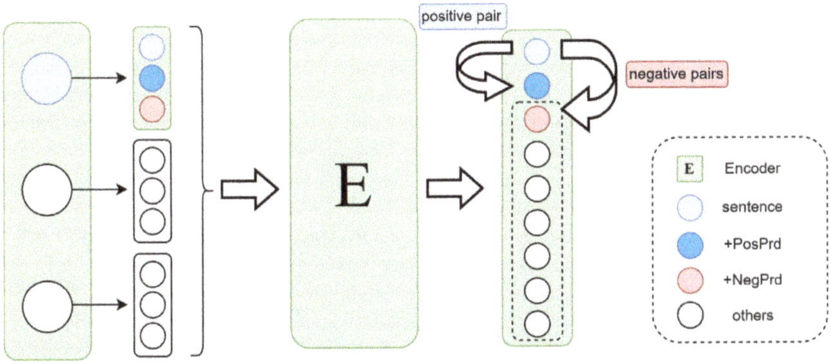

Figure 2. PrdSimCSE constructs positive and negative samples with different prefixes.

4.2. Experimental Environment Setup

Table 2 presents the computational environment of our model, and all experiments were conducted within this setup. We used Python 3.8 as our programming language. Additionally, we employed PyTorch (version 1.7.1) and the Transformers library (version 4.2.1) for the training, evaluation, and testing of PrdSimCSE.

Table 2. Experimental Environment Setup.

Attribute	Details
System Development Environment	Ubuntu22.04
Development Environment	Visual Studio Code (version 1.83)
CUDA version	11.8
GPU	NVIDIA 4080 (16 G)
CPU	Intel i9 13900KF
Memory	32 GB

4.3. Parameter Settings

For PrdSimCSE, we trained the model for three epochs, conducting evaluations every 250 steps. We performed a grid search over batch sizes of 32, 64, 128 and learning rates of $1 \times 10^{-5}, 2 \times 10^{-5}, 3 \times 10^{-5}, 4 \times 10^{-5}, 5 \times 10^{-5}$ on the STS-B development set. The final hyperparameter settings are shown in Table 3. Additionally, we used dropout sampling with a dropout rate of 0.1 and employed AdamW as the optimizer, with a weight decay of 0.01. For evaluations, we selected the [cls] token as the sentence representation and retained the MLP layer. All experimental results were assessed using the Spearman correlation coefficient as the evaluation metric.

Table 3. Parameter Settings.

Model	$\text{Bert}_{\text{base}}$			$\text{RoBERTa}_{\text{base}}$		
Batch size	32	64	128	32	64	128
Learning rate	4×10^{-5}	4×10^{-5}	3×10^{-5}	3×10^{-5}	2×10^{-5}	1×10^{-5}

4.4. Datasets

The training corpus was derived from an unlabeled dataset collected by Gao et al. [13], consisting of 1 million English sentences randomly extracted from Wikipedia, with each data entry being a single English sentence. For the PrdSimCSE's evaluation, we employed seven semantic similarity datasets and nine transfer task datasets, which are briefly introduced here.

The semantic similarity tasks includes STS12 [31], STS13 [32], STS14 [33], STS15 [34], STS16 [35], SICK-R [36], and STS-B [37]. STS 12–16 are the datasets from the SemEval competitions from 2012 to 2016, respectively. STS-B and SICK-R are also datasets from the SemEval competition. In these datasets, each text pair was scored by humans on a scale of 0–5, indicating the level of similarity between the texts. For evaluation, we used the test sets from all the semantic similarity tasks.

The transfer tasks included MR [38], CR [39], SUBJ [40], MPQA [41], SST-2 [42], TREC [43], MRPC [44], BQ [45], and LCQMC [46]. Among these, MR, CR, SUBJ, and SST-2 are sentiment classification datasets; MPQA and BQ are question answering datasets; TREC and LCQMC are question classification datasets; MRPC is a dataset for sentence pair similarity. Additionally, BQ and LCQMC are Chinese datasets; we first translated them into English before inputting them into the model for testing. In essence, these tasks were all text classification tasks, where each sentence was associated with a label (or a matching sentence). During evaluation, the model received a sentence and then determined its category; finally, we compared this prediction with the sentence's label.

4.5. Baseline

Sentence embedding learning can be divided into supervised and unsupervised categories, with this study focusing on improvements in unsupervised contrastive learning. We used unsupervised models such as IS-BERT [11], CT-BERT [12], and SimCSE [13] as baselines. IS-BERT ensures maximal consistency between global and local features, CT-BERT aligns sentence embeddings of the same sentence from two different encoders, and SimCSE aligns different embeddings of the same sentence from the same encoder. Additionally, we compared our approach with postprocessing methods such as BERT-flow [9] and BERT-whitening [10], as well as with naïve baselines such as average GloVe embeddings [47] and average embeddings from the first and last layers of BERT. BERT-flow and BERT-whitening focus on eliminating anisotropy in sentence vectors at the BERT output without changing the encoder structure, whereas average GloVe embeddings and average first- and last-layer BERT embeddings retain the original information of the pretrained BERT. These were all reliable standards for evaluating the effectiveness of our model.

4.6. Main Results

In Table 4, we showcase the performance on the STS tasks. We replicated the results of SimCSE and, through comparison, we found that PrdSimCSE-BERT$_{base}$ substantially outperformed SimCSE-BERT$_{base}$ on STS13-STS16, STS-B, and SICK-R in terms of Spearman correlation coefficient, notably by 2.01% on STS-B. On STS12, PrdSimCSE performed consistently with SimCSE, producing an increase in the average Spearman correlation coefficient from 76.25% to 77.33%. Compared with the unsupervised models, PrdSimCSE outperformed CT-BERT by 5.28% and IS-BERT by 10.75% in terms of the average Spearman correlation coefficient. For the RoBERTa model, PrdSimCSE-RoBERTa$_{base}$ also improved upon SimCSE-RoBERTa$_{base}$'s 76.57% to 77.10%, particularly outperforming SimCSE by 4.81% on SICK-R.

In Table 5, we present the results for transfer tasks. Compared with SimCSE-BERT$_{base}$, PrdSimCSE-BERT$_{base}$ performed better on five of the datasets. However, on the TREC task, the accuracy of PrdSimCSE was 7.89% lower than that of SimCSE—a substantial difference that requires further consideration. TREC is a widely used dataset in the field of information retrieval, employed for evaluating the performance of information retrieval systems. The Text REtrieval Conference (TREC) Question Classification dataset contains 5500 labeled questions in the training set and another 500 in the test set. The dataset has 6 coarse class labels and 50 fine class labels. During testing, each sentence is assigned a label. We speculate that the reason for this discrepancy is because PrdSimCSE uses prefix data augmentation, resulting in a large number of identical sentence prefixes in the training corpus, which leads to considerable semantic bias when encoding sentences. This was further discussed in the ablation experiments.

Table 4. Sentence embedding performance on STS tasks (Spearman correlation, "all" setting). We highlight the highest numbers among models with the same pretrained encoder. ♣: results from [6]; ♡: results from [11]. ◇: results from ourselves; all other results are from [13].

Model	STS12	STS13	STS14	STS15	STS16	STS-B	SICK-R	Avg.
GloVe embedding (avg.) ♣	55.14	70.66	59.73	68.25	63.66	58.02	53.76	61.32
$BERT_{base}$ (first–last avg.)	39.7	59.38	49.67	66.03	66.19	53.87	62.06	56.7
$BERT_{base}$-flow	58.4	67.1	60.85	75.16	71.22	68.66	64.47	66.55
$BERT_{base}$-whitening	57.83	66.9	60.9	75.08	71.31	68.24	63.73	66.28
IS-$BERT_{base}$ ♡	56.77	69.24	61.21	75.23	70.16	69.21	64.25	66.58
CT-$BERT_{base}$	61.63	76.8	68.47	77.5	76.48	74.31	69.19	72.05
SimCSE-$BERT_{base}$	68.4	82.41	74.38	80.91	78.56	76.85	72.23	76.25
PrdSimCSE-$BERT_{base}$ ◇	68.21	83.56	75.44	81.71	79.79	78.86	73.75	77.33
$RoBERTa_{base}$(first-last avg.)	40.88	58.74	49.07	65.63	61.48	58.55	61.63	56.57
$RoBERTa_{base}$-whitening	46.99	63.24	57.23	71.36	68.99	61.36	62.91	61.73
SimCSE-$RoBERTa_{base}$	70.16	81.77	73.24	81.36	80.65	80.22	68.56	76.57
PrdSimCSE-$RoBERTa_{base}$ ◇	69.29	83.52	75.02	81.13	78.84	78.52	73.37	77.10

Table 5. Transfer task results of different sentence embedding models (measured as accuracy). ♣: results from [6]; ♡: results from [13]. ◇: results from ourselves. We highlight the highest numbers among models with the same pretrained encoder.

Model	MR	CR	SUBJ	MPQA	SST-2	TREC	MRPC	Avg.
GloVe embedding(avg.) ♣	77.25	78.3	91.17	87.85	80.18	83	72.87	81.52
BERT-[CLS]embedding ♣	78.68	84.85	94.21	88.23	84.13	91.40	71.13	84.66
SimCSE-$BERT_{base}$ ♡	81.18	86.46	94.45	88.88	85.5	89.8	74.43	85.81
PrdSimCSE-$BERT_{base}$ ◇	81.32	87.32	94.67	88.11	86.81	80.91	76.23	85.01

In Table 6, we present the evaluation results of PrdSimCSE on the two Chinese transfer task datasets. Because our model was trained on English corpora, direct evaluation using Chinese datasets resulted in very poor performance. We used Google Translate to translate all the data into English before conducting the evaluations. PrdSimCSE-$BERT_{base}$ outperformed SimCSE-$BERT_{base}$ by 1.63% on the BQ dataset and by 2.17% on LCQMC. PrdSimCSE-$RoBERTa_{base}$ exceeded SimCSE-$RoBERTa_{base}$ in performance by 0.85% on the BQ dataset and by 1.37% on LCQMC.

Table 6. Sentence embedding performance on two Chinese datasets.

Model	BQ	LCQMC
SimCSE-$Bert_{base}$	45.38	56.46
PrdSimCSE-$Bert_{base}$	47.01	58.63
SimCSE-$RoBERTa_{base}$	47.97	62.41
PrdSimCSE-$RoBERTa_{base}$	48.82	63.78

5. Ablation Studies

The success of PrdSimCSE can be attributed to two factors: positive and negative prefixes. Therefore, we conducted experiments from these two perspectives. Unless otherwise specified, all models described in this section were trained based on $Bert_{base}$ and were compared on the STS-B development set.

5.1. *Progress of Prefix Data Augmentation*

We aimed to understand the extent of improvement PrdSimCSE could achieve over SimCSE and, specifically, the contributions of positive and negative prefixes to PrdSimCSE. As shown in Table 7, both positive and negative prefixes were found to be effective data augmentation methods, and their combination led to further improvement in PrdSimCSE.

Table 7. Improvement on STS-B development sets produced by PosPrd or NegPrd over SimCSE. ♡: results from [13].

Model	STS-B
SimCSE ♡	82.5
+PosPrd	83.4
+NegPrd	82.9
PrdSimCSE	83.5

Sentence embeddings play a pivotal role across a spectrum of downstream tasks including text matching, sentiment analysis, and question answering systems. The advancements facilitated by Predix data augmentation in sentence embedding models hold the promise of enhancing the efficacy of these specific downstream applications. Drawing insights from the findings presented in Tables 4 and 5, when benchmarked against SimCS-BERTbase, PrdSimCSE exhibited notable performance gains: a 2.01% enhancement in the STS-B text matching task, a 1.31% improvement in sentiment analysis as observed in the SST-2 task, and a 1.67% increase in accuracy for the question answering task BQ. Central to these tasks is the precise vectorization of textual data, a cornerstone in contemporary natural language processing (NLP) research. Retrieval methods relying on text embeddings have garnered significant traction within the NLP community. Text embedding libraries, by segmenting and organizing textual data followed by vectorization utilizing sentence embedding models, serve as pivotal components. Notably, the efficacy of these libraries hinges greatly upon the performance of the underlying sentence embedding models. With robust storage and retrieval capabilities, text embedding libraries stand poised to drive further innovation in NLP applications. The PrdSimCSE framework proposed herein is poised to catalyze advancements in this domain, bolstering the widespread adoption and utility of text embedding libraries.

5.2. Determining Positive Prefixes

The primary criterion for positive prefixes is that they should not distort the original semantics of the sentence. Before specific experiments, we deployed a semantic similarity calculation tool using the pipeline of the Transformers package. By adding prefixes to several example sentences and calculating their similarity to the original sentences, we selected sentence pairs with the highest semantic similarity to preliminarily determine several positive prefixes. For the convenience of later discussion, the abbreviations and meanings of these positive prefixes are explained here. one-[CLS], one-[MASK], one-um: a single [CLS], a single [MASK], and a single 'um' as prefixes, respectively. level-[CLS], level-[MASK], level-um: As sentence length increases, the number of prefix words also gradually increases, as demonstrated in the Table 8 outlining the specific rules. Subsequently, we used the corresponding positive prefixes for data augmentation in sentence embedding learning. The experimental results are shown in Table 9, where the positive prefix "level-um" achieved the best results. Additionally, using "level-[CLS]" as a positive prefix also yielded accurate results, whereas "one-[MASK]" performed poorly. Other prompting sentences led to a decrease in performance.

Table 8. Relationship between sentence length and number of words added as prefix

Sentence Length	Number of Words Added as Prefix
<8	0
[8, 16)	1
[16, 24)	2
[24, 32)	3
≥32	4

Table 9. Results of different types of PosPrd on STS-B. ♡: results from [13].

Type of PosPrd	STS-B
SimCSE ♡	82.5
one-[CLS]	81
one-[MASK]	81.8
one-um	81.5
level-[CLS]	82.8
level-[MASK]	80.6
level-um	83.4

5.3. *Determining Negative Prefixes*

Similar to the method of positive prefixes, we also experimented with various negative prefixes. Simply covering the original sentence by adding long prefixes loses the meaning of prefix data augmentation. However, short prefixes cannot reverse the semantics of the entire sentence. Based on this, we identified several appropriately sized semantic reversal cues. For the convenience of later discussion, the abbreviations and meanings of these negative prefixes are explained here. one-reversal: Using 'reversal' as a prefix. prefix1: "Sentence contradicts in time, place, people, number, emotion, type". prefix2: "Contradictory in time, location, individuals, quantity, emotion, and category within the sentence". prefix3: "The expression in terms of time, location, persons, number, emotion, and type in the following sentence is contradictory". Prefix3 did not override the original sentences, but reversed the meaning of the sentences as much as possible. Table 10 lists the performance of the negative prefixes in semantic similarity tasks.

Table 10. Results of different types of NegPrd on STS-B. ♡: results from [13].

Type of NegPrd	STS-B
SimCSE ♡	82.5
one-reversal	80.4
prefix1	81.3
prefix2	81.1
prefix3	82.9

5.4. *Semantic Bias Caused by Prefix Data Augmentation*

To further explore the semantic bias introduced by prefix data augmentation and verify the impact of sentence length on the encoding results, we conducted experiments on the SICK-R test set [36]. Based on whether the length of the shorter sentence in a sentence pair was less than eight, we divided the SICK-R test set into two groups and evaluated them separately, comparing the Spearman correlation coefficients. As shown in Table 11, both PrdSimCSE and SimCSE performed much worse on sentences with lengths > 8 than on those with lengths ≤ 8. However, upon further analysis of the original SICKR test set results, PrdSimCSE exhibited larger fluctuations, especially in sentences with lengths ≤ 8, where the fluctuation in PrdSimCSE was notably wider than that of SimCSE. This indirectly confirmed our speculation that models trained with Prd tend to produce semantic deviations when encoding sentences.

In English transfer tasks, we observed that PrdSimCSE significantly underperformed SimCSE on the TREC dataset [43], a discrepancy related to this specific error. PrdSimCSE produced a larger error for sentences shorter than eight words. The TREC test set contains 500 sentences, with an average length of 10 words per sentence. Each sentence is associated with one coarse class label and one fine class label, with the label being a single word. We attempted to remove sentences from TREC that were shorter than eight and six words, respectively, and then re-evaluated PrdSimCSE; the results are shown in Table 12. After removing the shorter sentences, PrdSimCSE's performance improved by 6.23%, indirectly confirming our hypothesis. Due to PrdSimCSE's use of repetitive, meaningless prefixes during training, the encoder reduces its attention to the tokens at the beginning of sentences, thus weakening its understanding of short texts compared with SimCSE.

Table 11. Performance on sentence embeddings for SICK-R with different sentence lengths.

Model	Dataset	Spearman
SimCSE	Original	72.23
	>8	70.22 (−2.01)
	≤8	73.69 (+1.46)
PrdSimCSE	Original	73.75
	>8	71.68 (−2.07)
	≤8	75.59 (+1.84)

Table 12. Performance on sentence embeddings in TREC dataset with different sentence lengths.

Dataset	Original	Remove Length < 6	Remove Length < 8
PrdSimCSE	80.91	84.86	87.14

6. Semantic Similarity Event and Prefix Data Augmentation

6.1. Semantic Similarity Event

We assume that all sentences A can be mapped to the vector space Rn; thus, any sentence pair (A_1, A_2) can be mapped to the vector space R2n, with the resulting vector denoted as x. Then, we define the sample space $\Omega(\{\Omega = \mathrm{sim}(x)|x \in R^{2n}\})$, where $\mathrm{sim}(x)$ represents the vector similarity of the sentence pair (A_1, A_2). The event space $\mathcal{F}$ is the set of combinations of any events (e.g., $\mathrm{sim}(x) > 0.6$); $\mathcal{P}$ is the probability function mapping events to $[0, 1]$. We define a probability space $(\Omega, \mathcal{F}, \mathcal{P})$ based on the similarity of sentence vectors. As such, we can define the occurrence of semantically similar event E in the sample space as

$$E = \{\mathrm{sim}(x) > \tau\} \tag{3}$$

where $\tau \in [0, 1]$ is a threshold parameter. Therefore, the probability of the occurrence of a semantically similar event is represented as

$$P(E) \tag{4}$$

In practice, determining whether two sentences are similar is based on specific contextual information. Therefore, only conditional semantic similarity events exist based on different contextual information, and their probability is

$$P(E|C) \tag{5}$$

where C is an event implying contextual information (e.g., $C = \mathrm{sim}(x) > 0.5$, $E = \mathrm{sim}(x) > 0.8$). In this paper, $P(E|C)$ represents our trained PrdSimCSE model. For any given pair of sentences, based on the training corpus, $P(E|C)$ can provide their semantic similarity score, thereby determining whether the pair belongs to a semantic similarity event. According to Bayes' theorem, the estimation of the probability of a semantic similarity event can be considered as

$$\hat{P}(E) = \frac{P(C)P(E|C)}{P(C|E)} \tag{6}$$

The alignment of the sentence vector space using positive samples strongly impacts contrastive learning. This is because the selection of positive samples is directly related to the quality of sentence pairs in the semantic similarity set. Additionally, Prd can expand contextual information; namely, the precision of semantic similarity event probability estimation is improved by adding higher-quality negative samples.

6.2. Advantages of Positive Prefixes

The term "positive prefix" refers to a positive data augmentation method that uses meaningless modal particles as prefixes. This approach changes the position of tokens within the sentence without altering the original sentence's semantics. In contrast, dropout merely deactivates some positions in the sentence embedding. Hence, our PrdSimCSE does not incur errors due to positional information. From the perspective of semantic similarity events, semantic events derived through dropout only contain sentence pairs of the same length, which fails to provide an accurate estimation of semantic similarity event probabilities. The proposed PosPrd, by expanding the sentence pairs within semantic similarity events, increased the precision of estimating unconditional semantic similarity event probabilities. We adjusted the proportion of sentences with added prefixes in the training set, as shown in Table 13, to verify our hypothesis. By gradually increasing this proportion, the training results progressively improved. As illustrated in Figure 3, gradually increasing the proportion of sentences with added prefixes—equivalent to expanding the yellow area—resulted in a smaller probability estimation error for semantic similarity events.

Table 13. The performance of sentence embeddings with gradually increasing proportions of positive prefixes.

Model	STS-B
SimCSE	82.5
+20%	82.3
+40%	82.6
+60%	83.1
+80%	82.9
PrdSimCSE	83.5

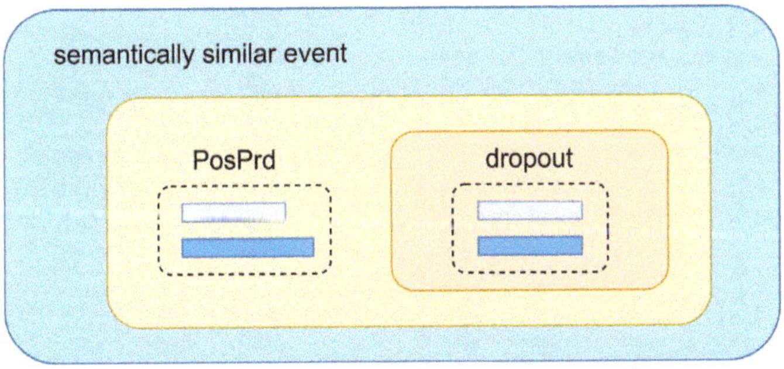

Figure 3. The difference between PosPrd and dropout in constructing positive samples, as well as the relationship between the two and the inclusion of semantically similar events.

6.3. Role of Negative Prefixes

"Negative prefix" refers to a negative data augmentation technique that uses semantic inversion prompts as prefixes. The goal of the negative prefix is to change the original sentence's meaning as much as possible, shifting the meaning to a semantically different category. When training the model using corpora, we were essentially estimating the probability of semantic similarity events using conditional semantic similarity events. During training, negative samples were considered the contextual information of conditional semantic similarity events; hence, we assumed that anchor and positive samples were similar. In Table 14, we attempted to replace sentences with negative prefixes with empty characters, finding that reducing the replacement proportion also improved the results.

This confirms that by adding negative prefixes, which enrich contextual information, the estimation of conditional semantic similarity probability becomes more accurate.

Table 14. The performance of sentence embeddings as the proportion of negative prefixes replaced with empty characters becomes smaller.

Model	STS-B
100%	75.2
80%	78.6
60%	79.3
40%	81.4
20%	81.9
PrdSimCSE	83.5

7. Conclusions

We developed a novel text augmentation method, prefix data augmentation. By using modal words as prefixes to construct positive samples, we avoided the positional information error that arises when SimCSE constructs positive samples. Constructing negative samples by employing specific semantic inversion prompts as prefixes effectively distinguishes negative samples. Based on these methods, we developed an unsupervised sentence embedding contrastive learning model enhanced using prefix data augmentation. The results of the experiments showed that compared with SimCSE, PrdSimCSE achieved comprehensive performance improvements on semantic similarity task sets, achieving a 2.01% increase on STS-B and a 1.08% increase on average.

We conducted a search on the form of prefixes. For positive prefixes, we found that as sentence length increases, adding more semantic word prefixes improves the model's performance. For negative prefixes, we discovered that semantic inversion cue sentences are suitable choices, where the shorter the cue sentence, the larger the performance loss of the model. Additionally, we found that in some transfer tasks, PrdSimCSE's understanding of short texts is not as strong as that of SimCSE. Through multiple ablation experiments, we observed that although PrdSimCSE avoids the semantic biases caused by positive samples of the same length, it loses some ability to comprehend short text. In summary, PrdSimCSE produced improvements compared with SimCSE on 16 tasks, also proving the feasibility and effectiveness of prefix data augmentation.

PrdSimCSE not only addresses the bias issues experienced with previous approaches but also provides a new approach to constructing negative samples for contrastive learning. We think that the method presented in this paper offers valuable references for researchers in the NLP field.

Author Contributions: Conceptualization, S.L. and C.W.; methodology, C.W.; software, C.W.; validation, S.L. and C.W.; formal analysis, S.L.; investigation, C.W.; resources, S.L.; data curation, C.W.; writing—original draft preparation, C.W.; writing—review and editing, S.L.; supervision, S.L. All authors have read and agreed to the published version of the manuscript.

Funding: This study received no external funding.

Institutional Review Board Statement: Not applicable.

Informed Consent Statement: Not applicable.

Data Availability Statement: The data presented in this study are available in [13].

Conflicts of Interest: The authors declare no conflicts of interest.

ferences

Kiros, R.; Zhu, Y.; Salakhutdinov, R.R.; Zemel, R.; Urtasun, R.; Torralba, A.; Fidler, S. Skip-thought vectors. *Adv. Neural Inf. Process. Syst.* **2015**, *28*, 3294–3302.

Hill, F.; Cho, K.; Korhonen, A. Learning distributed representations of sentences from unlabelled data. *arXiv* **2016**, arXiv:1602.03483.

Conneau, A.; Kiela, D.; Schwenk, H.; Barrault, L.; Bordes, A. Supervised learning of universal sentence representations from natural language inference data. *arXiv* **2017**, arXiv:1705.02364.

Logeswaran, L.; Lee, H. An efficient framework for learning sentence representations. *arXiv* **2018**, arXiv:1803.02893.

Cer, D.; Yang, Y.; Kong, S.Y.; Hua, N.; Limtiaco, N.; John, R.S.; Constant, N.; Guajardo-Cespedes, M.; Yuan, S.; Tar, C.; et al. Universal sentence encoder for English. In Proceedings of the 2018 Conference on Empirical Methods in Natural Language Processing: System Demonstrations, Brussels, Belgium, 31 October–4 November 2018; pp. 169–174.

Reimers, N.; Gurevych, I. Sentence-bert: Sentence embeddings using siamese bert-networks. *arXiv* **2019**, arXiv:1908.10084.

Gao, J.; He, D.; Tan, X.; Qin, T.; Wang, L.; Liu, T.Y. Representation degeneration problem in training natural language generation models. *arXiv* **2019**, arXiv:1907.12009.

Ethayarajh, K. How contextual are contextualized word representations? Comparing the geometry of BERT, ELMo, and GPT-2 embeddings. *arXiv* **2019**, arXiv:1909.00512.

Li, B.; Zhou, H.; He, J.; Wang, M.; Yang, Y.; Li, L. On the sentence embeddings from pre-trained language models. *arXiv* **2020**, arXiv:2011.05864.

Su, J.; Cao, J.; Liu, W.; Ou, Y. Whitening sentence representations for better semantics and faster retrieval. *arXiv* **2021**, arXiv:2103.15316.

Zhang, Y.; He, R.; Liu, Z.; Lim, K.H.; Bing, L. An unsupervised sentence embedding method by mutual information maximization. *arXiv* **2020**, arXiv:2009.12061.

Carlsson, F.; Gyllensten, A.C.; Gogoulou, E.; Hellqvist, E.Y.; Sahlgren, M. Semantic re-tuning with contrastive tension. In Proceedings of the International Conference on Learning Representations, Addis Ababa, Ethiopia, 26–30 April 2020.

Gao, T.; Yao, X.; Chen, D. Simcse: Simple contrastive learning of sentence embeddings. *arXiv* **2021**, arXiv:2104.08821.

Chuang, Y.S.; Dangovski, R.; Luo, H.; Zhang, Y.; Chang, S.; Soljačić, M.; Li, S.W.; Yih, W.T.; Kim, Y.; Glass, J. DiffCSE: Difference-based contrastive learning for sentence embeddings. *arXiv* **2022**, arXiv:2204.10298.

Wu, Z.; Wang, S.; Gu, J.; Khabsa, M.; Sun, F.; Ma, H. Clear: Contrastive learning for sentence representation. *arXiv* **2020**, arXiv:2012.15466.

Wang, T.; Isola, P. Understanding contrastive representation learning through alignment and uniformity on the hypersphere. In Proceedings of the International Conference on Machine Learning (PMLR), Virtual, 13–18 July 2020; pp. 9929–9939.

Srivastava, N.; Hinton, G.; Krizhevsky, A.; Sutskever, I.; Salakhutdinov, R. Dropout: A simple way to prevent neural networks from overfitting. *J. Mach. Learn. Res.* **2014**, *15*, 1929–1958.

Wang, H.; Dou, Y. Sncse: Contrastive learning for unsupervised sentence embedding with soft negative samples. In Proceedings of the International Conference on Intelligent Computing, Zhengzhou, China, 10–13 August 2023; Springer: Berlin/Heidelberg, Germany, 2023, pp. 419–431.

Nishikawa, S.; Ri, R.; Yamada, I.; Tsuruoka, Y.; Echizen, I. EASE: Entity-aware contrastive learning of sentence embedding. *arXiv* **2022**, arXiv:2205.04260.

Edunov, S.; Ott, M.; Auli, M.; Grangier, D. Understanding back-translation at scale. *arXiv* **2018**, arXiv:1808.09381.

Wang, X.; Pham, H.; Dai, Z.; Neubig, G. SwitchOut: An efficient data augmentation algorithm for neural machine translation. *arXiv* **2018**, arXiv:1808.07512.

Wei, J.; Zou, K. Eda: Easy data augmentation techniques for boosting performance on text classification tasks. *arXiv* **2019**, arXiv:1901.11196.

Xie, Q.; Dai, Z.; Hovy, E.; Luong, T.; Le, Q. Unsupervised data augmentation for consistency training. *Adv. Neural Inf. Process. Syst.* **2020**, *33*, 6256–6268.

Mikolov, T.; Chen, K.; Corrado, G.; Dean, J. Efficient estimation of word representations in vector space. *arXiv* **2013**, arXiv:1301.3781.

Devlin, J.; Chang, M.W.; Lee, K.; Toutanova, K. Bert: Pre-training of deep bidirectional transformers for language understanding. *arXiv* **2018**, arXiv:1810.04805.

Wang, S.; Fang, Y.; Sun, S.; Gan, Z.; Cheng, Y.; Jiang, J.; Liu, J. Cross-thought for sentence encoder pre-training. *arXiv* **2020**, arXiv:2010.03652.

Yang, Z.; Yang, Y.; Cer, D.; Law, J.; Darve, E. Universal sentence representation learning with conditional masked language model. *arXiv* **2020**, arXiv:2012.14388.

He, K.; Fan, H.; Wu, Y.; Xie, S.; Girshick, R. Momentum contrast for unsupervised visual representation learning. In Proceedings of the IEEE/CVF Conference on Computer Vision and Pattern Recognition, Seattle, WA, USA, 13–19 June 2020; pp. 9729–9738.

Liu, Y.; Ott, M.; Goyal, N.; Du, J.; Joshi, M.; Chen, D.; Levy, O.; Lewis, M.; Zettlemoyer, L.; Stoyanov, V. Roberta: A robustly optimized bert pretraining approach. *arXiv* **2019**, arXiv:1907.11692.

Chen, T.; Kornblith, S.; Norouzi, M.; Hinton, G. Simclr: A simple framework for contrastive learning of visual representations. In Proceedings of the International Conference on Learning Representations, Addis Ababa, Ethiopia, 26–30 April 2020; Volume 2, p. 4.

31. Agirre, E.; Cer, D.; Diab, M.; Gonzalez-Agirre, A. Semeval-2012 task 6: A pilot on semantic textual similarity. In Proceedings of t * SEM 2012: The First Joint Conference on Lexical and Computational Semantics–Volume 1: Proceedings of the Main Conferen and the Shared Task, and Volume 2: Proceedings of the Sixth International Workshop on Semantic Evaluation (SemEval 201 Montréal, QC, Canada, 7–8 June 2012; pp. 385–393.
32. Agirre, E.; Cer, D.; Diab, M.; Gonzalez-Agirre, A.; Guo, W. * SEM 2013 shared task: Semantic textual similarity. In Proceedings the Second Joint Conference on Lexical and Computational Semantics (* SEM), Volume 1: Proceedings of the Main Conferen and the Shared Task: Semantic Textual Similarity, Atlanta, GA, USA, 13–14 June 2013; pp. 32–43.
33. Agirre, E.; Banea, C.; Cardie, C.; Cer, D.; Diab, M.; Gonzalez-Agirre, A.; Guo, W.; Mihalcea, R.; Rigau, G.; Wiebe, J. Semeval-20 task 10: Multilingual semantic textual similarity. In Proceedings of the 8th International Workshop on Semantic Evaluati (SemEval 2014), Dublin, Ireland, 23–24 August 2014; pp. 81–91.
34. Agirre, E.; Banea, C.; Cardie, C.; Cer, D.; Diab, M.; Gonzalez-Agirre, A.; Guo, W.; Lopez-Gazpio, I.; Maritxalar, M Mihalcea, R.; et al. Semeval-2015 task 2: Semantic textual similarity, english, spanish and pilot on interpretability. In Proceedin of the 9th International Workshop on Semantic Evaluation (SemEval 2015), Denver, CO, USA, 4–5 June 2015; pp. 252–263.
35. Agirre, E.; Banea, C.; Cer, D.; Diab, M.; Gonzalez Agirre, A.; Mihalcea, R.; Rigau Claramunt, G.; Wiebe, J. Semeval-2016 task Semantic textual similarity, monolingual and cross-lingual evaluation. In Proceedings of the SemEval-2016: 10th Internatior Workshop on Semantic Evaluation, San Diego, CA, USA, 16–17 June 2016; ACL (Association for Computational Linguistic Stroudsburg, PA, USA, 2016; pp. 497–511.
36. Bentivogli, L.; Bernardi, R.; Marelli, M.; Menini, S.; Baroni, M.; Zamparelli, R. SICK through the SemEval glasses. Lesson learn from the evaluation of compositional distributional semantic models on full sentences through semantic relatedness and textu entailment. *Lang. Resour. Eval.* **2016**, *50*, 95–124. [CrossRef]
37. Cer, D.; Diab, M.; Agirre, E.; Lopez-Gazpio, I.; Specia, L. Semeval-2017 task 1: Semantic textual similarity-multilingual a cross-lingual focused evaluation. *arXiv* **2017**, arXiv:1708.00055.
38. Pang, B.; Lee, L. Seeing stars: Exploiting class relationships for sentiment categorization with respect to rating scales. *arXiv* **20** arXiv:cs/0506075v1.
39. Hu, M.; Liu, B. Mining and summarizing customer reviews. In Proceedings of the Tenth ACM SIGKDD International Conferen on Knowledge Discovery and Data Mining, Seattle, WA, USA, 22–25 August 2004; pp. 168–177.
40. Pang, B.; Lee, L. A sentimental education: Sentiment analysis using subjectivity summarization based on minimum cuts. *arX* **2004**, arXiv:cs/0409058.
41. Wiebe, J.; Wilson, T.; Cardie, C. Annotating expressions of opinions and emotions in language. *Lang. Resour. Eval.* **20** *39*, 165–210. [CrossRef]
42. Socher, R.; Perelygin, A.; Wu, J.; Chuang, J.; Manning, C.D.; Ng, A.Y.; Potts, C. Recursive deep models for semantic compositic ality over a sentiment treebank. In Proceedings of the 2013 Conference on Empirical Methods in Natural Language Processir Seattle, CA, USA, 18–21 October 2013; pp. 1631–1642.
43. Voorhees, E.M.; Tice, D.M. Building a question answering test collection. In Proceedings of the 23rd Annual International AC SIGIR Conference on Research and Development in Information Retrieval, Athens, Greece, 24–28 July 2000; pp. 200–207.
44. Dolan, B.; Brockett, C. Automatically constructing a corpus of sentential paraphrases. In Proceedings of the Third Internatior Workshop on Paraphrasing (IWP2005), Jeju Island, Republic of Korea, 14 October 2005.
45. Chen, J.; Chen, Q.; Liu, X.; Yang, H.; Lu, D.; Tang, B. The bq corpus: A large-scale domain-specific chinese corpus for senten semantic equivalence identification. In Proceedings of the 2018 Conference on Empirical Methods in Natural Language Processi Brussels, Belgium, 31 October–4 November 2018; pp. 4946–4951.
46. Liu, X.; Chen, Q.; Deng, C.; Zeng, H.; Chen, J.; Li, D.; Tang, B. Lcqmc: A large-scale chinese question matching corp In Proceedings of the 27th International Conference on Computational Linguistics, Santa Fe, NM, USA, 21–25 August 20 pp. 1952–1962.
47. Pennington, J.; Socher, R.; Manning, C.D. Glove: Global vectors for word representation. In Proceedings of the 2014 Conferen on Empirical Methods in Natural Language Processing (EMNLP), Doha, Qatar, 25–29 October 2014; pp. 1532–1543.

applied sciences

MDPI

ticle

ausal Reinforcement Learning for Knowledge Graph easoning

ezhi Li, Yunjun Lu *, Jianping Wu, Wenlu Zhou and Guangjun Zeng

School of Information and Communication, National University of Defense Technology, Wuhan 430019, China; ldzfreedom@sina.com (D.L.); wjp860343510@sina.com (J.W.); zhouwenlu17@nudt.edu.cn (W.Z.); guangjun_zeng@nudt.edu.cn (G.Z.)

* Correspondence: luyunjun@nudt.edu.cn

Abstract: Knowledge graph reasoning can deduce new facts and relationships, which is an important research direction of knowledge graphs. Most of the existing methods are based on end-to-end reasoning which cannot effectively use the knowledge graph, so consequently the performance of the method still needs to be improved. Therefore, we combine causal inference with reinforcement learning and propose a new framework for knowledge graph reasoning. By combining the counterfactual method in causal inference, our method can obtain more information as prior knowledge and integrate it into the control strategy in the reinforcement model. The proposed method mainly includes the steps of relationship importance identification, reinforcement learning framework design, policy network design, and the training and testing of the causal reinforcement learning model. Specifically, a prior knowledge table is first constructed to indicate which relationship is more important for the problem to be queried; secondly, designing state space, optimization, action space, state transition and reward, respectively, is undertaken; then, the standard value is set and compared with the weight value of each candidate edge, and an action strategy is selected according to the comparison result through prior knowledge or neural network; finally, the parameters of the reinforcement learning model are determined through training and testing. We used four datasets to compare our method to the baseline method and conducted ablation experiments. On dataset NELL-995 and FB15k-237, the experimental results show that the MAP scores of our method are 87.8 and 45.2, and the optimal performance is achieved.

Keywords: Priori knowledge; counterfactual; reinforcement learning; knowledge graph reasoning

1. Introduction

In recent years, knowledge graphs have been widely used in several fields. However, for various professional fields, the constructed knowledge graphs are usually sparse and the implicit relationship between entities has not been fully examined, resulting in a poor practical application effect. Therefore, it is necessary to complete the knowledge graphs; the typical method is knowledge graph reasoning.

Knowledge graph reasoning tasks include Knowledge Graph Completion (KGC), quality verification, path prediction, relationship reasoning, and conflict detection [1]. This paper mainly focuses on KGC and transforms the knowledge graph reasoning problem into a problem predicting the missing part of the triple. For example, as depicted in Figure 1, we obtain two paths based on the existing knowledge graph: "Christopher Nolan$\xrightarrow{\text{Born in}}$London" and "London$\xrightarrow{\text{Located in}}$Britain". Our task is to complete the triple: (Christopher Nolan, nationality, ?). Since we do not have the path "Christopher Nolan$\xrightarrow{\text{Nationality}}$British", we use the dotted line to represent the edge of the relationship. From knowledge graph reasoning, the above two paths are equivalent to "Christopher Nolan$\xrightarrow{\text{Nationality}}$British". So, we complete the triple: (Christopher Nolan, nationality, British).

In the above reasoning process, we start from the Nolan node. For the relationship of "nationality", the association degree of the edges linked to the Nolan node differs, highlighting that "Born in" is more relevant to finding a relationship of nationality than "Direct" and "Partner". This is because humans have prior knowledge that "place of birth" is more likely to determine "nationality" than "director" and "partner".

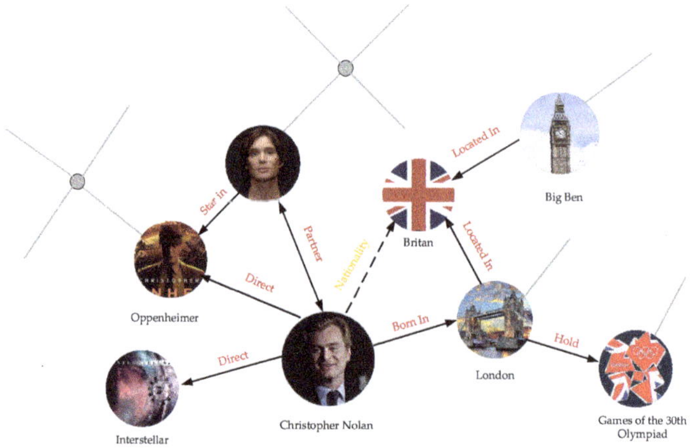

Figure 1. Schematic diagram of knowledge graph reasoning. The dotted lines represent relational paths that were unknown before reasoning.

Reinforcement learning is applied to knowledge graph reasoning tasks owing to its adaptability to complex environments [2]. Reinforcement learning regards the above reasoning process as the following problem: finding a path connecting the known head entity and tail entity, modeling this problem as a sequential decision problem, and solving it using the method based on policy gradient [3]. Since the existing reinforcement learning models do not conduct in-depth research on the knowledge graph, this paper employs causal inference to analyze the knowledge graph and obtain prior knowledge, thereby improving inference performance. For instance, in Figure 1, we want to complete the triple (person, language, ?), and there are two paths in the knowledge graph: "person$\xrightarrow{\text{Star in}}$film $\xrightarrow{\text{Country}}$Britain" and "person$\xrightarrow{\text{Star in}}$film $\xrightarrow{\text{Language}}$English". We obtain prior knowledge through causal inference, i.e., the relationship "language" in the second path is more related to the relationship in the triple to be completed than the relationship "country" in the first path. So, we obtain the importance of the relationship in the path and thus guide the path selection.

The major contributions of this work are as follows:

1. We propose a prior knowledge generation method based on causal inference. Specifically, it is implemented through the relationship importance identification module. The generated prior knowledge is mainly used to measure the contribution of the relationship in the triple to be completed.
2. We introduce a new method combining causal inference and reinforcement learning that applies to knowledge graph reasoning. Specifically, the prior knowledge is integrated into the control strategy of the reinforcement model, allowing the agent to select the relation more accurately in each step. Our model also applies to large-scale knowledge graphs.
3. The experiments demonstrate that our method's performance outperforms the current baseline methods in most cases. Additionally, we conduct ablation experiments to highlight that our method is more effective than solely employing reinforcement learning.

The remainder of this paper is organized as follows. Section 2 briefly introduces the related work. Section 3 presents the methodological details, and Section 4 conducts experiments and analyzes the experimental results. Section 5 summarizes this work and provides future research directions.

2. Related Work

2.1. Knowledge Graph Reasoning

The existing methods in the field of knowledge graph reasoning involve two categories: methods based on distributed representation and based on relational path [4]. Knowledge graph methods based on distributed representation predict the missing tail entities by learning the low-dimensional embedded representation of known entities and relationships in triples. The most common method is TransE, which was proposed by Borders et al. [5]. Since the TransE method can only deal with the one-to-one relationship problem, many subsequent methods evolved from it. For instance, Wang et al. [6] and Lin et al. [7] introduced hyperplanes and mapping matrices to deal with the many-to-one relationship problem and proposed the TransH method and TransR method, respectively. In addition, Ji et al. [8] introduced a dynamic matrix and proposed the TransD method to solve this problem. However, these improved models cannot model and simultaneously infer all kinds of relationships (symmetry and composition). Thus, Pasquale et al. [9] developed ConvE, a two-dimensional convolutional link prediction method. Furthermore, Trouillon et al. [10] proposed the ComplEx method, which introduced complex number space into knowledge representation. The model structure of ComplEx is relatively simple, since only Hermitian dot products are used.

The above methods cannot solve the problem of multi-step knowledge reasoning, and therefore, solutions based on the relational path have been developed. Such a traditional model is the PRA (Path Ranking Algorithm) [11], characterized by strong interpretability and automatic rules discovery. However, this model is ineffective in dealing with low-frequency relationships and low-connectivity graphs (sparse data). In addition, when the graph is large enough, path extraction is time-consuming. Thus, Xiong et al. [12] and Das et al. [13] introduced reinforcement learning into knowledge graph reasoning, considering the relational path selection problem as a Markov decision process with better reasoning effect and interpretability. On this basis, Wan et al. [14] proposed an improved multi-level reinforcement learning model, which encodes historical knowledge and action space, achieving appealing results. The attention mechanism introduced by Wang et al. [15] enables the reasoning process to be memorized, and the graph neural network can enhance the entity semantics. It should be noted that the models introduced above do not fully employ the knowledge graph. Therefore, the accuracy and efficiency of their methods can be further improved.

2.2. Casual Inference

Causal inference mainly refers to inferring the relationship between the cause-and-effect variables. Specifically, appropriate intervention on variable X will lead to a change in the distribution of variable Y, but intervention on Y will not lead to a change in X. In this case, X is the cause variable of Y, and Y is the effect variable of X. A causal inference model mainly solves two kinds of problems. One is the intervention problem, i.e., the variable is set to a certain value, and the causal relationship is analyzed according to the data distribution change. The other problem is the counterfactual problem, i.e., the probability that events A and B do not occur is inferred when events A and B occur [16–20]. Since the problem of relational path selection in knowledge graphs can be transformed into a counterfactual problem, this paper focuses on counterfactual problems [21].

Counterfactual reasoning generally comprises three steps: (1) Traceability: Updating the value of a noise term using evidence. This step accounts for a particular noise with evidence in mind; (2) Intervention: Modifying the original model, replacing the structural equation with counterfactual variables, and obtaining the modified model; (3) Prediction: The modified model and noise are used to re-estimate the outcome variables, and the counterfactual results are obtained [22]. Some studies investigate the counterfactual problem, with counterfactual reasoning improving the reinforcement learning algorithms' sample efficiency and interpretability [23]. For instance, Madumal et al. [24] proposed a behavioral influence model based on a structural causal model, which used the causal model for counterfactual analysis to improve the interpretability of the model. Lu et al. [25] developed a counterfactual-based data enhancement algorithm, which used the Structural Causal Model (SCM) to model the environment dynamics and estimate the causal effect based on the commonalities and differences in multi-domain data. Buesing et al. [26] introduced a CounterFactually Guided Policy Search algorithm CF-GPS, which counterfactually evaluates any policy based on SCM to improve policy performance and eliminate the model prediction bias. However, there are few studies on the combination of counterfactual problems and knowledge graph, and how counterfactual problems will help knowledge graph research remains to be explored.

2.3. *Reinforcement Learning*

Reinforcement learning is an important method in behavioral decision-making and control [27]. Specifically, the agent takes action at any time according to the next step's current status and reward [28]. The way an agent chooses an action is called a policy, and reinforcement learning maximizes the cumulative reward by constantly improving the policy.

Reinforcement learning algorithms can be divided into model-based and model-free methods depending on whether the agent uses the dynamic model of the environment in policy updating. In the model-free reinforcement-learning method, the agent directly interacts with the environment and optimizes the policy end-to-end, which is easier to implement and has better asymptotic performance. Classic algorithms include SARSA (State-Action-Reward-State-Action) [29], Q-learning [30], deep Q-networks [31,32], and their variants [33]. Many studies have recently applied reinforcement learning to knowledge graph reasoning [34,35]. Indeed, Lin et al. [36] extended MINERVA and proposed the MultiHopKG model to solve the above problems. Wang et al. [14] proposed AttnPath to quantify the difficulty of relation learning through MSR and MRR and redesigned the model's control strategy. At the same time, to avoid the stagnation of agents on the same entity, AttnPath designs a new learning mechanism that enables the agent to move forward at every step. Shen et al. [15] solved the problem of reward sparsity using a Monte Carlo search to improve the efficiency of knowledge reasoning. However, these models are highly data-dependent and perform poorly in non-stationary and heterogeneous scenarios.

2.4. *Causal Reinforcement Learning*

Causal reinforcement learning combines causal inference theory and reinforcement learning, allowing agents to understand the causal relationship and make correct decisions. Additional assumptions or prior knowledge is often required to achieve the above goals. Specifically, causal inference empowered reinforcement learning using improving sample efficiency, enhancing the generalization ability of agents, and reducing the impact of correlation on agents [37].

Maximilian et al. [38] measured the causal effect of an action on an object through constructing a causal quantity, thereby guiding the agent to explore the environment more effectively. Jiaxian et al. [39] enhanced the model's generalization ability through measuring the controlled direct effect and reducing the encoding of the state irrelevant to the action into the context information. Pim et al. [40] believed that more information is not necessarily better, revealing the false causality's misleading effect on reinforcement learning control strategy. Zhihong et al. [41] investigated the problem of false correlation in offline reinforcement learning and avoided uncertainty by pessimistic criteria to neglect the influence of false correlation on the model control strategy.

3. Proposed Method

This section describes the proposed model. First, the KGC problem is defined in detail. Then, the general framework of the proposed method is described, as well as how to extract prior knowledge through the causal inference module. Finally, the reinforcement learning framework is introduced.

3.1. Problem Definition

Let H denote the set of head entities, T is the entity found in the triple, and R represents the relation in the triple. G represents a known knowledge graph, $G = \{(h_i, r_i, t_i)\} \subseteq \{H, R, T\}, h_i \in H, r_i \in R, t_i \in T, i \in (1, n)$, where i represents the number of steps the agent moved on the knowledge graph with h_q as the starting point and the target entity as the endpoint. Our mission is to find the missing tail entity t_q given the triple $(h_q, r_q, ?)$. The proposed method solves the KGC problem based on a relational path. Therefore, we must find a path to the target tail entity in the knowledge graph, i.e., our goal is to find such a path denoted $p = \{h_q, r_1, r_2, \cdots, r_n, t_q\}$. This goal is equivalent to finding a path with semantics equal to r_q.

3.2. Overall Architecture

Figure 2 illustrates our method's framework. First, according to the triple $(h_q, r_q, ?)$ and the path extracted from the knowledge graph, the prior knowledge is obtained through the counterfactual theory in causal inference. The prior knowledge is represented using the relationship weight in each path relative to the relationship to be queried and obtained using the relationship importance identification module. The relationship importance identification module will be described in detail in the next section. After obtaining the prior knowledge, we combine it with the policy network to guide the agent to make the right choice. The policy network mainly uses a Long Short-Term Memory (LSTM) to represent semantic information, which will be described later. Then, the reasoning step and the tail entity to be queried will be obtained, and finally, the knowledge graph will be updated.

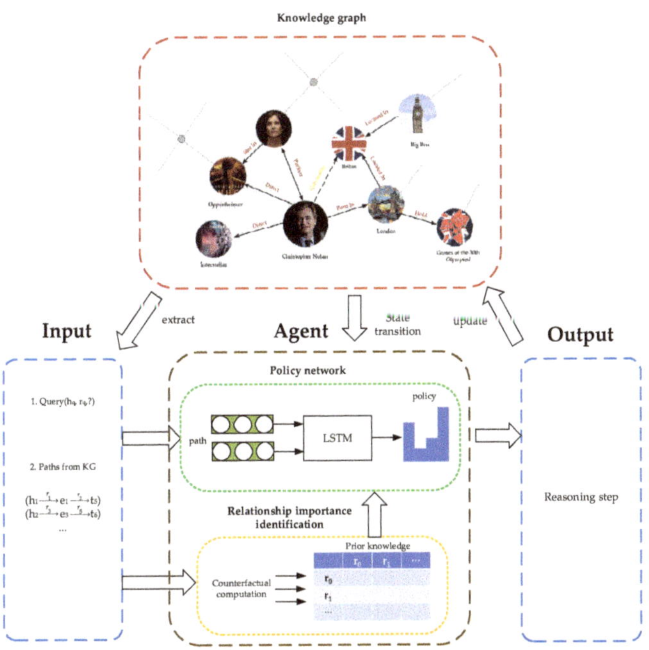

Figure 2. Overall framework of the casual reinforcement learning model. Combined with the question to be queried, starting from the target entity, the possible paths are extracted from the knowledge graph. In each step of the agent movement, the prior knowledge is obtained through the relation importance identification module, the reinforcement learning policy network is adjusted, and the state after the movement is updated. The agent updated the knowledge graph after reaching the target entity.

3.3. Relationship Importance Identification

Acquiring prior knowledge from the knowledge graph can assist in efficiently selecting the path closest to the real answer from the relational paths and better completing the missing tail entity. We introduced that prior knowledge is represented by the weight of the relationship in each path relative to the relationship to be queried. In this way, we quantify the importance of each relational path in the knowledge graph. This weight is implemented through a counterfactual question in causal inference. Specifically, for triple (h_q, r_q, t_q) with multiple paths from h_q to t_q, we obtain the following conclusion through the counterfactual definition: when the relation r_q changes, the tail entity will also change.

For the example in Figure 3, for the relationship R_0, if we change r_2 to r_4 in the path, and the rest remains unchanged, the relationship R_0 changes to R_6. Thus, we can obtain prior knowledge, as r_2 is more important for the relationship R_0. Then, we record this prior knowledge and the corresponding relationship individually.

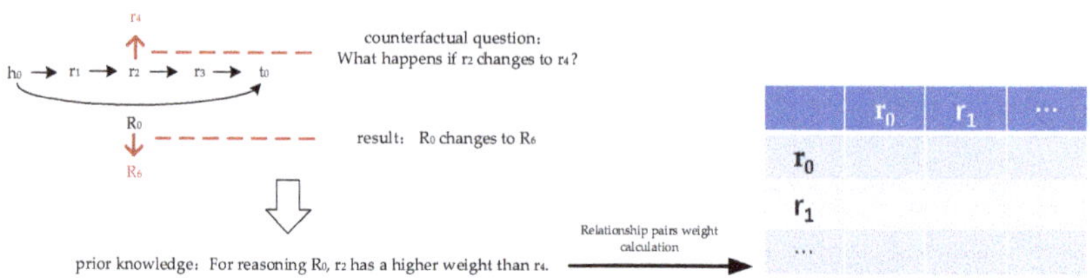

Figure 3. Relationship importance identification module based on causal inference.

Next, we construct a table of prior knowledge to represent the importance of the relationship. We denote this table by f, where r_i represents the relationship between the currently pointed entity and the next-hop entity after the agent moved i steps and the number of times we obtain the prior knowledge that "r_i is important for r_q" by $f[r_q][r_i]$. Thus, the weight of r_i to r_q is:

$$\omega_R[r_q][r_i] = \frac{f[r_q][r_i]}{\sum_{r_i \in R} f[r_q][r_i]} \tag{1}$$

where ω_R denotes the set of weights and the set of extracted prior knowledge. A larger weight of r_i indicates that r_i should be selected first when selecting a path.

Similarly, we use ω_E to represent the weight of the entity:

$$\omega_E[r_q][e_i] = \{\omega_R[r_q][r_j] | (e_i, r_j, e_k) \in G, e_k \in T\} \tag{2}$$

where $\omega_E[r_q][e_i]$ is the importance of the edge from entity e_i concerning relation r_q.

Figure 3 depicts the structure of the relationship importance identification module based on causal inference. Since we have obtained the knowledge graph, it is easier to obtain prior knowledge through counterfactual methods in causal inference. In contrast to graphical models that require negative sampling, the proposed model only requires the correct triples, thus avoiding the noise introduced by false negative samples due to negative sampling.

3.4. Reinforcement Learning Framework

This section describes how to design a reinforcement learning model with the relationship importance identification module. Compared with the traditional reinforcement learning framework, we introduce prior knowledge to enhance the performance of our method. Specifically, we transform the path selection problem into a partially observable Markov decision process. Suppose the following triple $(h_q, r_q, ?)$ is looked up in the knowledge graph. The agent starts from h_q and chooses a relation according to the inference problem, thus jumping to the new entity. Based on the new entity jumped to, we continue to select the relationship and iterate several steps until we find the ultimate goal. In this process, the agent prefers the most promising relationship for state transition according to the optimization process and updates the policy network through the reward function to find the same correct path as the r_q semantics.

3.4.1. Environment

Next, we represent the environment using five elements: (S, O, A, P, R).

S (State). The agent moves until it finds the target entity, so the state space at time t can be expressed in the following terms. One is the head entity h_q, which is the starting position of the agent. The second is the relation r_q, which is known in triples, and it is necessary to find a path in the knowledge map that is semantically equal to the relation r_q. The tail entity t_q is the target to be queried, which can test the accuracy of the inference algorithm. The third is entity e_t, representing the entity the agent is pointing to. According to the description of the above three parts, we can express the state space as: $s_t = (h_q, r_q, t_q, e_t)$.

O (Optimization). The optimization aims to quantify the prior knowledge obtained using the relationship importance identification module, i.e., to express the importance of the relation as a weight value. Taking entity e_t as the starting point, the prior knowledge is expressed as $\omega_E[r_q]$, and the optimization function is defined as $o_t = O(s_t = (h_q, r_q, t_q, e_t)) = (h_q, r_q, e_t, \omega_E[r_q])$.

A (Actions). The action space is the set of all edges from the current entity to the next entity. Therefore, the action space can be expressed as $A_t = \{(r_{t+1}, e_{t+1} | (e_t, r_{t+1}, e_{t+1}) \in G)\}$. Based on this, we represent the case where the inference terminates, which can be represented using an edge pointing to the entity.

P (Transition). The state transition space refers to the transition of the relationship path between the agent and the head entity and the transition of the current entity after the agent moves from one entity to another. The target entity to be searched remains unchanged during the agent's movement. Thus, the state transition space can be expressed as: $P(S_t, A_t) = P((h_q, r_q, t_q, e_t), (r_{t+1}, e_{t+1})) = (h_q, r_q, t_q, e_{t+1})$.

R (Rewards). Agents must constantly select actions from the action space, move forward in the knowledge map, and finally find the target entity. Therefore, we define the reward in the following form:

$$R = \begin{cases} 1 & \text{if } e_T = t_q \\ 0 & \text{otherwise} \end{cases} \tag{3}$$

where T denotes the last time the agent moves on the knowledge graph.

3.4.2. Policy Network

We use the policy network to guide the agent to make the right choice in the action space. The policy network is constructed using the prior knowledge extracted using causal inference and the neural network. Specifically, we first set a standard value φ, while the current time is t, and the entity pointed by the agent is e_t. The agent obtains the weight value of each edge from the optimization space and compares it with φ. If $\max(\omega_E[r_q][e_t])$ is larger than φ, the edge with the largest value is selected from the optimization space. Otherwise, the corresponding edge is selected according to the reinforcement learning model.

When the neural network selects an action, a path memory component (LSTM) is considered to encode the path information so that the history exploration is memorized [42]. History embedding h_t represents encoding the path that the agent moves on the knowledge graph before time t. The path is the composition of a series of entities and relationships, which can be represented as $\{h_q, r_1, e_1, r_2, e_2, \ldots, r_t, e_t\}$. Then, h_q, r_q, and e_t are concatenated and input into the nonlinear Multi-Layer Perceptron (MLP) [21]. The policy network π is defined as follows:

$$\pi(r_t|r_q,e_t,h_t,h_q) = \begin{cases} \omega_E[r_q][e_t] & \text{if } \max(\omega_E[r_q][e_t]) \geq \varphi \\ soft\max(A_t(W_2RELU(W_1[h_t;h_q;r_q;e_t;a_t]))) & \text{otherwise} \end{cases} \tag{4}$$

where W_1 and W_2 are weighting matrices.

3.4.3. Training

During training, according to the above strategy network, we update the parameter φ to maximize the expected cumulative reward J:

$$J(\varphi) = E_{(e_1,r,e_2)\sim D}E_{a_1,a_2,\ldots,a_{T-1}\sim\pi}[R(s_T\big|h_q,r_q)] \tag{5}$$

where D represents all real and observed triples, the first E is the empirical average over the training dataset, and s_T is the entity to which the agent is ultimately directed. The gradient update formula of the policy network can be expressed as follows:

$$\frac{\partial J(\varphi)}{\partial\varphi} = \frac{\partial}{\partial\varphi}\log\pi(r_t|r_q,e_t,h_t,h_q) \tag{6}$$

The specific training steps are described in Algorithm 1. First, the parameter θ (Line 01) is initialized. Next, for each episode (Line 02), a path p (Line 03) is created, and the history embedding h_0 is initialized to 0 (Line 04). Next, for the historical path of the current node (Line 05), the agent calculates the history embedding, trains the policy network, and obtains the next action vector (Line 06 and Line 07). Next, the environment will transition to the next state and reward the agent for its choice (Line 08). By continuously using the formula to update φ (Line 09), the relationship path is determined to obtain the location of the target entity.

Algorithm 1. Training Procedure

01 Initialize φ
02 **for** episode←1 to N **do**
03 Initialize path p
04 Initialize entity representation h_0
05 **for** $j \leftarrow 1$ to $|p|$ **do**
06 Calculate history embedding $h_t \leftarrow LSTM(h_{t-1},[a_{t-1};r_q;h_q;e_t])$
07 Obtain reward *R(p)*
08 $\nabla J \leftarrow \frac{\partial}{\partial\varphi}\log\pi(r_t|r_q,e_t,h_t,h_q)$
09 Update φ
10 **end for**
11 **end for**

4. Experiments

4.1. Datasets

This work employs several classes of data sets that are widely used in knowledge graph reasoning, including (1) FB15K-237 [43], (2) WN18RR [44], (3) NEL-995 [45], (4) YAGO3-10 [46]. Table 1 reports the details of the four datasets.

Table 1. Detailed of datasets FB15k-237, WN18RR, YAGO3-10 and NELL-995.

Dataset	E	R	Training Triples	Test Triples
FB15K-237	14,541	237	272,115	20,466
WN18RR	40,943	11	86,835	3134
NELL-995	75,492	200	154,213	3992
YAGO3-10	123,182	37	1,079,040	5000

FB15K-237 is a subset of FB15K, while FB15K is derived from the Freebase dataset. Freebase is a huge, multi-domain dataset created by Google, which collects a large amount of entity, attribute, and relationship information. The WN18RR dataset is derived from the WN18 dataset, and the WN18 dataset is derived from the WordNet dataset. Compared with the WordNet dataset, the WN18RR dataset removes the inversion relationship, retains other relationships, and has fewer relationship types. The NELL-995 dataset is an open-source machine learning dataset developed by OpenAI, which is constructed by unsupervised learning and automatically extracts entities and relationships through semantic analysis and pattern recognition of massive web content. YAGO3-10 is a subset of the YAGO dataset, with data from open-source websites or datasets such as Wikipedia, WordNet, and GeoNames.

4.2. Baseline Methods

We use typical representatives of methods based on distributed representation and based on a relational path as the baseline. The former methods comprise TransE, ComplEx, and ConvE, and the latter comprises PRA, DeepPath, and MINERVA.

4.3. Evaluation Protocol

We mainly evaluate the performance of each method through the following two tasks:

Relation Link Prediction. This is one of the common tasks to evaluate the reasoning performance of knowledge graphs. Specifically, first, we construct incomplete triples as negative samples, and second, we construct a test dataset containing both positive and negative samples. Then, we employ the Mean Average Precision (MAP) score for the specific evaluation index, which considers both the prediction accuracy and the relative position difference in the sequence.

Entity Link Prediction. This is also one of the common tasks used to evaluate the performance of knowledge graph reasoning. Specifically, we used Hit@N and Mean Reciprocal Rank (MRR). For the value of N in Hit@N, we take N as 1, 3, and 10 to obtain a more comprehensive evaluation result. The specific indicator should be selected in combination with the baseline method.

4.4. Implementation Details

In the experiment, we also need to determine the path length, the number of hidden layers of the neural network, the learning rate, the standard value, and other hyperparameters. We finally choose a path length from 2 to 6, the number of hidden layers from 50 or 100, and the learning rate from 0.01 to 0.05. The standard values are determined based on prior knowledge of each dataset. In addition, the training epochs must also be determined according to different data sets, ranging from 300 to 3000.

4.5. Results

This paper conducts relational link prediction tasks on the NELL-995 and FB15K-237 datasets. Table 2 reports the MAP scores of TransE, PRA, DeepPath, MINERVA, and our model, highlighting that although our model does not perform optimally on every sub-task, it outperforms the baseline model on most tasks, especially on the NELL-995 dataset. Indeed, most individual tasks and the final mean scores were better than the baseline model. Although the highest scores were achieved on only three sub-tasks, the average scores of our model were also very close to the highest average scores on the FB15k-237 dataset.

The entity link prediction task was conducted on the NELL-995, WIN18RR, FB15K-237, and YAGO3-10 datasets. Table 3 reports the corresponding results, which reveals that our model performs better on all four datasets compared to the baseline models. Specifically, our model performs best in Hit@1 and Hit@10 and is second only to the ConvE model in Hit@3 and MRR on the NELL-995 dataset. This is because the ConvE model increases the embedding dimension by convolution, making it better at capturing complex information. Our model generally performs well on the FB15k-237 dataset because the FB15k-237 dataset has the most relationship types and fewer relationship patterns, and the model based on the relational path has an insufficient generalization ability. On the WN18RR and YAGO3-10 datasets, the relational path-based model outperforms the distributed representation-based model, and our model performs best among them. This is because prior knowledge contains more effective information.

Table 2. The MAP scores on NELL995 and FB15K-237.

Dataset	Tasks	TransE	PRA	DeepPath	MINERVA	Our Model
NELL-995	AthletePlaysInLeague	77.3	84.1	92.7	95.2	**95.4**
	AthletePlaysForTeam	62.7	54.7	75.0	82.4	**86.9**
	AthleteHomeStadium	71.8	85.9	89.0	89.5	**90.7**
	TeamPlaySports	76.1	79.1	73.8	84.6	**85.5**
	OrgHeadquaterCity	62.0	81.1	79.0	**94.5**	93.6
	BornLocation	71.2	66.8	75.7	79.3	**82.2**
	OrgHiredPerson	71.9	59.9	74.2	85.1	**86.4**
	PersonLeadsOrg	75.1	68.1	75.5	**83.0**	81.4
	...					
	Overall	71.0	72.5	79.4	86.7	**87.8**
FB15k-237	adjoins	**68.4**	41.8	69.1	71.8	60.1
	contains	**56.7**	32.5	39.8	41.5	40.8
	personNationality	44.2	42.1	52.8	**62.1**	42.9
	filmDirector	41.5	32.8	45.6	38.9	**46.3**
	filmLanguag	**61.5**	45.1	52.5	58.9	46.1
	filmWritten	56.1	32.1	36.5	**59.1**	36.2
	capitalOf	42.5	25.8	43.8	48.9	**50.6**
	musicianOrigin	38.2	18.5	23.7	23.8	**38.7**
	...					
	Overall	**45.3**	31.5	39.8	42.3	45.2

Bold indicates the highest score.

Table 3. Link prediction results (Hits@N and MRR) on datasets WN18RR, FB15k-237, NELL-995 and YAGO3-10.

Dataset	Metric	TransE	ComplEX	ConvE	MINERVA	Our Model
NELL-995	Hit@1	0.514	0.612	0.672	0.663	**0.684**
	Hit@3	0.678	0.761	**0.808**	0.773	0.797
	Hit@10	0.751	0.827	0.864	0.831	**0.871**
	MRR	0.456	0.694	**0.747**	0.725	0.740
FB15K-237	Hit@1	0.248	0.303	**0.313**	0.217	0.228
	Hit@3	0.401	0.434	0.457	0.329	**0.464**
	Hit@10	0.450	0.572	**0.600**	0.456	0.491
	MRR	0.361	0.394	0.410	0.293	**0.422**
WN18RR	Hit@1	0.289	0.382	0.403	0.413	**0.440**
	Hit@3	0.475	0.433	0.452	0.456	**0.485**
	Hit@10	0.560	0.480	0.519	0.513	**0.542**
	MRR	0.359	0.415	0.438	0.448	**0.474**
YAGO3-10	Hit@1	0.248	0.260	0.350	0.355	**0.380**
	Hit@3	0.412	0.405	0.490	0.498	**0.510**
	Hit@10	0.315	0.550	0.620	0.650	**0.678**
	MRR	0.308	0.360	0.440	0.470	**0.492**

Bold indicates best performance.

4.6. Analysis

4.6.1. Setting of Standard Values and Ablation Study

We take the experimental results on the NELL-995 dataset as an example to study the influence of different standard values and further measure the influence of prior knowledge introduced by causal inference. Since the maximum weight of most relationships on the NELL-995 dataset is 0.1, we chose three standard values of 0.01, 0.05, and 0.1 for the following experiment. Furthermore, to ensure the consistency of the experimental results, we still use the Hits@N and MRR indicators to measure the performance differences in this ablation study, where N is still 1, 3, and 10. The experimental results are illustrated in Figure 4.

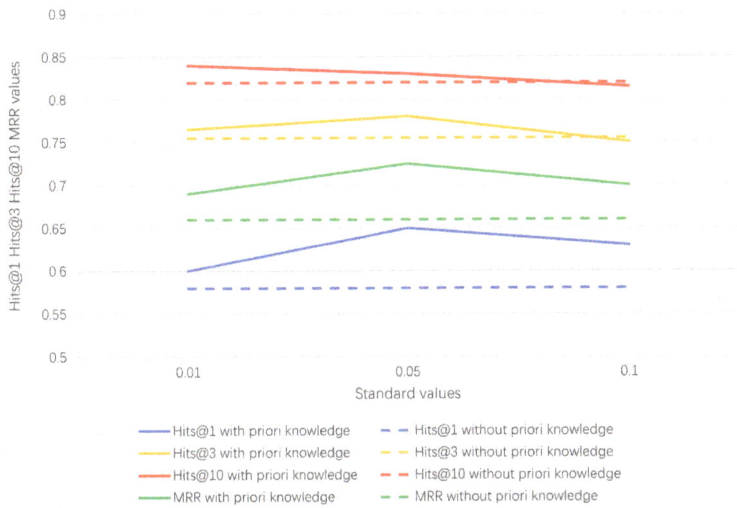

Figure 4. The effect of different standard values on the NELL-995 dataset.

As depicted in Figure 4, after introducing the prior knowledge, the performance of the reinforcement-learning method is significantly improved, demonstrating our method's effectiveness. It should be noted that the method's performance is related to a standard value, as within a certain range, the larger the standard value, the better the method's performance, preserving the standard value between 0.01 and 0.05. Beyond a certain range (for example, the standard value is between 0.05 and 0.10), the method's performance decreases with the standard value's increase. This is because setting the standard value too high may introduce noise. Therefore, it is necessary to set the standard value reasonably, according to different data sets, so that the model obtains the optimal performance.

4.6.2. Impact Analysis of the Number and Length of Paths

In the reasoning process, the agent will face the choice of multiple paths at each step, and the total number of these paths will impact the method's performance. In addition, the length of the relationship path through which the agent reaches the target entity will also affect the method's performance.

Therefore, we first analyze the impact of the total number of optional paths of agents on the method's performance, taking the experimental results on dataset NELL-995 as an example. We first set the length of the agent's relationship path to 4, then set the standard value to 0.1, and finally set the total number of agents' optional paths to 3, 5, 10, and 50. In order to keep the consistency of the experimental results, we still use Hits@N and MRR to evaluate the method's performance, where N is 1, 3, and 10. Figure 5 illustrates the corresponding results, which reveal that the method's performance increases as the number of paths increases within a certain range (the number of paths is less than 5). Beyond a certain range (for example, the number of paths is greater than 10), the number of paths increases, and the method's performance decreases. This may be due to errors in the knowledge graph or inaccurate prior knowledge obtained using the relationship importance identification module. Hence, the more prior knowledge is introduced, the greater the deviation is.

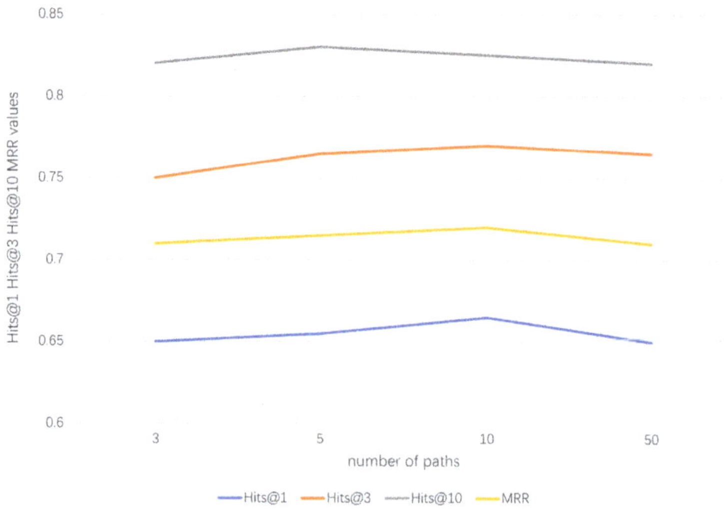

Figure 5. Influence of the number of paths on NELL-995 dataset.

Next, we analyze the impact of path length on the method's performance and conduct experiments on the dataset NELL-995. We fixed the number of paths to 5, set the standard value to 0.1, and set the path length to 2 to 6. The results in Figure 6 infer that within a certain range (path length less than or equal to 4), the method's performance increases with the path length increase. The path length increases beyond a certain range (greater than or equal to 5), but the method's performance is stable. This may be because the increase in path length brings more prior knowledge, which enhances the performance of the method, while the increase in path length also introduces more errors in the knowledge graph itself, which reduces the performance of the method, thus achieving a steady state.

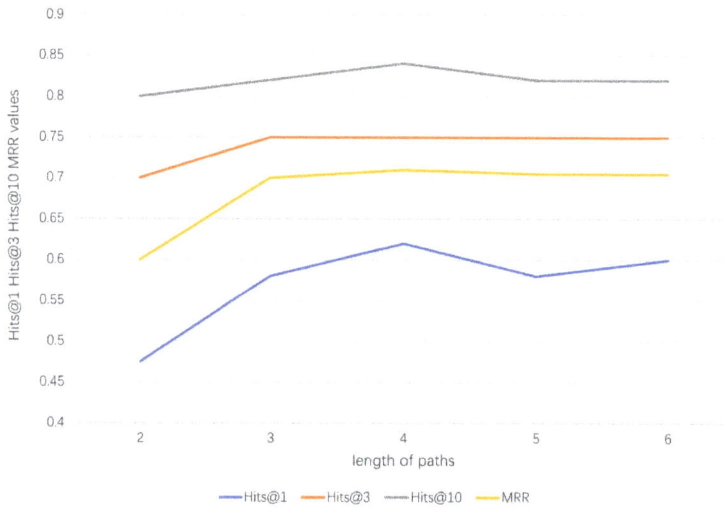

Figure 6. Influence of the length of paths on NELL-995 dataset.

5. Conclusions

This paper proposes a new method of knowledge graph reasoning based on causal reinforcement learning, as existing knowledge graph reasoning methods do not effectively use prior knowledge. Specifically, we use the counterfactual method in causal inference to obtain the weight of the relationship path, obtain the prior knowledge, and introduce it into the reinforcement learning reasoning model. The agent starts from the head entity and then selects the edge through the neural network when all the edge weights are small. Otherwise, it selects the edge according to the prior knowledge. Experiments on four datasets demonstrate the effectiveness of the prior knowledge. Follow-up research will focus on how to make the model automatically learn the standard value and how to effectively combine prior knowledge with semantic information to further improve the performance of reasoning.

Author Contributions: D.L.: conceptualization, writing—original draft, writing—reviewing and editing, methodology, validation, formal analysis. Y.L.: supervision, writing—reviewing and editing. J.W.: supervision, data procession, formal analysis. W.Z.: supervision, writing—editing. G.Z.: supervision, writing—editing. All authors have read and agreed to the published version of the manuscript.

Funding: This research received no external funding.

Institutional Review Board Statement: Not applicable.

Informed Consent Statement: Not applicable.

Data Availability Statement: The dataset and code generated during the current study are not publicly available because the data and code also form part of the ongoing study, but they can be obtained from the corresponding authors according to reasonable requirements.

Acknowledgments: The authors would like to thank all the reviewers and language editing organizations who helped to improve this manuscript.

Conflicts of Interest: The authors declare no conflicts of interest.

Abbreviations

KGC	Knowledge Graph Completion
SCM	Structural Causal Model
CF-GPS	CounterFactually Guided Policy Search
SARSA	State Action Reward State Action
LSTM	Long Short-Term Memory
MAP	Mean Average Precision
MRR	Mean Reciprocal Rank

References

Xiong, C.; Merity, S.; Schoer, R. Dynamic memory networks for visual and textual question answering. In Proceedings of the 33rd International Conference on Machine Learning, Honolulu, HI, USA, 23–26 July 2016; pp. 2397–2406.
Logan, R.; Liu, N.F.; Peters, M.E. Using knowledge graphs for fact-aware language modeling. In Proceedings of the 57th Annual Meeting of the Association for Computational Linguistics, Florence, Italy, 22–24 August 2019; pp. 5962–5971.
Xiong, W.; Yu, S.; Guo, X. Improving question answering over incomplete KBs with knowledge-aware reader. In Proceedings of the 57th Annual Meeting of the Association for Computational Linguistics, Florence, Italy, 22–24 August 2019; pp. 4258–4264.
Linardatos, P.; Papastefanopoulos, V.; Kotsiantis, S. Explainable AI: A review of machine learning interpretability methods. *Entropy* **2020**, *23*, 180–192. [CrossRef] [PubMed]
Bordes, A.; Usunier, N.; Garcia-Duran, A. Translating embeddings for modeling multi-relational data. *Adv. Neural Inf. Process. Syst.* **2013**, *26*, 2787–2795.
Wang, Z.; Zhang, J.; Feng, J. Knowledge graph embedding by translating on hyperplanes. In Proceedings of the 28th Association for the Advancement of Artificial Intelligence, San Francisco, CA, USA, 3–6 June 2014; pp. 1112–1119.
Lin, X.; Liang, Y.; Giunchiglia, F.; Feng, X.; Guan, R. Compositional learning of relation path embedding for knowledge base completion. *arXiv* **2015**, arXiv:1611.07232.
Ji, G.; He, S.; Xu, L. Knowledge graph embedding via dynamic mapping matrix. In Proceedings of the 53rd Annual Meeting of the Association for Computational Linguistics and the 7th International Joint Conference on Natural Language Processing, Beijing, China, 26–31 July 2015; pp. 687–696.
Pasquale, M.; Pontus, S.; Sebastian, R. Convolutional 2D Knowledge Graph Embeddings. *arXiv* **2018**, arXiv:1707.01476.
Trouillon, T.; Welbl, J.; Riedel, S. Complex Embeddings for Simple Link Prediction. *arXiv* **2016**, arXiv:1606.06357.

11. Lao, N.; Mitchell, T.; Cohen, W.W. Rotate: Random walk inference and learning in a large scale knowledge base. In Proceedin of the 2011 Conference on Empirical Methods in Natural Language Processing, Scotland, UK, 8–11 July 2011; pp. 529–539.
12. Xiong, W.; Hoang, T.; Wang, W.Y. Deeppath: A reinforcement learning method for knowledge graph reasoning. *arXiv* **201** arXiv:1707.06690.
13. Das, R.; Dhuliawala, S.; Zaheer, M. Go for a walk and arrive at the answer: Reasoning over paths in knowledge bases usi reinforcement learning. In Proceedings of the ICLR, Vancouver, BC, Canada, 28–30 March 2018; pp. 688–696.
14. Wan, G.; Pan, S.; Gong, C. Reasoning like human: Hierarchical reinforcement learning for knowledge graph reasoning. In Proceedin of the 29th International Joint Conference on Artificial Intelligence, Yokohama, Japan, 7–15 January 2021; pp. 1926–1932.
15. Wang, H.; Li, S.; Pan, R. Incorporating graph attention mechanism into knowledge graph reasoning based on deep reinforceme learning. In Proceedings of the 2019 Conference on Empirical Methods in Natural Language Processing and the 9th Internation Joint Conference on Natural Language Processing, Hong Kong, China, 3–7 November 2019; pp. 2623–2631.
16. Peter, J.; Micheal, D.; Nachiketa, C. A framework for causal discovery in non-intervenable systems. *Chaos* **2021**, *31*, 123–142.
17. Eric, J.; Isabel, F.; Ilya, S. Auto-G-Computation of Causal Effects on a Network. *arXiv* **2019**, arXiv:1709.01577.
18. Nicola, G.; Jonas, P.; Sebastian, E. Causal discovery in heavy-tailed models. *arXiv* **2020**, arXiv:1908.05097.
19. Bi, X.T.; Wu, D.; Xie, D. Large-scale chemical process causal discovery from big data with transformer-based deep learnir *Process Saf. Environ. Prot.* **2023**, *173*, 163–177. [CrossRef]
20. Cui, Y.; Pu, H.; Shi, X. Semiparametric Proximal Causal Inference. *J. Am. Stat. Assoc.* **2023**, *11*, 211–224. [CrossRef]
21. Wang, Z.; Li, L.; Zeng, D. Incorporating prior knowledge from counterfactuals into knowledge graph reasoning. *Knowl.-Bas Syst.* **2021**, *223*, 1307–1323. [CrossRef]
22. Pearl, J.; Creager, E.; Garg, A. *Causal Inference in Statistics: A Primer*, 1st ed.; John Wiley & Sons: Chichester, NY, USA, 201 pp. 254–256.
23. Pitis, S.; Pan, S.; Gong, C. Counterfactual data augmentation using locally factored dynamics. In Proceedings of the 34th Internation Conference on Neural Information Processing Systems, Vancouver, BC, Canada, 6–12 December 2020; pp. 2906–2922.
24. Madumal, P.; Miller, T.; Sonenberg, L. Explainable reinforcement learning through a causal lens. In Proceedings of the 34th AA Conference on Artificial Intelligence, New York, NY, USA, 7–12 February 2020; pp. 2493–2500.
25. Lu, C.C.; Huang, B.W.; Schölkopf, B. Sample-efficient reinforcement learning via counterfactual-based data augmentation. *arX* **2020**, arXiv:2012.09092.
26. Buesing, L.; Weber, T.; Zwols, Y. Woulda, coulda, shoulda: Counterfactually-guided policy search. In Proceedings of the 7 International Conference on Learning Representations, New Orleans, LA, USA, 1–5 May 2019; pp. 1693–1710.
27. Moerland, T.M.; Broekens, J.; Plaat, A. Model-based reinforcement learning: A survey. *Found. Trends Mach. Learn.* **2023**, 101–118. [CrossRef]
28. Yi, F.; Fu, W.; Liang, H. Model-based reinforcement learning: A survey. In Proceedings of the 18th International Conference Electronic Business, Guilin, China, 2–6 December 2018; pp. 421–429.
29. Singh, S.; Jaakkola, T.; Littman, M. Convergence results for single-step on-policy reinforcement-learning algorithms. *Mach. Lea* **2000**, *38*, 287–308. [CrossRef]
30. Watkins, C.; Dayan, P. Q-learning. *Mach. Learn.* **1992**, *8*, 279–292. [CrossRef]
31. Mnih, V.; Silver, D.; Graves, A. Playing Atari with deep reinforcement learning. *arXiv* **2013**, arXiv:1312.09092.
32. Mnih, V.; Silver, D.; Graves, A. Human-level control through deep reinforcement learning. *Nature* **2015**, *518*, 529–533. [CrossR
33. Fortunato, M.; Azar, M.; Piot, B. Noisy networks for exploration. In Proceedings of the 6th International Conference on Learni Representations, Vancouver, BC, Canada, 12-16 August 2018; pp. 1321–1330.
34. Kaelbling, L.P.; Littman, M.; Moore, A. Reinforcement learning: A survey. *J. Artif. Intell. Res.* **1996**, *4*, 237–255. [CrossRef]
35. Wang, H.; Huang, T.; Wang, W. Deep reinforcement learning: A survey. *Front. Inf. Technol. Electron. Eng.* **2020**, *21*, 1726–17 [CrossRef]
36. Williams, R. Simple statistical gradient-following algorithms for connectionist reinforcement learning. *Mach. Learn.* **1992**, 229–246. [CrossRef]
37. Deng, Z.; Jiang, J.; Long, G.; Zhang, C. Causal Reinforcement Learning: A Survey. *arXiv* **2023**, arXiv:2307.01452.
38. Maximilian, S.; Bernhard, S.; Georg, M. Causal Reinforcement Learning: A Survey. *arXiv* **2016**, arXiv:2106.03443.
39. Guo, J.; Gong, M.; Tao, D. A Relational Intervention Approach for Unsupervised Dynamics Generalization in Model-Bas Reinforcement Learning. In Proceedings of the 10th International Conference on Learning Representations (Virtual), Toul France, 25–29 April 2022; pp. 3453–3470.
40. Pim, D.H.; Dinesh, J.; Sergey, L. Causal Confusion in Imitation Learning. *Statistics* **2022**, *11*, 1467–1480.
41. Deng, Z.; Fu, Z.; Wang, L.; Yang, Z.; Bai, C.; Zhou, T.; Wang, Z.; Jiang, J. False Correlation Reduction for Offline Reinforceme Learning. *IEEE Trans. Pattern Anal. Mach. Intell.* **2023**, *46*, 1199–1211. [CrossRef] [PubMed]
42. Hochreiter, S.; Schmidhuber, J. Long short-term memory. *Neural Comput.* **1997**, *9*, 1735–1780. [CrossRef]
43. Carlson, A.; Betteridge, B.; Kisiel, B. Toward an architecture for never-ending language learning. In Proceedings of the 25th AA Conference on Artificial Intelligence, Atlanta, GA, USA, 10–15 June 2010; pp. 1306–1313.
44. Bollacker, K.; Evans, P.; Paritosh, T. Freebase: A collaboratively created graph database for structuring human knowledge. Proceedings of the 2008 ACM SIGMOD International Conference on Management of Data, New York, NY, USA, 6–10 May 20 pp. 1586–1604.

Bordes, A.; Weston, R.; Collobert, Y. Learning structured embeddings of knowledge bases. In Proceedings of the 25th AAAI Conference on Artificial Intelligence, San Francisco, CA, USA, 16–22 August 2011; pp. 301–306.
Sun, Z.; Deng, Z.H.; Nie, J.Y. Rotate: Knowledge graph embedding by relational rotation in complex space. In Proceedings of the 7th International Conference on Learning Representations, New Orleans, LA, USA, 9–12 May 2019; pp. 1–18.

MDPI AG
Grosspeteranlage 5
4052 Basel
Switzerland
Tel.: +41 61 683 77 34

Applied Sciences Editorial Office
E-mail: applsci@mdpi.com
www.mdpi.com/journal/applsci

www.ingramcontent.com/pod-product-compliance
Lightning Source LLC
Chambersburg PA
CBHW040820250926
51850CB00007BA/1221
* 9 7 8 3 7 2 5 8 4 9 2 3 9 *